U.S. BUSINESS IN SOUTH AFRICA

The Economic, Political, and Moral Issues

DESAIX MYERS III with Kenneth Propp, David Hauck, and David M. Liff

INVESTOR RESPONSIBILITY RESEARCH CENTER, INC.

Indiana University Press
Bloomington and London

This book is published in the United Kingdom,
Europe, and Africa by Rex Collings Limited.

Manufactured in the United States of America

Library of Congress Cataloging in Publication Data

Myers, Desaix B. III
      U.S. Business in South Africa.

    1. Investments, American--South Africa. 2. Corporations, American--
South Africa. 3. South Africa--Commerce. 4. Labor and laboring classes
--South Africa. I. Investor Responsibility Research Center. II. Title.
HG5851.A3M92   332.6'7373'068   79-3638
ISBN 0-253-11486-1

Contents

III. THE DOMESTIC DEBATE OVER SOUTH AFRICA

APPENDICES

Acknowledgements

The authors gratefully acknowledge support from the Investor Responsibility Research Center and from its executive director, Margaret Carroll, in the preparation of this book. Special thanks are due to Shirley Carpenter for her extensive work on the manuscript and to Eileen Marsh for her assistance.

The authors would like to thank particularly Carolyn Mathiasen for her thoughtful editorial advice and, on behalf of IRRC, to express appreciation to the Ford Foundation for providing funds in support of IRRC's work on South Africa and to the Carnegie Corporation of New York for its contribution to production and distribution of this book.

Introduction

For years foreign policy activists have been tantalized by the possibility that business links to South Africa could be used as a lever to force changes in that country's apartheid laws and practices. They have repeatedly questioned the role of American companies in South Africa. At annual meetings, the chairmen of major U.S. corporations have been faced with dissident shareholders challenging the sales policies and labor practices of South African subsidiary operations. Institutional investors holding stock in companies or banks doing business in South Africa are being pressured by their constituents on the policies governing those investments. Successive U.S. administrations have put limited restrictions on sales to South Africa. And on college campuses, no corporate responsibility issue has gripped students with greater concern since the war in Vietnam.

The Soweto demonstrations in 1976, the bannings and arrests in October 1977 of people involved in the black consciousness movement and the death in detention of black leader Steve Biko greatly accelerated the growth of concern over the situation in South Africa and focused attention on the role of business there. The attention has continued in the United Nations, on campuses, at meetings of church shareholders and union organizers and in Congress. Some institutional investors, particularly those associated with universities, have been forced to reexamine their portfolios; some have drawn up new guidelines for their investments; some have sold stock or withdrawn funds from banks active in South Africa. And at least partially in response to these pressures, more than 100 American companies have endorsed a code of conduct known as the Sullivan principles pledged to improving working and living conditions for employees in South Africa.

These developments, events in southern Africa, and pressures growing both within South Africa and abroad have encouraged a small and fragile momentum for change in that country. The changes that have taken place in the last few years have had little impact on the overall political structure in South Africa or on the government's apartheid policies. But they have begun to affect the role and practices of foreign companies operating in South Africa, and they may have implications for greater change in the future.

At the focus of concern over the American role in South Africa are some of the largest companies in the United States. More than half of Fortune's top 100 companies in the United States have South African subsidiaries. Approximately 350 American companies have subsidiaries or affiliates in that country and an additional 6,000 U.S. firms do business there on an agency basis. American companies employ nearly 100,000 workers, approximately two-thirds of whom are black. The size of U.S. direct investment was estimated by the U.S. Commerce Department at $1.99 billion in 1979, a slight increase over the 1978 figure of $1.79 billion. Indirect investment--through shares held in South African companies, gold stocks or bonds--is estimated at about $2 billion, and loans by U.S. banks total about $2.2 billion. Direct investment is about 37 percent of total American investment in the continent of Africa, 17 percent of all foreign investment in South Africa, and about 4 percent of private investment there. More importantly, U.S. investment has served as a stimulus to trade.

U.S. trade with South Africa has increased regularly during the last decade and a half. By 1976, it had grown to $1.35 billion in exports and $925 million in imports, and the United States had become South Africa's second largest trading partner after the United Kingdom. This position changed slightly in 1977--U.S. exports dipped to $1.05 billion, while imports grew to $1.3 billion. During 1978 exports grew only slightly, to $1.08 billion, as imports expanded to $2.3 billion.

This book evolved from research conducted over several years in the United States and in South Africa by the staff of the Investor Responsibility Research Center, based in Washington, D.C. For some time, the Investor Responsibility Research Center has been studying the activities of U.S. corporations in South Africa as part of its efforts to report on issues of public policy and corporate social responsibility. Founded in 1972, the Center now provides more than 170 institutional investors--universities, foundations, insurance companies, banks, and other commercial institutional investors--with impartial research on controversial issues relating to the role of business in society.

In 1978, at the request of subscribers, the Center initiated a review service specific to the conduct of American companies in South Africa. The aim of the service has been to provide background on the situation in South Africa, the role of companies there--particularly in certain strategic sectors of the economy--and the debate in the United States about corporate investment in South Africa. During the last year, the Center has issued the series of reports that provides the basis of this book. Information in the studies is drawn from four visits to South Africa between 1975 and 1979, and includes the findings from interviews with managers and workers at more than 50--some South African and European, although the majority American--companies in South Africa, labor union members, both black and white, journalists, South African and U.S. government representatives, and academics. The results published here are intended to provide people interested in the debate over American involvement in South Africa with information useful to an informed judgment on the issues raised by that involvement.

The book is comprised of three sections. The first, "Business and Labor in South Africa," provides background on the situation in South Africa and the positions of business and labor in the South African society. It is divided into six chapters. Chapter I discusses the historical background and development of the system of apartheid in South Africa. Chapter II describes the impact of apartheid on business and labor, discussing the government's migrant labor policy; laws restricting labor mobility; land tenure and housing for blacks; controls over dissent in South African society; education and training for blacks; labor representation; and recent developments affecting workers. Chapter III examines the role of foreign capital in South Africa. It looks at the economic attractiveness of the country to the foreign investor and the role of the South African government in attracting foreign capital. This chapter also discusses the attitude of South African blacks toward foreign investment. Chapter IV describes the broad role of business in South Africa, the historical divisions between Afrikaner-dominated politics and British-dominated business, business efforts to mobilize opinion in South African society, and the limits on and potential of business lobbying. Chapter V discusses the actual labor practices of specific companies in South Africa--the constraints on improved practices, the effectiveness of pressures resulting from recently developed labor codes of conduct, the recent improvement of labor practices in specific areas, and the areas in which little progress has been made. It looks at how U.S. companies stack up when their labor practices are compared with those of other companies in South Africa. Chapter VI examines the controversy over economic sanctions against South Africa. It discusses South Africa's efforts to protect itself against sanctions, U.S. government policy on South African investment and sales, and foreign attitudes toward sanctions. The potential impact of sanctions on South Africa is analyzed.

The second section, "Case Studies of Foreign Investment," contains chapters on four strategic sectors of the South African economy--oil, computers and electronics, motor vehicles, and minerals--describing for each sector: its importance to the South African economy; the role of foreign companies; labor practices; concerns about foreign activities and the debate over foreign investment; and the potential impact of a curtailment of foreign company operations in the sector.

The third section of the book, "The Domestic Debate," discusses the debate within the United States over investment in South Africa, the pressures mounting on investors in companies with activities there and the steps they are taking to respond to the pressures. Chapter I surveys the range of steps institutional investors have taken to partially or totally divest stock in firms active in South Africa or to participate actively as shareholders in attempts to influence corporate performance there. Chapter II describes the pressures from Washington--from Congress and the Carter administration--on companies involved in South Africa. Chapter III summarizes the responses of companies to investor and governmental pressures. It studies the costs of such investor pressures for companies, as well as the costs of federal trade restrictions. The report concludes with an evaluation of the changes in activist pressures on corporations over the last year and a look at the evolution of the positions of institutional investors. It assesses the current and likely future effectiveness of investor pressures.

The book contains a number of appendices. Appendix A describes the key apartheid laws that affect labor in South Africa. Appendix B contains the three major labor codes of conduct--the U.S. Sullivan principles, the European Economic Community code, and South Africa's Urban Foundation code--that have been adopted by a number of companies in recent years. Appendix C lists the 116 U.S. companies that have signed the Sullivan principles. Appendix D contains charts showing the number of black students enrolled in technical courses. Appendix E contains individual summaries of the South Africa-related investment policies of 88 of America's best-endowed colleges and universities. Appendix F discusses actions by schools that have decided to divest. Appendix G shows U.S. and British exports to South Africa as a percentage of their total exports. Appendix H gives support levels for shareholder resolutions involving South Africa that were proposed to companies in 1977, 1978 and 1979.

Terminology: The words used to describe the various racial, cultural and linguistic groups in South Africa are often a source of confusion and some controversy. We use "African" to refer to the black African population of South Africa. The term "colored" refers to the population group descended from intermixing of the white settler population and Africans or Malays. "Asian" includes the small Chinese population but is primarily the larger group descended from immigrants from the Indian subcontinent. The term "black" includes the African, colored and Asian populations as one group, often called "nonwhite" or "non-European" by white South Africans. We use "white" to refer to South Africans of European stock--"Afrikaner" for that portion of the white population descended from German, Dutch and French Huguenot settlers whose native language is Afrikaans; "English-speaking" for the remaining white population.

* * *

The first section of this study, "Business and Labor in South Africa" was written by Desaix Myers III, deputy director of the Investor Responsibility Research Center. The second section, "Case Studies of Foreign Investment," was written by IRRC research analysts. David M. Liff wrote the case studies on the oil industry and the computer and electronics industry, David Hauck wrote the study on the minerals industry, and Kenneth Propp wrote the study on the motor industry. Kenneth Propp also wrote the third section of this study, "The Domestic Debate." Appendices E and F were compiled by IRRC intern Leslie Kautz. IRRC's editor, Carolyn Mathiasen, edited the study.

I.
Business and Labor in South Africa

I. BACKGROUND - THE DEVELOPMENT
AND CONTEXT OF APARTHEID

At the heart of the debate over investment in South Africa are the South African government's discriminatory racial policies. Despite growing pressures, both internal and external, the government continues to follow a policy of separation of the races--apartheid--developed as an ideology after the National Party assumed power in 1948.

The government's policy--which it describes as designed to encourage "separate" or "plural" development--is based on the premise that South Africa's heterogeneous population must be divided into separate nations, that integration of the country's 26 million people is not possible, and that the country must evolve as a commonwealth of separate states--10 African, one white.

All government programs, including those for education, health and social welfare, industrial development and agriculture, have been designed to encourage separation of the races. Of South Africa's land, 13 percent has been divided into 10 homelands for the 18.6 million Africans who comprise more than 70 percent of South Africa's total population. Three of these areas--Transkei, Bophuthatswana and Venda--have already been declared independent, and others are slated to follow in the next few years. The remaining 87 percent of the land has been reserved for the nation's 4.3 million whites who comprise 17 percent of the population. (The South African government asserts that as much as 65 to 70 percent of the land in South Africa is not arable, and that land in the homelands represents 45 percent of all arable land. Other observers report that much of the land in the homelands is eroded, suffers droughts, is poorly cultivated. In fact, the homelands provide less than 5 percent of total agriculture production and hold relatively few of South Africa's mineral resources.)

Africans are to be granted the rights of citizens in "independent" homelands; they are denied any political rights in the areas designated by the government as "white." The position of South Africa's 740,000 Asians and 2.4 million coloreds remains undefined, although proposals to restructure the parliament introduced in 1978 would include these groups as South African citizens with political representation in a three-parliament system with a separate parliament each for whites, coloreds and Asians.

The racial policy in South Africa reflects the concern whites have for their position as a minority in an extremely heterogeneous population. The government states that separation is required "to avoid racial tension." Apartheid also divides blacks by race and language, thus permitting the whites to perceive their own position as that of only one minority among many, rather than as a unique minority surrounded by a black majority. South African figures in mid-1976 showed:

	Total population
Whites	4,320,000
Colored	2,434,000
Asians	746,000
Africans	18,629,000
Total	26,129,000

The government further divides the African population by tribal language:

Africans born in South Africa	Total
Xhosa	4,897,000
Zulu	5,029,000
Swazi	590,000
Sepedi	2,011,000
Tswana	2,103,000
Seshoeshoe	1,698,000
Shangaan	814,000
Venda	449,000
Others	615,000
Foreign Africans	423,000
Total	18,629,000

There is no officially mandated language division for those people the government has classified as "colored"--about 95 percent of whom speak Afrikaans as a first language--nor for Asians, who may have any one of several subcontinental Indian languages as their mother tongue but most of whom speak English as well. And the government makes no distinction between those whites largely of British origin who speak English--about 40 percent of the white population--and those white descendants of German, Dutch or French Huguenot settlers who have Afrikaans as a mother tongue.

Apartheid has a profound impact on the country's black population. The rights and opportunities for blacks within the white areas--about two-thirds of all Africans and virtually all coloreds and Asians live in areas designated white--are severely limited by law and custom. The government places restrictions on where blacks can live, where they can move, how they are educated and what work they can do. The restrictions fall particularly heavily on the African population, and critics argue that government policies exacerbate rather than diminish tensions. They describe separate development as an effort to divide and rule in order to maintain a system of race privilege and domination.

The effect of the government's policy has been to reinforce separation that already exists--between white and black, between language groups and between rich and poor. South Africa is a developing country. Its gross national product per capita is somewhere between the GNPs of Panama and Uruguay. But government policy, incorporating historical patterns of development, laws and customs, has effectively split South Africa into two divisions--one developed and one underdeveloped--separated largely along racial lines.

South Africa as a developing country: South Africa has many of the problems of any developing country. Its population, particularly its black population, is growing at a dramatic rate. By 2000 the African population will have doubled its current size. The rate of population growth and its composition--nearly half of the Africans are under 15 and African birth rates are nearly double those of whites--place real strains on the economy. Education, health services and housing in South Africa have not kept pace with this growth. And as a developing country, South Africa suffers from job shortages at some levels, skills shortages at others, a rural-urban migration that imposes new pressures for services in urban areas, and maldistribution of wealth.

But South Africa differs from other developing countries in several respects. A major difference is the strength, sophistication and potential of its economy. With 6 percent of Africa's population, South Africa produces 50 percent of all the electricity generated there and 25 percent of the continent's GNP. It has an abundance of resources, including 65 percent of the world's gold reserves, 50 percent of its diamonds and manganese and 25 percent of its uranium. Its consumer economy is among the most sophisticated in the world. Ten major automobile manufacturers assemble cars in 39 models with 257 variations. South Africa spends more on computers per capita than any country in the world other than the United States and the United Kingdom, and almost any brand name available in the United States is stocked on the grocery shelves of South Africa.

But the most important difference between South Africa and other developing countries is the racial overlay and the government's decision to emphasize racial differences and to divide the country along racial lines. Access to the country's wealth, participation in the political system and the economy are restricted by race. Although there is agricultural and mineral potential in the homelands set aside for Africans, the bulk of South Africa's known mineral reserves, the vast majority--95 percent--of its agricultural production, and virtually all of its industry are in areas set aside for whites.

In this environment, population growth not only represents an economic challenge to the system, but to a minority white population constantly shrinking in relation to the faster growing black population, it represents a political threat as well. Vastly outnumbered now, whites by the year 2000 will be outnumbered 5.3 to 1 (37 million Africans to 7 million whites). And because wealth is divided unevenly along racial lines--whites control 70 percent of the economy, blacks 30 percent--the funds for providing goods and services to this population will have to come in large part from increased taxes on the white population, forcing cuts in the high standard of living for whites. As one consultant to South Africa's Urban Foundation wrote recently, "Notwithstanding its enormous potential for wealth, the resources of the society are limited. Any gain in the benefits extended to the black people must result in a reduction of the benefits available to the other communities, particularly the wealthiest of these which is the white community."

Reflecting this threat, the government's policies seek to separate and limit the demands--both political and economic--that the black population makes on the white population. By establishing separate areas--independent homelands where Africans are to exercise political and economic rights--the government hopes to limit the responsibility of white South Africa to grant those rights in the areas it has selected for itself. Thus, according to the government plans, much of the underdeveloped area in South Africa would no longer belong to the country, but would be independent, self-governing entities, participating with South Africa in some sort of confederal or consociational arrangement. The policy of decentralization, encouraging industry to establish itself in or adjoining the homelands; the migrant labor policy, which restricts the rights of Africans to be in the white designated areas except to work; and policies on training and education, which limit opportunities for Africans to develop skills in white areas--all have bolstered the over-all philosophy of separate development. They minimize the responsibility of government to provide opportunities, resources and rights to Africans in the areas where those opportunities, resources and rights would be the greatest.

A final distinction between South Africa and other developing countries is the strength of its political system--its police and military strength, the political will of the government and its power to control events to bring the economy into line, to protect its borders, and to monitor and suppress internal dissent. The system has been tested recently by the growing threats outside South Africa--the independence of Mozambique and Angola and the continuing wars in Rhodesia and Namibia (South West Africa)--but to date the government has been able to set its own course, including active intervention in Angola, rejection of United Nations pressures in Namibia, and support for the internal settlement in Rhodesia, without serious opposition from within and with moderate and largely ineffective pressures from abroad. It has responded harshly to what it sees as threats to its internal security and has a variety of laws that grant it the authority to quell opposition. Moreover, it has a degree of control in parliament that permits it to pass any additional legislation it considers necessary. The opposition Progressive Federal Party, with 17 of 165 seats in parliament, provides only token opposition to the National Party's policies, and the often highly critical English-speaking press and the relatively independent judiciary lend a legitimacy to the government's claim of an open and democratic society that belies the government's ability and will to influence events when it perceives a threat to its interests. The government's ability to monitor and control internal dissent is enhanced by a police system that includes a number of informers, sophisticated monitoring equipment and a supportive legal structure. Its ability to withstand outside threats is supported by Africa's most modern army of 65,000 men and a reserve force of more than 400,000, including some 800 coloreds and 130 Africans, and by sophisticated military technology that may well include nuclear weaponry.

How long this control will remain effective, in light of the frustrations created by the government's policy of separate development, is impossible to determine. Despite a flurry of announcements affecting racial relations in the last year, there is little evidence that the government has given serious consideration to an alternative strategy. The policy has deep historical roots, and it is unlikely that it will be easily replaced.

The roots of apartheid: The policy of separate development is a unique combination of history, religion and self-interest forged out of three centuries of struggle by Afrikaans speakers to establish an independent nation in Africa. The first battle was against English-speaking settlers in the Cape, and conflict over a century-and-a-half there launched Afrikaner pioneers in 1836 on a "Great Trek" away from the coast, over the Drakensberg mountain range into South Africa's center. The Trek severed Afrikaners' connection with Europe. They became what they considered "the white tribe in Africa," and in successful battles over land with Africans they developed a belief that they had a special destiny as a people. This belief was tested in two wars with the English; the second, the 1899-1902 Boer War, introduced effective guerrilla warfare as 20,000 Afrikaner commandos opposed the British army of 400,000. The war ended with the Afrikaners' defeat after Britain adopted a scorched-earth policy, burning farms and putting women and children in concentration camps where eventually 20,000 died. It left Afrikaners with a lingering distrust of English speakers despite the formation of the Union of South Africa, which combined Boer and English states into an independent country in 1910. This distrust continues to affect relations between the two white groups today.

Political hostility between Afrikaans and English speakers was compounded by English control of the economy--primarily the mines in the late 1800s and later the growing commercial and industrial sectors. Traditionally rural, those Afrikaners who began to move to the cities in the 1920s and 1930s had little confidence in English managers. When the Chamber of Mines sought to bring in additional cheap African labor in the early 1920s, miners--including an increasing number of Afrikaans speakers--struck, a rebellion began and white unions became a political force to be reckoned with. Industrial legislation growing out of this period sought to develop a "civilized labor policy" to protect "persons whose standard of living conforms to the standard of living generally recognized as tolerable from the usual European standpoint" against those "persons whose aim is restricted to the bare requirements of the necessities of life as understood among barbarous and undeveloped peoples." Discriminatory industrial laws and policies that built upon earlier discriminatory legislation, such as the 1913 Native Land Act, restricted the areas in which Africans would own land.

During and immediately following World War II, increasing numbers of whites and blacks moved from rural areas to settle, often in shanty towns, around the urban areas. Whites threatened by the influx of labor, from a social as well as an economic point of view, sought to control the immigration. The Afrikaner-dominated National Party which came to power for the first time in 1948 began to enact a body of legislation restricting the rights of Africans to live and work in urban areas. The laws institutionalized, for the first time, a system of discrimination that had been evolving informally for nearly three centuries. The laws were explained in Afrikaner ideology as "apartheid," the need for each national group to maintain its own identity and to be responsible for its own growth. Originally, the roots of apartheid were found in the Afrikaners' desire to protect their ethnic identity from being absorbed by British cultural imperialism, not merely to separate whites from blacks.

To many whites in South Africa, the Nationalists' ideology of apartheid struck a responsive chord. Of those in opposition, including a majority of the English speakers, it was often said that "they talk Progressive, they vote for the United Party, but in their hearts they thank God for the Nats (the National Party of the Afrikaners)." To Afrikaners, now comprising about 60 percent of the white population, apartheid was a logical outgrowth of their own experience--their struggle for an individual national identity, independent of Britain; and perhaps more importantly, it gave them assurance that the position of power and privilege that they finally attained in 1948 would be protected. It was seen by many Afrikaners as a natural outgrowth of their history--a Calvinist predestination--and it was supported by many members of the Dutch Reformed Church, the predominant church among Afrikaners, as God's will.

Religion and apartheid--Religion and history have played a critical role in shaping Afrikaner political thought, providing the spiritual rationale and affecting the structure of leadership. The Great Trek, the battles against Africans, successive wars against the British, devastation during the Boer War, and redemption with the Nationalist victory at the polls in 1948, all contributed to Afrikaners' perception of their people as a chosen race. December 16, the Day of the Covenant, is a day of thanksgiving in South Africa, celebrating the day in 1838 when 470 Afrikaner pioneers resisted successfully the attacks of 15,000 Zulus. The evening before the battle, the Afrikaners entered into a covenant with God to commemorate the day as a sabbath if they survived; that they survived is interpreted as a sign of their special "calling as God's people."

The struggles of the early Afrikaners also lent themselves to the development of a great faith in individual leaders. Afrikaners who saw themselves as predestined to a special calling as a people chosen by God have assumed, until recently, that their leaders were also special. Traditional Afrikaner politics have been dominated by patriarchal leaders, and leadership once assumed or conferred has generally gone unquestioned.

Political leadership and religious leadership, both infused with the special calling of protection and development of the Afrikaner nation, have been intertwined. Many Afrikaner politicians have been drawn from the cloth, and the major Dutch Reformed Church to which 1.5 million of 2.5 million Afrikaners belong (an additional 338,000 belong to other Dutch reformed churches) has sometimes been called the "National Party at prayer." The church has practiced separation of the races since 1857, and deeply religious Afrikaner theorists have used teachings of the church in support of apartheid. The special calling of the churches and the political leaders, in addition to looking after Afrikaner interests, has been described as "the preservation of racial and cultural variety." Apartheid was designed to provide a structure to Afrikaner society, justified by history and by religion. It was, according to historian W.A. de Klerk, "an attempt to remake society in the total vision of a socio-political ideal." Chosen by God to establish and protect a unique white Christian nation in Africa, many Afrikaners also justified their actions by arguing that they had a larger responsibility to assume a paternal role toward the African population. De Klerk writes, "the policy of apartheid was designed to ensure the survival of the white race. Justice towards (Afrikaner) 'posterity' was at the heart of it, but also justice toward the Bantu, whose survival as a separate race with their own culture, and whose development toward higher levels, would be ensured by it."

This justification of apartheid developed at length by Afrikaner theorists in the mid-1940s has had the full support of the Dutch Reformed Church. As recently as 1974, the church wrote following a synod that "the new testament does not regard the diversity of peoples as something sinful." References in the Bible to "neither Greek nor Jew in Christ," the church argued, were to be interpreted as referring to spiritual unity, not social or political integration. And in December 1978, the white Dutch Reformed Church refused to allow its sister churches--African, Indian and colored--to join in a common secretariat.

The degree of racial separation: The enforced separation of races has encouraged people in South Africa to believe that there are irreconcilable differences between the races. And there are still few opportunities that allow whites to test this perception.

Outside observers cannot help but notice the degree to which Africans and whites have been separated--if not physically, psychologically. An American company, Weyerhaeuser, commented in a report to shareholders in 1974 that "we were surprised when visiting even heavily African rural areas to find that most of the whites we talked to have never been physically present in an African community." Despite some changes since 1974, virtually the same could be said today. Of 21 liberal white professionals at a gathering in northern Johannesburg in November 1977, only one had ever been in Soweto, the main black township, which is but 10 miles away. The one had last been there in 1948. A number of South Africans say that the riots in Soweto in 1976 seen on South African television (introduced in southern Africa for the first time in 1975) gave many whites their first view of life in an African township. Newspapers in Johannesburg covering events in Soweto carried small maps to show readers where the township for 1.5 million of Johannesburg's workers is located. By requiring whites to obtain a permit to enter Soweto, by placing it in an area outside the major metropolitan district, the government has created enough of a disincentive to discourage many South Africans from ever seeing it.

But the separation is not limited to the townships. It is evident in rural areas as well. One professor at Stellenbosch--the preeminent Afrikaans university--after surveying students for two years as to whether they knew the last names of any of the coloreds in their home towns, excluding personal servants, reported in 1978 that fewer than 20 percent answered affirmatively. And many South African whites said that they had never heard of black consciousness leader Steve Biko until he died in detention.

The separation has important implications for the way in which whites and blacks view each other and themselves.

Separation in living areas and in work helps maintain a perception among whites that blacks are somehow different from whites. According to O.S. Graupner, personnel manager for a South African company, Barlow Rand, "Separation helps to perpetuate the ideas of differentiation of the races in the minds of all races....Public policy and legislation requiring separation at work keeps the races apart because separate toilets, washrooms, dining and mess rooms are also provided." There is no public place for blacks and whites to go naturally to drink tea or to talk. Graupner continues: "Contact between the races is thus confined only to contact on the job. This contact is invariably of the master-servant type with the white worker in the more senior 'master' position." U.S. visitors to South Africa are often struck by the way many people--particularly American executives living temporarily in South Africa--use practically identical phrases to describe the attitudes and characteristics of the African and colored population. A common disparagement of an African worker is that he never saw a screwdriver before he took his present job. Some Africans come to believe such characterizations themselves. One African computer repairman told an American visitor that Africans lacked experience with tools--seeming to sense no inconsistency between that statement and his own experience. He had taught himself to repair radios as a boy in the township and was a customer service representative for a computer company.

"Because Africans are seen to be different," writes Dr. Simon Biesheuvel of the University of Witwatersrand Graduate School of Business, "it is argued that they need to be treated differently. Because black workers lack certain skills and may have difficulty in understanding or making themselves understood, deference is easily translated into inferiority. Thus a rational justification for keeping them in a subordinate position is readily provided." The rationalization not only applies in the work place but carries over into the political arena as well. There is hope among most whites in South Africa that Africans will be satisfied by a lesser form of political participation than whites would accept themselves.

Whites' assumptions are also affected by South Africa's degree of isolation in the world. For the most part, white South Africans are cut off from the rest of Africa because of the government's apartheid policies and have only limited contacts with the rest of the world through free but government-guided channels of communication. As a result, they have increasingly come to view themselves as the last bastion of western European civilization in Africa. Many whites in government, and in the public at large, argue that South Africa's fight is not black against white, but Christian and democratic values against communism. And the concern about communism in Africa and within South Africa itself is reminiscent of concerns felt in the United States during the height of the cold war.

Events of the last five years in southern Africa have brought pressures and challenges to many of the assumptions that had provided the basis of the government's policy of separate development. They have produced a level of discussion in South Africa, particularly within the National Party, that is unusual. They have led the government to take steps--in Angola, in the repression following Soweto, in Namibia, in the efforts by the Department of Information to win support at home and approval abroad, and now in current efforts to soften racial practices--that have in turn produced both new pressures and new challenges.

Chapter I Sources

Books

Heribert Adam, Modernizing Racial Domination, University of California Press, Berkeley, 1971.

Heribert Adam and Herman Giliomee, Ethnic Power Mobilized, Can South Africa Change, Yale University Press, New Haven, 1979.

Jeffrey Butler, Robert I. Rotberg and John Adams, The Black Homelands of South Africa, University of California Press, Berkeley, 1977.

T.R.H. Davenport, South Africa, A Modern History, University of Toronto Press, Toronto, 1977.

W.A. de Klerk, The Puritans in Africa, Pelican Books, New York, 1976.

John de St. Jorre, A House Divided, Carnegie Endowment for International Peace, Washington, D.C., 1977.

Muriel Horrell, Laws Affecting Race Relations in South Africa, South African Institute of Race Relations, Natal Witness (Pty) Ltd., Pietermaritzburg, Natal, South Africa, 1978.

D. Hobart Houghton, The South African Economy, Oxford University Press, Capetown, 1976.

John Kane-Berman, Soweto, Black Revolt, White Reaction, Raven Press, Johannesburg, 1978.

T. Dunbar Moodie, The Rise of Afrikanerdom: Power, Apartheid and the Afrikaner Civil Religion, University of California Press, Berkeley, 1975.

Barbara Rogers, White Wealth, Black Poverty, Greenwood Press, Westport, Conn., 1976.

South Africa Institute of Race Relations, A Survey of Race Relations in South Africa (annual surveys, Natal Witness (Pty) Ltd., Pietermaritzburg, Natal, South Africa.

Leonard Thompson and Jeffrey Butler, Change in Contemporary South Africa, University of California Press, Berkeley, 1975.

Ivor Wilkins and Hans Stryden, The Super Afrikaners, Inside the Afrikaner Broederbond, Jonathan Ball Publishers, Johannesburg, 1978.

Articles

S. Biesheuvel, "Black Industrial Labor--Cornucopia or Pandora's Box?," Witswatersrand University Press, Johannesburg, 1973.

O.S. Graupner, "Observations on Race Relations in South Africa," Barlow Rand, Johannesburg, 1975.

Stanley B. Greenberg, "Public Order and Business Response 1960 and 1976," unpublished paper, Yale University, 1977.

J.L. Sadie, "The Afrikaner in the South African Economy," unpublished paper written in 1967 for the Canadian Royal Commission on Bilingualism and Biculturalism.

J.L. Sadie, "Projections of the South African Population 1970-2020," University of Stellenbosch, 1978.

Reports

Barlow-Weyerhaeuser Packaging Investments (South Africa), "Weyerhaeuser: Employee Status Report, 1975".

L.E. Cortis and A. Ratcliffe, "Contingencies of Black Advancement," unpublished study for the Urban Foundation, Johannesburg, 1978.

II. IMPACT OF APARTHEID: CONSTRAINTS ON BUSINESS

A number of constraints--some real, some merely perceived--affect the ability of companies to follow progressive labor practices in South Africa. Perhaps the most serious constraint is the system itself--a system of separate development that affects labor's mobility, its level of training and education, its opportunity for advancement and its rights to representation. Fewer companies now argue that South Africa's laws prevent them from implementing equal opportunity programs. But the laws, the regulations and the interpretations and perceptions surrounding them create a context that makes it necessary for companies to make a conscious and concentrated effort if they are to combat successfully the inequality inherent in the South African system.

The Migrant Labor Policy

Much of the legislation supporting separate development seeks to establish a pattern of migratory labor. Since the early days of settlement, whites have been concerned about encroachment by Africans in areas the whites have reserved for themselves. The concerns centered first on grazing lands and then on farm lands. As increasing numbers of Africans began to work on white farms, white farmers worried about encampments of squatters on their property. With the growth of industry, white workers began to fear that cheap black labor would be used to undercut their position, and white politicians sought to stem the influx of African squatters moving to the outskirts of urban centers. But although the whites disliked the growing numbers of Africans in white designated areas, they recognized the need for African labor. The answer that evolved was a system of migrant labor. Africans could be forced to stay in reserved areas, eventually known as homelands, and migration to white areas would be restricted to those whose labor was required. The concept of migratory labor became a critical aspect of separate development--hypothetically, it would enable the economy to grow without a vast increase in Africans in urban areas because only those Africans with jobs would be allowed. Some legislation already existed that restricted the flow of Africans to the cities. As the policy of separate development evolved, new legislation was introduced to supplement and strengthen existing laws.

The policy has had limited success. Nearly half--43 percent--of African males working in South Africa are migrants. But it has failed to stem the rural-urban migration. Soweto, for example, has grown from a city of about 500,000 in 1960 to an estimated 1.5 million in 1977. And the laws designed to enforce the pattern of migrancy have had a severe impact on Africans' advancement.

Critics condemn the government's policy of migrant labor as cruel and degrading. Separating men from their families, they argue, provokes mental and physical hardship which leads to prostitution, illegitimacy, alcoholism, violence and malnutrition. It prevents Africans from having a stable existence, it limits opportunities to acquire job skills, it creates the reserves as empty dumping grounds for the unskilled, aged and infirm, and it is inefficient--it creates unnecessary administrative expenses for the government.

The government accepts these costs as part of the cost of separate development. It argues that the system of migrant labor prevents the formation of large slums characteristic of most developing countries; it provides jobs and boosts economic output. The government says that South Africa cannot be viewed in isolation, but that its migrant worker policy should be compared to the guest worker programs in Europe and other migrant labor programs in Africa. Finally, it argues that many African men prefer to keep their families in the reserves where their wives can tend the family farms.

For increasing numbers of Africans, however, the homelands hold little attraction. They wish to settle with their families in urban areas, or they have lived for decades in an industrialized environment already. Some Africans may favor controls on rural urban migration to protect their own jobs from unskilled and cheaper labor, but for most urban workers, those who already have some skills, the threat holds little meaning. Their jobs are not threatened by the unskilled. For them, the laws designed to control the in-migration of Africans are only oppressive. They impose severe social costs on blacks, they carry real costs to the economy, and they have direct implications for business: They affect the quality of work, the competitiveness of the labor market, turnover, absenteeism and worker productivity.

Laws Restricting Labor Mobility

Among the most restrictive of the laws are those that relate directly to the mobility of labor--the pass laws and the laws that define the areas in which Africans can live and work.

Through a variety of laws, regulations and policy the government has sought to define the territorial rights of blacks in South Africa. The Native Land Act of 1913, for example, set aside the 22.5 million acres now allocated to nine areas as reserves for Africans. Whites were prohibited from owning land in these areas, and Africans were not permitted to buy land outside the reserves. The Native (Urban Areas) Act of 1923 required local authorities to establish separate living areas or "locations" for Africans. The local authorities were to be held responsible for controlling the "influx" of Africans from rural areas and were charged with seeing that any "surplus" Africans were removed to the reserves.

The pass laws: In response, local authorities developed a plethora of laws--often referred to as the pass laws--in an effort to set up a permit system that would control the rural migration to the cities. Some municipalities established curfews on Africans, others required work permits, and others based their control process on housing permits. The conflict and confusion of regulations developed by local authorities, and their lack of effective implementation, led the government to try to rationalize their efforts with the Native (Urban Areas) Consolidation Act of 1945. The act authorized the central government to establish a system of influx control and with later amendments set strict conditions under which Africans would be permitted to stay in areas that had been "proclaimed" for whites. (Details, Appendix A) Under the act, more than 900,000 Africans were removed from urban areas to the homelands between 1960 and 1972. To facilitate monitoring of Africans in white areas, all Africans over the age of 16 are required to carry passbooks at all times. As recently as 1975-76, an average of more than 1,000 Africans a day were arrested for pass law violations.

The government's concern about pass violations has appeared to decrease slightly in the last few years. By the end of 1976, pass arrests had dropped to an average of 680 per day--250,000 during the year--and most of these resulted in minor fines. About 9,200 people were removed from urban areas and sent to the homelands that year on the grounds that they had violated the 1945 Natives--now Bantu--(Urban Areas) Consolidation Act and that they were considered "idle," or "undesirable."

But recently, the government has begun to step up arrests under the pass laws. In 1978, there were 55,030 pass arrests in Johannesburg alone--the average fine was $86--compared with 46,030 in 1977. And during the first three months of 1979, the West Rand Board, responsible for administering Johannesburg, removed 1,252 Africans from its area because they did not have their passbooks in order.

Designated living areas: In addition to defining the African's right to be in urban areas, the act establishes where he should live within the area. Africans working in Johannesburg, for example, are assigned to live in a township like Soweto, a settlement of about 1.5 million people, located about 10 miles from the center of the city. In addition, within the township, housing areas are assigned according to language group. Africans classified as Zulus are expected to live in a Zulu section. Xhosas are assigned to a Xhosa-designated section. Similarly, the government has zoned certain areas exclusively for coloreds and Asians.

The Group Areas Act of 1950 authorized the central government to define certain zones by race. Between 1950 and 1976, using the act, the government forced more than half-a-million people to move. Most of these were blacks, but 7,000 were whites. The government estimates that an additional 157,000 may need to move in the future to comply with existing determinations.

There has been little slackening of the government's efforts to establish separate living areas. Often, areas that have long been the home of certain race groups or mixtures of race groups are reclassified, and tenants or owners are forced to move. In 1976, for example, the government proclaimed 47 new group areas--17 white, 20 colored and 10 Indian--and some 32,000 people were moved. Only 26 of these were whites. In the process of reclassification, the government may elect to raze existing buildings. In the eight years to 1977, 121,000 houses were cleared as a result of the Group Areas Act.

One of the best-known examples of reclassification of an area occurred in District 6 in Capetown, long the home of a thriving and vibrant community of nearly 30,000 coloreds, Cape Malays, Asians, whites and a few Africans who lived in an area of old Victorian houses and narrow streets near the Capetown docks. District 6 was declared a white residential area in 1966. Despite opposition from the city council and many of the city's residents, the government has proceeded with plans to turn the area into a commercial and residential area for whites. Many of the homes have been razed, and 7,000 colored families have been moved into several townships outside of Capetown. Government supporters argue that District 6 can be used more effectively as a modern business area. They liken what has occurred in District 6 to successful urban renewal efforts elsewhere in the world and they argue that the government has constructed modern townships such as Mitchell's Plain, 30 miles outside of Capetown, to house coloreds from District 6. Critics cite the destruction of what they describe as one of the most vibrant and successful communities in South Africa. They say that many coloreds are unable to afford Mitchell's Plain, because of the higher rents and the cost of transportation to the city, and are forced to live in desolate and bland housing tracts. By 1978, the government had spent 27 million rand in demolition and expropriation of properties in District 6, but few white investors were interested in construction in an area which had become something of a living memorial to apartheid policies. The local government has lost 600,000 rand in revenue and, with one exception, by the beginning of 1979 there had been no new development in the district.

Land Tenure and Housing

Until recently, the policy of the National Party denied the right of Africans to land tenure in urban areas. The policy was articulated as early as 1952. The locations or townships were to be considered white-owned property belonging to the local authority. "The natives who reside there," then Prime Minister Dr. H.F. Verwoerd said, "reside there just as native farm laborers live on the farm of a European owner....The only native areas in South Africa...are the scheduled areas and the released areas."

Just as whites had been concerned about squatters on white farms, they also became worried about the growing numbers of squatters settling around urban centers. During and after World War II, thousands of people moved from the rural sections of South Africa to settle in camps around the major industrial areas. The new Nationalist government after its election in 1948 sought to clear these camps, separating their populations into racial groups to be housed in separate locations and forcing Africans without jobs to return to rural areas. At that time, the government began to build subsidized housing for all races, and since the end of the war it has constructed more than 250,000 houses for Africans.

But construction of government housing has not kept pace with the burgeoning demand, and regulations limiting the rights of Africans to land tenure have affected the ability of African workers to build their own houses and their interest in doing so. Unable after 1968 to obtain long-term lease rights to the land on which they were living, Africans living in white areas have lacked the collateral that would have allowed them to obtain loans to buy or build their houses and few have done so. (Until 1968, Africans in white areas had been able to obtain a 30-year leasehold on home sites in African townships; the right was removed in 1968, forcing Africans to rent the land on which they lived from the local governing authority.) The government in 1975 reinstated the concept of the 30-year leasehold, eventually extending it to 99 years and, in December 1978, issuing regulations that give Africans the right of title required by building societies for mortgage loans. The first title was granted to an African under the new regulations in April 1979, but bureaucratic delays in conducting surveys of townships and in clearing up questions relating to title have cooled any early enthusiasm among blacks.

The housing shortage: The changes in housing policy have come at a time when South Africa is plagued by a severe housing shortage.

H. Joubert, Under Secretary of Bantu Administration and Development, testified in April 1977 that the government needed to spend 510 million rand to meet the current shortage of 170,000 houses for Africans in urban areas. The government has plans to build 89,000 houses over the next five years, but experts predict that this will only allow the shortage to increase to more than 200,000 houses. To deal with the backlog, the government announced in May 1979 its intention to spend an additional 89 million rand on African housing over the next three years, a sum that should provide for an additional 40,000 houses.

As a result of the shortage, houses in African townships are overcrowded. For example, Soweto has an estimated 110,000 houses for a population of about 1.5 million. A number of migrant workers are housed in single-sex hostels; nevertheless, government statistics show an average of 6 persons per house in Soweto. Private studies estimate eight per family dwelling, but some homes may house as many as 26 people. Rent is low--6 to 20 rand per month--but the houses are small, the average house being 48 square meters, built of brick and divided into four rooms. About 15 percent of the houses have electricity; most burn coal for heat; 21 percent have running (cold) water inside the houses; 3 percent have showers or baths; 98 percent burn coal for cooking and heating.

The waiting list for houses in Soweto is officially estimated at close to 12,000. Helen Suzman, Progressive Federal Party Representative from a suburb near Johannesburg, says that at least 20,000 families are waiting. Between 1974 and 1976 the local government built 1,009 houses in Soweto; in 1978 320 houses were built, 110 by local authorities and 210 by private owners.

The lack of housing construction in part reflects a lack of resources committed to the development of African townships. According to historian T.R.H. Davenport, it also reflects the government's commitment to a policy of separate development. He writes that in the late 1960s the policy of the government "required a reduction in the number of Africans permanently residing in urban areas and an increase in the number of workers migrating from the homelands and living in hostels." Thus there was "an enforced cutback on municipal housing." In May 1979 Pieter Riekert, former economic advisor to the prime minister, confirmed this analysis, stating that "the comparatively small sums spent on black housing in white areas must be seen in the context of the emphasis on housing in the black states (homelands)."

Squatters' communities: The shortage of housing, however, has encouraged the development of squatters' communities, particularly in Natal and in the Western Cape. Overcrowded or unable to get housing in the township areas, increasing numbers of Africans and--especially in the Cape--coloreds as well have moved to areas on the outskirts of town and established their own communities. These communities are shanty towns, with makeshift shelters fashioned from whatever the dwellers can scavenge. In some instances, the move to a squatters' community is an act of protest against the government's policy on migrant labor. The Financial Mail quotes one African worker living in Crossroads, a squatters' village in the Cape: "We are trying to say that we are no longer prepared to accept a situation which demands, as a condition to the pursuit of man's basic aspirations, that we spend our working lives away from our families." Crossroads has grown from an estimated 7,000 people in 1975 to 20,000 in 1978. Most of the Africans living there--some 80 percent of the males--have jobs in Capetown, and many have worked there for as long as 20 years.

The African squatters' communities in the Western Cape pose a particular problem for National Party theorists. The Nationalists consider the Western Cape as an area where coloreds should be given preference over Africans. In 1955, Dr. W.W.M. Eiselen, Secretary for Native Affairs, said it was the government's policy eventually to remove all Africans from the Western Cape. A "freeze" was to be placed on Africans living in the regions, women and children who did not meet specific criteria were to be removed, and future influx was to be limited to migrant workers. This policy continues. The policy in the Western Cape is described in a recent study by a South African government commission: "All Bantu in that area--workers and others--must in time (by degrees and judiciously) be replaced with coloreds but in such a way as not to lead to any really serious economic dislocation." As many as 200,000 Africans may now be living and working in the Western Cape.

The contrast between the numbers of Africans in the Western Cape and the government's stated policy on replacing Africans there with coloreds points to the growing contradictions in the Nationalists' policy on housing and locations. Under increasing pressure, particularly from business, but also from the "verligte" (enlightened) wing of its own party, to recognize the permanent reality of increasing numbers of Africans in urban areas, the government has relaxed to some extent its policy on land tenure for Africans. The 99-year lease is the fruit of this relaxation as is the limited commitment to new expenditure on housing for Africans. Yet at the same time, the government is taking great pains to assure its more conservative constituents that there will be no real change in its policy of separate development, and it has taken a number of tangible steps to reinforce this assurance. It continues to shift population groups, and in 1977 and 1978 it moved repeatedly against squatters' communities in the Western Cape. The most visible actions included the destruction of the squatters' camps at Modderdam and Unibell in the Cape Province in 1977. Modderdam had been a community of 15,000 people, and its destruction sent a fresh flow of Africans into Crossroads. The government had repeatedly stated its intention to remove Crossroads, and the threat of its destruction became an increasingly political issue in South Africa until April 1979 when Piet Koornhof, Minister for Cooperation and Development (black affairs), announced the government's intention to build permanent housing for most of the Africans living in Crossroads. In a telephone interview with Washington Post correspondent Caryle Murphy, Koornhof said of his decision, "Yes it is a change of policy, but don't present it as a change of policy." The 99-year leasehold has not been extended to Africans living in the Western Cape, still considered a colored preference area, and Crossroads may not necessarily represent a precedent.

The Decentralization Policy

The government has also made efforts to discourage rural-urban migration by limiting the availability of jobs to Africans in urban areas and by discouraging the construction or expansion of labor-intensive factories. The efforts are part of the government's program to decentralize industry in South Africa. Decentralization is important, former Prime Minister John Vorster has said, both because industry in South Africa is overconcentrated and because enterprises providing Africans with jobs in or near the homelands further the policy of separate development by reducing Africans' interest in moving to the urban centers in white areas.

Trade and industry in South Africa now are heavily centralized. Nearly 55 percent of industrial production comes from four industrial centers representing less than 4 percent of the land area of the country; six industrial centers account for more than 60 percent of the country's purchasing power. Large numbers of Africans have moved to the township areas surrounding these centers.

Incentives and disincentives: To stimulate decentralization, the government has developed incentives for companies willing to move to or to establish operations in one of several growth points in or adjoining the ten homelands. It will provide loans at subsidized rates; income tax concessions, including deductions for expenditures on wages paid to workers or capital equipment; housing subsidies for white workers; and wage-law exemptions allowing companies operating in the border areas or homelands to pay wages lower than those required in other areas.

At the same time, the government has sought to discourage companies from setting up or expanding labor-intensive operations in the white areas. The Environment Planning Act restricts expansion of operations that will require increased numbers of African workers and requires industries in certain urban areas to maintain specific racial ratios in their work force. The government reports that since the introduction of the act in 1977, 2,002 applications for factory extensions that would have provided jobs for 101,557 Africans have been refused. (Details of act, Appendix A)

Failure of decentralization: Creation of jobs in the border and homelands areas has not approached the number of jobs required. To meet the government's objectives, the decentralization program is supposed to establish 20,000 new jobs for Africans per year. Since the program started in 1960, the government has spent nearly 1 billion rand in the homelands to create about 120,000 jobs. During 1976, 8,311 jobs were established in the homelands, at an average cost of 4,070 rand per job. Over the last 18 years nearly 800 million rand has been spent in the border areas adjacent to homelands--about 500 million rand provided by private industry--on plant development, housing and services. Some 70,000 jobs have been created in the process.

Many South Africans recognize that the decentralization program has failed essentially in its objective of creating sufficient jobs in the homelands and border areas so that Africans would be drawn back from white areas. According to then-Prime Minister Verwoerd's plan, as developed in the early 1960s, 1978 was to be the year that the tide turned and greater numbers of Africans were to begin migrating from white areas to independent homelands than were migrating from the homelands to urban centers in white areas. The decentralization program has not met the policy objective, but no alternative has been developed by the National Party.

Restrictions on African Entrepreneurship

On the premise that the right to engage in business is available to Africans in the homelands and that those Africans interested in developing businesses should move there, the government has used a variety of restrictions to actively discourage African entrepreneurship in the areas designated as white. Until recently African businessmen operating in urban townships were limited to 22 types of businesses--primarily small-scale retailing to "supply essential domestic requirements" of Africans living there. Shop sites were limited to 150 square meters in size, and an African businessman could operate only one kind of business, with one outlet. He could not form a partnership and could operate only in the area where he had been born or had worked for 10 to 15 years. Because Africans were not allowed to own land in the township, they lacked collateral for business loans.

The restrictions have had several consequences. The opportunities for Africans to get business experience have been extremely limited, and commercial services available to Africans living in the townships have been minimal. Soweto, for example, a city of about 1.5 million, had in January 1978 1,600 traders--including 394 variety stores, 226 grocers, 194 butchers, 17 undertakers, 165 coal and wood yards and 46 dry cleaners. The result is a severe constraint on the degree to which Africans are able to share the "trickle-down benefits" of a growing economy. Most of the increased discretionary income earned by Africans is spent in white-owned stores, not in the black community.

The government began to relax some of the restrictions on African traders in 1976. The kinds of businesses permitted were expanded from 26 to 66, including automotive maintenance and repair and dry cleaning. Traders were allowed sites up to 350 square meters, and in 1978 that limitation was abandoned. There is now no restriction on the size of site, and since September 1978 African businessmen have been able to carry on more than one business at a time. The National African Chamber of Commerce has launched an independent African bank, an insurance company and, most recently, a construction company.

But serious restrictions remain. Africans are not permitted to operate in downtown business centers--it is not possible for an African to lease office space in Johannesburg or Capetown, for example. Africans still cannot form partnerships with whites, although partnerships between Africans are now possible. Africans are not allowed to run industrial manufacturing operations in white areas, and the local government boards maintain their monopoly on liquor, movie theater and hotel businesses in the black townships.

Controls Over Dissent

The pass laws and the restrictions on housing for Africans, coloreds and Asians ignore the heavy costs imposed on those populations--direct costs in terms of losses during population shifts, transportation costs, the costs of separate domiciles. They also ignore severe psychological and human costs in the forced uprooting of communities and separation of families. They have been resisted repeatedly, and the government has developed a body of law to restrict and control the protest. The strength and flexibility of South Africa's system of legal controls over dissent are vital realities with which those seeking change must deal and present severe limits under which they must operate. The most significant laws affecting political discussion and action are the Suppression of Communism Act of 1950 (later incorporated in the Internal Security Act of 1976), the Riotous Assemblies Act (1956), the Terrorism Act of 1967 and those laws affecting the press and censorship. (See Appendix A) Under these acts and subsequent amendments, the government has the authority to suppress ("ban") dissent, and to arrest and indefinitely detain without charge persons suspected of political offenses. Individuals served with banning orders may be restricted to certain areas and prohibited from publishing or making speeches. The language of the laws is vague and a great deal of discretion is left to lower-level law officers and to the Minister of Justice.

On repeated occasions, when the government has considered demonstrations against the pass laws, education or other aspects of separate development as a threat to its security, it has not hesitated to invoke those laws. In March 1960, mass demonstrations against the passbook system culminated in the deaths of 69 unarmed people at Sharpeville, and the government moved aggressively to stop further protest. It banned African political organizations--the African National Congress and the Pan-African Congress--and in the first few months after Sharpeville it detained more than 18,000 people, eventually charging and sentencing more than 5,000. The demonstrations that began in Soweto in 1976 resulted in more than 600 deaths. The government detained more than 6,000, and it brought 3,000 to court in Port Elizabeth alone. In October 1977, it banned 18 organizations associated with the black consciousness movement. An estimated 700 people were under five-year banning orders in July 1978. Some 41 people were being detained under the Terrorism Act in November 1978, according to Minister of Justice James Kruger; some 35 cases involving 138 people had yet to be tried under the Internal Security Act. Since 1976, 26 prisoners have died while being held in detention. In September 1978, the government charged eight men--including six white detectives--with the death of one black prisoner and the beatings of five others.

The position of the press: South Africa has a traditional policy of a free and open press, although the government operates an active censorship program that limits information from abroad, affects local writers, and has played an important role in shaping the view South Africans have of their society and its world context. Under the 1974 Publications Act, the Directorate of Publications reviewed 2,121 publications or files in 1977, and 1,246 items, including 44 films, books by Xaviera Hollander, Harold Robbins and eminent Afrikaans author Etienne LeRoux, were found undesirable and banned.

In addition, the government has moved directly against newspapers and journalists when it considers their efforts detrimental to state security. On Oct. 19, 1977, the black newspaper, the World, was banned, its editor Percy Qoboza was detained, white editor Donald Woods was banned, and the Union of Black Journalists was banned. Subsequently, limited bans have been issued on the ecumenical black paper, The Voice, and numbers of journalists have been detained for questioning. The government introduced in parliament in 1977 a Newspaper Bill containing a press code and providing for fines and imprisonment for violators of the code. The bill was revoked after stout protests by the National Press Union, but the Prime Minister stated that the newspapers should consider themselves on a one-year probation and the National Press Council would be expected to discipline its members.

The censorship laws and the actions taken by the government against writers, film makers and members of the media have had a dampening effect on the degree of freedom exercised by the press and the level of public debate within the society. Nevertheless, public criticism of the government continues and, in fact, it has been so effective in one case relating to the activities of the Department of Information as to force the resignation of the Minister responsible and the revamping of the entire information program. And public debate and criticism, traditionally the private reserve of the English language press, is increasingly finding its way into the Afrikaans press. But editors and writers complain of the necessity to look constantly over their shoulders. Andre Brink, a well-known Afrikaans writer, told Tiiu Lukk of The Washington Star that the actuality of banning is not as great a danger as "the atmosphere of uncertainty built around it. Writers begin to write with one eye on the censors, the other eye on the page. Publishers fear to print, because printers can also be prosecuted. Young writers, struggling for a market, are inhibited."

The press appears relatively powerful after its recent efforts to unravel what has been dubbed South Africa's Watergate, but few journalists are unaware of the limits under which they operate and the potential consequences of becoming overly political in their writings. Prime Minister P.W. Botha has repeatedly warned reporters about "gossip mongering," and in 1979 parliament passed legislation making it an offense to publish "any untrue matter" about the police "without having reasonable grounds for believing the statement is true." The burden of proof lies with the press; reporters and editors are liable to fines of up to nearly $12,000 and five years in jail and reporters may be required to reveal their sources under any circumstances--they are already required to do so in criminal cases. The parliament also passed legislation that would forbid press discussion of South Africa's supplies of oil and other strategic materials--defined by the Financial Mail as raw, intermediate or manufactured goods.

Education Under Apartheid

Many companies say that the chief obstacle to blacks' advancement in South Africa is the lack of adequate education and training available to Africans, Asians and coloreds. There are simply too few blacks around with the skills required for business, company officials say, and the shortage of trained workers is likely to grow more severe. A number of South Africans describe South Africa's educational deficiencies as those familiar to all developing countries--too many students, too few teachers, inadequate resources. But South Africa's problem is vastly more complicated. It is only partially a reflection of the massive demands that development makes on scarce resources. At its root is the government's lack of political will to make sacrifices for black advancement and its desire, instead, to move forward with a policy of separate development.

Government policy: The government's program for education has been developed in line with its policy of separate development and has long been a target of resentment among blacks. There are 17 departments of education in South Africa; Africans, Asians, coloreds and whites are assigned to separate schools, and Africans are further segregated according to tribal language. The government has argued that such separation is necessary to allow the development of separate cultures and to avoid unnecessary racial friction. Its critics maintain that the policy consciously holds Africans back, limiting their opportunities for education by forcing them to attend inadequate schools, with inadequate staffs and an inadequate syllabus.

Afrikaners have viewed education as an important part of their own national development, and the National Party leaders have stressed this view in their educational policies for other such groups. The Eiselen Commission, formed to examine African education, commented in a 1954 report that was to become the keystone of the National Party's platform for African education, "Educational practice must recognize that it has to deal with a Bantu child, that is, a child trained and conditioned in Bantu culture, endowed with a knowledge of a Bantu language, and imbued with values, interests and behavior patterns learned at the knee of a Bantu mother. These facts must dictate to a very large extent the content and methods of his early education." The commission emphasized the importance of using schooling as a method for the transmission and development of African cultural heritage.

But separation of the races in school had other practical advantages as well for the ruling white elite. It permitted education to be structured according to the roles that individuals were to assume in the society. H.F. Verwoerd, then Minister of Native Affairs and the principal architect of apartheid, later to become Prime Minister, told parliament in 1953 that teaching should be geared to the opportunities that would later be available in the society. Verwoerd argued against a policy for education of Africans that would foster the development of unrealistic expectations. There was no place for the African in the white community above a certain labor level, and education for Africans in white areas should be limited. He argued that all doors would be open to Africans in their own areas--the homelands--and it was there that education should "stand with both feet...and have its roots in the spirit and being of a Bantu society."

Soon after the publication of the Eiselen report, the government moved to take over education from the church, to ensure that the educational programs in African schools conformed with state policy. Until 1954, a majority of the schools operating in South Africa were run by the churches; in 1976, the number of church schools had fallen to 230. After the Bantu Education Act of 1954 was passed, government funds for church-run schools dried up; churches were required to offer their schools for sale or lease to the government or to go without government funds. The government refused to purchase or lease church schools operating in white areas, and without government subsidy many churches were forced to abandon their schools. The government's policy was not to build schools in white areas, and the number of schools in urban areas declined. The policy has relaxed somewhat in recent years, although the emphasis on school construction remains in the homelands.

The government has maintained that schools should be funded by the populations they serve. In 1954, for example, the Minister of Native Affairs stated that furniture for state, community and farm schools should be constructed, to the extent possible, by African vocational schools or workshops and that students should be held responsible for care and maintenance of the buildings. The government proposed to allocate 13 million rand to African education that year, with the remainder of the budgeted 17 million rand to come from taxes and fees levied on the African population. The size of the central government's contribution to Africans' education remained at 13 million rand until 1968, when the government recognized that the funding was insufficient and permitted the Department of Bantu Education to obtain funds on loan from other government departments. Since 1972, the government has raised its budget for education of Africans 350 percent, but the amounts spent remain relatively small—less than three-fourths of 1 percent of gross domestic product. The gap between the amount spent per capita on whites and that spent on other races remains wide and is growing wider. In 1977-78, for example, the government spent an average 57 rand per capita for education of Africans and 654 rand per capita for whites, a ratio of 1 to 11.5. In 1953, the ratio was 1 to 7.5: 17 rand for blacks, 128 rand for whites.

The government argues that its education system for blacks is the best in Africa. It claims 59-percent literacy for the African population—compared with an estimated 20 to 25 percent for Africans living in neighboring Angola and Botswana—and says that literacy among those Africans in the 15- to 22-year age group is much higher, approaching 80 percent. It says that it is building an average of one new school per day, has promised to provide free text books for all students through standard 10 (grade 12) by 1979, and has made education compulsory for Africans through standard 2. (Education already is free and compulsory for whites.)

Dissatisfaction with the education system: But critics raise considerable doubts about the quality of education for Africans, and in 1976 the government's decision to make Afrikaans a mandatory subject in African schools provided the spark that set off the demonstrations in Soweto. The Afrikaans language issue provided African students with a focus for their anger at an educational system that they consider grossly unequal, and their anger grew rapidly to encompass the whole of the apartheid structure. In protest, more than 25,000 secondary school students in Soweto alone boycotted schools during most of 1977. Nearly 500 teachers resigned, and at the end of 1977 only 12 of 40 secondary schools in Soweto were in operation.

The school boycott has ended, although the number of students attending school has not returned to normal. In Soweto, some 12,000 secondary school students were unaccounted for in 1978, and it is suspected that they were either continuing an individual boycott, they had left Soweto to get schooling elsewhere, or they had fled the country to join the several thousand in studies abroad or students in military training in neighboring countries.

The government acknowledged Africans' dissatisfaction with the system (as well as Africans' dislike of the word Bantu) by changing the name of the administering department from the Department of Bantu

Education to the Department of Education and Training. There has been no major new commitment of funds to education of Africans, however, and without a dramatic reversal of past policies, it is unlikely that the government's program for African education will begin to approach the needs of the population. In terms of Africans' education, the country faces many of the problems of any developing country--a rapidly expanding student population (43 percent of all Africans are under 15, compared with 30 percent of the whites), inadequate numbers of teachers and inadequate training. The lack of resources and trained personnel are compounded by government policies that require schooling for Africans in the primary grades to be conducted in tribal languages in the urban as well as the rural areas; students who do not reach secondary school may have little training if any in English or Afrikaans. Those students who do reach secondary school where English and Afrikaans are major subjects as well are far more likely to have a background in three languages than to have a grounding in math and science when they graduate.

The weakness of education for Africans, particularly when compared with that available for whites, is apparent in figures on student-teacher ratios and size of enrollment. In 1977, the student-teacher ratio for Africans was 52 to 1; for whites it was 20 to 1. These ratios compare with a ratio of 36.1 to 1 for Africa as a whole, 44 to 1 in Lesotho, and 34 to 1 in Botswana--although in South Africa a far greater percentage of the school-age population is in school. Only 14.3 percent of African teachers had received their matriculation diploma--equivalent to a junior college diploma; many had less than a standard 5 (grade 7) education.

South Africa would have to train 14,000 African teachers a year to overcome the deficit of trained teachers. In 1976, there were only 8,171 graduates from high school and 6,579 from teacher-training colleges. Teacher shortages are compounded by the government's policy that teachers should come from the racial communities in which they teach--that is, whites should not teach in black schools. Of 63,868 teachers in African schools, some 930 are white and these are mainly consigned to teachers' colleges. At the same time, in certain subjects and sectors, there is a surplus of white teachers.

To cope with the shortage of teachers, more than 900,000 African students are on double sessions. The drop-out rate among students is very high; nearly one-quarter of all students drop out after their first year and more than two-thirds have left school by the sixth grade. Two-tenths of 1 percent graduate from secondary school.

The limited number of these graduates is reflected in the university attendance figures. The three universities established for Africans had a combined enrollment of just under 5,000 in 1977; an additional 6,320 were enrolled by correspondence at the University of South Africa in 1977. In 1977, 403 Africans graduated from universities, predominantly in the liberal arts, language and history. Few Africans graduate in the professions. In 1977, two Africans received university degrees in engineering and 15 qualified as doctors. There are now about 100 African lawyers in South Africa, 25 African pharmacists and one certified accountant.

University opportunities for blacks began to open slightly in 1977, primarily at the graduate level, as the government allowed increasing numbers of blacks to attend white universities. In 1977, some 1,277 blacks--including nearly 500 Africans--were attending white universities. One hundred eighty-nine Africans were approved for admission to white universities in 1978 and 360 were turned down. The government denies that the increased admissions constitute a revision of its policy of separate education, but it explains that blacks are only being admitted for courses of study that are not available at their own universities. In 1979 the government formed a committee of inquiry to examine the need for university education for Africans in "white" areas. Gerrit Viljoen, rector of Rand Afrikaans University and head of the Afrikaner secret society, the Broederbond, told IRRC in 1978 that increased numbers of Africans could be admitted to white universities, particularly at the post-graduate level, but he predicted it would be two years before African undergraduates could be accepted at RAU. The pace, he said, was dictated by attitudes in the university community more than by government policy.

Training Opportunities for Blacks

The opportunities for blacks--particularly Africans--to acquire trades and technical training have been severely inhibited by government policy, white union activity and, to a lesser extent, lack of interest in the private sector. In line with its policy of separate development, government has sought to restrict the training opportunities for Africans to the homelands; few opportunities have been available to Africans in areas designated for whites. In the private sector, white unions have refused to train blacks for certain positions and, in agreements with companies, have excluded blacks from work in certain positions. While many companies increasingly recognize the importance of greater training opportunities for black employees, only in the last few years have they begun to establish formal training of their own. As a result of these three factors, the number of Africans with training in trades and higher technical subjects remains extremely limited, and for those companies actively recruiting blacks for higher positions, the universe from which they may draw is far smaller than their needs demand.

Government policy: The government's policy of limiting training to the homelands has had two objectives: first, to encourage those Africans interested in training in the trades or in technical subjects to move to the homelands--with the subsequent result of encouraging industry requiring these skills to locate either in the homelands or in the adjoining border areas--and second, by limiting the availability of skilled Africans in white areas, to protect the interests of the white skilled workers there. It is the government's policy, the Minister of Labor said in August 1975, that "each race group would as far as possible serve its own community in its own area. The blacks are therefore destined to develop their full potential in their own areas where there is no limitation whatsoever on their progress or achievements." As with education, Africans should only receive training to the levels for which there are jobs available, and the training should only take place where the jobs are available.

Formal training in trades and technical subjects for Africans is provided by four types of programs: (1) trades training designed to provide Africans with the basic skills required for certification as an artisan; (2) technical education at the secondary or high-school level designed to qualify Africans for higher technical training; (3) advanced technical education for professionals--to the level of hospital technician or technical engineer; (4) industrial training in pre-service or in-service training centers.

Trades training: Most formal training in the trades for Africans takes place in the homelands. There are 19 trade and semi-trade schools located in the homelands and one in Soweto. The schools offer a curriculum required for a national technical certificate and are open to students who have already passed standard 7 (grade 9). The curriculum includes a certain amount of theory as well as practical training. Following the program, which may take up to three years, and a period of in-service training, the duration of which depends on the trade, graduates may take tests that would qualify them to be artisans. In 1977, 3,150 Africans were enrolled in trade schools in a variety of subjects (see chart A, Appendix D). The government offered trade tests to 2,986 Africans in 1977; of these, most were being tested to qualify as skilled or semi-skilled workers in the building trades; 207 were being tested to see whether they could qualify as artisans. (By contrast, in 1976, 27,515 whites were enrolled in national technical certificate courses and nearly 10,000 whites were tested after completing their work for the national technical certificate.)

Secondary technical training: Following standard 7, African students may enroll in one of five technical high schools--three in the homelands, two in urban areas--for courses that include six hours a week on theory and practical work in building construction, electronics, woodwork, motor mechanics and welding. The government describes this curriculum as designed to prepare students for advanced technical or university training. Some 1,146 Africans were enrolled in secondary technical courses in 1977. (This compares with more than 32,000 whites studying full- and part-time at technical institutes in 1975.) (See chart B, Appendix D)

Advanced technical education: Advanced technical education for Africans, including studies to prepare Africans for careers as technicians in engineering, surveying, geology, telecommunications or paramedical work, is available at two colleges in homelands. One of the two colleges is described as "inter-ethnic," open to all Africans; the other is reserved to Nguni speakers. In 1977, 541 students were enrolled in the two schools. (About 27,000 whites were enrolled for advanced technical training in 1976.) (See chart C, Appendix D)

Industrial training for Africans: In 1975, the government modified its policy restricting training for Africans in white areas. The Bantu Employees In-Service Act passed in 1976 provided for the establishment of pre- and in-service training at public as well as private centers in urban areas. Eight centers were to be established--six are now in operation--to provide 30 to 40 higher primary and junior high schools in black townships with facilities for pre-service training. The training consists of an introduction--two to two-and-a-half hours a week--to wood, metal and plastic working, welding, electrical work and brick work. During 1977, 13,326 students from standard 5 to standard 8 participated in the program.

The act also provided for the establishment of eight private in-service training centers for industry. The government is committed to providing funding--some 2 million rand in total--for the land and buildings required for each center, and industry, through trade associations, is responsible for the staffing and administration of the training programs. The centers provide training for such jobs as repair shop assistants, body shop assistants, fork lift operators, storemen, switchboard operators, salesmen and punch card operators. The centers, the government states, are designed to "provide in-service training to black workers to increase productivity in permissible job categories." During 1977, 3,843 people participated in courses at these centers.

In addition, the government has approved subsidies to 19 ad hoc industrial training centers in border areas which were responsible for training some 3,500 employees in 1977. Although the employer is responsible for the instructors, the center itself and any special equipment or materials, the government pays the instructors and exercises control over the curriculum. The government also reviews and provides tax deductions of up to 250 percent to private employers who have developed training programs approved by the Department of Education and Training. In 1977, 48 training programs were approved.

The success of the industrial training programs has been limited by a combination of government policy, business needs and lack of company interest. The government states that "the industrial training of operators is limited to only those skills and techniques essential to the efficient performance of the operators' task. The duration of this training is much shorter than is the case with the training of artisans." The pre-service centers are designed to introduce urban Africans to industrial skills; the in-service centers will offer courses in woodworking, metal working, keypunch operation and lower-level welding, designed to help improve "operative" skills. Neither the pre-service nor in-service centers provide the kind of skills training required to allow blacks to qualify as skilled or artisan labor.

Company representatives have criticized the government's policy. The Johannesburg Star reported May 18, 1978, that R.J. Ironside of General Motors had made what it described as an "unprecedented call for government to open artisan training to all races." Ironside said that even entry of Asian and colored workers into trades would not meet South Africa's demand for skilled labor. Failure to open training facilities to all races, he said, would cripple industry's capability to "even sustain present reduced levels of activity, let alone support the upswing which seems on its way." And companies' support for the centers has been limited.

The supervisor of one center commented in February 1978 that his center was desperately short of trainees as well as funds. The "support these centers are getting comes from only a few industries. Most industries and commercial organizations are not making use of the centers." Many companies argue that they can provide in-service and pre-service training to employees better themselves. As a result, two of the centers are barely breaking even and one is operating at a loss. The supervisor at Chamdor, which is the most advanced center and has received support from a number of American companies--most notably IBM--reports that the center is breaking even but could double the number of trainees. Joos Lemmer of Chamdor commented, "It is a shame that we are not being used enough at a time of large-scale unemployment. But we are in-service institutions which means that we can provide only for employed people." Chamdor has trained some 1,500 people since it opened.

Legal limits on blacks' training and advancement: In addition to the limits imposed by the nature of public training available to blacks in trade and technical schools, training and advancement are further inhibited by the body of legislation governing black labor. The government says its policy is "not to stand in the way of changes in traditional work patterns which allow non-whites to move up into job categories for which they will require higher skills and in which they can earn higher wages than previously, provided these changes come about in an orderly fashion and with the concurrence of the trade unions." But the laws leave a good deal of discretion to the white trade unions, and the unions, acting under the laws, have sought consistently to delay blacks' advancement. Africans, in turn, are inhibited by law from making protests against the limits imposed on their advancement.

Among the laws effectively restricting the development of black labor are the Apprenticeship Act of 1922 and its 1944 and 1963 amendments. While non-discriminatory in language, the act has been used by white trade unions to exclude Africans and other blacks from apprenticeship training. The act, according to an adviser to the Urban Foundation in South Africa, "has been one of the most powerful barriers to the economic advancement of Africans and to a lesser extent of colored and Asian workers." It has "contributed to the scarcity of skilled labor, which has the effect of retarding economic growth during the last economic upswing," he writes. The act establishes apprenticeship committees that must approve apprenticeship training. Because the committees are composed equally of representatives of industry and white unions, no Africans have been apprenticed outside the homelands. In 1975, throughout South Africa in the steel and engineering trades, there were 15,079 apprentices; 13,952 were white, 983 colored, 73 Asian and 72 African. In the same year, in the electrical trades, of 7,649 apprentices, 7,181 were white, 316 were African, 77 Asian and 75 colored. The lack of training available to Africans, either through trade schools or through apprenticeship programs, is reflected directly in the number of African artisans. In 1975, there were a total of 4,862 African artisans in South Africa, 2,635 of whom were in the building trades; this compares with 170,993 white artisans in South Africa the same year.

Other key laws restricting blacks' job advancement or the position of blacks in the workplace include the Industrial Conciliation Act of 1924; the Bantu Labor Act of 1964 and amendments; the Mines and Works Act of 1911, as amended in 1926 and 1956; the Factories, Machinery and Building Work Act of 1941, amended in 1960; and the Shops and Offices Act of 1964. These laws have prevented Africans from joining registered trade unions, limited their ability to strike, reserved specific jobs for whites, and separated work facilities by race. (Details of the laws restricting black labor, Appendix A)

The Limits on Labor Representation

The ability of African workers to negotiate for better working and living conditions has been severely constrained by a combination of legal and historical factors and company attitudes.

Labor committees: The Industrial Conciliation Act bars Africans from joining registered trade unions and provides no legal protection to unions that are not registered. African workers are represented at industrial council meetings by an official of the labor department. Agreements reached at the meetings are binding on all workers in the industry, including Africans, but the official representing Africans' interests is not allowed to vote at the meeting. Moreover, until 1973, only a white official was allowed. In that year, the government agreed to allow African members of what were then called regional Bantu labor committees to attend industrial council meetings to speak for Africans' interests. Neither they nor the official could vote, but they could speak in the discussion and had the right of appeal to a minister if they had objections to the decisions reached.

Within companies, Africans are allowed to deal with company officials through works committees and liaison committees. Under the 1953 Bantu Labor (Settlement of Disputes) Act, companies were permitted to establish works committees composed entirely of representatives elected by African workers. (Works committees differ from liaison committees in that half the members of the liaison committees are elected by African employees, including the chairman and secretary, and the remaining members are appointed by management.) Few companies chose to sponsor works committees, and by the end of 1973 only 125 works committees and 773 liaison committees had been established in the more than 30,000 factories and commercial establishments in South Africa.

Strikes of 50,000 African workers in Durban in 1973 led the government to amend the labor act to give African workers the right to demand that a company establish a works committee unless it already had established a liaison committee. The 1973 act gave liaison committees authority to "communicate the wishes, aspirations and requirements of the employees...to their employer and to represent the said employees in any negotiations with their employer, concerning their conditions of employment or any other matter affecting their interests." It was further amended in 1977 to allow committees the power specifically to negotiate wage agreements and to state that the agreements once reached are legally binding on the employer.

Most companies, including the majority of American companies, have decided to establish liaison committees rather than be faced with workers' demands for a works committee. Since 1973, 2,503 liaison committees and 301 works committees have been formed. Urwick International's annual survey of labor in South Africa found in 1978 that 60 percent of the companies questioned had liaison committees and 18 percent had works committees.

Despite the proliferation of committees, and although the committees have now been granted greater power to represent workers, there is strong criticism of the committee system from companies as well as from black unions. Eleven trade unions submitted a memorandum to the Wiehahn Commission, a commission considering labor law reform, protesting that the works and liaison committee system contained structural weaknesses and permitted employers to avoid dealing with independent African trade unions. Some company officials, as well, disputed the effectiveness of the system. The personnel manager for Brynzeel Plywoods, a South African company, said that committee representatives were forced to confront their own employer in negotiations, lacked financial independence, and were faced with the possibility of being fired from their jobs because of activism. A representative of Anglo American commented in 1977 that a refusal to recognize the rights of Africans to join trade unions would leave the way open for "political agitators." And the head of the Wiehahn Commission, Nicholas Wiehahn, suggested training of Africans in the principles of trade unionism, arguing that without such training, workers would be vulnerable to "outside influences." (Details on Wiehahn Commission, below)

   History of union movement: There has been no legal restriction on the formation of African unions. African trade unions have existed with varying numbers of members since the turn of the century. But the government has moved swiftly to detain or arrest African union leaders suspected of any political activity. It has also denied African unions the right of recognition, and thus any agreements reached by African trade unions have lacked the force of law and have been dependent on the good will of the negotiating parties. Finally, the Bantu Labor Act of 1964 makes it illegal for companies to issue checkoffs (called stop orders in South Africa) on employees' paychecks. The stop order would allow deduction of union dues from the weekly or monthly wage checks, and union organizers consider them critical to the effective financing of a union. Companies can make deductions, however, for government-approved welfare or insurance programs, and African unions have been formed around funeral benefit societies. Stop orders have been issued on behalf of the societies, and African union representatives have been allowed to keep a portion of the funds collected as their fees for administration of the societies.

   But the obstacles placed in the path of the African trade union movement have contributed to wide swings in membership. A union formed in 1918, the Industrial and Commercial Workers Union, had an estimated 100,000 members in 1927 before it dissolved following a political split. By the early 1940s some 23 African unions had grown up and, following the war, between 100,000 and 160,000 workers were organized in African unions. Some white unions accepted black members--until 1963 African women but not men were allowed to join unions--but interest in the unions dropped sharply when a number of union leaders and organizers were accused of political activity. Since the mid-1950s, hundreds of African union leaders and whites assisting in the organization of African unions have been arrested, detained or banned under the Suppression of Communism Act, because the government has said they were promoting the aims of communism as those aims are broadly defined in the act.

   Government harassment has been a powerful deterrent to black unionism. Muriel Horrell of the South African Institute for Race Relations wrote in 1969 that "active leaders who voice workers' grievances run the risk of finding themselves dubbed as 'agitators,' being dismissed from their jobs and, under the pass laws, being ordered out of the town concerned, thus losing their homes. The police have raided the offices of many of the unions, confiscating the records. Some employers are understanding; but it is said that others do not want their employees to join trade unions and, if the organizer visits the place of work, threaten to call the police and have him arrested for disturbing the workers." Consequently, Horrell said, "most Africans are afraid to become members of trade unions."

Nevertheless, the 1973 Durban strikes led to a resurgence of the African trade union movement. Since then, the number of Africans participating in independent African unions has increased dramatically. Twenty unions have been launched in the last 10 years and, despite the banning, arrest or detention of some 30 union organizers since 1976, 28 African unions now represent an estimated 115,000 workers (50,000 paid members).

The growth of African unions has received some international support. In addition to the encouragement in the codes of conduct, several international unions have pressed parent companies to get their subsidiaries to recognize African unions. The Trade Union Council of the United Kingdom has been active for a number of years on South African issues and, to a lesser degree, American unions--the United Auto Workers, the United Mine Workers and some members of the AFL-CIO--have expressed interest in the development of a black union movement in South Africa. One American company--Kellogg--and one British company-- Smith & Nephew--have officially recognized African trade unions. Ford has informally recognized an African union, as have several British companies and about a dozen South African companies.

Recent Developments Affecting Workers

There is little doubt that a number of important, although limited, developments that affect labor and living conditions for workers in South Africa have occurred in the last few years. The South African government has not deviated in its broad policy of separate development, but economic pressures, political pressures from abroad, and efforts within South Africa have combined to alter to some extent the environment in which companies operate. Several of the changes reflect modifications in government policy or its implementation; others are the result of foreign pressures and the increased attention being paid by home offices and shareholders abroad to corporate activities in South Africa; and some changes reflect developments within South Africa. Together they have brought modest but measurable improvements in the labor practices of companies in South Africa and in the living conditions for employees and their dependents.

In the private sector, a number of companies, some voluntarily, others under pressure from their home offices, began to spend more time on programs for employees and their dependents. For some companies, interest in the training and promotion of blacks began in the late 1960s and early 1970s, prompted by the necessity to deal with shortages in skilled and semi-skilled positions. But for many, initiation or the revamping of employee programs received impetus from the attention--and additional home office capital and expertise--that has come with outside pressures. The Sullivan principles--developed under the aegis of General Motors board member Leon Sullivan and now endorsed by more than 130 U.S. companies--and similar codes of conduct developed by the European Economic Community and the South African Urban Foundation provided companies with a framework and an incentive for judging their own performance. After an initial assessment, a number of companies moved to develop programs to improve their performance, and there is evidence that a number of companies today are considering changes in training, wages, job evaluation, housing and desegregation of facilities that were not under consideration two to three years ago. (Details on the effect of the codes, Chapter V)

Employers' efforts to ease white concern about--and opposition to--black advancement have borne some fruit. In June 1978 the Steel and Engineering Federation of South Africa (SEIFSA), representing employers in a sector that accounts for about 450,000 workers, concluded an agreement with white workers that the South African Financial Mail described as "the biggest blow in decades...struck at the jobs color bar." The agreement theoretically opened for the first time middle- and higher-level skilled jobs to Africans; it also assured whites already holding positions at those levels that their jobs were secure. Signing the agreement did not herald a sudden advance for Africans--by and large whites still control advancement of blacks by controlling the training required for Africans to advance to higher levels--but it did represent a theoretical breakthrough that many hoped would be a precedent for similar agreements in other industries.

A further precedent was set when mining companies chose to ignore wildcat strikes called by white miners in March 1979. The strikes, called in protest to a management decision at O'okiep Cooper Co. to promote three colored workers into positions formerly reserved for whites, received little public support and no support from the government. After two weeks, the miners were forced to return to their jobs. The strikes' failure, observers remarked, demonstrated a growing recognition on the part of both the government and the general public that "racial job protection is a lost cause."

The Wiehahn and Riekert Commissions: More important potentially than the changes introduced by private companies are those developments that are taking place within government policy. Following the Soweto riots in 1976 and reflecting the mounting pressures from the business community concerning the government's policies toward black workers, the South African government announced in 1977 the formation of two government commissions. The first, the Wiehahn Commission, under the chairmanship of Pretoria academic and expert on industrial relations Nicholas Wiehahn, was asked to investigate labor legislation affecting Africans. A second commission, headed by Pieter Riekert, then the prime minister's adviser on economic affairs, was charged with reviewing the body of legislation affecting the utilization of African manpower. The initial recommendations of both commissions were made public in May 1979.

The Wiehahn report, described at first glance by South Africa's Financial Mail as "a major step forward," recommended that Africans be allowed to join registered trade unions, that statutory job reservations be abolished, that Africans working in urban areas be allowed to be indentured in apprenticeship training programs that would enable them to qualify as certified skilled artisans, and that requirements for separate toilet, eating and work areas for each race be abolished. The report also called for the establishment of a National Manpower Commission--to do research, plan and advise on labor policy--and an Industrial Court to arbitrate disputes. It did not recommend whether unions should be segregated or mixed, but left that decision to individual unions. Nor did it say what would constitute a legitimate union; all parties--employers and existing unions--making up an industrial council were to be given the right to veto the application for admission of any newly formulated union.

The Riekert Commission report submitted May 8, 1979, to South Africa's parliament supported continuation of the government's policy of "influx control" to control rural-urban migration, but advocated adjustments in the "pass" system to make it less onerous. The report stated that "controlled employment and controlled accommodation are the two pillars on which the ordering of the urbanization process and sound and orderly community development ought to rest." The right of Africans to live in white-designated areas should be decided by the availability of jobs and housing with the approval of regional labor bureaus. Africans meeting these criteria should be able to move freely, and should be allowed to have their families join them if housing is available. The commission also recommended that the rights of Africans to remain in white areas without the proper pass--now limited to 72 hours--be extended. It argued that controls on flow to urban areas are absolutely necessary, but the burden of responsibility could be accepted to a greater extent by employers. The commission suggested that the government begin to fine employers for hiring Africans who were working in white areas without proper passes--thus possibly reducing the degree to which African workers are harassed directly. Finally, the commission called for free economic competition, a relaxation of the restrictions on African entrepreneurs, and new opportunity for white employers to purchase housing for employees living in African townships.

The long-awaited commission reports met with a mixed reception. Conservative white union leaders branded the Wiehahn report as a betrayal of white workers' interests. Wessel Bornman, chief secretary of the Iron, Steel and Allied Industries Union, called the commission's report "a slap in the face of every white worker" and the "biggest embarrassment to white unions in the history of South Africa." Less conservative white workers saw its recommendations as inevitable and necessary, and business leaders heralded them as opening a "new labor era." Blacks were cautious in their reactions. African trade unionist Skakes Skikhakahne told the Financial Mail that he welcomed the report but was afraid its provisions "may control rather than strengthen black unions." Soweto community leader Dr. Nthato Motlana stated that "the principle underlying the proposals is commendable but there has been no suggestion that discrimination in industry should be outlawed." Without that, he said, "all the fine intentions mean nothing."

Observers described the Riekert Commission report as creating new opportunities for Africans already living in urban areas, while providing for a continuation of the strict controls on Africans seeking work or already employed as migrant labor. One critic of the commission, Sheen Duncan, the head of Black Sash--a women's organization established to assist Africans and to protest government racial policies--argued in response to the report: "Isolating a privileged group of blacks in the urban areas is going to take place at the expense of a vast number of people in the homelands, whose only safety-net up till now has been the inefficiency of the influx control system, which has enabled them to survive by getting jobs, albeit illegally, in the informal sector in the urban areas." The commission's recommendations offered a tangible step forward by easing some of the restrictions on many Africans living in urban areas. But for more than half of the Africans living in South Africa--those who lack the rights to permanence in white areas--they signaled a tightening of the system's controls.

The government announced that it accepted the recommendations of both commissions "in principle." In fact, its white paper on the Riekert Commission accepted most of the commission's proposals, only rejecting the suggestions that the 72-hour limit on Africans not permitted in urban areas be dropped, but accepting Riekert's major points that permission for Africans to live in white-designated areas be tied to jobs and housing.

In its white paper on the Wiehahn Commission and in the legislation following from it, the government's response fell far short of that hoped for by those who were initially enthusiastic over the report's recommendations. A major concern among black union officials was the acceptance by the government that existing unions and employers operating as an industrial council can act to prevent admission of new members. Thus a white union can veto an African union's admission to the council, effectively eliminating its rights as a bargaining agent. White unions could start up black parallel unions and choose to recognize them rather than recognizing an existing, but perhaps more activist, African union. A second concern has been the operation of the industrial court which could, according to South Africa's Financial Mail, "if it wishes, restrict and control factory floor change." Nor does the new legislation ensure Africans access to apprenticeship training in white areas. The apprenticeship process is left intact. But most importantly, the new legislation extended the right to join unions only to those Africans already living in white-designated areas--thus excluding the two million or so frontier "commuters" who live in townships located in the homelands but work in adjacent urban areas that are designated for whites. The omission of these workers would have made meaningful African union organization nearly impossible in Pretoria, Durban and Port Elizabeth, and by requiring all existing black unions to register while forbidding them to have migrant "frontier commuters" among their members, the government could effectively eliminate a number of the largest existing African unions. Either they would be forced to drop many of their members or they would be forced to forego registration and to operate without legal sanction.

The government later made a dramatic reversal of policy when, under pressure from business and from black unions, it agreed to drop the restriction on "commuters." Exercising his right as Minister for Manpower Utilization, S.P. Botha announced in the fall of 1979 that all Africans in South Africa, except those migrant workers from outside either the homelands or white-designated areas, could join recognized unions. The change, based on an exception in the regulations rather than new legislation, typified the process of change in South Africa. Willem de Klerk, editor of the Afrikaner paper Die Transvaler, described in 1978 the stages of policy change in South Africa as "never; no, not now; perhaps; yes but; yes, but keep it quiet; good, go ahead but beware of repercussions." Implementation of the recommendations of the Wiehahn and Riekert Commissions is likely to go through stages, fits and starts; it will take some time, and some steps could be greatly if not permanently delayed by the internal squabbles taking place within the National Party.

The Information Department scandal: Any major changes in government policy can only be made after thorough discussion within the

National Party. (The policy-making process is discussed in Chapter IV, The Broad Role of Business in South Africa.) For several years the Nationalists have presented a unified front to outside viewers, carefully covering up the ongoing struggle between those favoring a verligte (enlightened) strategy and those who supported a verkrampte (narrow) approach to policy issues. The effort to maintain unity has been difficult at times, however, and has certainly constrained the speed at which changes have been introduced. Former Prime Minister John Vorster stated that "a leader cannot move any faster than his sheep or they tend to stray." And he was particularly concerned that any changes made by the government not be viewed as alterations in the basic ideology of separate development, that conservatives not be offended by the pace of change, and that the unity of the National Party not be threatened. Debate over racial ideology split the party in 1969, shortly before Vorster became prime minister, resulting in the formation of a splinter right wing party--Herstigte Nationale Partie. Many observers said Vorster was traumatized by the event and committed to avoiding any similar public split. They describe the desire to avoid public dissent as severely inhibiting any decisive action.

The continued unraveling of a scandal involving the Information Department over the last two years further aggravated tensions within the party and, observers say, slowed any progress toward ending discrimination the government might have been able to make. The scandal, centering on the expenditure of more than $75 million over five years for some 150 secret projects to bolster the image of South Africa at home and abroad, shook, at least temporarily, the unquestioning faith of many Afrikaners in their elected leaders. Questions about who was actually involved, the extent and timing of their involvement, and the degree to which they may have benefited personally plagued the government in a fashion reminiscent of Watergate. Cornelius Mulder, the former Minister of Information who was nearly elected prime minister in October 1978--he lost by 24 votes in a 172-member party caucus--was forced to resign, not only from office but from the party. A second member of parliament was forced to resign, and several government officials are under investigation or have been tried. At the same time, the conservative wing of the party successfully elected as leader of the powerful Transvaal Province branch of the National Party, Andries Treurnicht, a staunchly traditional idealogue. His new position is considered as second only to the prime ministership in terms of political power, and more progressive whites viewed his election as a signal of a backlash from the right. They were concerned that Treurnicht will use his position to inhibit implementation of changes such as those recommended by Wiehahn. The extent to which he is able to do so will depend in large part on Prime Minister P.W. Botha's ability to end the scandal surrounding the Information Department's activities and to bind the party together.

For the moment, at least, P.W. Botha seems to have successfully gained control of the party. A series of by-elections held in the fall of 1979 demonstrated a decline in support for the National Party--Nationalists won all the seats contested with pluralities well below the previous election--and a fair amount of confusion among the voters. But Botha stood up to his critics in the round of National Party Congresses and has won the support of important Afrikaner journalists, academics and businessmen. He is apparently intent on forcing moderate change in the workplace in his efforts to develop a black middle class. He has removed the banning orders on several union leaders in addition to broadening access to African unions, and he has stated his willingness to sacrifice some of his more conservative support--particularly among white labor--in order to ensure efficient use and development of manpower. The Wiehahn Commission was scheduled to publish additional reports, covering such subjects as mixed unions, trade union administraton, labor in the mines, toward the end of 1979 or early 1980. Exactly how important are the recommendations already made by Riekert and Wiehahn or how significant are the changes suggested in subsequent reports will depend on how they are eventually translated into legislation, what regulations flow from the legislation, and how new regulations are carried out. It may be some time before the real impact of the changes could be measured. There is, however, a growing momentum for greater changes--still very much within the separate development structure--and the labor attache at one foreign consulate commented in October 1979 that it was "no longer possible to view South Africa's labor scene with the static glasses of the past."

Chapter II Sources

Books

Muriel Horrell, Laws Affecting Race Relations in South Africa, op. cit.

South Africa Institute of Race Relations, Annual Surveys, op. cit.

Francis Wilson, Migrant Labor in South Africa, Christian Institute of South Africa, Johannesburg, 1972.

Reports

South African Government:

"Annual Report of the Department of Bantu Education," Department of Education and Training, Government Printer, Pretoria, 1977.

"Industrial Conciliation Amendment Bill," Government Printer, Pretoria, 1979.

"Information on Trade Training, Advanced Technical Training, Industrial Training," Department of Education and Training, Pretoria, 1978.

Report of the (Riekert) Commission of Inquiry Into Legislation Affecting the Utilization of Manpower (excluding mines)," Government Printer, Pretoria, 1979.

Report of the (Wiehahn) Commission of Inquiry Into Labor Legislation, Part I," Government Printer, Pretoria, 1979.

White Paper on "The Report of the Commission of Inquiry Into Legislation Affecting the Utilization of Manpower (excluding mines)," Government Printer, Pretoria, 1979.

White Paper on Part I of the Report of the (Wiehahn) Commission of Inquiry Into Labor Legislation, Government Printer, Pretoria, 1979.

U.S. Government:

Frank Golino, "South Africa's Black Trade Unions," unclassified cable from the U.S. Consulate General in Johannesburg, Feb. 7, 1977.

Private:

Franz Auerbach, "Discrimination in Education," Centre for Intergroup Studies, University of Capetown, Capetown, 1978.

Fine Spamer Associates (Pty) Ltd., "Advancement in South Africa, Asiatic, Black, Colored," Johannesburg, 1978, 1979.

Janet Graaf, Kim Weichel, "Employment Survey of Black Workers Living in Crossroads," Urban Problems Research Unit, University of Capetown, Capetown, 1978.

Jill Nattrass, "Economics of Rising Expectations," address to the South Africa Institute of Race Relations, July 4, 1979.

Sean Maroney and Linda Ensor, "The Silenced: Bannings in South Africa," South Africa Institute of Race Relations, Johannesburg, 1978.

"Quotso," (survey of Soweto), published marketing report, Markinor, 1973, 1975.

Urwick International, "The Definitive Study of General Staff Remuneration Benefits and Employment Practices," South Africa, 1978.

Francis Wilson, "Economics of Rising Expectations," address to the South Africa Institute of Race Relations, July 4, 1979.

Articles

Financial Mail:

"African housing: land not for sale," Dec. 2, 1977.
"What do black shops offer," Dec. 9, 1977, pg. 17.
"Black housing: that 250 million," May 5, 1978, pg. 349.
"Citizenship and leases," May 5, 1978, pg. 357.
"Colour bar breakthrough," June 2, 1978, pg. 697.

"Cape squatters, hell no, we won't go," Sept. 22, 1978, pg. 1055.
"Black business: less hamstrung," Sept. 29, 1978.
"Soweto expansion: westward ho?," March 9, 1979, pg. 758.
"Pass laws: new deals for old," March 16, 1979, pg. 848.
"The iron curtain," March 23, 1979, pg. 948.
"Tension mounts," March 30, 1979, pg. 1038.
"The Riekert report: laagers around the towns," May 11, 1979, pg. 475.
"Wiehahn white paper: a formula for control," May 11, 1979, pg. 476.
"Urban Africans: Riekert in a nutshell," May 11, 1979, pg. 481.
"Riekert white paper: a rose by any other name," June 22, 1979,
    pg. 1050.
"99 year leases: the cost of living," June 29, 1979, pg. 1145.

Johannesburg Star:

"Churches defy new bar on mixed schools," Feb. 24, 1979, pg. 2.
"End of mine strike may mean start of new era," March 17, 1979.

To The Point:

"Changing the face of South Africa," Aug. 3, 1979, p. 8.

The New York Times:

John F. Burns, "Pass laws aspect of apartheid blacks hate most, bring
    despair and pent-up fury," May 24, 25, 26, 1978.
"20,000 South Africa blacks fight regime's effort to uproot them,"
    Nov. 29, 1978, pg. 1.
"South Africa prepares new contraints on the press," April 5, 1979.
"South Africans grant all indigenous blacks the right to organize,"
    Aug. 26, 1979.

The Washington Post:

Caryle Murphy, "South Africa increasingly restricts press," Aug. 12,
    1979, p. A-12.

The Washington Star:

Tiiu Lukk, "South Africa censors' wide reach," Sept. 9, 1978, p. 1.

III. FOREIGN CAPITAL IN SOUTH AFRICA

Foreign capital and foreign trade have been critical to the economic development of South Africa, providing the foreign exchange required for industrialization and for the expansion of an increasingly capital-intensive economy. South Africa's imports of goods and services each year are equal to about one-third of the country's gross national product. Expanding exports--primarily agricultural products and minerals--have covered a portion of rising import costs, but in eight of the last 10 years South Africa has run a balance-of-payments deficit on current account. Loans and investment from foreign countries have served to cover this deficit and to supplement domestic savings, and their role in the South African economy has become increasingly important in recent years. Between 1974 and 1976 the flow of foreign capital to South Africa was more than $6 billion, which offset the current account deficit for those years.

South African economists estimate that foreign capital alone is responsible for about one-third of the growth in the country's gross domestic product. It has provided funds to critical growth sectors of the South African economy--computer, electronics and telecommunications; petroleum processing; motor vehicle production; and to a lesser, though still important degree, to mining. For the decade and a half to 1975, South Africa's gross domestic product grew at a rate of about 6 percent annually. Foreign capital, economists say, generated about 2 percent of that.

Foreign investment has been important not just for the capital provided but also for the technology that has accompanied it. A former director of Barclay's National Bank of South Africa has said that figures on foreign investment "can be misleading in that they do not reflect the true extent to which we have had to rely on foreign investment (and in particular the know-how skills normally accompanying foreign investment) in respect of specific projects or key economic sectors." One British economist, John Suckling of York University, suggests that foreign technology accounted for 40 percent of the growth in South Africa's gross domestic product during the period between 1957 and 1972.

Foreign companies dominate several of the most important sectors of South Africa's economy. Five multinationals--Shell, British Petroleum, Mobil, Caltex and Total--collectively control close to 83 percent of the petroleum market in South Africa and generate 91 percent of the service stations. Volkswagen, Ford, GM, Datsun and Toyota hold the major share of the automobile market; the sole South African company, Sigma Motors, has acquired 14 percent of the market by manufacturing Chrysler, Peugeot, Citroen, Mazda and Leyland cars. Mainframe computer sales are split between IBM and British-owned ICL, each with one-third of the market, and Burroughs, Control Data, Sperry Univac and Siemens play lesser roles. Only in mining and agriculture are the companies and operations primarily South African, and even in those sectors, some major international corporations such as Exxon, Union Carbide, U.S. Steel, Phelps Dodge, Del Monte, Tate and Lyle, Rio Tinto Zinc and Newmont Mining play an important role.

Foreign capital has also served to spur international trade. South Africa relies heavily on foreign trade; its exports in 1978 amounted to

$15.3 billion including gold and services against $13.7 billion in imports. And imported technology plays a particularly critical role in selected sectors of South Africa's economy. A study in 1978 by a South African bank, Nedbank, shows that machinery and transport equipment account for more than half of the imports from South Africa's six largest trading partners, and the study concludes that the figures suggest "unless the South African manufacturing industry makes fundamental adjustments to its production processes, or greatly expands its domestic market, it will remain very dependent on imported capital goods." In addition to high technology goods in data processing, telecommunications and electronics, South Africa depends on imported heavy equipment such as earth movers and long wall miners for its mining sector and imported oil for its transportation sector. Foreign oil meets about 25 percent of the South African energy requirement.

   Foreign capital and employment: Without foreign capital, South Africa cannot hope to achieve a rate of economic growth sufficient to provide jobs for its rapidly expanding population. Between 1975 and 1978, South Africa suffered through its worst recession since the Depression of the 1930s. Unemployment among whites, coloreds and Asians, while still small, increased 117 percent between 1976 and 1977. Unemployment among blacks was far greater. Government figures showed 633,000 Africans unemployed in October 1977. By February 1978, the number of unemployed Africans had dropped to 569,000, but many analysts argue that government figures are low and some knowledgeable observers say that between 1.5 and 2 million Africans, more than 25 percent of the African work force, may now be unemployed or underemployed.

   South African government officials estimate that a growth rate of 5.5 percent will be required in future years to absorb the workers coming into the job market. To attain such a rate of growth, the Unit for Forward Research at Stellenbosch University has estimated, South Africa would need somewhere between $1 billion and $2 billion a year in new foreign capital. The rate of growth in 1978 was 2.5 percent; economists predict it may be no higher in 1979. J. Adendorff, managing director of the Corporation for Economic Development, says that South Africa will need to create 8.5 million jobs by the turn of the century, 1,100 jobs every working day for the next 21 years. There is little evidence that such a pace of growth will be possible unless there is a dramatic turnaround in the South African economy. However, the stupendous increase in the price of gold during 1979 led many South African economists to predict that such a turnaround was on its way.

Foreign Exchange Flows in Recent Years

   Sources of foreign capital: In addition to the foreign exchange brought in through a surplus in the balance of trade, foreign capital enters South Africa through three major paths--investment in the South African economy, long-term loans, and short-term loans primarily used to finance international trade. Investment in the economy is the preferred method of obtaining foreign capital--not only is it by nature long-term, but it brings with it foreign technology and expertise and lets foreign investors assume the economic risk. It also indicates a certain belief in the stability of South Africa's political and economic system, a belief that is cheering to South Africa. As one South African embassy official commented privately, "if not exactly the Good Housekeeping seal of approval, the presence of companies like Ford and GM is at least a sign of international support."

Long-term loans force the borrower to accept the risk; foreign technology and expertise may be purchased with the loan but do not accompany it automatically as is the case with direct investment. But like direct investment, the South African government encourages long-term loans as evidence of the creditworthiness and the acceptability of its policies.

The least attractive sources of foreign capital are short-term loans and trade credits. They are made for less than a year, carry higher interest charges than long-term loans, and have little impact on international assessments of South Africa's credit rating. They provide, however, the funding that enables South Africa's businessmen to import goods from the world market and, because the loans are from foreign banks, permit South Africa's domestic supply of short-term capital to be used for other purposes.

The switch from investment to lending: For years, most of the foreign capital moving to South Africa came through investment--equity investment in subsidiaries and joint ventures with South African companies or stock purchases. Until the late 1960s, foreign investment accounted for two-thirds of South Africa's total foreign liabilities. In the 1970s, however, the situation began to change. Foreign investment as a percentage of total capital flow began to drop off, first to 63 percent in 1972 and eventually to 41.3 percent in 1976. Foreign loans were becoming increasingly important.

Several factors were responsible for the increased importance of foreign lending to South Africa. One was that South Africa's major source of capital, Great Britain, was no longer willing or able to invest the large amounts it had in the past. South Africa out of need--and, to some extent, inclination--began to look elsewhere for money to diversify its sources. Many investors in Europe and the United States did not share Britain's preference for direct investment and preferred to make loans.

A second factor affecting the balance between loans and investment was the increasingly large role the South African government and its state-owned corporations began to play in the economy during the 1970s. Buoyed by expanding exports and a rising price for gold, South Africa committed itself in the early 1970s to an ambitious $20-billion development program. The program included a number of projects run by South Africa's state-owned corporations to boost electricity production, port capacity, energy resources and mineral exploitation. It was heavily dependent on imports, and the foreign exchange requirements of these projects could only be met through loan or bond financing.

The government's increased demand for imported goods came at a time when South Africa's import costs were expanding. The Arab oil embargo and the quadrupling of oil prices added to those costs, and with the arrival of independence and black majority rule to neighboring Mozambique and Angola, the South African government felt obliged to increase its defense budget, a large portion of which is devoted to imported arms. The government increased the defense budget 46 percent in 1974 and continued to expand it at an average 25 percent each year for the three succeeding years. The defense budget for 1979 increased 20 percent over that for 1978. Approximately 25 percent of South Africa's arms were imported before the 1977 UN arms embargo.

The growing cost of South Africa's imports could not be covered by the foreign exchange earned by exports or by that entering South Africa through private investments. The world recession cut into South Africa's export market, and the price of gold dropped precipitously, from $196 an ounce in 1975 to $103 in August 1976. (Gold sales abroad pay for about 40 percent of South Africa's imports, and a change of $10 per ounce is roughly equivalent to a $230-million change in South Africa's balance of payment figures.) The government helped to bridge the gap in its balance of payments by stepping up its foreign borrowings. At the end of 1976, South Africa's debt had reached $7.6 billion, almost three times the $2.7 billion outstanding in 1974. Loans by U.S. banks and their overseas branches provided nearly one-third of the credits to South Africa--$2.2 billion. More than 50 U.S. banks were involved in these loans.

Long-term lending--The majority of the loans were long-term, with maturities of more than one year. The World Bank reported more than $2.7 billion worth of long-term international bonds and Eurocurrency credits for South Africa between 1974 and 1976. However, by late 1976, many banks in Europe and the United States had begun to reach their ceilings on long-term lending to South Africa, forcing the government to borrow at higher interest rates and for shorter terms. Long-term lending was also discouraged by concerns about South Africa's political and economic future following events in Soweto, the government's moves against the black consciousness organizations, and the death of black activist Steve Biko, as well as the continuing recession in South Africa and the escalating pressure on banks to stop lending to South Africa.

The effect of these factors on long-term lending was striking. In 1977, South Africa raised only $33.2 million in the international bond and Eurocurrency markets, a mere 3 percent of the 1976 figure. There was little sign of new foreign investment. In 1977, the Business Environment Risk Index, at the School of Business Administration at the University of Delaware, moved South Africa from its acceptable risk category to the top of its moderate risk category. The Index predicted that by 1980 South Africa would be in the middle of its prohibitive risk category and at the top of the prohibitive risk category by 1985.

Reflecting concern about the political and economic situation, foreign companies began to repatriate a greater portion of their earnings from South African operations. Traditionally, the South African subsidiaries of American companies had retained more than 60 percent of their earnings for reinvestment but, in 1975, the amount dropped to 50 percent, and in 1976 and 1977 American companies sent home nearly two-thirds of their profits.

Short-term lending and consequences--South Africa compensated in part for the lack of availability of long-term funds by increased reliance on short-term financing. Although banks were unwilling to provide long-term credit to the South African government or its public corporations, they were more than willing to make short-term loans for trade with South Africa. In fact, by the end of 1977, South Africa's total debt (both long-term and short-term) to its major foreign creditors was $7.95 billion--some $350 million more than a year earlier. Most of this increase was in the form of short-term credits.

Recognizing the dangers inherent in continued deficits in its balance of payments on current account--the balance between merchandise, goods and services imported and those exported--and in over-reliance on short-term loans, the South African government moved in 1976 and 1977 to curtail imports. From mid-1976 until early 1977, it required importers to deposit for six months a sum equivalent to 20 percent of the value of their imports, and in March 1977 it imposed a 15-percent tax surcharge (eventually reduced to 7.5 percent in April 1979) on all imports.

The measures had a strong impact on the South African recovery. Imports dropped and their decline hurt an already declining economy. Heavily dependent on imported capital goods, South Africa's economy slowed down as imports dropped off. The growth in South Africa's real gross domestic product (GDP) slipped to 0.3 percent in 1977. The sacrifice in growth, however, was rewarded by a dramatic shift in South Africa's balance of trade. The efforts to discourage imports, together with a drop in import demand as a result of the recession in South Africa and a rising price for its exports, all contributed in late 1977 and all of 1978 to a dramatic turnaround in South Africa's balance on current account. In contrast to massive deficits registered in each of the three preceding years--$1.5 billion in 1974, $2.4 billion in 1975, and $1.9 billion in 1976--1977 witnessed a $580-million surplus. This was followed by a current account surplus of $1.6 billion in 1978.

The turnaround on current account was not matched by the balance on capital account--the account that tracks all financial and capital transfers. Capital flows moved from a positive balance of $660 million in 1976 to a deficit of $677 million in 1977 and $1,073 million in 1978. The capital outflow from South Africa was in part due to the South African government's repayment of loans; a major portion, however, was from the private sector, a sign of waning business confidence in South Africa's long-term economic prospects.

But if investors were skittish about long-term investment, bankers were impressed by the turnaround on current account and the government's ability to control the economy. Foreign lenders--primarily Swiss and German, but also a few from the United States--who had held back in 1977 began to return to South Africa in 1978. The World Bank recorded $565 million in new bond issues and Eurocurrency credits for South Africa in 1978--up from $33 million in 1977, almost two-thirds the amount received in the heavy borrowing years of 1975 and 1976. Moreover, the terms associated with these 1978 bond issues and loans improved to South Africa's benefit.

Current demand for capital: Events in 1979 have had a real impact on South Africa's demand for foreign capital. At the beginning of the year it looked as though South Africa's need to pay off old loans, finance new industrial development, compensate for the net outflow of capital, and achieve a rate of economic growth sufficient to provide jobs for its rapidly expanding population assured continued interest in foreign trade, investment and loans. The immediate need for foreign capital appeared to be aggravated by the fall of the Shah of Iran--supplier of about 90 percent of South Africa's oil. The end of an assured supply of Iranian oil sent South Africa to the expensive spot market and clandestine sources. In 1978, oil cost South Africa $1.7 billion, equal to one-fifth of total merchandise imports. Early estimates suggested that the Shah's fall could add $400 million to South Africa's oil bill, contributing to an increased interest in foreign capital.

In hopes of stimulating foreign investment, as well as of stanching the outflow of capital, the South African government accepted in February 1979 recommendations of the De Kock Commission that modify the existing foreign exchange regulations. The commission had been established to review South Africa's monetary policy. The changes it recommended are designed to allow foreign investors to use rands purchased at a discounted rate for a wider range of--and ostensibly economically more productive--investment purposes than was previously possible. By November 1979 the Reserve Bank had approved applications for investments with discounted rands worth some 350 million rand. The government also made overseas financing of trade more attractive than domestic borrowing by providing discounted dollars through the South African central bank to South African importers to pay off short-term trade loans. Finally, the government is extending forward cover--a type of insurance to cover risks in foreign exchange rate fluctuations--to private sector borrowers in order to encourage greater foreign long-term borrowing. (Previously only state-owned corporations had such protection.) Shell has used discounted rands to purchase prospecting rights; General Motors and Volkswagen have bought them to use in desegregating their dining rooms and constructing new training and eating facilities, and Union Carbide is using them to pay off loans incurred during a 1976-77 expansion of its facilities.

What appeared to be a likely increase in the demand for foreign capital failed to develop. Government steps to reduce oil consumption--reduced speed limits, restricted gasoline sales hours, drastically increased prices--succeeded in cutting oil imports by 40 percent. A dramatic increase in the price of gold gave South Africa a windfall of foreign exchange. If the price of gold averages $300 in 1979, it will mean an additional $2.8 billion in foreign exchange earnings over 1978. And structural factors and a government desire to check inflation prevented the gold boom from being translated into economic growth. The economy after three years of recession, awash with liquidity, plagued by unemployment and excess plant capacity, remained in the doldrums. Much of the windfall gain in foreign reserves supplied by the buoyant gold prices went to pay off existing government loans, and, in order to prevent the sudden increase in foreign exchange from overheating an already inflationary economy, the Reserve Bank kept domestic interest rates far enough below world rates so that importers borrowed from local banks rather than seeking trade financing from abroad.

Until the economy picks up pace significantly, the immediate demand for foreign loans and investment will be limited. But the government, seeking to stimulate growth, is likely to loosen up some of the restrictions on the economy in the near future. When it does, and most certainly over the long term, South Africa's interest in attracting foreign capital and investment will grow--to finance trade, to demonstrate foreign confidence and to bring in new technology. And having paid off old government debts and financed increased trade locally, South Africa is apt to find its credit rating high once its economic growth rate begins to pick up and it begins to seek foreign capital actively.

SOUTH AFRICA'S IMPORTS FROM AND EXPORTS TO
ITS LEADING TRADING PARTNERS

(in billions of U.S. dollars)

IMPORTS FROM:

	1974	1975	1976	1977	1978
U.S.	1.160	1.302	1.348	1.054	1.080
U.K.	1.234	1.520	1.172	1.012	1.281
Germany	1.410	1.382	1.240	1.124	1.543
France	0.350	0.424	0.489	0.498	0.610
Japan	0.962	0.873	0.710	0.764	0.910*

EXPORTS TO:

	1974	1975	1976	1977	1978
U.S.	0.653	0.881	0.976	1.340	2.340
U.K.	1.398	1.390	1.100	1.538	1.450
Germany	0.755	0.884	0.895	1.106	1.222
France	0.251	0.288	0.321	0.504	0.755
Japan	0.773	0.880	0.763	0.909	0.946*

* figures for Japan are for the first 11 months of 1978

Source: IMF Direction of Trade Annual, March 1979

Trade and investment sources: Most of South Africa's trade is with western Europe, the United States and Japan, and the vast majority of investment in South Africa comes from the EEC countries and the United States. South Africa's merchandise exports to the United Kingdom, the United States, Germany, France and Japan constitute 78 percent of its total exports, and approximately 65 percent of its imports come from those countries. Traditionally, the United Kingdom has been South Africa's major trading partner, as well as its most important investor. The United States and West Germany are increasingly close rivals, however, and in 1978 the United States surpassed the United Kingdom to become South Africa's largest trading partner for the second time in five years.

European and American investors also supply the dominant portion of South Africa's foreign investment. British assets in South Africa and holdings by British shareholders in South African companies total about $12 billion--some $6.8 billion in direct assets, $5.1 billion in shares--equal to approximately half of total foreign investment in South Africa. U.S. citizens, with $1.8 billion in direct investment in 1977 and approximately $2 billion in shares--primarily in mining companies--provide about 17 percent of total foreign investment. The remaining third of foreign investment in South Africa comes almost entirely from European Economic Community or sterling bloc countries. Japan, although it does extensive business in South Africa through its licensing arrangements, does not permit direct investment in South Africa.

European and American banks have supplied the majority of South Africa's loans; most in the last five years have come out of the Eurodollar market in London. American banks, with more than $1 billion in short-term loans and trade credits and nearly $1 billion in long-term notes, provided about one-third of South Africa's foreign loans during this period.

South Africa's demand for new loans has declined slightly in the last year, but a slumping economy, strategic concerns and the need to pay off existing loans are likely to keep the country interested in increased foreign lending.

The Economic Attractiveness of South Africa

Recognizing the importance of foreign capital to its own development, South Africa has actively sought foreign investors. Its investment terms have been generous. All current income may be repatriated, and the government offers numerous concessions to companies interested in establishing operations in government-designated growth areas, including low-interest loans, preferential transportation rates, cash rebates and tax concessions. The latest effort to spur foreign investment is the De Kock Commission's recent recommendation to allow companies to use rand purchased at a discounted rate (financial rand) for a variety of investments.

The number of foreign companies attracted to South Africa has been impressive. Some 350 American companies--including more than 50 of Fortune's top 100 U.S. corporations--have subsidiary operations in South Africa, and an additional 6,000 firms do business there on an agency basis. West Germany has at least as many companies--nearly 400 by some estimates--operating in South Africa and as many as 1,000 United Kingdom companies may have direct investments there.

No figures are readily available on the number of workers employed by foreign companies, but it is estimated that U.S. companies employ about 100,000, anywhere from 50,000 to 70,000 of whom may be black. The South African employees of American firms account for roughly 1.7 percent of the entire work force in South Africa; other foreign companies may employ an additional 5 to 6 percent of the total work force. Based on an assumption that, particularly among blacks, one worker supports a family of five, U.S. companies affect indirectly some 300,000 to 350,000 blacks and 165,000 or more whites.

To most foreign companies, South Africa has offered an attractive--and in the case of mining companies, a uniquely attractive--business opportunity. The rate of return on investment there has traditionally outpaced investment elsewhere in the world. Return on investment in manufacturing by U.S. companies in South Africa during the two years before 1975, for example, averaged 16 percent and for some companies was much higher. The U.S. Department of Commerce estimated that for all U.S. investments in South Africa the rate of return was 17.9 percent in 1974 and 18.6 percent in 1973. (The 1974 rate of return on manufacturing operations worldwide was 13 percent in developing countries, 12.4 percent in developed.)

U.S. operations in South Africa in 1975 felt the impact of that country's recession. Return on all U.S. investment in South Africa dropped to 9 percent in 1975; return on manufacturing investments fell to 8 percent. Worldwide returns for total U.S. investment and for U.S. investments in manufacturing that year were 13 percent and 14 percent, respectively.

But by 1976 recovery from the recession began. The rate of return for U.S. manufacturing companies in South Africa returned to 14 percent in 1976 and stayed steady in 1977 and 1978. And for some companies, most notably computer and electronics manufacturers, South Africa continued to be a booming market. Several computer companies expect to continue to expand at 20 to 30 percent a year for the indefinite future.

The role of the South African government in the economy: In addition to government incentives and an acceptable rate of return, many company directors say that they like to operate in South Africa because of the lack of political instability or government interference. In 1973, a study by the University of Delaware placed South Africa among the 10 countries offering the most favorable business opportunities. The study measured "business environment risk" in terms of political stability, government attitude to foreign investment, economic growth, and the availability of labor, capital, and technology. Many businessmen agree. "South Africa is attractive," Colgate-Palmolive's managing director, John McLean, told IRRC in 1975, "because of its stability and because the government doesn't poke fingers into the economic picture. It lets market forces work their will." McLean continued, "The situation appears secure for the next decade."

In fact, the South African government plays an active role in the economy. It is directly involved, through large government corporations, in iron and steel production, transportation, communications and utilities. It also is involved through legislation and regulation affecting business operations. But government involvement has not been troublesome; where the government has made decisions affecting business operations, managers of U.S. companies in South Africa say, those decisions generally have favored business interests. Managers describe government actions affecting business--such as requiring automotive manaufacturers to use a prescribed percentage of locally produced items or placing price controls on certain industries--as reasonable and say that the government has allowed a reasonable rate of return on investment.

Protection of business information--The government has also sought to protect businesses against what might be termed "strategic intrusion" from abroad. Responding to a subpoena threat to De Beers Industries in 1974, the government passed the Second General Law Amendment Bill to protect South African companies against outside demands for information on their operations. The provisions of the bill--later incorporated in the Business Protection Act of June 1978--are designed "to restrict the enforcement in the Republic of certain foreign judgments, orders, directions, arbitration awards and letters of request; to prohibit the furnishing of information relating to businesses in compliance with foreign orders, directions or letters of request; and provide for matters connected therewith."

The Minister of Economic Affairs is authorized to permit exceptions, to allow business to supply information abroad. A private law firm in South Africa after consultations with South Africa's Department of Commerce said the legislation "is not intended to prohibit or restrict the normal business information passing between a South African business and a foreign parent or affiliate," but it does, however, offer business "the machinery to refuse to furnish the information (requested by an official body) if it does not wish to do so."

A number of companies have cited the law as a factor limiting their ability to supply information on their activities in South Africa. Before the signers of the Sullivan principles filed their first reports, the American Chamber of Commerce in Johannesburg approached the Minister of Economics on behalf of U.S. companies for permission to file information on labor practices regularly with their respective home offices. The minister asked that they send to his office copies of reports they intended to file, but said that the government would not oppose company efforts to supply the information requested. (Sullivan principles, Appendix B)

National Supplies Procurement Act--In addition, the South African government has introduced a number of laws affecting business that seek to protect what the government views as the strategic role of business in South Africa. The National Supplies Procurement Act, passed in 1970 and activated in 1977, authorizes the South African Minister for Economic Affairs to order any company operating in South Africa to manufacture and deliver any goods that the government determines are essential to national security. Should a company fail to comply with the minister's order, he has the power to seize the goods or make use of the company's facilities to provide the goods in question. The Financial Mail commented in November 1977 that "it is the general impression that foreign controlled firms supplying the Department of Defense could be commandeered if their parents instruct them to stop supplying goods which (the government) needs. These go beyond arms and ammunition. Motor vehicles, telecommunications and lighting equipment, ball bearings and other electronic goods are among the strategic materials produced by foreign-controlled firms. The Economics Minister, Christian Heunis, explained the act: "Most recently, there has also been much talk about the active use of coercive steps against the South African economy, with the object of forcing political concessions from us." We would be foolish, Heunis said, "if we should fail to take into consideration the need to prepare ourselves adequately for any conceivable range of coercive economic measures which may be put into effect against South Africa."

In addition to activating the National Supplies Procurement Act in 1977, the government passed a law designed specifically to protect a major strategic sector--oil. The Petroleum Products Act of 1977 gives the Minister of Economic Affairs the authority to regulate the purchase, sale or use of any petroleum product. U.S. company officials refuse to say whether a standing agreement on sales to the government exists. Officials say that disclosure of such information is forbidden by the Official Secrets Act, but some say that they have been notified by the government that they are legally prohibited from imposing any conditions on the sale of oil products to creditworthy South African customers--thus they cannot prevent sales either to South Africa's military or police or, through third parties, to Rhodesia. After the 1979 cutoff of Iranian oil, the government introduced legislation that bans publication of details relating the country's supply of oil. The Minister of Economics justified the legislation as necessary "because of the sensitive position we have in the world."

Blacks' Attitudes Toward Apartheid and Foreign Investment

As frustration mounts, there is growing evidence that urban blacks--many of whom have extolled the benefits that foreign companies bring to blacks--are increasingly questioning the role of foreign investment in South Africa, although accurate assessment of this change is extremely difficult. There are real limits on the extent to which blacks can speak openly. Publicly calling for withdrawal of foreign investment, for example, could be interpreted as a crime punishable under the Terrorism Act. And there are few organizations that provide political representation or participation for blacks. In addition, a number of important or potentially important black leaders have been arrested, detained, banned or forced underground and several have died in demonstrations or in detention.

Nevertheless, in the last three years there have been visible signs of changes in blacks' perceptions of the future, convincing many observers that a dramatic alteration of the political situation in South Africa is inevitable. Development of an increasingly large urbanized, sophisticated and economically secure black population living in white areas--about 30 percent of South Africa's African population now lives in urban townships--has further contributed to the growth in black aspirations. Significant economic advances for blacks in the early 1970s went unmatched by a growth in political rights, and the contrast between the growing importance of blacks to the economy and the stagnant rights of blacks in the society became increasingly apparent. A Johannnesburg stockbroker estimated in July 1975 that the discretionary spending power of Africans--defined as the income earned above that required for absolute subsistence--grew 300 percent in the five years to 1974. Nevertheless, a survey of Soweto by Markinor, a Johannesburg marketing firm, showed that more Africans interviewed in 1975 thought that their financial situation had deteriorated in the last year than thought so in 1973. Only 9 percent of the Africans interviewed thought that black-white relations were improving, against 32 percent in 1973.

Economic frustrations and violence: Blacks' frustrations erupted in the demonstrations that began in Soweto in 1976. The demonstrations and the government actions to repress protest by blacks gave international visibility to the black consciousness movement that began in the mid-1960s and focused primarily on self-help activities. After the student demonstrations of June 1976, this movement became the rallying point of opposition to apartheid. In contrast to earlier black movements--the protests that led to Sharpeville in 1960, or the African National Congress or the Pan African Congress--the black consciousness movement penetrated beyond the politicized Africans and swept into its orbit relatively apolitical Africans--parents, teachers, businessmen and members of the middle class. It has few recognizable leaders--most have been arrested or detained or have fled the country--and no real structure.

But its goals of African political rights in a unitary South African state have been accepted generally by blacks living in urban areas, and its supporters are available to organize spontaneously around single issues that provide a focus of their frustration. Since the spate of arrests and bannings of black consciousness organizations in October 1977, protest has been relatively passive. The boycott of the community council elections, however, when about 5 percent of eligible voters voted, demonstrates the strength of the opposition. And occasional outbursts of violent protest signal the direction opposition might take.

Data from a survey taken in urban areas shortly after Soweto, under the auspices of the Arnold Bergstraesser Institute, indicate that Africans in South Africa consider economic change more important than political change, but that there is widespread support for the demonstrations in Soweto and that "the readiness for conflict is growing, especially among urban black youth." According to the survey, 28 percent of those polled believe violence will be necessary to achieve change, although 65 percent believe improvement in living standards can be achieved through negotiation. The 28 percent believing in the necessity of violence, however, represent nearly half of the more educated and economically advantaged of the groups surveyed, and the survey report remarks that as blacks become urbanized and educated they become more disillusioned and less hopeful that peaceful change can accomplish what needs to be done in South Africa.

The survey also points to the growing strength of one major African movement with political overtones that has not been banned. It reports that the 150,000-member Inkatha movement--formed in 1975 and described by its founders as a "national cultural liberation movement"--"represents by far the strongest organized political tendency among urban blacks" and that 44 percent of the Africans polled view Inkatha's president, Gatsha Buthelezi, as their leader. Buthelezi also is the hereditary chief of the Zulus--South Africa's largest tribe--and the appointed head of the kwaZulu homeland, a position that makes it difficult for the South African government to move against him. His use of the platform provided for him by the government's homelands policies cuts two ways. It affords him some protection from the government, allowing him to criticize its policies more freely than most other blacks and it has made the government hesitant to challenge Inkatha; but, at the same time it alienates him from potential supporters in the urban areas who view him as a tribal leader or as an overly active participant in the government's policy of separate development. In light of the criticism he has received from some urban Africans and the direct abuse he has received from African students--most recently at the funeral of Robert Sobukwe, Pan African Congress leader--the degree of support reflected in the survey was impressive. It also may have some implications for pressures brought to bear by Africans on foreign companies operating in South Africa.

Blacks' attitudes toward foreign investment: Blacks' attitudes toward foreign investment have been varied. Many have argued that foreign investment creates jobs, improves the economy, providing trickle down benefits, and gives companies an opportunity to influence the situation in South Africa by following model employment practices and by improving working and living conditions for black employees. Lucy Mvubelo, head of the 24,000-member black clothing workers' union, recently stated "the multinational companies have been an asset to us....Why should the world be so cruel as to call for these companies to withdraw when we are only now getting some sunshine in that very dark country of ours?" and Chief Buthelezi told Forbes magazine in 1978, "it is morally imperative that American firms remain active here--and support us in our struggle--even though the business aspects may well present problems." He rejected withdrawal because foreign investment feeds growth and, "as industry expands, propelled by domestic and foreign investment, a severe shortage of qualified men is increasingly appearing, and black people are of necessity being advanced to more responsible positions." He said a "call for a slow down on investment, or actual disinvestment...(is a) call for an aggravation of exactly the conditions that we are struggling against....What kind of struggle for independence can you wage from a level of utter impoverishment?"

But both Mvubelo and Buthelezi put caveats on the performance of companies operating in South Africa. "It's very important," Buthelezi argued, "that your American companies, when they come here, do more than just invest. They must take an active role, not just a passive one." They must use their influence, he said, "wherever they can, to promote peaceful change." And Mvubelo argues that pressure by Americans on U.S. companies can help improve opportunities for blacks in South Africa.

Seeking a position short of withdrawal, Buthelezi, as spokesman for the Inkatha movement, announced in July 1978 Inkatha's intention to monitor the behavior of corporations in South Africa in order to encourage them to adopt and implement the principles included in labor codes of conduct and to press companies to recognize black trade unions. Inkatha has made contact with overseas employer organizations, trade unions and governments. Its objective is to impress upon companies the importance of following the progressive employment codes developed by the European Economic Community, the Canadian government, American companies acting under the aegis of Leon Sullivan, and the Urban Foundation in South Africa. Gibson Thula, an Inkatha representative, has said that Inkatha wants to make workers on the shop floor aware of what the codes say and to further the cause of black unions. "Our main purpose," Thula said, "is to strengthen the existing trade union movement." And Inkatha has some potential leverage with which to encourage corporations to pay attention. (Details of codes, Chapter V)

In addition to its membership of 150,000, Inkatha in 1977 formed an alliance with the two major political parties representing coloreds and Asians. The organization, called the South African Black Alliance, has called for a national constitutional convention to draw up a revised configuration for political representation. It has also endorsed Inkatha's decision to monitor and enforce labor codes.

Representatives of Inkatha have talked about the potential leverage Inkatha and the Black Alliance have over companies in terms of consumer demand. They may also have eventual power through the withholding of labor. "A work stay away is our major weapon," Buthelezi has said, but it must be more than a few days. "Strikes have failed in the past because half-baked plans have been presented to the people....To succeed the people must be politicized enough and prepared for the trauma of losing their jobs." Forms of pressure that have been suggested include: pressure on management in South Africa, pressure on the parent company, protests by Inkatha to the government of the county in which the home office is based, calls by Inkatha on trade union movements and political interest groups to seek influence on the company's performance.

A number of urban Africans also advocate business pressures on the government. Percy Qoboza, editor of South Africa's largest black paper, member of the Soweto Committee of Ten--an ad hoc group of community leaders in Soweto--and a recent detainee under South Africa's security laws, argued against sanctions in 1978. "To impose economic sanctions on South Africa would be to acknowledge total abandonment of a peaceful and negotiated settlement," Qoboza told Time magazine. "What is more, the creation of economic chaos here would expedite the very thing we are all trying desperately to avoid: a bloody racial confrontation." Qoboza argues that companies "must be compelled to play a far more active role in helping to remove the walls of discrimination in our country."

Increased demands for foreign action: But as blacks become increasingly frustrated by the government's response to protest and by their own inability to effect change, the demand for foreign countries to take action to affect the situation increases. A sense of impotence within South Africa has contributed to growing support among blacks for an end to foreign trade and investment--no matter what the cost to blacks.

In a diplomatic cable written in March 1978, U.S. Ambassador William Bowdler reported that "among more politically oriented blacks, (the) question is increasingly being weighed of whether foreign investment should be seen as an ally or obstacle in pursuing (the) goal of a more democratic and non-racial society." The cable concluded with the embassy's impression "that blacks who reflect on foreign investment as an issue are now roughly divided between those favoring disinvestment and those who would like to see it remain in instances where it contributes to black aspirations directly and in the near term. A smaller segment," Ambassador Bowdler wrote, "continues to favor investment on any basis." He suggests that "with radicalization of black attitudes, (the) tendency to call for disinvestment grows stronger,...(the) role of American firms here will become increasingly controversial and (the) rationale for continued presence will seem less and less persuasive to growing numbers of blacks."

To many critics of the government, foreign investment provides a potential lever in their protest against apartheid policies. Steve Biko, explaining the position taken by the South African Students Organization (SASO) and the Black Peoples Convention (BPC), said at a terrorism trial of nine SASO leaders in 1976 that SASO leaders "never, for a moment, thought that foreign firms would, as a result of this kind of stand, withdraw." They recognized that there were limitations that made it "impossible for anybody intimately involved with the South African economy to withdraw at will." A major theme of the campaign for withdrawal, he said, was "to increase pressure on South Africa." Biko testified that the foreign investment issue provided a political forum because of

> ...the relationship between a foreign government and its companies which invest (in South Africa)--and we believe South Africa is particularly sensitive like any normal country to criticism by the world of its policies. We believe that part of our political campaign is to make sure that as many people as

possible criticize South Africa for its policies. Now, putting pressure on foreign companies about their participation in this kind of what we would regard as an immoral set-up was also calculated to make sure that the foreign governments also equally begin to feel unhappy about the fact of the participation of their firms in this country and assist generally in building up pressure to make South Africa shift its attitudes gradually to a more acceptable stance. It was a political stance which was calculated to bring about political pressure to bear on South Africa to shift policies to make them more flexible, more acceptable to the world and to us as blacks....

In July 1978, the South African Council of Churches issued a statement that "foreign investments and loans have largely been used to support the prevailing patterns of power and privileges" in South Africa, and called upon foreign countries and businesses "to revise radically their investment policies and employment practices...in such a way as to benefit the total population." Although considering withdrawal of existing capital investments a largely rhetorical issue because of foreign exchange restrictions, the council's general secretary, Desmond Tutu, has called for other economic actions against South Africa, such as a boycott of South African coal. Any suffering by blacks resulting from such a boycott, he said recently, would be "suffering with a purpose."

Chapter III Sources

Books

Millard Arnold, Steve Biko: Black Consciousness in South Africa, Random House, New York, 1978.

Merton Dagut, Appraisal: A Sovereign Risk Analysis, Nedbank, Johannesburg, 1977.

John Suckling, Ruth Weiss, Duncan Innes, The Economic Factor, Foreign Investment in South Africa, Africa Publications Trust, Uppsala Offset Center, Uppsala, Sweden, 1975.

Reports

South African Government:

Annual Report and Quarterly Bulletin, South Africa Reserve Bank, Horters Printers, Pretoria.

U.S. Government:

Survey of Current Business, U.S. Department of Commerce, Bureau of Economic Analysis, U.S. Government Printing Office, Washington, D.C.

"U.S. Corporate Interests in Africa," Report to U.S. Senate, Committee on Foreign Relations Subcommittee on African Affairs, U.S. Government Printing Office, Washington, D.C., 1978.

Articles

Forbes:

John Train, "South Africa: U.S. don't go home," Nov. 27, 1978, p. 33.

Johannesburg Star:

"Inkatha to fight for unions," July 13, 1978, p. 2.

Southern Africa:

"Confidential diplomatic cable reveals black hostility to U.S. investment in South Africa," Vol. XI, No. 3, April 1978, p. 2.

Time:

"Qoboza--a role for the U.S.," April 17, 1978.

The Washington Post:

"South African church unit urges shift," Religious News Service, July 21, 1978.

Other

Review, monthly newsletter of the Standard Bank, Standard Bank of South Africa, Johannesburg.

"Direction of Trade Annual," International Monetary Fund, Washington, D.C., March 1979.

IV. THE BROAD ROLE OF BUSINESS IN SOUTH AFRICA

Both business and its critics agree that companies in South Africa have an important role to play in effecting change there. In discussing the impact that business can have, executives in both foreign and South African companies tend to focus on labor practices and economic growth as the two areas in which they can make the greatest contribution. By providing investment, they contribute growth; growth creates jobs and allows improved labor practices. Those opposed to the current role of companies in South Africa take a larger view. They argue that labor practices represent only one aspect of the problem in South Africa; improvements in the work place and the changes that are being bought with economic growth are not enough. They see business as the major tangible link between western countries and South Africa and, therefore, the primary link by which pressures can be brought to bear on the South African government. They argue that this link can be used by companies lobbying for change in South Africa to try to influence the government by withholding loans or investment or by withdrawing completely.

Writing in the January 1978 issue of Foreign Affairs, William Cotter and Clyde Ferguson describe recent changes in South Africa as "desegregation of the deck chairs on the Titanic," and offer a list of 41 steps that the U.S. government might take to get the South Africans to institute substantial political changes. Many of the steps are economic--discouraging new investment in South Africa, eliminating Export-Import Bank facilities, curtailing imports from South Africa, or cutting oil supplies--and affect companies operating in South Africa directly. The steps would also, the authors argue, increase the cost of Afrikaners' intransigence, support the internal efforts of blacks and, perhaps, cause moderate whites in the society to take to the streets in civil disobedience.

Whether or not economic pressures would be effective is a question of considerable debate. Former Under Secretary of State George Ball wrote in The Atlantic of the "ineffectiveness of economic denial in persuading governments to accept benign change." He cited UN Ambassador Andrew Young as recognizing that "unfocused economic sanctions against South Africa would only intensify an already nascent siege psychology, while forcing even liberal South Africans to support their government against a common enemy." John Purcell of Goodyear has written to Foreign Affairs in response to the Ferguson-Cotter article that "any manipulation with the intent of damaging the economy of South Africa can have no other short-term result but human misery." Purcell argues that economic pressures will not encourage nonviolent social change in South Africa, which he said will be brought about by "economic growth, expanded contact with the outside world, and time."

The effectiveness of economic pressures depends on how they are perceived by those responsible for political decisions in South Africa, a perception that may be shaped by the role that business is willing and able to play there. Business is the first hit by economic pressures. People in business, officials in government offices working directly with business, and business economists are likely to have the best understanding of the consequences of economic pressures and to draw the connection between South Africa's domestic political policies, external pressures, foreign investment and internal economic growth. How and whether they are able to convey this understanding to those responsible for political decisions--in effect to lobby for change--will play a significant role in determining the degree to which economic pressures are translated into political change.

Company representatives have long maintained that it is not the role of business to formulate political policy. Companies in South Africa, South African as well as foreign, have been particularly apolitical. As Afrikaner insurance baron A.D. Wassenaar has said, the government has provided them with "law, order, stability and profits," and business has minded its own store. Foreign companies challenged on the operations of their subsidiaries have repeatedly argued that they cannot get involved in the politics of South Africa. A recent statement by Kodak is representative of the position taken by many multinationals: "Kodak regards its proper role in South Africa, as elsewhere, as a business dedicated to normal commercial transactions within the law of the land, and not as an instrumentality involved in political activity."

This position has come under increasing pressure, not only from critics abroad, but from people within South Africa--including representatives of a number of companies. One of the most outspoken, A.H. Bloom, the managing director of a South African company, Premier Milling, recently questioned:

> Why should it always take a crisis to evoke our conscience? Compare the magnitude of the shrieks of anguish over the increase in the butter price (or eggs) with the deafening silence over the years of business leaders over the issues such as land tenure for Africans in urban areas or forced squatter removals. I totally reject the notion that businessmen must stay out of the political field....Let us discard the semantics of whether business opinion should be characterized by consultation or confrontation (with government)--let us settle for business opinion that is characterized by involvement, by honesty and by integrity.

Some companies have begun to explore the broader role business can play in the society. On the heels of the Soweto protests, South African businessmen formed the Urban Foundation; American companies signed the Sullivan principles and launched the American Chamber of Commerce. American companies, William Norris of Control Data testified in 1978 before the House subcommittee on international trade, "need to operate cooperatively and leverage their common interest in social change."

The effectiveness that a business lobby may have in South Africa is difficult to measure. Change in South Africa comes by stealth, and rarely, if at all, is the government willing to admit that it has made a decision in response to lobbying efforts by concerned constitutents or outside pressures. There are some signs that government is hearing, several businessmen have said, but it is difficult to determine to what extent government is listening.

There may be real limits to the broader, more political and as yet largely untested role business can play in South Africa. The limits relate to the traditional role of business; the separation between business and government, aggravated by conflicts between English and Afrikaans speakers; the entrenched civil service bureaucracy; and the importance of ideology and history to businessmen, government and civil servants.

Historical Divisions Between Business and Government

The ability of business to influence government is greatly affected by the historical division between Afrikaans and English speakers. In describing the relationship between business and government in South Africa, Etienne Rousseau, a prominent Afrikaans-speaking businessman, said in 1977 that one only need to look at the centers for each. Pretoria, the political capital of South Africa, is the historic capital of the old Boer republics, he said, and Johannesburg, the commercial center of the country, is a city built by uitlanders (outsiders or foreigners), he said, who came to South Africa for its wealth and remain uncommitted to its future. The two centers are separated by distance and by history.

The historic separation between business and government, while slightly less visible than it once was, is still very strong. Business has long been the preserve of the English speaker. Politics, government, agriculture and labor have become the preserves of the Afrikaans speakers. There is considerable mistrust between the two.

Afrikaners have viewed business as allied with the English-speaking community in opposition to their own nationalist aspirations and policy objectives. The perspective has strong roots. For years business was seen as part and parcel of the British Empire, and the image of the two inextricably interwined fades slowly if at all in the Afrikaner minds. Early traders establishing themselves on the Cape in the late 17th century represented the British East India Company. The adventurers and fortune seekers of the late 1800s who invaded Afrikaner farming areas in search of mineral wealth were tied to British interests. British capital built South Africa's mines, and profits from the mines were repatriated to Britain or reinvested in South Africa on behalf of British shareholders. The Empire kept a strong hold on its colony, and Afrikaners, excluded from business by inclination, education, language, or lack of the old school ties that made entry into business natural for English speakers, resented both the economic and the political domination.

The interests of British businessmen have repeatedly conflicted with Afrikaners' nationalist aspirations. British troops operating on behalf of British interests in South Africa crushed Afrikaner nationalism in the Boer War at the turn of the century. As a British colony, South Africa was called to participate on Britain's side in two world wars. Many Afrikaner nationalists opposed South Africa's participation in the wars, arguing that they were wars to protect Britain's interests, not South Africa's. Nationalists organized around a call for "South Africa first." Some participated in an active rebellion against entry into the war in 1914, and a number of nationalists--including the former Prime Minister, John Vorster--were imprisoned during World War II for their anti-British sentiments.

Entry into the industrialized economy was often difficult and often painful. Afrikaners leaving their farms to enter the industrialized sector of the economy entered on the lowest levels. The first to abandon agriculture began to move to the cities following serious droughts after the Boer War. Carrying resentment from the war and the loss of their farms, family members and cattle, Afrikaners were forced to seek work in the mines, working for managers who had supported the armies that had defeated them. Normal suspicion between management and labor was compounded by the fact that much of the labor in the mines and increasingly in the manufacturing sector was Afrikaans-speaking and management was exclusively English-speaking. Afrikaner workers formed unions that together with rural support eventually became the backbone for Afrikaner nationalist politicians.

The battle against British capitalism in many respects paralleled the fight against British political domination. A.D. Wassenaar, former chairman of the Afrikaans-run corporation, Sanlam Mutual Life Insurance Co., argues that the Boer War "implanted in the minds of Afrikanerdom the impression that there was an indestructible link between wealth in the hands of foreigners and a political threat to Afrikanerdom's independence, if not to its very existence." As Afrikaner nationalists were arguing for "South Africa first," a number were seeking to establish a counter-attack against uitlander capital. Denis Worrall, one of the few English-speaking Nationalist members of parliament, wrote in 1971 that, "The essentially capitalist economic system in terms of which South Africa had developed was seen as an import and something foreign to the Afrikaner's national character." Afrikaner farmers formed agricultural cooperatives, and rural communities pooled funds in a funeral insurance scheme that became the base of what eventually became South Africa's largest insurance company. Funds from the insurance payments were invested in Afrikaner businesses and provided support for the development of Afrikaner entrepreneurs. The effort in the early 1930s and 40s, one Afrikaner professor told Worrall, was "not to allow the Afrikaner nation to be destroyed by trying to adapt to the alien capitalist system, but to mobilize the nation (Afrikaner) with the purpose of conquering this alien system and transferring it into something more akin to the Afrikaner character."

Access to business, however, remained limited for most Afrikaners. Ambitious Afrikaners left their farms in the period between the world wars and sought jobs in teaching, the church or politics--where their preponderance in population gave them an advantage over English speakers. Some pursued professions in journalism, law or medicine, but there were few jobs available in business at levels above the hourly paid workers.

Following World War II, however, the new Nationalist government began to push the development of state-owned corporations--there are now 22. The Industrial Development Corporation was formed, according to Wassenaar, "to strengthen Afrikaner participation in the industrial progress of the country" and "to serve as a bulwark against the (English-speaking-controlled) Anglo American Corp., which had caused concern because of its wide involvement in a large number of sectors." The government became a major employer--today it is estimated that 30 to 40 percent of the white population works for the government or its public corporations, and by 1992 the majority of economically active whites will work in the public rather than the private sector.

Some inroads were being made in the private sector as well. With the establishment of Federale Mynbou in 1953, Afrikaans speakers moved into mining for the first time, and in 1964 Anglo American agreed to sell

General Mining to Federale, thus giving Afrikaners their first major control in gold mining. (The sale was opposed by a number of more traditional Afrikaners who felt that Federale was entering a partnership with Anglo.)

Nevertheless, even today, the vast majority of private business remains in the hands of the English-speaking community. Afrikaner insurance companies control just under 50 percent of the insurance industry, according to former Sanlam Chairman Wassenaar. Afrikaans speakers control about 20 percent of gold production and 20 to 30 percent of the platinum production, but over all, economists estimate that companies controlled by Afrikaners represent less than 20 percent of the total gross domestic product. Companies controlled by the English-speaking community represent close to 90 percent of manufacturing and 85 percent of banking. One company alone, the giant Anglo American Corp., produces the equivalent of 16 percent of South Africa's gross domestic product.

The continued dominance of business by English speakers contributes signficantly to the distrust between business and government and has distinct political overtones. Many Afrikaners see English speakers in business against the background of their former colonial status. To them, English speakers exist as a potential fifth column, working against Nationalist government policies. One Afrikaner banker told IRRC that it is only in the last decade or so that the control of South African business has moved from London to Johannesburg, and Afrikaners say that the interests of many English speakers continue to center in England rather than South Africa. A significant number of English speakers continue to hold British passports despite South Africa's withdrawal in 1960 from the Commonwealth, many send their children to England for school or for vacations, and an increasing number have begun to emigrate in the last several years. Perhaps more important, at least in the eyes of the government, has been the continued English-speaking support for the opposition parties, a support that many Afrikaners view as linking business to the opposition. This link is most tangibly seen in the financial support given by Anglo American's chairman Harry Oppenheimer to the Progressive Party in South Africa. Former Prime Minister Vorster in 1977 described Oppenheimer as "the spiritual father" of the Progressives and stated "it is time that he told South Africa where he stands and what he is doing."

Government Policy-Making

The historic predominance of English speakers in business has not been duplicated in politics. In fact, since the Afrikaner-controlled National Party assumed power in 1948, English speakers have played an increasingly ineffectual role in South Africa's electoral politics. Outnumbered among whites three to two, English speakers have had their potential influence cut further by a gerrymandering of constituencies that has given disproportionate representation to largely Afrikaans-speaking rural areas. Those people opposing National Party policies, including most English speakers, have been unable to develop a party platform with sufficient drawing power. The traditional opposition party--the United Party--collapsed several years ago, a victim of its inability to attract a sufficiently broad constituency. It has been succeeded by the smaller but not more successful New Republic Party, and a number of its supporters have joined the Progressive Party to form the Progressive Federal Party. Combined, the New Republic Party and the Progressive Federal Party hold a total of 27 seats in the 165-seat parliament.

The role of the cabinet: The almost complete absence of English speakers from the National Party, combined with their domination of business, has meant that few policy makers in South Africa today come from what could be considered a corporate business background. Policy-making in South Africa is highly centralized. Major policy decisions are made almost exclusively by members of the cabinet, and there are no former business executives in the current cabinet.

The cabinet is composed of a maximum of 18 members, ministers and deputy ministers, selected by the prime minister and charged with direction of the more than 40 departments of the government. By law, cabinet members must become members of parliament within three months of their selection; in practice, they almost always already are. Parliament has been controlled by the Nationalists since 1948, and most of the National Party representatives have been drawn from small towns, from law firms, newspapers, schools, churches or a lifetime of political party organization. The National Party caucus, composed of party members elected to parliament, has contained only a handful of former businessmen, most of whom were owners or employees in relatively small business concerns, and there have been few if any cabinet members with corporate backgrounds in recent years. Professor G.C. Olivier, of the University of Pretoria, writes: "One generalization which can be made is that the majority of South Africa's cabinet ministers fall within the 'intelligent layman' category. Apart from a few exceptions, members of the present cabinet are politicians of long standing without notable achievements in professional careers outside politics."

There is little precedent in South Africa for drawing cabinet ministers from outside the traditional party hierarchy as there is in the United States. South Africa has no revolving door, with corporate executives moving to positions of power within the government and returning to business once the terms of their patrons have expired. Most ministers in South Africa have been active in party politics for an extended period of time and not only hold a seat in parliament but carry substantial weight within party circles as well. The National Party, as Professor R.A. Schrire of the University of Capetown has said, "plays a critical role in determining the leadership pool from which government leaders are drawn."

Once selected for the cabinet, ministers tend to stay in office for lengthy terms. Newell Stultz, political science professor at Brown University, notes that South Africa has demonstrated a remarkably "slow circulation of elites." The cabinets have been highly stable with long terms in office and low turnover. Stultz writes that "all these features have been somewhat more apparent since 1948 (when the Nationalists assumed power) than before, although the Vorster cabinet to January 1972 proved more unstable than its immediate predecessors."

Prime Minister Vorster's government was exceptional in that several of the members of his cabinet came from outside the traditional party ranks and had relatively short or no service in party politics. Roelof (Pik)

Botha, for example, was Ambassador to the United States immediately before he became Minister of Foreign Affairs. His quick accession to the cabinet, without a lengthy waiting time in parliament, has imposed some limits on his power within the party itself, despite his apparent popularity among the voters. Polls taken shortly before the election for prime minister in October 1978--a position elected by the party caucus in parliament, not by popular vote--showed overwhelming popular support for Pik Botha. He lost badly in the caucus vote, however. Although he carries one of the most important portfolios in the cabinet, he still is considered by many Nationalists to lack the seniority required for party leadership.

The lack of businessmen among Nationalist ranks in parliament, and the difficulty of bringing someone in from outside the normal party structure, has greatly limited the likelihood that corporate executives will be appointed to serve in the cabinet. Even if there were representatives from the private sector in the cabinet, their power might well be limited by their strength within the party. "A minister who is outside the ideological mainstream of the cabinet and caucus will not be as influential as several of his colleagues, irrespective of his department or his personal ability," Professor Schrire comments. Five or six members of the cabinet form an informal advisory group for the prime minister. The more powerful members, Schrire writes, will usually attempt to reach agreement amongst themselves informally before a cabinet meeting. If this consensus is achieved, the structured meeting (the cabinet meets weekly on a formal basis) for the full cabinet will be used to inform other ministers of this consensus and to have the decision ratified. When Vorster was prime minister, the Ministers of Defense, Information, Bantu Affairs and Justice were among those most frequently consulted. The Ministers of Economics and Finance, the positions most likely to be responsive to business concerns, played little role in discussions on political and strategic issues.

The methods by which cabinet members are selected, the degree of authority granted the prime minister, and the importance of ideology, religion and history to the National Party itself all combine to create a certain homogeneity to the cabinet. Peter Harris of the University of Hong Kong commented in 1971 that there "exists an almost unique harmony of ideas regarding the policy in the cabinet." While this harmony has deteriorated slightly in the last few years as a result of mounting pressures on the government, a generalized agreement remains and cabinet members guard a traditional facade of unanimity. Ministers rarely publicly oppose policies advocated by other ministers and, Schrire writes, "despite personal disagreement with colleagues, it is customary for the cabinet to display a united front to the outside world. Especially on sensitive issues such as race relations, sports and state security, ministers are extremely careful not to overstep the policy line collectively agreed upon by the cabinet."

Changes in the role of the party in policy-making have paralleled, to some degree, changes within the cabinet itself. Just as it has become impractical for the cabinet as a whole to deal with all major policy decisions, resulting in greater authority to informal groups of individual ministers and to cabinet committees, so has it become impossible for the party to play a major role in initiating policy. Instead, the cabinet, the caucus and the party as a whole have come to play a more legitimizing consultative role, reviewing policies developed by smaller groups of decision makers, but not actually making policy themselves.

The position of the civil service: Thus the areas in which business could play a role in policy formulation have shrunk to focus on a few members of the cabinet or certain members of the civil service. The power of a minister for a particular department depends on his relationship to the secretary of that department, a permanent civil servant. The minister is dependent on the secretary and his staff for information used both to formulate and carry out policy. Some ministers play a very active role in administering a department and in guiding the gathering of information required to develop new policies and programs. Other ministers choose to play a more passive role, leaving many of the policy decisions to their department secretaries.

Few members of the civil service have been drawn from business, and increasingly the civil service is having difficulty attracting younger talent. Since the end of World War II, the private sector has offered greater job opportunities to white South Africans than has the civil service, and where once the civil service was one of the few means by which Afrikaans speakers could gain power, increasingly it has lost its drawing power. At the same time, expanding demands both within the departments and with the growth of the public corporations have overtaxed the resources of the limited numbers of whites available to the bureaucracy. The bureaucracy has been stretched thin, the economic adviser to the prime minister told IRRC. "Real policy changes have to come out of commission reports," he said, "because civil servants are busy with day-to-day operations," and are unable to prepare policy documents. More commission studies have been launched in the last two years than ever before, several analysts say, a sign that the bureaucracy and the government recognize that they can no longer handle problems alone and that the pressures for change are being felt as never before.

Business participation on government commissions: Participation on commissions offers business one opportunity for participation in policy formulation and review. Commission members are selected generally by the ministers to whom the reports will be made and may include representatives from a variety of constituencies, business, labor, universities, churches. The Wiehahn Commission on laws affecting African labor, for example, included representatives from several labor organizations and business groups, some academics, and, for the first time, one African. Moreover, business representatives are invited to present testimony or statements to the commissions. The American Chamber of Commerce in Johannesburg submitted a statement both to the Wiehahn Commission and to the Riekert Commission on laws affecting Africans living in areas designated for whites.

Ministers are granted a great deal of authority within the cabinet over issues relating to their department--party members tend to respect ministerial jurisdiction--and the ministers are responsible for preparing legislation based on the reports of commissions they have ordered. Nic Wiehahn had been asked by the Minister of Labor to draw up legislation in line with his report's recommendations even before the report was accepted by the cabinet. The ministers' authority is not politically sacrosanct, however, and a number of people suggest that the report of the Wiehahn Commission was delayed as a result of the election of hard liner Andries Treurnicht as head of the Transvaal wing of the National Party. Commission reports may be ignored or even suppressed.

Business may also play a formal role in policy discussions through its participation on the Economic Advisory Council to the Prime Minister. It is possible for representatives of foreign as well as South African companies to participate on the EAC. The managing directors of at least two American companies have served on the EAC--both have been South African citizens. The EAC is composed of 55 representatives from the major business and labor organizations, from academia and from the relevant government departments. The council meets three times a year to discuss a variety of problems relating to the national economy. Past discussions have covered some subjects relating to apartheid, such as blacks' land tenure and blacks' trading rights, but the council focuses primarily on the national budget discussions and the government's economic program. A major topic of discussion over the last several years has been the degree to which the government should stimulate the economy with increased spending programs. The council has no staff of its own. The office of the economic adviser to the prime minister provides staff work; it has one standing committee on manpower utilization and a number of subcommittees. Topics for discussion are proposed by non-government members of the council. No formal report of the meetings, which extend over a two- to three-day period, is made public, but minutes are kept and the economic adviser reports directly to the prime minister on the major issues or proposals raised during the meetings.

The Role of Interest Groups in South Africa

There are less formal means by which business or other interest groups may seek to influence policy. Alone or in concert, interest groups lobby those people in government responsible for making or carrying out policy. Much lobbying takes place unseen, at backyard barbecues, cocktail parties, sporting events, on the golf course or at other social gatherings. Or it may be done, in the words of political scientist Peter Harris, using "the time-honored techniques of interest groups everywhere. Ministers will be bombarded with letters, public petitions and press announcements; above all, interest groups will employ the technique of the urgent telegram."

In seeking to influence government policy on limited day-to-day issues rather than political issues, interest groups in South Africa differ little from groups in the United States. Both the breadth of groups seeking to influence the government on issues--from farmers and church groups to women's organizations and businessmen--and the tactics they employ are often reminiscent of U.S. interest groups. The difference between interest group politics in the United States and in South Africa is not in the groups and their methods, but rather in the way their role is perceived by the government and the government's responsiveness to their concerns.

Kinds of interest groups: Essentially, South Africa has two kinds of interest groups. Members of the first kind are interested primarily in influencing policies that affect them directly. Farmers may want transport rebates, or businessmen may want lower taxes. They may have complaints with regulations or specific day-to-day problems. Their goals are limited and well-defined, and often their efforts are aimed at representatives in the bureaucracy responsible for administering areas specific to their concerns. They are able to influence department heads and ministers by their expertise on the matters at hand.

The second kind of interest group has broader interests and longer-term goals. Members of this group are interested in influencing national priorities and shaping legislation that affects national issues. Their efforts are focused almost exclusively on the cabinet ministers responsible for decision-making, and the lobbyists' ability to obtain a hearing or to influence policy-makers at this level is dependent on the degree to which their objectives are congruent with those of the National Party.

Interest groups and the political system: Politicians in South Africa are far less dependent on interest group support than they are in the United States. Campaigns are financed through the party; ministers generally rise to the cabinet as a result of their service in the party ranks. In only a few exceptional cases, such as the trade unions, do interest groups have the power to influence elections and therefore obtain special right of access. Thus, the party is the predominant line of access for an interest group, and those interest groups most likely to have an influence on policy decisions are those that are perceived as aligned with the party. Because the parties are largely divided along ethnic lines, influence also divides along ethnic lines. "In general," Schrire writes, "influence is related to ethnic membership and Afrikaner groups are more influential than English groups and white groups more influential than black groups."

The National Party draws its support from the Dutch Reformed Church, farmers organizations, the labor unions and Afrikaner cultural organizations. One interest group that has been particularly successful in shaping government policy has been the Afrikaner secret society--the Broederbond--an organization of 12,000 Afrikaans-speaking men established in 1920 to promote Afrikaner interests. The Broederbond has members throughout South African society and explains its influence, in the words of its official historian, A.N. Pelzer, as the result of an understanding between government and the Broeders "that has always been of the best." "This fortunate state of affairs," he writes, "can be attributed to the fact that political leaders were normally members of the Afrikaner Broederbond and problems were discussed in a spirit of brotherhood." The prime minister and all but two of his cabinet ministers are members of the Broederbond, and cabinet members attend meetings of the Broederbond's executive council when policies affecting their departments are being reviewed.

The years in power with only token opposition from other political parties have colored the government's perception of the role of interest groups and, according to many observers, have limited its responsiveness. Opposition to National Party policies has often been viewed as opposition to the government itself; criticism of party ideology or policy may be viewed as unpatriotic or even treasonous. The government does not hesitate to use counterpressures to prevent interest groups from having too great an influence--the numerous clamp-downs on black organizations, the bannings of blacks and liberal whites, are examples of government counterpressure. Even when criticism comes from the Afrikaner community, if it comes in public, the government's response can be swift and strong. Party stalwarts and government officials may label Afrikaans speakers who publicly criticize government policy as traitors not only to the party but to their people, and public criticism can lead to ostracism of an Afrikaner by his religious and cultural community.

Thus, while interest groups can and do play a role in South Africa's political system, they are constrained by the political sensitivity of the government. Schrire describes interest groups as playing a role in "the politics of detail," but says that they are largely excluded from participation in the "politics of principle." Another political scientist comments, "interest groups have many of the good cards, but they are not the ones that shuffle them."

Business Efforts to Mobilize Opinion

There are several organizations through which business can mobilize opinion on specific issues, and foreign as well as South African companies participate in them. The Associated Chambers of Commerce (ASSOCOM) represents the 110 chambers around the country and has 16,000 business members. The Federated Chamber of Industries (FCI) acts as the umbrella group for South Africa's major manufacturers. Although its membership is predominantly English-speaking, its executive director until fall 1979, Dr. Hennie Reynders, is an Afrikaner. The Chamber of Mines, representing the seven major mining houses and 85 percent of the mining industry, acts as spokesman for the sector. It is again largely English-speaking (six out of seven of the mining houses are run by English speakers, although the seventh, General Mining, often serves as spokesman for the group). The Afrikaanse Handelsinstituut (AHI), an exclusively Afrikaans-speaking organization, is the Afrikaner counterpart to the Associated Chambers of Commerce. And the Steel and Engineering Industries Federation (SEIFSA) represents the major employers in the steel industry.

Most policy analysts say that despite the existence of these organizations business has played a relatively small role in shaping political policy in South Africa. David De Villiers of the Nationale Pers (National Press) told IRRC that political issues in South Africa rarely have grown out of economic concerns. Politics has been more a question of ideology, and political lines have infrequently been drawn around economic issues, he commented. Only recently has the situation begun to change.

A part of the change may be attributed to the extent to which political policies are viewed by business as having an economic impact. The traditional role of business has been to steer clear of politics. For many years, there has been no real reason to become involved, A.D. Wassenaar told IRRC in 1977. The economy has been good and business has felt little reason to complain. In general, political scientist Peter Harris comments, it is "true to say that business accepts government as long as government refrains from interfering in the day-to-day activities of economic life....Business is quite prepared to work as closely with the National Party government as is felt necessary and desirable."

When business has become involved, its involvement has been limited for the most part to practical business issues--price control, import permits, exchange control--or issues relating to the economy, such as increased government expenditures or efforts to curb inflation. Issues of political policy, particularly questions concerning race relations or national security, have become topics of business discussion only on rare occasions.

The impact of Sharpeville: One such occasion followed the events at Sharpeville in 1960 when protests against the pass laws ended in the shooting deaths of 69 unarmed Africans. Occurring at a time in which much of black Africa was on the edge of independence, the massive demonstrations against the government's policy of influx control, the shootings, and the government's subsequent declaration of a state of emergency appeared to threaten the fundamental structure of South Africa. The government banned the two major black nationalist organizations, the Pan African Congress and the African National Congress, detained more than 18,000 people, and eventually convicted and sentenced more than 5,000. In the next 18 months, 248 million rand left the country, and the country's reserves of gold and foreign exchange dropped 50 percent.

Investors' confidence plummeted and business began actively to question government policy. The president of South Africa's Chamber of Mines stated that "every effort must be made to restore investors' confidence in the inherent soundness of investment in gold mining," and the Associated Chambers of Commerce was the first business organization to suggest publicly the efforts the government might make. The Executive Council of ASSOCOM issued a statement calling for collective bargaining rights for African workers, the right to freehold title and a relaxation of influx control. Eventually, writes Stanley Greenberg, Yale political scientist, "when it became evident that the tide of political unrest and economic instability would not readily subside, the five major business associations--AHI, ASSOCOM, FCI, SEIFSA and the Chamber of Mines--joined in a general assault on the labor environment." They signed a joint memorandum that called for the replacement of the passbook system and a revision of the administration of influx control to "reduce the number of incidents of harsh methods adopted in applying the regulations."

But business hesitated to attack the basic foundation of separate development. FCI, according to Greenberg, sought to reassure the government that the international business community is "not asking for a change in policy," but "a more elastic implementation." In a trade publication, FCI representatives said that "various outside interests, including one of our industrial magazines, have been counseling organized commerce and industry, especially of late, to make their collective weight felt in the political field. We must underline this point," FCI stated, "namely that we have to work within the compass of what parliament determines." The AHI was even more chary of appearing critical of government policy. In its journal Volkshandel, it wrote, "The Afrikaanse Handelsinstituut can accept the policy of separate development and strive for close feeling and cooperation with the government and its departments in order to watch over the interests of the businessmen and to be helpful to the authorities with sober and practical advice."

ASSOCOM alone continued to argue for policy change. Greenberg notes that more than a year after Sharpeville, ASSOCOM said that "the abolition of influx control and job reservation, with positive action to develop the Bantu areas, would reduce the danger of unrest and lead foreign investors to take a more optimistic view of our future." The president of the Johannesburg Chamber commented, "If the Republic is to be a viable state, separate development in all spheres will have to depend more on the natural inclinations of people and less on repressive legislation."

But the government response to business criticism was not favorable. Prime Minister Verwoerd accused the business critics of being "traitors" who were more concerned with profits than with the survival of the white man. He argued that ASSOCOM's statements were part of an organized campaign against the state. Criticism of party policy was considered unpatriotic.

Post-Sharpeville business attitudes: The business activism that appeared immediately after Sharpeville faded quite quickly with the economic boom of the 1960s. The government encouraged the boom, and tried to channel it for political as well as economic gains. Arthur Hammond Tooke of the Federated Chamber of Industry argues that government during this period sought to "use business for political ends" in launching its program of decentralization. Several South African economists point to efforts to get business to decentralize in the mid- to late 1960s as evidence of the government's willingness to sacrifice a portion of economic growth to further its own political objectives.

Many business representatives objected to legislation such as the Environment Planning Act (then known as the Physical Planning Act) that furthered decentralization, but most objections were not publicly stated. Business cites examples of real costs to overly visible dissent. In 1969, FCI had proved to the government that there was a more efficient way of achieving the ends of the Physical Planning Act through administration of a selective employment tax. The plan was released to the Financial Mail in advance of government approval, however, and the government then refused to accept the plan because it did not want to appear influenced by the Financial Mail. One FCI spokesman characterized its two efforts to influence the government through public campaigns--against influx control in 1954 and decentralization during the 1960s--as "unmitigated disasters."

Toward the end of the 1960s and during the first part of the 1970s, FCI and other business organizations began to discuss revisions in the government's policy on training of blacks. Recognizing the cost of skills shortages, companies began to urge the government to remove the restrictions on training for blacks in urban areas. Business representatives claim responsibility for the government's decision in 1975 to allow pre- and in-service training centers for Africans living in white areas, and many businessmen attribute the formation of the Riekert and the Wiehahn commissions to business pressures.

But aside from efforts to get revisions in training and in job opportunities, most companies felt little compunction to speak out on policy issues until the beginning of the recession in 1975. Hennie Reynders of FCI commented to IRRC in 1977 that business has tended to stay out of the gray area between business and politics. "Until 18 months ago," he said, "business viewed the gray area pretty conservatively. The recession has increased business interest in policy, however, and political aspects of policy now affect business confidence."

<u>Business activism after Soweto</u>: The importance of political ramifications of government policy became dramatically apparent in 1976 and 1977 with the demonstrations in Soweto, the government's actions to quell the protests and the reaction of the outside world to Steve Biko's death and the bannings and arrests in October 1977.

The impact of Soweto and subsequent events on foreign investors and the implications of outside reaction to events inside South Africa for the South African economy were brought home to business by the drying up of foreign loans, declining new investment and outflow of foreign capital. "Steve Biko's death," one businessman stated, "was equivalent, in the short term, to a $30 drop in the price of gold." Continued political unrest was directly tied to South Africa's recession, some analysts said. It was a vicious triangle. Slow economic growth contributed to blacks' dissatisfaction; the venting of blacks' anger led to government reactions against black dissidents and their white supporters; government actions led to a further decline in business confidence; failing business confidence prolonged the recession.

In response to the recession, unrest among blacks, declining foreign investment and local business confidence, business began to criticize government policies more publicly than was normally the case. The extent of business's willingness to take issue with government policies, however, varied greatly between business organizations and their members and, for the most part, business remained cautious.

As it had been in the past, ASSOCOM was the most outspoken business group in the early days following Soweto. Soon after the initial demonstrations, ASSOCOM issued a call for an end to discrimination based on race. ASSOCOM members asked for an end to job reservation, restrictions on blacks' training and limits on blacks' land tenure in white areas, and they spoke in favor of black unions. ASSOCOM's position was reiterated at its annual conference in October, despite clear warnings from government to business to stay out of politics. In his keynote speech, Henri de Villiers, head of Standard Bank Investment Corp., complained that: "A continuation of social instability and the present lack of progress towards a solution which is acceptable to the rest of the world must result in direct and indirect external pressures growing stronger. These pressures will be manifested in limited availability of long-term loans to South Africa, a lack of direct foreign investment and possibly trade boycotts or embargoes." Representatives to the conference argued that "Politics is causing the complete and utter disruption of the economy. The prime minister is being unfair when he tells us we can't bring this to his attention," and one commented, "If Vorster and his colleagues won't listen to us, maybe other members of his party will."

A similar position was taken by the Transvaal Chamber of Industry independent of its mother organization, the National Federated Chamber of Industries. Representing many of the largest manufacturers in the country, the TCI submitted a memorandum to the prime minister saying that, "The only way in which a stable and contented work force can be established and maintained is to look at all the legitimate grievances which workers and their families have and to do whatever is practical to overcome such grievances." The memorandum cited "the need to encourage a stable, contented, urbanized black community in our metropolitan and industrial. areas" and to create a "middle class" of blacks. Specifically, the TCI called for the development of a "coordinated manpower policy," the expansion of training and job opportunities, a revision of statutes affecting blacks, "with a view to alleviating whenever possible the feeling in the blacks that they are being discriminated against." It recommended that "the legal provisions and the practical administration of influx control be streamlined and minimized to what is really necessary, and that time-wasting procedures and procedures which cause friction and embarrassment be eliminated." Finally, the chamber asked that steps be taken to improve the lot of urban Africans in terms of schools and law and order in the townships.

The two potentially most influential business organizations in the country--the Federated Chamber of Industries and the Afrikaanse Handelsinstituut--hesitated to comment publicly. The AHI declined to issue a joint statement with ASSOCOM and AHI's executive director stressed the need to couch any proposals to the government in a form that would not antagonize the political leadership. AHI's monthly journal urged better conditions for blacks living in white areas, but one foreign official commented, there is "little reason to hope that the Handelsinstituut is ready to challenge the government's basic approach or to press for more than gradual upgrading of the status of urban blacks." After all, an AHI official told IRRC in 1977, "most of our member organizations are supporters of government policy."

The Federated Chamber of Industries initially said little about Soweto and subsequent events. In its October 1976 annual meeting, four months after the first demonstrations in Soweto, the only reference to race was a resolution asking for an end to job reservation. Eventually, in February 1977, the FCI issued a statement expressing publicly "its concern at the seriousness of the current economic situation in South Africa and to again call for a new initiative in the country." It said South Africa's economy had suffered from signs of distress since 1969 (when the FCI had first begun to speak out on the need to train additional blacks) with a serious misallocation of resources responsible for distorting the country's growth pattern. The statement suggested that the government had acted according to political rather than economic demands, and said that the economy could not indefinitely withstand the effects of decisions taken with a political rather than economic framework. It called for the need to develop a stable black middle class. Reynders, FCI's executive director at the time, said that the FCI had decided to make a public statement as a result of its dissatisfaction with the degree of progress growing out of private meetings with government officials.

Government Response to Business Criticism

The government response to business criticism has come in three steps. The first step was an effort to quiet the voices of complaint. In a speech to the Associated Chambers of Commerce in October 1976, Prime Minister Vorster told business, in the words of one journalist, "to mind its own business." His statement is a clear articulation of the government's perspective on the limited role of business, and although Vorster is no longer prime minister (he is now State President) and is under attack for his alleged role in the Information Department scandal, his views as stated in 1976 reflect the current attitudes of many top-level National Party politicians. He defined the limits of dissent permitted business and accused some critics of seeking to circumvent the political process. He questioned the propriety of business organizations raising matters of a broadly defined political nature. He said:

> (T)he way to change overall, broad directions of policy is through the political processes provided for in our constitution....(T)he government derives its legitimacy from a mandate given the governing party by the electorate on the basis of the policies it has espoused at successive elections, and for the government to let itself be dissuaded from the terms of that mandate by extra-electoral pressures, be they from business organizations or from other sources, would amount to adulterating the whole basis of our political system.

He concludes, once again counseling against too much involvement by business in political issues: "I wish to repeat that the government cannot obviously abdicate its basic political responsibilities and principles to business or other organizations or any other extra-electoral groupings, and that efforts to use such organizations to bring about basic changes in the broad direction of government policy are bound to fail and can only give rise to unnecessary and harmful tensions between the government and the private business sector." Comments "voiced by individual businessmen and by business organizations in reaction to political events (Soweto)," he said, really amounted to a call for a restructuring of "our political framework, regardless of the consequences." He warned business against "very subtle attempts...to bring about a new socio-economic order where there will be little room, if at all, for free enterprise."

Establishment of commissions: The second step taken by the government was the establishment of a number of commissions to investigate the causes of the demonstrations and to review legislation affecting Africans living in the designated white areas. In the aftermath of Soweto, the Cillie Commission was set up to look at events that let to the demonstrations. During the spring parliamentary session of 1977 the minister of labor announced the formation of the Wiehahn Commission to investigate labor legislation affecting Africans. Soon after the formation of the Wiehahn Commission, the government established the Riekert Commission to review the body of legislation affecting the utilization of African manpower. (Wiehahn, Riekert recommendations, Chapter II)

Other government moves, business response: The third step, taken in part as a response to mounting pressures from South African business as well as from abroad, has been minor changes affecting opportunities for blacks--limited desegregation of restaurants and hotels, lifting of some job reservations, opening of some private schools to several hundred African students. In addition, the government has offered tacit support to employment codes of conduct--although making occasional references to outside intervention--by not overtly opposing the codes. And one change that the government has made largely in response to business pressure has been the granting of the 99-year leasehold.

To the few business activists in South Africa, the government's first response appeared inadequate. In August 1977, the Transvaal Chamber of

Industries wrote directly to the prime minister stating its concern:

> We have followed with dismay the hardening attitude of overseas investors towards the Republic, and noted the very clear message from the traditional suppliers of foreign loans that they expect to see visible evidence of the move away from discrimination before again recommending long-term investment in South Africa. We have been confused by conflicting ministerial statements, often on matters of important principle. We have realized more and more the indivisibility of political and economic issues in South Africa's present circumstances.

In its memorandum, the TCI found a need for "a definite statement from the government regarding the nature and timing of the planned changes in South Africa...(to) restore internal business confidence." The chamber asked for recognition of the permanency of Africans in the urban areas, a recognition the chamber said "need not be incompatible with the separate development cornerstone of government policy," and reiterated the points made in its 1976 memorandum.

The Associated Chamber of Commerce continued to advocate substantive change and argued for the development of a five- to 10-year socio-economic plan for blacks. Such a plan, ASSOCOM argued, would not only remove uncertainty and present concrete evidence of a better dispensation for all races, but would also provide both the public and the private sectors with a framework within which to operate. The president of ASSOCOM called for "genuine 'freehold title' for all, better educational institutions, improved housing and transportation, the rights to free trade and marketing of labor, and the removal of all discrimination." The government had commented frequently during this period on the threat from outside South Africa, the enemies seeking to force change upon the country. ASSOCOM responded, in the words of the president:

> If one analyzes the current situation then it should be obvious that housing, transport, electricity, education and the right to work are as much part of the defense program as is the maintenance of a well-trained and equipped force on our borders.
>
> We cannot afford to have an Achilles heel within our borders and look only for signs of danger on the outside. Our biggest threat lies within the country and we have at our fingertips a peaceful means of overcoming it, and overcome it we must.
>
> Finally, and at the risk of repeating myself, we have to instill confidence in all those domiciled within the country, and at the same time provide something tangible for those living elsewhere to see, so that they too will have confidence in us and what we stand for.

Business Involvement in Expanding Rights for Blacks

The Urban Foundation: Shortly after the first demonstrations at Soweto, two of South Africa's major industrialists--Harry Oppenheimer of

Anglo American and Anton Rupert of Rembrandt Tobacco--met in London to discuss how the private sector might react. Eventually they settled on convening a conference of businessmen, Afrikaans- as well as English-speaking, to discuss "the quality of life in urban communities." The conference focused on the status of blacks and provided the basis for the establishment of the Urban Foundation, a business-backed organization, "to serve as a catalyst in combining efforts of the (black) communities involved, concerned business and the authorities." Clive Mennell, an Anglo officer and regional director of the foundation, explained the companies' interest in the foundation to John Burns of The New York Times: "We became involved because we were scared. There was a concern for the country, of course, but there was also a selfish concern for our assets."

The objective of the foundation is "the improvement of housing standards, education in the broadest sense, community activities, recreational facilities, employment opportunities and other related matters." It solicited the support of business--aiming originally to collect 25 million rand in the first five years--and focused its attention initially on housing, education, and employment practices. Business funds were to serve as seed money in urban areas to demonstrate what could be done in response to the stated needs of the community. The foundation began in early 1977 to provide grant or loan money to a range of projects that included everything from garbage removal in Soweto to construction of health service facilities.

The aims of the foundation were not limited to project development. The group's involvement in projects provided it with an opportunity to try to build community participation at one level and to lobby the government (and business itself) for changes on another.

An initial problem the foundation faced was to win acceptance by the communities in which it hoped to operate. Black militants rejected the assistance from the foundation as "blood money." In a special report on the foundation, the Financial Mail quotes some blacks as opposing the foundation because they felt that improved living conditions would undermine the commitment to fight apartheid. "Keep it painful brother," they argued, "so the people stay motivated." Others viewed the foundation's work as palliative or stop-gap measures that delay the real changes that need to take place. And a number of blacks saw the foundation as another welfare agency. They sought contributions from it for projects, but were unwilling to accept the need to commit their own time and energies in the self-help mode the foundation was pushing.

Foundation leaders have spent extensive time in consultation with black communities and have made some inroads in obtaining blacks' support. The Financial Mail quotes Dr. Nthato Motlana, recent detainee and member of the Soweto Committee of Ten, in response to critics of the foundation: "Do we have to live in hovels waiting for the liberation without enough of even the basic facilities? Isn't there enough motivation without hovelism too?" Percy Qoboza, also a recent detainee and editor of the African paper, the Post, successor to the banned World, wrote in the Jan. 4, 1979, lead article, "the foundation is doing a magnificent piece of work and fulfilling a worthwhile need."

But support is tempered by the limits of the foundation's ability to achieve what the black community as a whole views as meaningful change. Before the government's decision not to destroy Crossroads, for example, the Financial Mail cited an African worker as saying, "If Crossroads goes, every white outfit operating down here, including and particularly the Urban Foundation, can just pack up. They will have lost the people forever and might just as well throw their money in the sea for all the good it will do them." And recognizing the potential problem in being branded an organization with only band-aids for major wounds, the foundation has sought to extend the impact of its projects well beyond the individual immediately affected.

Activists within the foundation see its projects not only as an opportunity to mobilize the black communities in self-help programs, but also as a means to provide talking points with government and with business itself. Assiduously disclaiming that it is intended as an interest or pressure group, the foundation's members have played as active a role in lobbying on sensitive political issues as any business group in South Africa's history. Their efforts have met with much frustration and limited, but noticeable, effect.

Buoyed by the general optimism shared by business executives who are used to achieving objectives, businesses participating in the early planning of the foundation were confident that they could overcome most of the major obstacles to changes in the urban black community. There was a certain "can-do" flavor to the early pronouncements by executives supporting the foundation, and there was considerable expectation that will, money and cooperation in the private sector could achieve quick results. Disappointment came early.

Reaction of the government to the foundation--Not only did the foundation face problems in winning acceptance among the black communities, but members found that politicians and the government bureaucracy were far more intractable on issues relating to political policy than on day-to-day issues relating to business. Few of the businessmen involved in trying to get the government to revise its policy on land tenure for blacks in urban areas had dealt actively with the government before on political policy issues. Confident from successes in lobbying on normal business issues, many believed that they would enjoy a similar hearing on the leasehold question. Instead, they encountered suspicion and wariness.

The government's initial reaction to the formation of the foundation was to view it as a threat. One knowledgeable analyst told IRRC that Prime Minister Vorster's first response to a visit from Afrikaner industrialist Willem de Villiers of General Mining to announce establishment of the foundation was to ask, "How long until it becomes a political party?" The foundation, launched with the support of Anglo American's chairman Harry Oppenheimer--a man with strong links to the Progressive Federal Party--was seen as potentially another means by which the opposition party could meddle in the policies of the governing National Party. Some members of government resented proposals by the foundation--despite the fact that it numbered among its members many of South Africa's most prominent Afrikaans-speaking industrialists. Afrikaner businessmen are seen in many National Party circles as tainted by their association with English-speaking businessmen so that they cannot be counted on to put party policies above profits.

Negotiations between Urban Foundation members and the government over leasehold rights dragged on, seemingly interminably. Although the government had announced a revision in land hold rights as early as 1975, and a 99-year lease was decided upon in 1977, sources close to the foundation say that the language of the leasehold would never have gotten out of parliament without substantial lobbying efforts in 1978. Foundation lawyers in Capetown worked and re-worked memoranda for government ministers during the parliamentary session. Eventually the foundation called upon its most important Afrikaans-speaking members to put pressures on members of the cabinet and top civil servants. The effort made by the foundation was reminiscent, one observer said, of corporate efforts to push legislation in the United States.

Even once the legislation was passed, however, considerable work was needed to ensure that it was translated into regulations that would meet the needs of the building societies, thus allowing loans to be made to blacks interested in home ownership. In October and November 1978, foundation officials met four or five times with Connie Mulder, then minister for black affairs, and with top civil servants. Finally, the language was worked out and the regulations rescheduled to take effect in April 1979. But bureaucratic delays in surveying house sites and what one source close to the Urban Foundation called "purposeful obstruction" by some members of the civil service set the program back further. By November 1979, only seven Africans had been given titles to leaseholds.

Foundation members who were surprised and frustrated by the problems encountered in achieving even the minimum objective of the 99-year lease were similarly frustrated for some time in their efforts to achieve agreement among companies on an acceptable code of conduct for employment practices. The code eventually promulgated by the South African Consultative Committee on Labor Affairs and the Urban Foundation went through 27 drafts, according to one source close to the effort; at one point the foundation almost splintered irreconcilably over the issue of integration of toilet facilities, he told IRRC. The issue was resolved with a pledge "to strive constantly for the elimination of discrimination based on race or color from all aspects of employment practice and to apply this principle in good faith...(to such things as) the provision of...physical working conditions and facilities relating thereto."

Other responses to the foundation--The response of companies to the Urban Foundation has not been universally supportive. The Financial Mail quotes the managing director of a small manufacturing company as saying "the Urban Foundation, that's for the big boys, the Oppenheimers and Ruperts of this world....I haven't got time to involve myself in committees." Some directors argue that it is not the responsibility of business to become involved in social service projects. Managers of several American companies told IRRC that they saw the Urban Foundation as "keeping the government's feet from the fire," helping to provide short-term improvements that actually delay real change. And within the foundation itself there has been tension between Afrikaans and English speakers and between those who see it focusing exclusively on project development and those who see it as a means of organizing black communities and raising issues with the government. The foundation's executive director commented to the Financial Mail that in the beginning some business people expected miracles--when they made a donation, they expected it to be translated into bricks and mortar within three months.

The foundation has gathered substantial support in its two years of operations. Including the foreign loans it has negotiated, the foundation has raised more than $100 million. It has received contributions in cash or service from nearly 100 corporations. Foreign companies have played a relatively minor role in the foundation's activities--in part because the foundation has not actively solicited foreign participation. Some companies like Caltex (250,000 rand), Ford (500,000 rand), Mobil (250,000 rand), and Otis (250,000 rand) have made major contributions; a few like Citibank, Kimberly-Clark and Carborundum have made small contributions (under 20,000 rand each); but most foreign companies have not participated at all.

Other business involvement: Some foreign companies--most notably the American ones--have sought a means of working on black development that offers greater visibility and national identification. An American Chamber of Commerce was formed in November 1977 and a French Chamber shortly thereafter. The first major project sponsored by the American Chamber is the construction of the first commercial high school and community center in Soweto. The cost of the project--nearly $3 million originally and $518,000 in annual operating costs--is to be borne by American companies. In a brochure developed for the American Chamber, the project is described "as a good way in which you can effectively act for good in South Africa and enhance the image of American business both here and overseas. It is an opportunity to participate in a highly visible manner towards the development of South Africa's black population, in a well-planned project. By doing so it offers you a way to create better worldwide acceptance of the continuing presence of your company in South Africa."

The American Chamber expanded the role of U.S. companies in South Africa in 1978 by making submissions to the Riekert and Wiehahn Commissions. In the memorandum prepared for the Riekert Commission, the American Chamber criticized the Bantu Labor Act of 1964 as "a primary cause of prevalent alienation, frustration and lack of commitment manifested by black workers." It argued for a "free labor market" and equal labor conditions for blacks and "called upon the government to grant permanent residence status to Africans in urban areas." It also recommended "full property ownership rights, the right to establish businesses and full security of terms." It said "the concept of human beings being subjected to curfew is a denial of basic human dignity," and criticized aspects of a number of laws affecting the rights of Africans in urban areas. In a March 15, 1978, letter to Wiehahn, the American Chamber recommended that "all forms of social discrimination written into existing labor legislation and associated regulations be eliminated," that the "principle of freedom of association apply to all workers of all population groups on a common basis," and that changes be made to enable education and training of workers.

Companies have also had an opportunity to speak out individually against government policies. In their 1976 and 1977 annual reports, the chairmen of many South African companies made reference to the need to take steps to quiet political uncertainties. They referred to the relationship between foreign investment, economic growth, employment and unrest and called for government efforts to respond to the unrest and to spur growth.

The government took steps to quell dissent and unrest--by bans and arrests of Oct. 19, 1977--which, several observers told IRRC, were taken to reassure the outside world that the government was in control of the situation. The outside world had just the opposite reaction, however, although the subsequent lull in open protests against the government has diminished any impulse among companies within South Africa to seek changes in political policy. Instead of pushing political change as a means of dealing with black dissatisfaction, business has turned back to economic issues--such as government stimulation of growth--as a means of encouraging further foreign investment. ASSOCOM has continued to recommend a five- to 10-year economic plan. FCI mentions the need for greater training opportunities and for rights in the workplace. Whereas for a brief period after Soweto in 1976 business began to look at the plight of blacks at least in part as a political problem, by 1978 it was again concentrating on economic issues. In their annual conventions in 1978 neither FCI nor ASSOCOM spent much time on issues specific to the black population. Instead, they focused on how best to spur growth in the economy. FCI's economist Hammond Tooke argued to IRRC that because economic growth would bring more jobs and better wages to blacks, references to economic growth were really code words for greater opportunity for blacks.

Others are more critical of the business role. Stanley Greenberg of Yale, in an initial comparison of the responses to the events in Soweto to those after Sharpeville in 1960, describes the events at Sharpeville and immediately following--particularly the precipitous flight of foreign capital--as temporarily stunning business into a strong unified statement for revisions in political policy. Within a year, however, as the situation cooled, business stepped back, and became removed from discussion of political issues. Soweto and subsequent events again provoked business to become involved in a political debate. The debate after Soweto was muted, however, Greenberg argues: "Unlike the Sharpeville aftermath, Soweto produced neither serious apprehension about economic collapse of a divided business community; nor for that matter did it force the business community to formulate a genuine political program. It produced instead a black unanimity around a program of self-help and increased expenditures on housing, sewage and electrification, while avoiding the more political issues, like African trade unionism, political rights and apartheid."

There have been exceptions to Greenberg's overview of business involvement. ASSOCOM has continued to argue for change and the American Chamber's submission to the Riekert Commission was outspoken by traditional business standards, although such outspokenness was still conducted with a government-structured form--the commission process. Also, the effectiveness of ASSOCOM as a foreign national chamber may well be limited by its very nature. Etienne Rousseau, Afrikaans-speaking chairman of Federale Volksbeleggings, told IRRC in 1977 that one could not "pay much attention to ASSOCOM because all they want is more trade. They are not really South African," he said, because they are all English speakers, and they are "not the least bit concerned with the political implications of their acts."

Rousseau's statement represents the views of an important segment of South Africa's power elite, but there are other members of the power structure who take a less extreme position. One government official told IRRC that the government's refusal to adopt a five-year plan such as the one suggested by ASSOCOM was less a question of language than one of style--it was simply not the style of Vorster's government to set out its course in advance. And under no circumstances would the government want to appear publicly to be acting at the suggestion of a pressure group. This view was confirmed by Hammond Tooke at FCI, who describes the incident in which efforts by FCI to get the government to accept a tax program in view of the Environment Planning Act were undercut by publication of a similar suggestion in the Financial Mail shortly before the decision was to be announced. The government then refused to go ahead as agreed, lest it appear as though it were acting on the suggestion of the press. It was months, he said, before the FCI felt it could approach the prime minister on any issue.

The Limits and Potential of Business Lobbying on Behalf of Blacks

The fear of jeopardizing whatever limited influence it may have by publicity in the press runs throughout business. This so-called "Rand Daily Mail kiss-of-death syndrome" is a prime rationale offered for the lack of public business criticism of government policies. Because government plays an active role in the South African economy, as both a regulator and a consumer, business is wary of appearing to be antagonistic, and foreign companies as guests in a host country are particularly cautious. "If a person criticizes the government publicly, he is apt to become a hero in the English-speaking press," one Afrikaaner businessman told IRRC. "Once his name appears in the press, he is apt to become a victim of doodswyg--kill by silence." He may suffer not only in his business, but in his personal life as well. He may be ostracized from his social and ethnic community. In describing their concern about government reaction to criticism, business executives often recount stories about what has happened to the most powerful in their community. One story relates to Anton Rupert's efforts in the late 1950s to start a partnership company with colored businessmen. Prime Minister Verwoerd criticized Rupert soundly, and, according to several sources, Rupert shifted his interest in social change to something less political--a concentration on historic preservation. More recently, Harry Oppenheimer, long a critic of the government, was denied the opportunity to buy Samancor, a government-owned manganese corporation, and most observers attributed the denial of the sale to government displeasure with Oppenheimer's politics. A third instance was the personal attack waged by Prime Minister Vorster on A.D. Wassenaar after Wassenaar published his book, Assault on Private Enterprise, criticizing the extent of state intervention in the South African economy. The prime minister challenged Wassenaar's thesis on the floor in parliament and later went further, questioning his party credentials and his loyalty to South Africa.

Thus the initial reaction to public criticism of government may well make it appear counterproductive. It is unlikely that active critical lobbying by business will have immediately demonstrable positive results. The government, traditionally, has avoided at all costs the appearance of responding directly to pressure.

Business effectiveness has been tempered as well, not only by the limits on the government's willingness to respond, but by its own willingness to raise issues. In the past, business interest in lobbying on political issues has resulted from black dissent within South Africa, foreign pressures, declining investment and an unhealthy economy. The extent of this interest and the degree to which it is sustained varies widely between sectors of the economy and between individual companies. Lawrence Schlemmer, South African sociologist, says that polls taken before the 1977 elections, but after Steve Biko's death and the October 19 bannings, showed that non-Afrikaans-speaking businesses, executives and members of business organizations appear to view international pressure more seriously than the general population, but the same is not true of Afrikaans-speaking and government-supporting businessmen." He concludes, therefore, that outside pressure affects most "those sections of the electorate with little influence on government."

There may also be a difference in the way various elements of the business community view internal unrest. Schlemmer reports that, generally, Afrikaans speakers take less seriously than English speakers the manifest discontent of South Africa's blacks. He attributes their greater complacency to "the fact that they find it easier to adopt scapegoat explanations for some of the threats to their future--for example, extrinsic forces such as agitators, communists and the like tend frequently to be seen as the cause of disturbances." It is a view that is commonly accepted among many Afrikaner businesses as well. Jan Marais, now one of the few Nationalist members of parliament drawn from business, formerly the head of the Trust Bank, has said, "Whatever we do, the 'red onslaught' against this part of the world will continue. Our survival is at stake. We, therefore, need total mobilization....We are the key to future world domination by an ambitious superpower. Those who control southern Africa in the future will, to a considerable degree, determine world destiny."

Whether businessmen share these concerns--and many do--they are generally in agreement on the need for stability and growth. Business interest in stabilizing may be what makes it more conservative about future political configuration. Schlemmer reports that as a group, businessmen, "together with those interested in Afrikaaner culture, are relatively more insistent than others on the maintenance of the power position of whites."

Even with these constraints there are signs that business pressures, public as well as private, have had some impact on inner party circles. Despite former Prime Minister Vorster's public rejection of Wassenaar's book, for example, the government has begun to study seriously the need to limit its role in the economy. ASSOCOM's urging of a five- to 10-year plan, while dismissed by many Afrikaners as English business propaganda, has gained currency in some government circles. Former Minister for Black Affairs Connie Mulder began to talk about a plan of his own. FCI's interest in training has borne some fruits; widespread business pressure following Soweto led to the establishment of the Riekert and Wiehahn Commissions; and business pressure helped push the government to reverse its position on granting "African" commuters the right to join unions. The codes of conduct forced the government to recognize publicly the need to allow desegregation in the workplace, and the Urban Foundation played a critical role in the government's decision to offer Africans a 99-year lease and in the government's change of policy on Crossroads.

These successes, moderate as they are, show both the potential and the limits on the ability of business to lobby for change. One manager closely involved in the Urban Foundation's efforts on the 99-year lease told IRRC that he found in dealing with the government it is "very hard to tell what is non-negotiable. There might be an ideological impasse, but except on issues relating to the security of the state, that impasse is not met at the first door. We can only think ahead a few steps at a time. Win some gains, build some new premises and move from there."

The Future Under P.W. Botha

There are some signs of change, both in the attitude of government and of business, that are likely to increase the potential influence of business on political decisions in the future. Perhaps the most important of these comes as the result of the new prime minister, P.W. Botha, whose approach to government and vision of South Africa's future are far different and considerably more sophisticated than those of his predecessor, John Vorster.

As prime minister, Vorster recognized the need for change in South Africa, but he greatly feared that rapid progress to dismantle race policies would lead to secession of the National Party's right wing. Avoidance of a party split became his obsession. Dependent on only a small group of political loyalists for advice, he generally waited for a public consensus before taking a major policy step. Any advances made during his tenure were inevitably cautious and conservative, as he sought to limit the risk of dissent within his party. Outside the party structure, he used political repression to control black political activism at home and a propaganda campaign under the auspices of the Information Department to combat critics abroad. His attitude toward anyone critical of his policies, including business, was defensive.

P.W. Botha has opted instead for a more flexible--"adapt or die"--approach. His basic premise is that South Africa must develop a black middle class to serve as a stabilizing force. He knows that some changes necessary to allow black advancement will alienate influential sections of his white constituency--particularly conservative union members, farmers and civil servants. The growing disillusionment among some voters is already apparent in recent by-elections in which traditionally heavy National Party pluralities have been cut measurably by both more liberal and more conservative opposition parties. But he is willing to accept the losses.

To succeed in his approach, the prime minister recognizes that he will need new political allies, and businessmen are a natural choice. Having learned as minister of defense the advantages of working closely with business, he recognizes as prime minister the consequences of interests between business and government in a way Vorster never did. Not only does he see that Afrikaners can be less defensive about business now that Afrikaner businessmen such as A.D. Wassenaar of Sanlam Insurance, Anton Rupert of Rembrandt Tobacco and Willem de Villiers of General Mining have come to play relatively prominent roles in the South African economy, but he needs business support. He needs business to invest, expand and provide jobs at home to create a black middle class, and he needs business to support him abroad, in effect to play part of the role that Vorster had envisioned for the Department of Information--combatting South Africa's critics overseas.

As a result, business access to government has improved considerably in the last year, through participation on commissions and task forces and because of P.W. Botha's willingness to recruit suggestions from academics, business and other outsiders. A.D. Wassenaar has commented that he has "the strong impression that the Republic has never had a prime minister so able to consult private enterprise and so capable of the physical exercise of listening as is the present prime minister."

In June 1979 Botha announced that he intended to restructure his cabinet radically, chopping the number of cabinet committees from 40 to five. Each of these committees will supervise working committees composed of department heads and senior civil servants who, in consultation with representatives from the private sector, will prepare recommendations for the cabinet. Business will have access to the cabinet through these working committees, but also through direct appointment. In June Botha selected three top South African executives to sit on the Public Services Commission. The commission is charged with revamping the civil service, restructuring departments and developing a system by which the government can attract executive level recruits from the corporate world. The commission will also preside over what has been described as the "desocialization" of government--selling off some of the public corporations to private buyers. The recent government offering of some $600 million worth of stock in the South African Coal, Oil and Gas Corp. (Sasol) to private investors is the first major step in this direction. The prime minister also assigned the Urban Foundation the delicate task of arbitrating which of Crossroads' residents should be permitted to move into new housing. He appointed the executive director of the Federated Chamber of Industries to heat the new National Manpower Commission. And he collected more than 200 business representatives together in November 1979 to discuss a "total strategy" for South Africa's future.

Business leverage: These developments give business a new leverage at a time in which it is institutionally more capable of playing an active role. The Urban Foundation has established itself as a useful business spokesman in the last three years, and another business organization formed after the Soweto demonstrations--the American Chamber of Commerce--offers U.S. companies the opportunity to speak collectively on policy matters. In interviews at American companies in 1979, executives asserted that the corporate community in South Africa has crossed a threshold over the last three years that has cemented its understanding of the need for fundamental change to ensure long-term survival. Negative foreign economic reaction to the government handling of black unrest, the squeeze of worsening skills shortages and the noticeable lack of business confidence in the future, despite the country's gold bonanza, have reinforced this thinking. "To lapse into apathy because of short-term economic gains would be foolhardy," one executive said. "Enlightened self-interest demands that we take an extended view of the country's development and move to eliminate those policies that have exacerbated inefficiency and aroused international ire." And Anglo American Chairman Oppenheimer has called upon white liberals "to move from the politics of protest to the politics of power."

But whether business will choose to play a more active role remains in doubt. Critics fear that business will allow itself to be coopted by government, encouraging gradual and largely apolitical change within South Africa while defending South Africa against its international opponents. Certainly, many in business, out of concern about government reactions or bound by their own perceptions of what the relationship should be between business and government, will hesitate to take overt political stands or lobby for change.

Despite the beating of wings on the surface of South Africa's political waters, there is no sign that the government is willing to deviate from its commitment to separate development. A South African magazine--To The Point--which has had government support in the past, commented recently that "what even the most verligte (enlightened) Nationalist espouses is not a change of political philosophy but one of style....As skeptical commentators have pointed out, the government obviously has no intention of abandoning basic aspects of the policy such as influx control, group areas, the racially based immorality laws or the political separation of blacks from the white, colored and Indian body politic."

Guided by their perceptions and concerns, most business representatives--with a few exceptions--are likely to limit their pressure on the government to marginally political issues, such as housing and training, that directly affect their work force, rather than challenge the system of separate development. Their efforts, through organizations such as the Urban Foundation or the American Chamber of Commerce, will probably continue to focus on project assistance and labor practices, although such efforts may offer opportunities for discussion of politically related issues. In the past, business has been provoked to comment on policy issues by a faltering economy. Should the economy continue to recover, should Botha press forward with his moderate reforms, and should black unrest not manifest itself again with the intensity of 1976-77, foreign and domestic pressures on companies in South Africa are likely to diminish, and so may the interest of business in becoming a more active political force.

Chapter IV Sources

Books

F. McA. Clifford-Vaughn, International Pressures and Political Change in South Africa, Oxford University Press, Capetown, 1978.

Anthony de Crespigny and Robert Schrire, The Government and Politics of South Africa, Juta and Co. Ltd., Johannesburg, 1978.

Gail Gerhart, Black Power in South Africa, University of California Press, Berkeley, 1978.

A.D. Wassenaar, Assault on Private Enterprise, Tafelberg Publishers Ltd., Capetown, 1977.

Denis Worrall, South Africa, Government and Politics, J.L. Van Schaile Ltd. Pretoria, 1975.

Articles

Heribert Adam, "Interests behind Afrikaner power," Social Dynamics, 3, No. 1 (June 1977).

George W. Ball, "Asking for trouble in South Africa," The Atlantic, October 1977.

Clyde Ferguson and William R. Cotter, "South Africa: what is to be done," Foreign Affairs, January 1978.

Stanley Greenberg, "Public disorder and public response," op. cit.

John Purcell, Letters, Foreign Affairs, April 1978.

Laurence Schlemmer, "White voters and change in South Africa," Optima, Anglo American Corp., Two 1978.

Financial Mail, "The Urban Foundation," special report, Feb. 16, 1979.

Speeches

Anthony Bloom, "The necessity for progress in the area of removal of discrimination in industry," address to the national convention of the Institute of Personnel Management, Sept. 27, 1978.

Harry Oppenheimer, "Why the world should continue to invest in South Africa," address to the International Monetary Conference, Mexico City, May 22, 1978; Official Opening, South Africa Institute of Race Relations, Fiftieth Anniversary Conference, July 2, 1979.

John Vorster, "Speech to the Associated Chambers of Commerce," Port Elizabeth, October 1976.

Other

American Chamber of Commerce, "Comments and recommendation to the inquiry into legislation affecting the utilization of manpower," April 6, 1978.

Transvaal Chamber of Industries, "Memorandum to the Honorable, B.J. Vorster, M.P., Prime Minister," July 29, 1976; Letter to the Honorable B.J. Vorster, M.P., Prime Minister, Aug. 2, 1977.

William C. Norris, testimony before the U.S. House of Representatives, Subcommittees on Africa and on International Economic Policy and Trade, July 12, 1978.

The Urban Foundation, "First Progress Report," Johannesburg, 1978.

V. LABOR PRACTICES IN SOUTH AFRICA

Perhaps the greatest new boost to the job advancement of South African blacks in the last three years has come from abroad with the development of the Sullivan principles and, later, the European Economic Community and Canadian codes of fair labor practices. These foreign codes spurred the South Africans to develop their own code under the aegis of the Urban Foundation and the South African Consultative Committee on Labor Affairs (SACCOLA). (Texts of codes, Appendix B)

Collectively, the codes have had a measurable impact on the way many companies evaluate their employee programs. The extent of this impact varies markedly from company to company, depending on a number of factors--type of operation, responsiveness of management, degree of home office pressure, business climate, attitudes of white workers or customers. Some companies have been relatively aggressive in pursuing the principles articulated in the codes; others emphasize the degree to which progress is constrained by the economy or by government policies or regulations. But the over-all impact of the codes has been positive.

Largely as the result of codes and the public's focus on companies' employee practices, both within South Africa and abroad, a number of companies have begun efforts to improve specific aspects of their employment programs. Many companies have begun to consider housing assistance for the first time. Some companies--particularly American companies--have begun a concentrated effort to desegregate their facilities, tearing down walls that divide races or constructing new dining rooms or restrooms. More companies have started training Africans for jobs that require essentially the skills of an artisan; although Africans may still be legally restricted from becoming qualified artisans, the companies say they plan to employ them in artisan-level jobs without qualifying certificates.

In addition to the codes, the growing demand for skilled workers in specific jobs has spurred improved labor practices for blacks in recent years. Although South Africa's economic boom died in 1975, companies still require increasing numbers of skilled workers and workers for white-collar clerical, management, administrative and technical positions. Shortages of whites for these jobs, together with the inadequate public education and training available to Africans, provide an incentive to companies to develop their own training programs to meet their employment needs.

The developments taking place in various companies must be viewed within the context of South Africa. They are important, particularly to the workers and the families of workers directly affected. At the same time, events taking place on the factory floor or in workers' housing have little impact on the greater structure of separate development. Their importance should not be exaggerated, but they should not be ignored simply because their impact is limited.

The sections that follow discuss what managing directors see as the major constraints on their employment programs; the pressures and incentives that encourage them to do battle with those constraints; and the impact of the codes and the steps that companies are taking to respond both to the constraints and to the incentives affecting their labor practices.

Constraints on Improved Labor Practices

In discussions with IRRC, company representatives have cited a number of factors that they see as major constraints as they attempt to improve their labor practices in South Africa. Among these are a lack of trained black manpower; opposition from white workers and customers; managers' perceptions of blacks, as well as blacks' perceptions of themselves; laws and regulations; government policies; and time and money.

Lack of trained manpower: In 1977 and 1978, as in earlier interviews in South Africa, nearly every company visited by IRRC cited the lack of trained manpower as the overriding constraint on the ability to hire and to promote blacks. In the words of Keith Partridge, managing director of Carlton Paper (38.6 percent owned by Kimberly-Clark), South Africa has "an abysmal lack of African graduates." Wally Life, managing director of Goodyear, concurs. He reports that in Uitenhage--a major industrial center near Port Elizabeth where a number of large companies including Goodyear and Volkswagen have factories--there were only 11 male African students in standard 10, the equivalent of the senior year of high school. Some of these would not graduate, he said, and only three were likely to have the training in math or science that would make them attractive to industry.

Not only are the numbers of students in school inadequate, companies say, but the training facilities that the government has allowed in white areas are inadequate as well. General Electric representatives describe the industrial training centers that the government has allowed to be constructed in white areas since 1975 as "still in their infancy and not really applicable to GE's needs." Officials from Barlow Rand, a major South African conglomerate, are harsher in their description. One representative described the centers as "white elephants," arguing that there is "no real shortage in the sort of semi-skilled labor the centers are established to train." The problem, he said, is that the government has "refused to allow the training centers to do any more than pre- and in-service training," and most companies think they can perform such training best themselves. As a result, the personnel director of the British-based company, Afrox, told IRRC, the "training centers may be among the best in the world, but a whole lot of the training is pretty useless" because what Africans need is higher skills training. He also faulted the government for limiting the centers to "those who were already employed," thus offering no opportunities for the growing number of unemployed blacks.

The results of inadequate training and education facilities are immediately apparent in the shortages of skilled, technical, managerial and administrative workers. The government's manpower survey shows shortages of skilled workers in the tens of thousands. C.H. Wyndham, professor of environmental and work physiology at the University of Witswatersrand and an adviser to the Chamber of Mines, has estimated that "by 1980 there will be a shortfall in the 'skills' categories of manpower of 2 million."

The situation is severe not only in the skilled worker category, but also in positions requiring management, administrative and technical expertise. In the United States, 15 percent of the economically active population is involved in management, administrative and technical positions; in South Africa the figure is less than 6 percent. Those people in decision-making positions are stretched thin. Many companies lack qualified staff for training and employee development programs. The former director of the Institute of Personnel Management in South Africa, David Jackson, told IRRC in 1975 that he estimated that the country could support 8,000 to 10,000 personnel and training professionals, "at least half of whom should be black." At that time there were about 3,000 personnel professionals, 350 of them black.

The lack of skilled workers is cited repeatedly as a problem by U.S. companies in South Africa. Union Carbide and Esso both complained to IRRC that they had been unable at various times to fill positions in white-collar areas at salaries more than twice the minimum effective level. Esso reported it had difficulties despite using four different employment agencies.

Whites' opposition: Managing directors of companies frequently cite their concern about whites' opposition as a major constraint to blacks' advancement. Within their plants, they are afraid that hiring or promoting blacks may irritate workers and lead to strikes, work stoppages or complaints to the South African labor department. They also say that customers may be offended by company policies and may refuse to deal with black salesmen. Most companies report that the situation is changing, that opposition to opportunities for blacks has lessened, but many managers say they must be careful not to move too fast.

The degree to which concern about whites' opposition is a question of perception and the degree to which it is grounded in the realities of apartheid varies from company to company. In a number of cases, concern about white workers' intransigence or white customers' reactions has proved far greater than the reality would warrant. Several companies argue that it is not the native-born white South Africans who resist the change so much as the recent European immigrants, and either time or their departure overcomes their opposition. In a recent survey of 167 companies employing more than 1 million people, Fine Spamer and Associates, a South African consulting firm, concluded that whites' reactions, whether from workers in the factory or from customers outside, presented far less of a constraint than company officials imagined. In companies where white workers are supervised by blacks, concerns about whites' opposition appear exaggerated, and customers seem far more concerned with the competence of the worker serving them or servicing their equipment than they do with the worker's ethnic or racial background. Nevertheless, whites' opposition and the perception of its potential continues to be an important factor affecting the pace of innovation in many companies in South Africa.

The white union factor--The most tangible form of whites' opposition to greater opportunity for blacks has come from the white trade unions. White trade unions have long resisted efforts to improve advancement opportunities for blacks. In an interview in 1975 Arrie Paulus, general secretary of the Mine Workers' Union, said, "As far as my union is concerned his (the African's) future is that of a laborer. Because all gold mines, all mines, fall within our white homeland, preventing blacks from gaining certain skills is justified. A Bantu can rise to be prime minister in his homeland, but I can't go there and become a prime minister. So why must he be able to rise here in South Africa, in my homeland, to the status of white miner?" Paulus's attitude has changed little in the last few years. In September 1978, he told the Capetown Graduate School of Business that "work integration leads to social integration leads to total integration."

A number of other white unions, although less concerned about blacks working in positions traditionally reserved for whites, take a similar position on the training of Africans. Wally Grobblar, head of the Artisan Staff Association of the railways workers, told IRRC in October 1978 that the rank-and-file vehemently opposed apprenticeship training for African workers. The indenturing of Africans, he said, would be "over the dead body" of the rank-and-file. Unions demand control of access to the artisan level. "Indenturing of Africans is merely the thin edge of the wedge," threatening the elite status of whites, he argued. Although workers recognized that some change in job reservation and access for blacks will have to occur, he said, they do not expect a dramatic change in the near future.

Despite whites' opposition, however, some change has begun to occur in the work place. The 1978 SEIFSA agreement represented a small breakthrough, as do the recommendations of the Wiehahn Commission.

A white backlash developed in response to the removal of some job reservations in 1977, to the SEIFSA agreement, and to the rumors about the Wiehahn Commission report before its publication. The conservative Mine Workers' Union capitalized on this and in 1978 began a successful recruiting effort among SEIFSA unions--recruiting more than 1,000 workers from the government's Iron and Steel Corp. Following the release of the Wiehahn Commission report, a number of white union members openly voiced dissent.

There is increasing evidence that the government no longer supports unconditionally white workers' demands for protection against blacks' advancement. In response to a decision by the American-owned O'okiep Copper Co. to hire three colored workers for jobs traditionally held by whites, the Mine Workers' Union at the company struck in March 1979 and was joined by illegal wildcat strikes by miners who struck at other companies in a show of sympathy. The Chamber of Mines refused to deal with the strikers, firing all strikers, saying that companies would review applications of those who sought to be rehired on a case-by-case basis, and stating that those not rehired or still striking would be evicted from the company-owned housing within a week. The government refused to intervene despite pleas from the miners and their families. About half the miners refused to join the strikes, which collapsed after two days. Analysts reported that this was the first time since 1922 that the government has not taken the side of a white union in a labor dispute concerning race. One union leader, Jimmy Zurich, president of the Railways Artisan Staff Association, said "this test of strength has shown that racial job protection is a lost cause."

Another less dramatic example of the government's changing attitude had come in 1978 when Minister of Labor S.P. Botha asked the Motor Industry Employees' Union to alter its policies on training African apprentices because of severe manpower shortages. After negotiations with the union, the Minister of Labor said that "the union has expressed some reservations but there has been some training taking place."

Moreover, the union had agreed to train some African mechanics for the first time in Soweto.

Managerial concerns--At many companies, however, the problem may not be with white trade unions at all. At a number of companies, white trade unions simply do not exist. Sixty-three U.S. companies participating in a 1979 survey of signers of the Sullivan principles reported that they had no employee unions. And some union representatives blame the companies themselves for the failure of blacks to advance. Clyde Pinnock, president of the Motor Industry Employees' Union, says employers "could have trained double the number they have if they had wanted to."

Managers may fear opposition from their white workers, whether they are unionized or not. The fear in some cases is that white workers will quit. Many administrative offices continue to employ only whites in secretarial positions, as telephone operators or receptionists. The managing directors argue that if they were to employ blacks in those positions, they might lose the whites working in those jobs.

A second concern is that businesses might suffer a loss of customers if black advancement programs become too visible. The concern about loss of customers is particularly strong in sales jobs. Few companies employ blacks in sales positions, and in those that do the black sales force is usually assigned to sell to black areas. Esso, for example, has no blacks in sales positions, a company official explained, because the company official does not consider its customers ready. "Customer attitudes," wrote Cliff Lyddon, managing director of Esso, are "not sufficiently evolved to avoid placing such an employee in an embarrassing and non-productive situation." Some managers argue that blacks cannot advance because of questions of background and training. Geoffrey Serrurier, personnel director for Mobil, told IRRC in 1975 that a man soliciting in competition with other representatives needs to establish a cordiality--something that is difficult for a man coming from a separate background. The problem may be compounded in the case of black sales people by the forced separation in the society. Black salesmen operating in white areas are limited because their choices of hotels, restaurants or other places where they may meet clients are limited.

Some managers have argued that they are unable to hire more blacks simply because to do so would require a costly revamping of their existing facilities, or because their employees would not tolerate desegregated facilities. Firestone has argued, as have several companies, that "desegregation of locker rooms in a factory situation is extremely difficult because of whites' opposition and the extensive modifications required."

Exactly how much companies are held back by whites' opposition or by their perception of what whites' opposition might be is the subject of much debate. When asked how they tell when they may be able to move blacks into new positions or when they may be able to desegregate facilities or put blacks in sales jobs, most managers argue that it is a subjective question of feel. Few want to be the front runners, but most want to be perceived as at least keeping pace with the pack.

Perception is a major constraint on black advancement. A manager in South Africa may be affected by the stereotypes that have developed through racial separation, and his willingness to hire or promote blacks is affected by his perception of their abilities. In 1975, one manager told IRRC that he did not hire blacks to work on assembly line operations, despite high turnover among the white workers, because he believed that black women were too emotional and black men too proud. At another company, the personnel manager said that even after two or three generations of living in an industrial environment, "the African man is still the fighter; manual labor is to be done by the women, whom many see as the providers."

These stereotypes, together with the system itself, have also affected blacks' perceptions of themselves--or at least white managers believe this is the case. Separation of facilities, separation of schools and living areas, and different social environments have meant that blacks and whites have minimal opportunity for social intercourse. Most conversations between blacks and whites take place at work, and they consist primarily of whites telling blacks what needs to be done. Blacks may feel uneasy asserting themselves in front of whites. And a number of companies replying to the Fine Spamer study listed blacks' own attitudes as a major limit on the potential for blacks' advancement. More than 40 percent of the companies reporting said that the effectiveness of blacks is inhibited because blacks view themselves as inferior, see little scope for advancement, or feel insecure. Several companies reported to IRRC that Africans had refused to accept promotions because they did not want to take the added responsibility or did not want to leave their immediate peer groups. A number of managers said as well that some Africans were not interested in extra shift work, and when the companies moved from four-day to five-day work weeks, they had difficulty in adjusting to the added work load. Cliff Lyddon of Esso told _Time_ magazine's William McWhirter in September 1978 that "blacks are reluctant to take advantage of opportunities because they have grown up in an environment that says that you stay in your place." He told IRRC that this reluctance is particularly common for Africans being considered for or employed in professional positions.

Many blacks would dispute these perceptions. Several African workers complained to IRRC about racial stereotyping. Nevertheless, some blacks agreed that fear of white management or even white workers often inhibits blacks from speaking out, and others talked about the limited exposure Africans have to industry.

Legal constraints: Despite recent alterations in several pieces of racial legislation, and despite the government's easing of its enforcement of regulations that limit opportunities for blacks, managing directors at many companies continue to consider legal restrictions to be among the most serious constraints on blacks' advancement. More than half--53 percent--of the companies reporting in the Fine Spamer study, for example, said legal restrictions prevented them from advancing blacks in their operations. They ranked legal restrictions with the lack of qualified staff as two of the greatest obstacles to equal opportunity, second only to whites' resistance. Fine Spamer concluded, "from the tenor of replies, that a great deal of confusion exists about what legitimately can be done within the framework of existing labor laws." "It seems," the study said, "that many companies see legal restrictions as more limiting than they really are in practice." (Details of labor laws, Appendix A)

In fact, the laws, as they are enforced, are steadily declining in importance as a constraint on the labor practices adopted by companies. The Environment Planning Act, for example, sets limits on the numbers of Africans who can be employed by companies located in certain areas. But most companies have been able to obtain exemptions, and few American companies claim that it has affected their hiring practices. The job reservation clause of the Industrial Act was largely scrapped with the lifting of many of the remaining reservations in November 1977. The positions still reserved in the clause cover only a handful of jobs and, except for jobs in mining, they are of no great importance. Gains have also been made in the desegregation of facilities, although there has been no change in the laws requiring companies to provide for separation of the races. Until publication of the Sullivan principles in 1977, most companies had argued that they were unable to desegregate their facilities because of the Factories Act and the Shops and Offices Act. But the South African government has not opposed the principles, and increasing numbers of companies are finding that they are able to desegregate their operations without government interference. In fact, their actions influenced the government's decision to scrap its regulations requiring separate facilities.

Training--A major legal restriction remains, however: The Apprenticeship Act, combined with the Industrial Conciliation Act, serves as an important barrier to training for blacks. As a result, the number of companies with apprenticeship programs for coloreds as well as Africans is extremely low. More companies are training Africans for semi-skilled and skilled jobs than was true a few years ago, but the numbers are still small and there is no guarantee that Africans will ever be allowed to qualify for artisans' certificates.

Mobility--The laws governing where blacks can live and work also put serious constraints on the mobility of labor, limiting the ability of companies to recruit Africans in one location for work in another. The amount of time Africans may have to spend in travel to and from work may affect productivity, and the fact that Africans are unable to sell their labor on a free and open market has led to a distorted wage structure that makes equal pay for equal work more difficult to achieve.

An employer cannot be certain that a worker recruited in one district will be given permission to move to another or, even if he is, whether he will be permitted to move his family with him or will be able to find housing there once he arrives. Consigned to townships at some distance from the industrial centers themselves, Africans have transportation difficulties different from those of persons of other races. Shift work may be unattractive because public transport is less available during off hours. For many Africans, leaving work after a certain time of day means long delays in transit to and from the township or hazardous travel through the township late at night or early in the morning. Some workers reported to IRRC that their travel to and from their jobs takes as much as two to three hours, and many who use public transportation are afraid of being robbed on their way home if they work beyond normal working hours.

Wages--The limitations on the mobility of black labor distort the market system and make equal pay for equal work difficult. While restricting blacks' ability to sell labor on a free and open market, South African laws have protected white labor, creating an artificial demand for increasingly scarce white workers to fill jobs that are legally available only to whites. The result has been artificially high wages for whites. The former personnel director of Sigma Motors (29-percent-Chrysler-owned) described white artisans as a class of "skilled mercenaries" who because of artificial scarcity were able to hold companies "hostage to a ransom in higher salaries." Companies replacing whites with blacks say that it is unreasonable for them to continue to pay wages that are not justified by the importance of the position simply because whites have extorted extravagant wages from them in the past.

The historic wages for whites have also made it difficult for companies to close the wage gap between white and black workers. In order to win the agreement of white workers to blacks' advancement, companies have promoted whites to supervisory positions or increased their wages. Moreover, even though companies may have increased wages faster for black workers (as a percentage of original base pay) than for whites, the wage gap between white and black continues to widen because the whites began at a much greater base level. And Africans, lacking the right to join registered unions, often lack the power and ability to bargain for higher pay.

Entrepreneurial restrictions--Another constraint imposed by the legal system affects both the ability of companies to do business with black firms and the opportunity for blacks to benefit from economic development by becoming entrepreneurs. Laws restricting the rights of Africans in white areas to sell, to form partnerships or to engage in manufacturing severely restrict the potential for black business. A number of restrictions on Africans' businesses in the townships have been lifted in the last year, but the inability of blacks to own or operate businesses in any white-designated area, including the central business districts of the major cities of South Africa, remains a critical constraint on the development of black companies and greatly limits the effectiveness of any corporate efforts to encourage black entrepreneurs.

Misconceptions--The impact of South African law or policy as a constraint on the employment practices of companies is compounded by companies' misconceptions. For example, many companies have believed incorrectly that African unions are illegal. Some still accept as law the National Party policy that no black should supervise a white in a white area. In fact, it is merely party policy. No company has ever been convicted of violating a law by hiring blacks for positions supervising whites. While the number of companies that do employ blacks as supervisors to whites is very small--and often the circumstances are such that the supervision is largely invisible, in positions in warehousing or quality control--in those companies where it has occurred, managers report little or no negative reaction. A number of white workers told IRRC that they had no objections to working under blacks as long as the blacks were qualified.

Time and money: Two final constraints are time and money. Managerial talent in South Africa is thin, and a number of smaller companies operate without full-time personnel or training staff. Without such staff, it is more difficult for a company to develop an innovative employee program.

Lack of managerial time may be compounded by lack of money, some managers say. The recession in South Africa that began in 1975 not only diminished the need for more workers in some companies, but also depleted the resources that might be used in training programs. It is difficult to think of expanding training programs, several personnel directors told IRRC, when you are trying to figure out how to cut back your labor force. Holding jobs becomes more important than training, they argued.

Managers at a number of companies, South African and European as well as American, maintained that there was a trade-off between improvement of wages and fringe programs and jobs themselves. Which is better, a common question ran, to pay 10 workers 10 rand a week or to pay one worker 100 rand a week? For most companies the question is largely hypothetical. With the exception of mining and a few labor-intensive manufacturing companies, labor represents a relatively minor portion of total costs--usually well below 20 percent. And black labor at many companies, even where more than a majority of workers are African, is often less than half of total labor cost. Few managers were planning to replace African workers with technological advances, although the possibility was often discussed. In areas where such changes are likely to occur, it is most likely to mean a loss in potential jobs rather than a displacement of workers currently employed.

Incentives to Improve Labor Practices

Although numerous constraints affect the ability of companies to adopt more progressive labor practices, countervailing pressures that encourage changes in labor practices have appeared in the last few years. Until recently, the greatest incentive for corporations to hire and train increasing numbers of blacks had been the performance of the economy. In the last 18 months, the greatest push has come from the increased political pressures on companies, particularly on American companies, and from the rising involvement of home offices spurred by the development of the Sullivan principles.

Economic pressures: The economy was the major incentive for companies to develop opportunities for blacks until 1975. Shortages of skilled workers, inflated wage demands by whites, high absenteeism, high turnover and low productivity among white workers all offered sound economic reasons for a manager in South Africa to make efforts to recruit and train blacks and place them in positions traditionally held by whites. The objective was simply to achieve a more stable and productive work force.

Most companies were aware of projections that showed that South Africa would need 1 to 2 million skilled workers by 1980. Some were concerned by projected shortages in specific areas: Honeywell's managing director told IRRC that, by 1980, South Africa would need 800 new instrument engineers a year; there were only 800 in the country in 1975. International Harvester reported that in a section of the motor trades the industry needed to have 6,000 apprentices in training each year. At the time, there were 1,300 apprentices in training. And Ford's managing director, Douglas Kitterman, said there were "no areas in white collar jobs without shortages."

The shortages created a seller's market for white labor. Employers were willing to pay inflated wages to whites--and even so, the extremely low unemployment rate and high demand for whites made absenteeism and turnover perennial problems for management. White unions ensured that all companies provide the full panoply of benefits, and white workers felt free to change jobs for increases in wages or fringe benefits amounting to pennies an hour. Turnover rates ran higher than 100 percent in some job categories. Goodyear reported that during the 1960s the annual turnover rate among its white workers ranged between 130 percent and 170 percent. Colgate in 1973 had a turnover of 120 percent in some job categories held by whites. International Harvester reported turnover at the rate of 100 percent a year for some artisan positions. A number of companies--Gillette and Honeywell are two--said their annual turnover rate for white collar staff and keypunch operators was more than 30 percent.

Several managers told IRRC that high turnover and absenteeism contributed, in turn, to low productivity. One said the shortage of white labor was forcing them to hire "the dregs of the white labor pool," the least skilled and the least dependable. At the same time, those blacks who were ready to move into white jobs were among the best trained and most capable of the black labor pool.

With the onset of the recession in 1975, the situation changed somewhat for the short term. Demand for workers declined, and many companies were faced with serious lay-offs. Otis cut its staff by one-third, as did International Harvester. The number of employees at General Motors dropped from 5,499 in January 1976 to 3,657 in January 1978. While the cutbacks primarily affected black workers, they affected some whites as well. The demand for artisans declined slightly, and the shortages, although continuing, were no longer as severe. Unemployment among whites could be measured for the first time. Absenteeism and turnover among whites dropped.

The importance of black development declined as a short-term economic pressure for many companies, but certainly not for all. A number of companies have continued to grow despite the recession. The computer companies, for example, continue to have a rate of growth of 20 percent or more. For some companies the recession offered an opportunity to rationalize employee programs. H.S. Stroh, the personnel manager at Consolidated Glass (20-percent-owned by Owens Illinois) said that his company had retrenched from 5,500 workers in 1976 to 4,669 in 1977, but that the reduction had encouraged the company to intensify its productivity efforts. The company increased its training staff to 20 workers--equal to an increase of more than 100 percent--and productivity improved measurably. Many others viewed the recession as only a short-term relaxation in the shortages that are certain to reappear in the longer term. Some managers saw the sudden downturn in the economy and the corresponding preoccupation with lay-offs as merely a distraction from the increasing demand for skilled labor that is expected to continue. Harry Oppenheimer, chairman of Anglo American, speaks of needing more than a million more skilled black workers in the next decade. As noted earlier, a number of companies expect to have shortages in skilled and white-collar technical, administrative and managerial positions. Nevertheless, the downturn in the economy eased at least temporarily the pressure on companies to expand their black development programs for economic reasons.

Home office pressure and the labor codes: The greatest and most visible incentive to improved labor practices of American companies in South Africa during the last two years has been the increased pressure that home offices in the United States are placing on susidiaries. Fueled by the rising pressures from shareholders--primarily church groups, universities and foundations--and by a dramatic increase in the press coverage of South Africa and American business there, the interest of home offices in the operation of their South Africa subsidiaries has grown considerably. Many home offices have made this interest known to subsidiaries through their endorsement of the Sullivan principles; the principles have offered a forum for home offices' involvement in the practices of their subsidiaries and have laid the foundation for a system by which subsidiaries can be held accountable to their home offices and home offices accountable to the public at large.

Sullivan principles and U.S. activism--The principles were first signed on March 1, 1977, by 12 American companies, which had been meeting under the aegis of the Rev. Leon H. Sullivan, a member of the board of General Motors. The principles were designed, according to Sullivan, as "a voluntary effort among companies to end racial discrimination in their operations in the Republic of South Africa and to help improve the living conditions for blacks and other non-whites there, and to take a stand against apartheid." By November 1979, a report prepared for Sullivan by Arthur D. Little Inc. said 135 U.S. companies had endorsed the principles.

Some of the momentum for endorsement of the principles has been supplied by the rapid rise in public interest in South Africa. Press reporting on South Africa increased dramatically after the Soweto demonstrations in 1976; the number of foreign journalists assigned to cover South Africa grew from a handful to more than 70. Daily newspapers carried regular reporting on South Africa, as did network news. Business Week, Fortune, Time and Saturday Review published major articles during 1977 and 1978 on the role of U.S. business in South Africa. And interest across the country, particularly on college campuses, has remained at a fairly constant, high level for several years.

Since early 1977, activist groups have pressed for divestment of South Africa-related holdings on more than 100 campuses, organizing demonstrations, sit-ins, petition drives and teaching seminars to publicize their cause. Some 1,000 people have been arrested during campus protests against American corporate involvement in South Africa. At corporate annual meetings, South Africa has continued to be a major topic of debate. In 1978, church shareholders, many of whom have been actively concerned about American involvement in South Africa since the 1960s, sponsored 24 resolutions relating to South Africa--urging non-expansion of operations, an end to bank loans, a cessation of sales, or withdrawal. Three universities joined with church groups in sponsoring resolutions and one--the University of Minnesota--proposed a resolution to 14 companies urging that they adopt and carry out the Sullivan principles. In 1979, church groups, two colleges and a student group proposed 35 resolutions dealing with South Africa. None of these asked a company to sign the Sullivan principles, reflecting the fact that most major corporations had become signers.

The public pressures undoubtedly encouraged a number of companies to sign the Sullivan principles. If they did not view the signing of the principles as a means of escaping the questions being asked of their subsidiaries, many companies at least saw them as a method of responding to inquiries and reducing the pressure. Sullivan, in testimony before the House Subcommittee on Africa in August 1978, expressed concern that the code not be used by companies merely as an easy escape from pressures. He said, "We do not want the principles to be regarded or used as a camouflage, or something for businesses to hide behind. All the companies who have signed the principles are expected to implement the plan, abide by the guidelines, and report progress on a regular basis."

Critics, particularly among church groups and university activists, have argued that the principles, even as amended in July 1978 to provide for union rights, fail to go far enough. The issue, they say, is not labor practices alone, but the contribution--economic, technical and moral--that companies make by continuing to operate in South Africa. In an early criticism of the principles, Timothy Smith, director of the Interfaith Center on Corporate Responsibility, quoted one South African church leader as saying, "These principles attempt to polish my chains and make them more comfortable. I want to cut my chains and cast them away." African union leaders in South Africa complained to IRRC that the principles were developed "without consulting the people they sought to affect--the black worker." (Text of principles and signers, Appendix B and C)

Despite such criticism, a number of universities, foundations and other institutional investors seeking guidelines for decisions affecting investment in companies with subsidiaries in South Africa have incorporated the principles in their review process. Harvard, for example, has said that as part of its policy on South Africa-related investments it will ask portfolio companies to follow progressive labor practices there, "even where such action impinges on profitability." It asks the companies to implement the Sullivan principles, and also to improve wages and to recognize and negotiate with African trade unions. Yale has said it will support shareholder efforts to liberalize the labor practices of portfolio companies involved in South Africa using the Sullivan principles as the basis of its policy, and several other universities have adopted similar positions.

Legislation has also referred to the Sullivan principles. In November 1978, Congress passed a bill prohibiting the Export-Import Bank from extending any credit for any export that would contribute to the maintenance of apartheid or for export to purchasers in South Africa unless the Secretary of State certifies that the purchaser has endorsed the Sullivan principles and is proceeding to put them into effect.

The increased focus on the principles and the efforts companies are making to carry them out has led a number of institutions to seek methods to monitor or review corporate performance. The companies endorsing the principles have formed task forces to review progress, and signers have agreed to report to Sullivan on a semi-annual basis. His organization agreed to release data on company performance in an aggregate form, and the first report, compiled by Arthur D. Little Inc., was released on Nov. 28, 1978, and a second was released on April 2, 1979. Sullivan describes the process of establishing the principles as evolutionary. He reported recently the formation of a "Monitoring Council" and said the next reports would "list progress of companies on an individual basis, in specific categories of progress." Moreover, he expects to send observers to South

Africa in 1979 for on-site inspection of company facilities and operations.

In addition to the monitoring by Sullivan's organization, IRRC in 1978 began a South Africa Review Service that includes questionnaires to more than 100 major corporations with interests in South Africa and to the 90 largest U.S. banks; reports on the role of several industry sectors in the South African economy; and profiles of 50 corporations active in South Africa.

EEC guidelines--In September 1977, soon after the Sullivan principles were developed, the foreign ministers of the member countries in the European Economic Community promulgated guidelines for labor practices that ask European companies to take steps that go beyond the principles established by the Sullivan statement. The EEC code of conduct requests companies to:

• permit the development of African labor unions;
• establish a minimum wage scale 50 percent above "the minimum wage required to satisfy the basic needs of an employee and his family";
• restrict the utilization of immigrant white labor and improve conditions for black migrant workers;
• provide equal pay for equal work, training programs, fringe benefits and integrated work facilities for non-white employees;
• report annually to their governments on the progress they are making in implementing the steps suggested by the guidelines.

(For full text of the EEC code, see Appendix B)

Other codes--Several other codes have been developed. The Canadian government adopted a code similar to that of the EEC, calling for equal pay for equal work, wages 50 percent above the subsistence level, bargaining rights for black unions, training for Africans, and desegregation of working, eating and other facilities as rapidly as possible.

And in South Africa, the Urban Foundation and the South African Consultative Committee on Labor Affairs developed a code for South African companies that asked companies to "strive constantly for the elimination of discrimination based on race or color from all aspects of employment practice." The companies should work toward equal pay for equal work and the creation of greater opportunities, and they should recognize "the basic rights of workers of freedom of association, collective negotiation of agreements on conditions of service, the lawful withholding of labor as a result of industrial disputes, and protection against victimization resulting from the exercise of these rights."

Monitoring--A number of South African organizations--the Trade Union Council of South Africa, the Federation of Black Trade Unions, the Black Peoples Alliance (which includes Inkatha, the Colored Labor Party and the Asian party), the SACCOLA and the Urban Foundation--have expressed an interest in monitoring the performance of companies in carrying out the Sullivan principles, as well as the codes developed by the European Economic Community, the Canadians, SACCOLA and the Urban Foundation. To date no formal process has been adopted by these organizations, although TUCSA and the BPA have both sought to inform their members on the codes and asked that their members report any violations.

General impact of the codes: It is still far too early to draw any final conclusions as to the effectiveness of the employment codes. Collectively, the codes have certainly focused a great deal of management time, attention and money on the plight of black workers. Individual companies' responses have varied, as has the interest of the governments of the multinational companies involved.

The methods by which the codes were developed differ and, at least initially, this difference has affected the response of corporations. The Sullivan principles and those included in the Urban Foundation code were established by the corporations themselves, drawn up after numerous meetings between company officials and made public only after companies had reached some agreement on what they might be expected to achieve and how they should report it. Consequently, both the principles and the Urban Foundation code were slightly weaker in substance and less specific than the EEC and Canadian codes--although additions were made subsequently to strengthen the Sullivan principles--but they enjoy a greater measure of corporate support than do the European and Canadian codes.

Commitment to the EEC code--The EEC code has suffered to some extent from the varying levels of interest demonstrated by the member governments. British sources say that Sweden and Denmark are considering making the code mandatory, whereas the French have distributed the code without great enthusiasm, and the Italians have adopted what can best be described as a relaxed view of the necessity to enforce the code. The British government, which had had a code of conduct for companies in South Africa since 1974, has taken the most active line, calling for regular reporting on companies' activities in South Africa.

The EEC code has also had less than active support from employers' associations in Europe and European companies in South Africa. Employers' associations in West Germany, France and the United Kingdom all resisted the code when it was introduced, arguing that they had not been included in its development. The home offices of many companies refused to take the code seriously, and some subsidiaries in South Africa resisted adoption of it. Several European companies--including Philips, Siemens and African Oxygen--said they had heard nothing from their home offices or foreign shareholders on the EEC guidelines and that the establishment of the code had little meaning for their operations. The managing director of Philips told IRRC that the employee relations were left to local management. He described the guidelines as a "paper tiger" and said it was not practical for the EEC to draw up guidelines that interfere with local marketing conditions. "We don't need them," he said. "Thanks very much, I'll put them in my drawer. A company that exists for 90 years with employees in 60 countries does not need to be told what to do," he commented. "We instinctively do what is required of our enlightened self-interest." Siemens's managing director agreed, saying the company already had an internal code: "We don't need outside forces to tell us how to run our labor program." However, representatives of Imperial Chemical and Rank Xerox told IRRC that their home offices had shown considerable interest in their ability to carry out the code.

Response to the Sullivan principles--The response by American companies to the Sullivan principles was generally less critical than that of European companies to the EEC code but was not universally supportive. Some companies argued that they were unnecessary. Several refused to sign them because they thought that would be interpreted as an admission of failure to be more progressive. A representative of Johnson & Johnson told IRRC that originally the company refrained from signing because the company thought it was already doing what the principles prescribed. R.J. Ironside, personnel director of General Motors, said that GM had been far along in its efforts to improve employee practices "before Dr. Leon Sullivan put any formality to it." GM has been involved with improving employee practices and social responsibility programs since 1969.

Signing the principles did not necessarily imply commitment to carrying them out. Ford's Fred Ferreira told IRRC in 1978 that "many companies signed the Sullivan principles but pay only lip service." An officer of one American company in 1977 said the signing of the principles had little impact on his company's program. "You have to remember who signed the principles," he told IRRC. "We didn't sign the principles, the home office did." He said that most of what the company was doing or had done would have occurred without the principles. Some South African companies and a few American managers saw the principles as outside interference. Willem de Villiers, chairman of the South African company, General Mining, a partner of Union Carbide in a chrome mine and smelter operation, took issue not with the substance of the principles, but with the fact that they came from outside South Africa and are being imposed on South African companies.

Despite Sullivan's desire that companies not use the principles as a protection against criticism, there is little doubt that this was at least somewhat on the minds of several of the signers. One company reported that it held off signing the statement for some time, until it realized that "the principles were being used to pacify critics in the States." But it also recognized that they could "be used internally as a club if necessary to spur whites for change."

Many companies report, however, that the Sullivan principles have had a measurable impact. They say that, regardless of what they had been doing in the past, the principles provided a useful focus for their programs. A Goodyear representative praised the principles for exposing the company to better management concepts. Union Carbide and IBM representatives described them as a catalyst. Ford said the principles had a significant effect on the company's practices--"not that they have led us to do more," Ferreira said, "but that they have led us to systematize our programs and to plan on a more systematic basis." As a result of the principles the company is reporting more frequently to the home office, it is receiving more visits, and it has done "some specific things that it had not expected to do as quickly--such as removal of signs and desegregation of facilities." The principles, he commented, "cannot be underrated."

The impact of the principles, several companies said, was at least as important to the home office as to the subsidiary. Gillette reported that interest in the London office to which the South African subsidiary reports directly has increased and there was greater receptivity to the subsidiary's personnel program proposals. Kodak's corporate management in Rochester reports that it has increased the attention it directs toward Kodak South Africa since the signing of the Sullivan principles, and the subsidiary's managing director in Capetown, Richard Ferris, confirms that he now has "a hot line to high places." And Burroughs officials report that the signing of the principles increased the home office's interest and prompted it to pick up in its budget a portion of new training costs that would normally have to have been covered by the subsidiary.

General acceptance of the principles, however, does not mean agreement on the pace at which they can be carried out. One subsidiary manager commented that "the principles cannot be implemented over a weekend." Another, Ian Leach, managing director of Caterpillar's subsidiary, told his home office in 1977 that he would need 18 months to develop programs that would carry out the principles--a process the company now says is complete. Other managers have said implementation will take five years, and some told IRRC that they simply could not see the time when toilets and lockers would be desegregated and blacks would supervise whites. Nevertheless, ripples from the signing of the principles are being felt at most companies, not only at the local management level and in the home offices, but where companies have discussed the principles with workers at the factory level as well.

When IRRC visited South Africa in November 1977, 57 companies had endorsed the Sullivan principles. Only a few, however, had communicated the principles to their workers and explained their implications. In only two of the 15 companies visited did the workers interviewed seem to understand the principles, even at companies such as Colgate that had published the principles in their company newsletter and talked to workers. William McWhirter said in Time magazine in September 1978 that none of the 60 companies he visited had posted copies of the Sullivan principles in an area accessible easily to black employees. The situation had changed somewhat by November 1978, however, and several companies were making a concerted effort to discuss the principles with workers. Union Carbide was circulating the code to its workers in Zulu as well as English. Abbott, one of the first companies to discuss the code with black workers, was sending copies in multiple languages to all workers, and several companies were holding meetings with workers to discuss the principles and the programs that were being developed to implement them. Where workers were aware of the principles, there were few objections from whites, and blacks responded favorably. Africans at two companies said they could positively date a change in the attitudes of white workers from the time when their managing directors spoke to all workers about the meaning of the principles and the companies' commitment to their implementation. It marked the first time that whites in the company began to treat blacks as colleagues rather than as lower-level workers.

The principles have also had some effect on the behavior of others in industry. Without the spur of the Sullivan and EEC codes, one South African businessman told IRRC, the Urban Foundation would not have developed its own code of conduct for South African corporations. And the head of Barlow Rand said that his company would not have moved ahead on desegregation of facilities if companies signing the Sullivan principles had not already begun their own efforts.

To sum up, response to the codes is measurable and sometimes impressive. A number of the signers have taken tangible and often dramatic steps toward improving opportunities for black workers. But the effort has not been universal among those affected by the codes or among those who have endorsed the principles. The speed and interest with which companies are carrying out the codes varies considerably. The layers of separation in South Africa do not dissolve easily; perception of what is possible and sense of urgency differs between home office and subsidiary and from one company to another. It is difficult and often misleading to compare one company's performance with another's. The ability of a company to take steps to improve its practices varies considerably from company to company, and it is influenced by a number of factors--the size of the subsidiary and its work force, the nature of the subsidiary's business, the location of its South African operations, management's attitudes toward unions, home office interest and commitment. The more dramatic steps being made today are the work primarily of a relatively few, highly visible companies. They have affected a small number of workers within South Africa's total work force, but they have also set a certain pattern that other companies may choose to follow.

Company Progress in Specific Areas

The signing of the Sullivan principles served as a catalyst for a number of American companies in South Africa. Companies, many of which had already begun to take steps to improve labor conditions in the early 1970s, formalized their programs in light of the six principles. Others began to look seriously for the first time at the possible improvements they could make. A number of companies had already been meeting in 1973-74 under the auspices of the United States-South Africa Leader Exchange Program, a private non-profit organization established to improve communication between the United States and South Africa. These meetings frequently centered on discussions of employee programs. More formal meetings between American companies began with the formation of the South African American Chamber of Commerce in November 1977. After the signing of the Sullivan principles, several American companies made individual efforts to compare labor practices. Colgate's personnel director visited some 11 other American companies to review their practices; Goodyear's personnel director surveyed operations at 18 companies. The products of these efforts--and the first visible result of the Sullivan principles--were the moves many companies began to desegregate facilities. Signs designating toilet or locker facilities by race came down at most companies, walls separating eating facilities for the races were torn down, and several companies made substantial commitments to build new, desegregated facilities.

In two other areas, in addition to the desegregation of facilities, companies seem to be making progress, at least in part, as a result of the Sullivan principles. More companies have developed or are developing training programs for blacks that will provide them with artisan level skills, if not with official papers, within the next three to five years. And a number of companies have been involved in developing housing programs that will allow Africans to buy or build their own homes.

Less visible but often important progress is being made in other areas at a number of companies--recruitment, selection, evaluation. The progress is usually not as dramatic as it has been in the area of desegregation of facilities, and much remains to be done. In reviewing an evaluation of the progress made by signers of the Sullivan principles, Sullivan commented in November 1978 that "we are making progress, but much, much more remains to be done to be really effective." He talked about the progress made as a "first step."

Desegregation of facilities: As mentioned in Chapter II, under the Factories Act and the Shops and Offices Act companies may be required to separate the races in the work places, in dining areas and in toilet and locker facilities. Moreover, under the Factories Act, signs are to be posted designating toilet facilities by race. The unproductive cost of constructing separate facilities has kept some companies from hiring any black workers. Until recently, most companies that do hire blacks have had segregated facilities. Many, at one time, even have separated workers on the factory floor with partitions or workers in administrative offices with filing cabinets. Segregation on the factory floor began to break down in the 1960s when the numbers of black workers increased, there were few blue-collar white workers, and separation of the races became impractical. White collar segregation began to dissolve in the 1970s, although in many companies blacks are still separated from whites by panels or open spaces.

Desegregation of eating, medical, locker or toilet facilities is a far more recent phenomenon. Managers have argued that African workers prefer African meals--mealie meal, a sort of gruel and stew--to European-style cooking. They have said that there is a need to separate the races not only because of the law, but also because of whites' opposition to desegregated facilities and because of differences in styles of eating and hygiene. Black workers at most companies have traditionally eaten in areas apart from whites. At some companies they have been required to take food and eat outside. Often, Africans have had separate kitchens, separate menus, and even different plates and utensils from those used by whites.

Until pressures from outside began to mount there had been little incentive to desegregate those facilities. Desegregation was avoided by some companies because they thought it impractical in strictly financial terms. As late as November 1977, R.J. Ironside of General Motors told IRRC that the company's eating facilities could not be desegregated without "tearing down the existing cafeterias and kitchens," and that "simply couldn't be justified under existing and foreseeable business conditions in a depressed economy." Other companies did not desegregate for fear of opposition from whites or reaction from the South African government.

When IRRC visited South Africa in 1975, most companies had desegregated their factory floors--with notable exceptions where white artisans were separated from the main factory area by chain mesh fences. Some administrative offices still were segregated, often by function--with most blacks working in accounting, warehousing, mail rooms, or quality control areas, although many companies had begun to remove the remaining barriers. A few companies were taking hesitant steps to desegregate facilities. Some had removed signs. One manager explained how he had desegregated the company's eating facilities by first replacing the wall dividing the dining areas with a long flower box on the floor, a trellis reaching to the ceiling, and some vines crawling up the trellis. Once the vines had reached the ceiling, he removed the trellis.

He then failed to water the vines. The vines died, and he removed them. Finally he removed the flower box as well. A personnel officer at a second company employed a similar technique to desegregate the medical facilities. He used a panel with a large window to separate the medical areas for blacks and whites. One evening he broke the window. He left the broken window for a while and then removed it. He left the open window space for a short period, and when there was no reaction, he removed the entire panel.

Following the signing of the Sullivan principles a number of companies began to move actively to desegregate. First, companies called in architects to redesign existing facilities or to design new ones. Several committed themselves to substantial outlays for new cafeterias, toilets or lockers. Colgate spent $250,000 for a new cafeteria; Goodyear committed $2.3 million for new toilets, locker rooms, eating and training facilities; Carlton Paper is spending $690,000 to revamp and desegregate existing facilities in 1978 and 1979; Firestone spent $300,000 on a new cafeteria and training center; Deere built new dining, toilet and locker areas for hourly workers; Ford, Caterpillar and Abbott Laboratories desegregated existing facilities; and General Motors, after explaining in 1977 how costly desegregation would be in terms of new facilities, confirmed its estimates by pledging to spend $4.5 million on new training, dining, toilet and locker facilities.

Several managers point out that desegregation has not necessarily meant integration. In some instances, companies replaced segregation of eating or locker areas by race with segregation by workers' status--hourly or salaried. Cafeterias, toilets and locker rooms formerly designated for blacks were assigned to hourly workers. White facilities were allocated to salaried workers or to artisans. Because the companies had no salaried blacks or hourly whites, the separation of the races has been perpetuated. At other companies, despite the desegregation of facilities, some workers continue to use the facilities they were accustomed to using. In a company poll at Abbott, for example, most African workers elected to eat European meals in what had been the white cafeteria, but a few chose to take African meals in the old African cafeteria. Some personnel directors found themselves telling black white collar workers where to eat--using black personnel officers to break the ice by being the first blacks to use previously all-white dining or toilet facilities. And one company official said that if blacks and whites continued to use the toilets that they had always used, he would simply close down one set of toilets, declaring it out of order, and forcing integration to take place.

The South African government's response has been to look the other way. Although removing signs from toilet facilities constitutes a violation of the Factories Act and the Shops and Offices Act, no company reported government resistance to efforts to desegregate. One company submitting plans for new facilities had marked in dotted lines the toilets ostensibly allocated to blacks. The company told the Labor Department that it had no intention of constructing the separate toilets but had blocked them in so that the plans would meet government requirements on paper. Department officials approved the plans and informed inspectors that there should be no harassment of the company for not constructing separate facilities.

Continuing resistance to desegregated facilities--Although active efforts toward integration are far more prevalent than they were two years ago among American companies, they are by no means universal. Parker Pen has separate toilets, lockers, dining areas and food services. Uniroyal writes that "separate facilities have traditionally been provided and our program supports a change by evolution. Forced integration will, we believe, only lead to disaster and will defeat the aims of the program." The level of desegregation not only varies between companies but within companies as well. Altech (36.3-percent owned by ITT), South Cross Television (100-percent owned by ITT), and African Telephone Cables (30-percent owned by ITT) have segregated facilities. Alfred Teves Engineering (100-percent owned by ITT) has integrated facilities, and Martin Directories (80-percent owned by ITT) has desegregated eating areas. Altech officials and those at African Telephone Cables say they have not removed the signs designating which race may use each facility because signs are required by law. Concern for the law was also offered by several other companies as a reason for not desegregating facilities. One company official told IRRC in 1977 that "there was no way that the company will break the law" requiring separation of the races. And some companies--Hewlett-Packard and Monsanto among them--argued that desegregation of facilities was complicated by their location in buildings that were shared with South African companies.

Some companies question the importance of desegregating facilities. The plant manager of one major U.S. company told IRRC that "desegregation of facilities was not the number one problem; training, education and housing are a lot more critical," and "there are many things more important to worry about than office toilets." An official at Firestone said that integration of facilities was not a particularly high priority among his black workers.

Companies have responded to whites' opposition in different ways. Many simply ignore the whites who complain. Colgate told workers that "if they don't like the situation here, better check other companies before you leave because they are likely to be subjected to the same principles." One company faced with a white worker who had complained to the government about the lack of separate facilities simply designated a toilet located in a storage area at the far end of the factory as the toilet reserved for whites. He was welcome to use it exclusively, he was told, if he so desired.

The symbolism of the desegregation of facilities appears to be of considerable importance to many black workers. A number of black workers with whom IRRC discussed the issue stressed the significance of having access to the same facilities as whites. Several workers at one company complained that black professionals were tucked away in a training building while white administrative workers were all assigned offices in a newly constructed office compound. Company managers said they were not aware that de facto segregation was being maintained, but black workers were well aware of the separation. At another company, a black woman professional told IRRC that she had been forced to use a toilet located in a store room well away from her office and those of her colleagues. One day, unaware that someone was using the toilet, a janitor locked her in the storeroom, she said, an incident that was both inconvenient and embarrassing. An African union leader spent nearly an hour with IRRC explaining how important it was for black workers in a cafeteria to be able to use the same crockery and utensils as white workers. The failure to provide the same utensils was just one more important sign to him and to the workers he represented that management was not willing to treat blacks equally.

Training: Training has been a second area in which a number of American companies have made some progress during the last three years. Interest in training began to develop in the early 1970s. Before that most training was acquired on-the-job, "sitting watching Nellie."

Interest in formal training received a boost from the economic boom of the early 1970s and development of the labor codes. John Clark, managing director of IBM, told IRRC in 1978 that the codes and an awareness of manpower needs "had produced an explosion of training. Three years ago there was no understanding of what the country faced. Now there is a new awareness."

The awareness is visible in several ways. Many companies have made modest but important changes in their own training programs. Gillette, for example, hired a full-time training officer in 1977; Carlton Paper has begun to formalize its training programs; several companies have begun programs to give workers basic background in how a company operates.

Increased interest in training is not limited to American companies. Large South African companies such as Barlow Rand, Anglo American and its subsidiary, South African Breweries, and Rembrandt Tobacco, as well as a number of European companies, have demonstrated a greater commitment to training recently than was apparent a few years ago. The personnel director of Afrox, the South African subsidiary of a British company, told IRRC in 1977 that the company had developed all its training programs in the last 18 months. Afrox hopes to train five to 10 artisans' assistants a year, he said, and 80 percent of them can be expected to be employed in artisan-level jobs. Officials at the South African subsidiary of the German company, Siemens, say they are now training Africans for metal and electrical work at the artisan level. In 1977, African Explosives, a subsidiary of a British company and Anglo American, took 40 African workers into the first phase of a five-phase artisan-level training program. The problem, an official of the company told IRRC, "is not in training the workers, but in being able to use them in a closed shop." Some Barlow Rand companies have initiated artisan-level training despite opposition from white union members.

Collective efforts--Perhaps the most tangible examples of the increased interest in training among companies are the collective efforts under way to develop new training facilities. Until recently, it has been nearly impossible for Africans to get training in white areas, although in the last two years, several companies--including Goodyear, Volkswagen, Ford and General Motors--have been bringing teachers from local white technical schools to teach very limited numbers of their African workers. The members of the American Chamber of Commerce announced in 1978 plans to provide some $3 million to construct a commercial high school in Soweto. The American Chamber decided to construct the school after conversations with the government and with Soweto community leaders, including representatives of the Soweto Committee of 10. Construction is to begin in 1979; the school is to open in 1980 and accommodate 600 pupils a year. In a separate effort, companies in Port Elizabeth--including Ford, General Motors and Firestone--are committed to build a $1.25- to

1.5-million technical institute to provide technical training through high school to 600 students a year. The school will allow Africans to acquire "technical certificates" and to get the background necessary for jobs as artisans, technicians and ultimately management positions. Backers of the project hope to have the school open in January 1980. The school has received the support of the National African Chamber of Commerce, the organization of African businessmen in South Africa, which has pledged $57,500 to the project. Goodyear and Volkswagen have committed $60,000 each to develop a branch of the Port Elizabeth School--eventually expected to accommodate 100 students--at Uitenhage, an industrial town near Port Elizabeth.

In addition to collective efforts to construct training facilities, several companies have made major commitments to existing outside facilities or to their own facilities. In developing plans for new training programs several companies discovered that they simply lacked the facilities required. A Ford spokesman said, "A review of current training facilities has revealed that they are totally inadequate to meet current training objectives. The result has been that a number of companies are planning new facilities." Ford began construction of its new facility in 1979. 3M has begun construction of its own training and education center. The Palabora Mining Co. (28.6-percent-owned by Newmont) has spent more than $850,000 for a training facility near its mine in the Lebowa homeland. The center opened in 1978 with 200 live-in students getting artisan-level training in motor mechanics, electronics, panel beating and boiler making. The company expects enrollment to double in the next two to four years. As part of the upgrading of its facilities, General Motors has allocated $900,000 to an in-company "mini-technical institute" that will provide training for workers between standard 5 and standard 10 in mathematics, commercial affairs and basic subjects required to make them eligible for technical certificates. The company expects to have 360 students in training at all times at a cost to GM that the managing director estimates at $800,000 per year. Union Carbide has built a training center at its Brits Mine and has begun artisan training for African workers. It now has 36 workers in its artisan training program.

The recent willingness of companies to provide the equivalent of artisan-level training for Africans is a new and important development. Two years ago few, if any, companies were willing to provide such training. Ford had no African apprentices in 1975. Between 1976 and 1978 the company increased its expenditure on training and development by nearly 140 percent to $1 million, two-thirds of which went for black workers. The number of African trainees more than tripled (from 14 to 50) during these years. By 1978 it had 19 Africans in what it called "workshop training," which it described as the same as the training provided to coloreds and white apprentices. Ford expects to double the number of Africans in the program by 1981. General Motors had no Africans and only three coloreds in artisan training as late as 1978; in 1979, however, the company has stated that it expects to have 20 coloreds and 7 Africans in training for artisan positions.

The degree of interest in the joint government-business training centers has been low, although a few companies, most notably IBM, have been active in their support. One executive at IBM has spent a considerable portion of his time on the development of the Chamdor training complex. IBM has contributed funds to Chamdor and also has lent an employee to serve full-time as its director. At least in part as a result of these efforts, Chamdor is the most advanced of the joint centers. 3M said in 1978 that 14 of its employees had spent or would spend time at Chamdor. NCR and Burroughs are among a number of companies that have trained employees there.

White-collar training--Some companies have shown a growing interest in providing basic business education and training for white-collar jobs. Colgate has launched a "business appreciation course"; Hewlett-Packard is offering a two-hour-a-week course to its black employees in language, geography and reading that could prepare them for a high school diploma; Gillette is now offering a business economics course at the tenth grade level that includes work on stock inventory, pricing, mailing, advertising and banking. Ford has four Africans in a commercial trainee program designed to prepare them for salaried staff, administrative and clerical positions, and three Africans and four coloreds in a management intern program. Caterpillar has four Africans in supervisory positions receiving managerial training. As of Dec. 31, 1978, IBM had 14 Africans training for what it considers professional positions, 14 in clerical training and 16 training for jobs as technicians.

Most training for white collar positions, where it occurs, is done within the company. Occasionally, companies have sent Africans abroad through programs developed under the aegis of the International Association of Students in Economics and Business Management. A number of American companies--Ford, General Motors, Cummins Engine, Gillette, Columbus McKinnon, Union Carbide, Polaroid and IBM--have sponsored interns for training periods of three to 12 months in their home offices. Most of these interns, although not company employees at the time of their selection, are employed by the South African subsidiaries upon their return.

At least two companies--Norton and IBM--have lent executives to work on black development. In addition to working at Chamdor, IBM has lent an executive to the University of Zululand to design a system analyst and data programming course. Norton has made two executives available on a full-time basis to small black businessmen to assist in development of entrepreneurial skills.

Resistance to training--Even though many companies have made substantial effort to develop training opportunities in the last three years, the numbers of blacks being trained remains very small. A 1978 study by Urwick International of several hundred companies employing thousands of workers concluded that most companies did their own job training. Sixty-eight percent of those surveyed had not allocated the responsibility for training to a specific individual and only half had what would be considered permanent training facilities.

Some companies have cut back considerably on training because of the recession. Others argue that artisan-level training is impossible in light of union opposition and the inability of Africans to get official certificates of qualification. A Firestone representative, for example, said it would be pointless to train an African to become an electrician because the worker would not be able to get his papers. If a problem were to arise from work done by a worker without his papers, the company official said, it would mean trouble for the company.

Others have argued that results of training may be too costly. One company spokesman told IRRC that the company opposed the concept of training Africans for artisan aides' jobs because it would require the promotion of white artisans to supervisory positions. In the end, he said, the company would be obligated to pay two workers to do one job.

Employee housing: A third area in which companies' interest has increased measurably in the last three years is employee housing. Interest began with the government announcement in 1975 of its decision to restore to Africans some form of right to land tenure in white areas. A number of companies began to examine the possibility of direct aid to African employees to enable them to buy or build their own homes, and several have begun home loan programs during the last three years. Despite the government's announcement of a change in its land tenure policy in 1975, it was not until December 1978 that officials issued the regulations clarifying the means of obtaining leases, and many companies that initially had been interested in a housing program have held back pending the release of the regulations. Thus the programs that have started in the last few years vary greatly among companies, and many are just in the first phase of development.

The few companies that were involved in housing before 1975--the mining companies and some manufacturers such as General Motors and Ford, for example--provided loans to local government authorities to build houses in township areas. The loans increased the government's capacity to construct homes for Africans and thus the likelihood that company employees would be able to get a home or that their waiting period would be shorter. They did not enable employees to acquire their own homes, however, nor did they change what the personnel director at one company described as the government's bureaucratic mentality that led it to build match box houses to fill the housing deficit. The government not only built too few houses, he said, but the ones it built were inadequate. To approach this problem, several companies before 1975 had home improvement loan programs. The employees with a certain seniority or wage level were able to obtain from the company interest-free or low-interest loans, usually under 500 rand, for home improvements. Since 1972, for example, Ford has provided loans up to 500 rand interest-free to 25 African and 183 colored employees.

As a result of the 1975 announcement on land tenure, companies began to review their housing policies. These efforts were bolstered later by the codes and the Sullivan principles. Many companies argued that they could do little until the government issued its regulations. Coca-Cola, for example, said it was looking at the possibility of a home purchase loan program but was waiting to see what would come out of the regulations. Abbott officials also said they were waiting for the regulations, as did officials of Schering Plough. Some companies continued to make home improvement loans. Abbott will provide its employees with 1,000 rand to be paid back at a rate of 7.50 rand a month. Caltex originally limited its loans to 600 rand, but it will now lend an amount equal to the amount an employee has in his pension plan. Some companies began home improvement programs. Pfizer began a loan program in April 1978 that provides two-year loans of up to 600 rand at 6 percent interest to employees who earn 400 rand a month or more and have five years' experience. Firestone started in 1978 a program of two-year loans--interest free for the first 12 months--of up to 750 rand for employees who earn 450 rand a month and have three years' experience.

A number of companies--including Caterpillar, Deere, IBM and Union Carbide, as well as several South African companies--began to move on home-loan programs without the regulations. "One dilemma which faced us was the argument that until freehold was granted to urban blacks, any move by private enterprise to provide black housing would be construed as support for unsecured leases," the chairman of a South African insurance company told the Financial Mail. "But several black community leaders told us that while freehold was the ideal, the need for more and improved housing took precedence," he said.

Caterpillar's efforts to provide housing offer an example of what companies could do even without the regulations. After interviewing all its African workers in 1977 to see what type of housing they might like and what sort of loan might be appropriate, Caterpillar agreed to deposit 65,000 rand with the Natal Building Society. The society agreed in exchange to lend money to the local government authority, which in turn lent the money for 25 years at 9 percent to Caterpillar's employees for the purchase of their homes. Twelve employees elected to purchase their homes--with monthly payments of 27.50 rand a month compared with their 16.50-a-month rental fee.

Similar programs are under way elsewhere. With company help, 33 African IBM employees had constructed or purchased new homes by Dec. 31, 1978. After a survey of employees, Deere is negotiating loans to 19 African employees to allow them to purchase new homes. But despite companies' commitment, bureaucratic delays abound. Union Carbide had hoped to build 40 new homes at its plant by November 1978 but actually had constructed 17. The company has agreed to lend employees up to 20 percent of the cost of the house or 1,000 rand, and it provides a monthly subsidy to workers with houses that is equal to the difference between their mortgage fee and the rental fee that they paid earlier.

A number of companies--GM, Ford and Gillette among them--are exploring means of lending more funds to the local authorities to spur house construction, and in December 1978 the Johannesburg Star reported that three American banks--Chase, Bank of America, and Morgan Guaranty--had agreed to make a 28.7-million-rand loan to South African banks to be used in a mortgage loan program for blacks.

The increased interest in housing is evident also in the findings of the 1978 survey of companies by Urwick International. The study found that 8 percent of the companies surveyed assisted black employees on their first mortgage bonds--compared with 2 percent in 1977--and that 12 percent of the companies were providing collateral security for housing loans for black employees--against 2 percent in 1977. Despite this increase, however, 60 percent of the companies responding to the survey said they made no contribution to employee housing.

Worker representation: Many of the people concerned about the role of business in South Africa see worker representation and efforts to form African trade unions as the most important labor issue. It has been the subject of the most debate, and it is the one area in which European companies have been visibly more progressive than U.S. companies. Despite most managers' lack of enthusiasm for African unions, a few companies have recognized African unions in recent years and some observers see a shift in momentum favoring increased recognition. "Though you find a whole range of views from employers (on the subject of African unions), the move is now increasingly that blacks will be unionized," D.L. Van Coller, head of the Institute for Industrial Relations, told the Financial Mail in July 1978. (The institute, formed in 1976, provides a forum for workers and management to discuss industrial relations.)

Most companies do not recognize African unions. Some companies are not faced with the prospect of a black union. The resurgence in the movement is still relatively young, and many industries are far from being organized. Other companies have not negotiated with unions for a variety of reasons. As late as 1978 a few still thought African unions were illegal; others said they did not recognize any unions, they were waiting for the Wiehahn Commission report, they thought their current grievance procedures were adequate, or they saw unions as having a potentially political role.

More British companies say they recognize African trade unions than do American companies. In reports submitted by some 150 British companies to parliament in 1979, eight companies claimed to recognize African unions--compared with one American company--although exactly what is meant by "recognition" may vary from company to company.

Some companies--such as Union Carbide and IBM--say that they prefer to deal directly with their workers, rather than through a union. They say that it is management's responsibility to look after employees' needs. "We try to run ahead of complaints," one IBM representative told IRRC; "we train managers to handle issues and have a speak-up program" for grievances. "Joining a union is an individual choice," he said, "and none of our employees have chosen to do so." Union Carbide says it tries to avoid unions worldwide and points out that it deals with no unions, "black or white," in South Africa.

Many companies take a position similar to that of Berec International. In responding to a trade union's question on Eveready's policies, Berec's chairman wrote that it considered its existing system of liaison committees very satisfactory. The company opposed recognition of a black union because, officials said, it would further entrench job reservation, and they said they were waiting for the Wiehahn Commission's report, which they hoped would provide for the establishment of multiracial unions.

Some companies oppose what they see as intervention by an outside body. A Consolidated Glass offical told IRRC that although 40 percent of African workers at its plant were involved in the African union, the company refused to recognize the union because management did not want to enter into a third party arrangement. The desire to avoid third party arrangements was also given as the reason why Smith and Nephew, a British subsidiary which in 1975 became the first company in South Africa to negotiate an agreement with an African union, refused to negotiate a second agreement. Company officials said they preferred to deal with liaison or works committees, although some observers commented that the company had been under pressure from the South African government to rescind the agreement with the African unions. (The company eventually ended up renewing its agreement with the African union.)

Others argue that they cannot recognize unions that do not have government sanction. A Barlow Rand representative told IRRC in 1977 that "black unions have no legal standing," and thus the company was not interested in negotiations with one. It would not negotiate with any union, white or black, he said, and would not issue stop orders to withdraw dues from employee paychecks for any unregistered union, even if a majority of the workers demanded it. In 1977, a Barlow Rand company, Heinnemann Electric (partially American-owned), suffered through what the representative described as an "unhappy and expensive" labor dispute over black union recognition, but the holding company did not intervene in the dispute.

A similar stance was taken in a strike at Leyland in 1975. When management refused to negotiate with a union, workers struck, management declared the strike illegal, and the company fired workers and informed the state internal security officials. To negotiate with an unrecognized union, management explained to IRRC, would take the company outside the law, and neither side would have legal recourse if the agreement reached in the negotiation were later broken. The company preferred to wait until unions were recognized; in the meantime, the company deputy chairman told IRRC, management had to be careful because "the Communist influence still lingered in the African labor movement."

Concerns about the politicization of black unions influence managements' attitudes at many companies. W.J. de Villiers, chairman of a South African company, General Mining, stated his opposition to African unions in 1975, "because the trade union movement is used by far left socialists as a political tool and not to improve the worker." Just as some companies used the argument that African unions must be recognized in order to avoid driving African workers into radical camps, others argue the reverse--African unions provide radical camps for politicizing workers.

Softening of opposition--Several companies that opposed unions have begun to soften their views. At Barlow, for example, the chairman said in June 1978 that the company would "like to see negotiations at industry or national level between employers' organizations and multiracial unions, rather than black unions, with supplementary negotiation on domestic issues at plant level between managements and multiracial commitees." But pending the changes that would allow such a situation to develop, companies within the Barlow Rand group "will be prepared to consult and negotiate with unregistered unions, provided that such unions are so constituted that they would satisfy the Industrial Conciliation Act's requirements for union registration, can demonstrate that the majority of the employees concerned wish to be represented by them, and accept that companies must continue to abide by the laws and agreements to which they are subject." Time correspondent William McWhirter quoted R.J. Ironside of General Motors in September 1978 as saying that the company had not issued stop orders to withdraw union dues from the paychecks of 298 employees who wished to join the African unions because "there are 114 ways a black can be relieved of his money and GM is not going to be one of them." Ironside later wrote IRRC that only 114 of the 249 employees that the union said had requested payroll deductions for union dues actually elected to have the deductions when questioned by the company. Three months later, however, the company not only had issued stop orders but was providing black union leaders with computer lists of those employees who had not joined the union in order to help the union's recruiting efforts.

Several companies, in addition to Smith And Nephew, have now negotiated agreements with African unions. Ford was one of the first, establishing aninformal relationship with an African union in 1977. Kellogg in 1979 became the first U.S. company to award formal recognition to an African union. The South African chain store, Pick 'n' Pay, with 3,000 African workers, has recognized the Commercial Catering and Allied Workers, and Anglo American has adopted guidelines for its more than 300 subsidiaries that provide for recognition of African unions. The guidelines are not binding, but they describe, according to the Financial Mail, "various facilities a company should grant a black union depending on its membership at the plant, leading up to full union recognition when the union represents a majority." Three Anglo companies, including Sigma (24.9-percent owned by Chrysler), have been approached by African unions seeking stop orders. Sigma has agreed to do so, and company officials say that they are waiting until a majority of workers at the other two companies join the union before issuing the stop orders at those companies. They say that managements at several Anglo companies have been willing to discuss workers' grievances with officials from unions that they have not yet recognized and have posted union notices on company bulletin boards.

Within the South African context, whether an African union succeeds has often depended less on workers' interest and organization than on companies' attitudes. Without government recognition of the rights of Africans to join registered unions, African employees have had few defenses if companies decide to take action against them for their pro-union activities. South African labor laws include provisions to protect Africans from victimization, but the government has not yet taken action based on those regulations, despite numerous complaints against victimization. As the Leyland case showed, not only may companies have the power to fire workers, but many also have the power to get employees or union organizers arrested. Whether, in fact, a company actually has the power to have its employees arrested, or would use it if it did, makes little difference to African workers who are being asked to join unions. It is their perception of management's power, both to fire employees and to call in the authorities, that acts as a major constraint on organization of African unions at companies that have opposed them. Virtually all African workers who spoke to IRRC about the development of African unions, both in 1975 and again in 1977 and 1978, have mentioned their fears of victimization--that if they joined a union they would be hurt at work, fired, or labeled as political activists, and, perhaps, persecuted by the government. Union organizers say that their efforts to organize Africans will continue to be an uphill battle against Africans' fears, real and imaginary, that it is too risky for them to join a union.

Finally, once a union is organized and negotiations carried out, workers have still been dependent on the company to uphold the agreement reached. Without legal standing, and restricted by ponderous procedures that had to be followed before Africans could strike legally, African unions have been dependent on the good faith of management to give meaning to the negotiating process and its subsequent agreement. Some of this will certainly change with the developments recommended by the Wiehahn Commission. Just how strong African unions or mixed unions (if they are allowed) will become remains to be seen. But some observers, including the U.S. labor attache in Johannesburg, were optimistic in 1979 that African workers, for the first time, were moving toward a position from which they could negotiate their wages, hours and working conditions.

Areas of Little Progress in Labor Practices

It is important to recognize that the momentum for change at companies operating in South Africa is fragile, that it is by no means universal, and that many of the first steps taken are among the easiest. Removing signs designating separate facilities by race, for example, posed few problems for most companies. Actual desegregation of facilities and the beginning of integration, similarly, has been far less traumatic than companies anticipated. Improved training of Africans has encountered slightly greater resistance, but in most places where it is occurring, the economic justification--the shortage of whites for the jobs--is such that any opposition that exists can be answered quite simply. Housing programs have not required significant new contributions by companies; financial commitments have been limited. And in worker representation, the one U.S. company that has experience with a black union--Ford--reports that the union has been reasonable in its relations with management and effective in representing black workers.

The real problems to be encountered by companies trying to implement progressive practices are likely to be encountered as companies try to move beyond the early steps: to train and promote blacks into white collar and management positions, to close the wage gap, to improve fringe benefits, and to end the system of migratory labor. In these areas, little progress has been made to date--with the possible exception of the closing of the wage gaps in those few positions where blacks and whites are working at the same jobs--and the systemic constraints and economic realities are likely to be much more severe.

Africans in white collar, salaried positions: Few companies employ many Africans in white collar, salaried positions, as higher level supervisors, managers or foremen. Arthur D. Little's analysis of the responses to the first Sullivan questionnaire reported that only 7 percent of the companies responding had Africans at the level of managers/officials. Moreover, only 10 percent had courses for management trainees. A number of companies--Bendix, Ferro, Nabisco, Parker Pen, Phillips Petroleum, Phelps Dodge and Uniroyal among them--have no Africans in any salaried positions. Most have very few. At General Motors, for example, in 1978 only four of more than 1,100 salaried workers were Africans. GM plans to add four more in 1979. Firestone's operations around the country have one salaried African worker. Goodyear has nine salaried Africans, equal to about 3 percent of its total white collar force. In many cases, the lack of Africans at the managerial level carries over to the factory floor. Colgate has no Africans among its 14 foremen. Otis had no Africans among its 80 supervisors until it added four to its rolls in 1977 for the first time.

The lack of Africans in higher level positions is not limited to U.S.

companies. It reflects in large part the inadequacy of training and educational opportunities for blacks in South Africa. It also reflects corporate managers' concerns about the reaction of whites to blacks in better jobs. A spokesman for Consolidated Glass told IRRC that the "occupational structure in South Africa mitigates against further advancement of blacks because it would require blacks to supervise whites," a situation which he described as politically unacceptable. He said he could not see blacks as supervisors for five years.

Dresser's managing director recounted an incident in 1974 in which management pulled back from a promotion of an African because of a white's opposition; the company later made the promotion after the white had left. A Colgate representative reported to IRRC that the company could not have African foremen until it had African artisans because foremen must supervise artisans and come from the artisan background. He said the company hoped to have its first African foremen in three or four years.

A few companies argue that Africans' labor progress should not be measured by whether workers are salaried. Uniroyal says that "traditionally the non-white has received weekly wage payments and this has resulted in his developing a weekly wage budget concept. To change this would cause hardship and resentment from the staff concerned and in many cases would result in the employees being unable to provide for their needs in the latter part of the month." But salaried or not, the company has only three Africans in a white collar population of 65. Some companies, such as Deere, have developed training courses for employees in budget management and savings to prepare them for a move to salaried wages or to assist them in avoiding unwieldy credit debts, and a few companies--Caltex and Caterpillar among them--have all workers on a salaried basis.

Wages: Until blacks have equal access to jobs, a measurable gap is likely to exist between wages paid to blacks and those paid to whites. Despite efforts in many companies to raise the wages of blacks more frequently and with larger increases than for whites, the gap between the two is growing. Companies that have adopted a policy of equal pay for equal work find that the policy has only limited meaning; there are few positions in which blacks and whites work side by side performing the same labor and, where they do, whites may earn more because they have greater experience or the company may pay them more in return for their agreement to the promotion of blacks. And because most blacks begin with a much lower wage than whites, percentage increases for them do not mean as much in real terms as percentage increases for whites. Thus, even with gains in wages for blacks in the last few years, the gap between blacks and whites continues to widen.

Setting a minimum wage--The government of South Africa sets the absolute minimum wage in an industry in one of two ways. If the job positions are not covered by union negotiation, a national wage board can establish a minimum wage. If a white union is active in a company, as it is in most cases, the company's operations and working conditions, including wages, will be set by negotiation between industry and union representatives at industrial council sessions. (There are no ceilings on wages.) In most cases, the minimum wage set by wage boards or industrial council agreement falls well below that being paid in the industry.

Usually, the minimum level prescribed by the government falls below other standards as well.

A company can measure its minimum wage in South Africa against several nongovernmental standards. The standard that is known most widely outside South Africa--although not necessarily the one used most inside the country--is the poverty datum line. The PDL, defined by a South African professor as a "line below which health and decency cannot be maintained," includes unavoidable expenses an African family must incur--food, transport, clothing, rent and fuel. It does not include such things as medical and educational expenses, bedding and utensils. These items are included in a second standard called the minimum effective level (MEL), which is estimated at 150 percent of the PDL. PDL and MEL figures have been published periodically in the past by a number of institutions, including the South African Institute for Race Relations and the Johannesburg Chamber of Commerce. Figures are based on a survey of the major township areas around Johannesburg and are updated to take account of changes in the cost of living. Minimum-wage levels prescribed by the government are often as much as 30 percent below the PDL.

Several other surveys that are taken with greater regularity and cover a larger number of geographical areas provide similar indices. Perhaps the most widely used by U.S. companies is the semi-annual survey of each of the major industrial areas done by the University of Port Elizabeth. That study establishes figures for a household subsistence level (HSL) and a household effective level (HEL), based on criteria similar to those used for the PDL and MEL, for both Africans and coloreds. The HSL generally runs slightly below the PDL. The University of South Africa's Bureau of Market Research also does surveys to establish standards called the minimum-living level and higher-living level. The bureau's levels are generally 10 percent below the University of Port Elizabeth's figures. Both the university and the Bureau of Market Research have conducted private surveys for companies that wished to determine living costs in areas outside those areas normally surveyed.

In addition to surveys of subsistence and effective living levels, a number of private companies conduct surveys that allow comparison of wages at higher job levels. Urwick International and Fine Spamer are two research and consulting firms that do annual industry-wide surveys of wages that companies are paying in job categories from tea server to chief executive officer, and some companies do surveys of their own.

The EEC code states under its third principle that "the minimum wage should initially exceed by at least 50 percent the minimum level required to satisfy the basic needs of an employee and his family," and the amended Sullivan principles include a reference to wages with a minimum tax "to be well above the appropriate local minimum economic living level. A number of companies have been inching their minimum wage levels up toward the minimum effective level in the last three years, but most companies continue to start workers at a wage below the MEL, and some companies still pay wages below the poverty datum or household subsistence level.

The South African Institute of Race Relations states that in more than half of the job categories listed in a 1977 Urwick study, African workers were paid average wages below 202 rand--the household effective level determined by the University of Port Elizabeth. Moreover, in 13 of

the 30 categories, according to the survey, companies were paying
workers less than the subsistence level.

Statistics for the performance of American companies similarly show
that most companies pay a minimum wage below the MEL or HEL and a
number start workers at wages below the PDL or HSL. Several
companies--Burroughs, Caltex, Caterpillar, Colgate, Esso (Exxon), Ford,
IBM, General Motors, Lilly, Mobil and Sperry Rand--report that their
minimum wage is at or above the MEL-HEL level. The practice is not so
widespread, however, as to be reflected in the early reporting by the
signers of the Sullivan principles. Nearly all--95 percent--of the U.S.
companies responding to the initial Sullivan questionnaire reported paying
a minimum monthly wage below 209 rand. (The MEL-HEL in 1978 for
Johannesburg was approximately 225.) At 17 companies the minimum
entry level wage was below 150 rand a month--the minimum subsistence
level in August 1978 was 146 rand--and four companies reported that their
average monthly wages fell below 125 rand. Bendix, Ferro, International
Harvester, Masonite, Nabisco, Phelps Dodge, and Quebec Iron and
Titanium all reported starting wages below the minimum subsistence
level. But analysis of wages may need to be tempered by extenuating
circumstances. The mining companies, for example, may provide housing
and board, pushing their total wage package above the HSL; International
Harvester says that the six workers earning less than the HSL at a plant it
acquired recently are being paid with wages set by the old employer, but
that it plans to rectify the situation.

Management arguments on wage levels--At some companies,
however, wages are low because of a management decision. Masonite
pays 165 male migrant workers on its forestry plantations 32.50 rand a
month, and 338 women are paid at the rate of 28.60 rand. (The company
also provides workers with free meals valued at 35 cents a day and has set
aside 24,000 rand a year for health services, welfare, ablution blocks and
on-site housing.) Masonite's chairman describes the company's wages at
its forestry plantations as "very low." The company's managing director
states, "Our performance at our plantations is far from meeting anything
like the PDL. All it will show is that there has been a big improvement
since 1972. In the light of forestry performances generally in South
Africa and at Masonite, in particular, higher wages can just not be
afforded. However, we ensure that our pay scales, based mainly on piece
work, are in line with what the industry pays. You will probably recall
that this profit center of ours has in the past at best broken even and
during the past three recession years has been in the red substantially and
will probably remain so until the demand for timber is such that we can
sell our full production."

A number of companies argue that a rapid increase in Africans' wages
may be difficult. They are not able to raise wages as fast as they might
like, several managers argue, because Africans and whites respond
differently to wage increases. One Firestone representative said that
because African and white workers measure the need to work differently,
if the company raised wages too rapidly, Africans would simply work less.
As an example, he said that when the company moved from a four- to a
five-day week, many workers preferred to remain on a four-day schedule.
Other companies have argued that increasing wages rapidly makes workers
suspicious that the company has been underpaying them in the past, and

some say, as did Palabora's manager in 1975, that Africans have a "limited absorptive capacity" for more wages. If salaries go up too quickly, workers will become victims of "hire purchase" credit buying schemes and will end up with greater debt than they had with lower wages. A few have argued against higher wages because it "will throw off others in the industry," and some have said that higher wages will force them to use fewer workers and to become more capital-intensive.

Some companies dismiss these arguments. Firestone's Peter Morum accuses some managers of using the argument that higher wages will force layoffs as a refuge because they oppose raising wages. And perspectives have changed within companies. At Rio Tinto Zinc's mine at Palabora, for example, officials told IRRC in 1975 that the company did not intend to provide equal pay for equal work. The mine manager reported to IRRC in 1975 that the mine and smelter operation, located in a relatively isolated rural area, is paying according to supply and demand. For the time being, he argued, it was not reasonable to pay the same wage for Africans and whites when the supply of Africans is great and the supply of whites is short. In 1978, however, the chairman of Rio Tinto Zinc announced that wages were to be raised, and that by the end of the year no African at Palabora would be paid less than the household effective level.

Equal pay for equal work--Most companies say they have adopted a policy of equal pay for equal work. The 1978 Fine Spamer survey reports that 69 percent of the companies responding to its questionnaire stated that they give equal pay.

But the actual impact of an equal pay program is often limited by the relatively few positions in which blacks and whites do equal or comparable work. Despite gains in blacks' advancement, there are still few positions where blacks and whites overlap and, where they do, whites usually have greater seniority and experience and draw higher wages. Rio Tinto Zinc's chairman said in November 1977 that Africans' salaries at Palabora were about 75 percent of whites' salaries, based on experience and productivity. In some instances, companies have only won the agreement of white unions to promote blacks with the understanding that whites are promoted to supervisory levels or are granted raises.

In many cases, companies continue to "fragment" jobs--giving a black a job that is much the same in substance, but not in title, as that held previously by a white. The job traditionally done by a white is broken down, and various responsibilities are included in a newly created job category to be filled by a black. Proponents of job fragmentation argue that it satisfies interests of all racial groups. They maintain that the black is paid a fair wage and more positions are opened up to blacks. The fact that whites earned higher wages for similar work should be disregarded, they argue, because the whites' wages are largely a reflection of the limited availability of white workers. Critics say job fragmentation denies blacks the opportunity to take over full responsibility and to be paid for the whole job. Often, they maintain, the black is paid a lower wage than the white he succeeded, and the white is advanced to a supervisory position with a wage increase. Thus, although the black receives a wage increase, he may not earn what was paid previously for essentially the same work. The white earns more, and the gap between the two widens, they point out.

For a number of companies, the problems of providing equal pay for equal work are compounded by the high wages demanded by whites. Even if it is possible to raise the wages of blacks to an appropriate level, it is not possible to lower whites' wages from the level to which they have been forced. Discussing this problem, a representative of Barlow Rand said that although the company had made equal pay for equal work an objective, it had not attained it yet.

Nearly one-third of the companies reporting to Fine Spamer that they did not provide equal pay for equal work cited the increased cost as the reason. Almost an equal number said they had to pay whites more because the whites demanded it. A number of managers told IRRC that raising blacks' wages to the inflated level of whites' would force their companies to hire fewer workers. And an official at one company--Dresser Industries--told IRRC that it paid African workers less because they had to pay less income tax. (In most cases, Africans earning the same as whites actually pay a greater tax because they are allowed fewer deductions than whites and have to begin tax payments at a lower income level. The government announced its intention to revise tax schedules in 1979 and predicts that by 1982 whites and Africans will be taxed according to the same schedule.)

Some companies do not know whether in fact they do pay equal wages. Abbott's managing director explained to IRRC that the company had no measure of equal pay for equal work because it had no formal job evaluation. The company planned to make a full evaluation of all jobs in 1979, he said, a process that it would not have undertaken at that time except for the Sullivan principles.

Evaluation of performance--Abbott is not alone in its lack of a formal evaluation program. In a 1977 survey Urwick found that 70 percent of the companies questioned had no formal system to assess the level of performance of workers, and 60 percent had no formal system by which to evaluate the importance of individual jobs.

A formal approach to the evaluation of jobs and the appraisal of an individual's performance within each job category are factors receiving increasing attention at a number of companies.

Once a minimum-wage level has been set, the next step for a number of companies is a company-wide job evaluation, defining proper job categories and setting wage levels for each category. Within each category, the company defines the tasks and responsibilities of the worker. Some companies assign points for each responsibility and rate each job according to its points. Jobs involving different tasks may have the same level of responsibilities, and by defining a job in terms of its responsibilities a company is able to compare different types of jobs, rate each, and assign a wage according to its points.

One objective of the redefinition of jobs by responsibility is to locate all jobs along a unitary wage curve, from the lowest paid unskilled labor up through the white collar workers. All jobs are placed along the curve, and all workers, regardless of race, will eventually be paid according to the job. By checking the wages paid in certain jobs along the curve against cost-of-living data, the company can make adjustments in the wages paid workers in all jobs in order to respond to inflationary trends. Finally, defined job categories allow the company to use private surveys by such consultants as Fine Spamer or Urwick International to compare their wages in certain job categories with those other companies are paying workers in similar categories.

Several companies have made or are making efforts to develop a unitary wage curve. Phillips Petroleum had not had a job grading system before but is now developing one. Union Carbide reports that it succeeded achieving a unitary wage scale at the end of 1978. Carlton Paper expects to be able to reach a unitary curve in 1979.

The wage gap--Despite successful efforts in the last four years to increase blacks' wages at a faster rate than that for whites, the gap between the average wages earned by the two sets of workers continues to grow. It is particularly severe between African and white workers and is likely to widen in the future.

The wages paid to African workers, according to Urwick's 1978 study, increased 119 percent between 1974 and 1978, while those going to whites went up 49 percent. Blacks' wages as a percentage of whites' also improved; in 1974 Africans' wages were equal to 37 percent of whites' compared with 54 percent in 1978. At the same time the discretionary income--that income not required to supply the essential requisites of daily life--of Africans rose faster than that of whites. Between 1974 and 1978 discretionary income for Africans went up 121 percent, and for whites, 67 percent. (Real discretionary income, after discounting for the increased cost of living, went up 71 percent for Africans, 17 percent for whites.) Urwick interpreted the increase in blacks' income "as a positive indication of a desire, at least on the part of the participating companies, to close the wage gap," and the survey's authors cited figures showing "a greater desire on the part of the international companies (surveyed) to close the gap" than on the part of local companies. Thirty-seven percent of the international companies responding planned increases in blacks' wages of more than 12.5 percent in the next year; only 20 percent of the South African companies participating in the survey said they had plans to make increases of the same magnitude.

Nevertheless, despite these efforts, 72 percent of the companies surveyed by Fine Spamer said they had a wage gap, and Urwick's study showed that the gap between the earnings of Africans and whites had gone from 218 rand a month in 1974 to 244 rand in 1978. The gap in discretionary income grew from 108 rand a month to 170 rand a month. That gap has grown more rapidly than the gap in average monthly wages because Africans are required to spend a greater proportion of their income on essentials, and the price inflation on essential consumer goods has been particularly high in the last four years.

There is a good deal of pessimism about how soon the wage gap can be closed. Few observers see the gap narrowing in the near future. Even companies that have made an end to the gap a specific objective say it will take time. Two-thirds of the companies responding to the Fine Spamer study stated it would take them at least three years to close the gap, and one-third of the respondents said it would take more than five years.

Affirmative action--The speed with which a company is able to close the wage gap through a policy of equal pay, training for more skilled positions and achieving a unitary wage scale may depend on the extent to which a company has a formal employment program. Formal programs in recruiting, selection, training and job evaluation contribute to a company's ability to promote and hire blacks for managerial and white collar positions. In some companies they have become part of a concerted effort to increase the numbers of blacks in the company. Several companies have developed specific manpower plans with hiring and promotion objectives designed to adjust the racial balance in the company. They have, in fact, adopted plans that resemble affirmative action plans in the United States.

The concept of an affirmative action program, reviewing manpower needs and designing the processes required to move increasing numbers of blacks into positions of increasing responsiblity, is relatively new to South Africa. Some companies argue against affirmative action programs. A Barlow Rand representative told IRRC that the company would have to change its basic management philosophy before it could endorse an affirmative action program. "It would be a change in the company's approach," he said, "to suddenly instruct subsidiaries on how to approach future manpower needs. It would not be Barlow's style." Other managers fear whites' resistance. An Afrox personnel director said his company could not afford to be seen pushing advancement of blacks. And some companies, such as ICI, say that "affirmative action would be discriminatory." Siemens argues that its policy is to develop the races separately, with each race supervising itself. "They understand each other best," a Siemens spokesman said.

Some companies said that in the wake of the recession they simply could not afford an affirmative action program. A Colgate official told IRRC in 1977 that the company "had no affirmative action program, per se." "It is difficult to come up with an affirmative action program," he said, "when we are preoccupied by how to preserve existing jobs."

But despite the reluctance of many companies to establish a formal affirmative action program, a number of companies have manpower plans that provide for increased numbers of black employees at higher skills and white collar jobs. Firestone's Peter Morum reports that by November 1980 the company expects to have 40 Africans in white collar positions. CPC says that more than 10 percent of its management should be black by 1980, and a consultant to Coca-Cola said that the company's work force should be 95 percent black by 1988. Borden reports that in the last 18 months the number of blacks as technicians, supervisors, professionals or managers has increased from 21 percent to 43 percent. "We are moving through specialized and on-the-job training programs to improve that record," James T. McCrory writes, "and to achieve our own target of 100 percent black operators and managers of our food plant in four years." Goodyear in 1976 established an operation "upgrade" designed to move Africans into positions held by whites. The original target was 56 positions by 1980; in 1977 the goal was raised to 64; and in 1978 the company expected to move Africans into 90 positions by 1980.

The ability of companies to reach these goals is affected by the effectiveness of their employment programs in training, selection and recruitment. In 1975, few American companies had formal training and selection procedures. Most companies continued to select employees on a relatively haphazard basis, or were at the early stages of developing recruiting programs. Unskilled workers were recruited, managers said, by selecting from the lines of workers standing outside the factory gate. The waiting list at some companies was long enough to fill expected vacancies for the next two years. Selection procedure often was minimal, limited to a short aptitude test and interview.

Since 1975 some companies have adopted formal procedures. At least one-third of the companies interviewed in 1978 had begun to recruit at black universities. Several had made contacts at the secondary school level, and more companies were participating in high school and university scholarship programs than in 1975. At the same time, many had adopted minimum education standards for workers, thus increasing the potential for future advancement within the company, and some were employing formal testing procedures to screen applicants.

Fringe benefits: Most companies say that they consider fringe benefits to employees--in health and education and through pensions, life insurance and charitable contributions--to be an important aspect of their personnel practices. They say they have made efforts to offer the same fringe benefits to all workers regardless of race. But some acknowledge that offering equal programs in South Africa may not always result in equal benefits. Customary or legal restrictions may inhibit or prevent full participation by blacks in some programs. Representatives of some companies say privately that the difficulties experienced by blacks in South Africa sometimes require a company to do more for its black workers than it does for whites in order to provide equal opportunity.

Some of the discrepancies between treatment of whites and blacks in practice are readily apparent. According to Urwick's 1977 survey, 92 percent of the companies surveyed provided retirement benefits to workers, and 25 percent of those said that their benefits were not equal for workers of all races. Every one of the companies provided medical assistance to whites; 54 percent provided assistance to Africans, Asians or coloreds; but of those 54 percent, one-quarter provided no medical assistance to their African employees.

Some companies justify a decision not to offer special benefits to blacks on the grounds that companies should avoid paternalism toward their employees. Thirty-five percent of the 81 companies responding to the initial Sullivan questionnaire indicated that they provide no assistance outside the workplace. Several managing directors told IRRC that although their companies had some benefit programs, they preferred to pay a good "clean" wage to the extent possible and leave to their employees decisions as to how their wages were to be spent.

International Harvester, for example, gives no educational assistance to employees because, according to the personnel director, the company would rather pay higher wages. "Paternalism is a failure," he told IRRC in November 1977; "we pay rate for the job." His remarks were similar to those made by Uniroyal in response to IRRC's 1978 questionnaire: "We do not lend assistance outside the work environment to any of our employees. Our policy on the uplifting of the non-white employees is to close the wage gap by granting increases at a considerably higher percentage than that granted to white employees."

But many observers say that as long as the political situation in South Africa remains unchanged, special fringe benefits are necessary both to ensure better opportunity for blacks and to increase the efficiency of the work force. Medical, legal, educational and health problems faced by blacks, particularly Africans, are different from those facing whites, and many observers argue that special fringe benefits for blacks are necessary to solve those problems.

Companies seeking to extend certain fringe-benefit programs to blacks continue to encounter certain difficulties. Until 1972, companies were not able to get private insurance firms to handle pension or medical insurance programs for Africans. "There were no actuarial tables for Africans," several managers said. Managing directors also said they have had difficulty in administering programs or getting Africans to participate. Several companies mentioned that they had encountered initial resistance to insurance policies because Africans feared that close relatives might kill them to take advantage of their life insurance. Others recounted difficulties in administering educational or medical programs for dependents of employees because the extended African family made identification of true dependents difficult.

Government regulations also have hindered companies' efforts in a few areas. For example, a company cannot obtain a license to run a bus service to provide transportation to employees.

Until recently, as mentioned earlier, government restrictions on ownership of property by Africans in white areas have prevented Africans from participating in company programs to assist employees through home-purchase loans. Some companies have also refused to make home-improvement loans to Africans because the Africans, unable to own their homes, have lacked collateral.

Lack of communication between management and workers has hurt the effectiveness of a number of company programs, particularly programs to provide education. In several instances, companies told IRRC that they had policies of providing educational aid to dependents of black employees. In discussions with black employees, though, it was apparent that they had little knowledge or understanding of the programs. Opportunities the company said existed were not known to the workers. Goodyear, for example, did a lengthy survey--including 90-minute interviews with 200 workers--to determine the effectiveness of its efforts to communicate the nature of its personnel programs to employees and to examine workers' concerns and needs. The company was surprised to find that both white and black workers were ill-informed about the company's programs. Sixty percent of its African workers did not understand who was eligible for its housing program, and 40 percent of the workers lacked a clear understanding of the company's training program. (It was worse for white workers, the personnel director told IRRC--62 percent of the white workers did not understand the training program.)

Medical benefits--By law, all companies with factory operations are required to have medical facilities for employees. Some companies make the clinics at their plants available to dependents of employees; others do not.

A number of companies argue that there is little need for company involvement in health care for Africans in addition to the clinic at the plant because they believe government-subsidized health programs provide adequate care for blacks. They argue that if they introduced a medical program for their African employees that would require those employees to contribute, the employees would not participate because they could get less expensive aid from the government clinics. Phillips Petroleum reports that black workers have turned down membership in medical programs on three occasions "on the basis that their costs for medical attention at a state hospital are extremely low."

Several companies, however, say that the government's program does not meet the health needs of blacks. In 1975, officials at ITT's then-subsidiary, Standard Telephones and Cables, reported that in the health clinic at their plant, of 1,148 blacks examined in the course of a year, 410 were treated for tuberculosis and 388 for venereal disease; of 6,967 whites examined, two were treated for TB, eight for VD. To limit blacks to the government medical program or to charge for participation in a private scheme, many companies say, is to discriminate against black workers in the lower wage levels. Burroughs's then-director Laurie Rushton said in 1975 that a company must provide better health benefits than the government and be "sensitive to blacks' desires to see their own physician." Not to provide assistance to blacks, Rushton said, would be like "forcing a white person to go to a clinic and wait half a day for service." To equalize opportunity, these companies say, companies should provide supplementary medical aid programs that blacks can afford. Phelps Dodge, for example, pays all medical, surgical and hospital services for black employees; Control Data has a non-white doctor who is available to attend employees in Soweto and supplies company transportation for visits to clinics and hospitals; and John Deere "has made arrangements with two white doctors to be on call and willing to go to the black township on request."

Some companies have started medical programs that are equivalent to those available to whites. According to Arthur D. Little's study of the Sullivan principles signers, 55 of 81 companies had equivalent programs. One can assume that those companies signing the principles are among the most progressive; the Urwick figures show fewer companies with equivalent programs, and the programs now operating are relatively recent. Standard Telephones and Cables claims that in 1975 it was "the first company in South Africa to negotiate and introduce a medical aid program for blacks along similar lines to that for white salaried employees." Other companies have instituted similar medical plans with private insurance companies. To ensure participation, the programs are made compulsory and in several cases the companies pay the full cost. If the program is not compulsory and the company does not pay the cost, companies said, few black workers participate.

Education benefits--Because education for Africans is neither free nor compulsory, a number of companies have made efforts to contribute to education of African employees, and, in some cases, their dependents. According to a 1978 Urwick International study, 83 percent of the companies surveyed gave some form of educational assistance to employees, and a number of companies gave aid to dependents of employees as well.

Thirty-nine of the companies responding to the initial Sullivan questionnaire said they subsidize schooling, 36 percent give tuition refunds, and 19 percent give bursaries or scholarships.

Among those companies giving assistance, the circumstances under which aid is given may vary considerably. Some companies stop aid at the primary school level; others only give aid in secondary school because that is where the highest proportion of dropouts occurs. Some offer university bursaries to promising students, others to all dependents of employees. Some prefer to give their education contributions directly to the school system and have participated in school construction projects. Companies may give a flat percentage--80 percent of total course costs--to cover education for employees. They may make their assistance in the form of a loan, or they may refuse to pay an employee who does not pass a course.

At a number of companies the participation of employees has been very small. At Schering Plough's facility only one of 50 black employees used the educational assistance program. A few, such as Caterpillar, have reported a much higher participation rate.

Pension and other benefits--Most companies say that pension plans, as well as provisions for vacation and sick leave, are the same for all workers, although this has not always been the case. General Electric, for example, wrote in a 1978 report that, "starting in 1979, pension plans within salaried and hourly paid categories will be equivalent, regardless of race."

Even if plans are equal, as with companies' medical and education programs, the existence of programs does not mean they are being used. Instability of African life may mean that large numbers of African workers are not able to work for one company long enough to gain significant benefit from a pension plan.

Charitable contributions--In the last several years, the new Urban Foundation--funded by corporate donations and with a goal of 25 million rand--has been a major focus of corporate contributions. In addition to grants from South African corporations, the foundation has received support from a number of American companies. Mobil has pledged $287,000 over the next five years, Caltex $287,000, Ford $575,000, Otis $287,000.

Participation in charitable contributions has grown more visible, if not actually larger, since the demonstrations in Soweto in 1976, but there has been no major change in companies' policies governing contributions. Although several companies have discussed the possibility of pegging their contributions to a level of earnings--2 percent--most argue that to do so could break the continuity of their programs should earnings fall. It also is likely, according to one knowledgeable observer, that most companies will not be willing to commit themselves to give away such a large portion of earnings.

How U.S. Companies Stack Up

For the last several years there has been debate over whether the labor practices of U.S. companies are any more progressive than those of other companies operating in South Africa. Many American companies have sought to defend their subsidiaries' activities there by arguing that American companies provide great opportunities for black workers and set an example in labor practices to be emulated by other companies. One U.S. manager commented somewhat sarcastically, "the Italians are about as interested in labor practices as are the Japanese."

At least one South African study says that American companies are better employers. Fine Spamer's 1978 report concludes that, "in general, companies with U.S. ties were ahead of the others in removing discriminatory work practices. South African companies tended to lag behind both U.S. and U.K. companies. However, the gap is sufficiently small to be closed quickly, given the will to do so." One black union leader told IRRC that U.S. companies were among the most progressive.

"The British companies," he commented, "are worse in their labor practices than the U.S. companies could ever hope to be."

But several analysts, including a number of managers of American companies in South Africa, take issue with this position. William Degenring of American Cyanamid commented to IRRC that "a lot of South African companies are a hell of a lot better than U.S. companies." South African managers know the situation better and are more committed to long-term prospects for their companies; American managers, some argue, are always looking on to their next post and thus take a short-term approach. Steve Pryke, executive director of the American Chamber of Commerce in Johannesburg, cautioned against reading too much into the Fine Spamer study. "It took the top 40 American companies," he said. A private survey by the American Chamber of 121 American companies showed that a number of companies still were having difficulties in setting an adequate minimum pay; at least three firms, he said, "were extremely bad."

In fact, an accurate comparison of companies in South Africa is extremely difficult. The performances of individual companies differ both from company to company and industry to industry, affected by myriad factors of which nationality of ownership is only one. Analysts have tried to determine whether nationality in management affects performance, but increasingly American companies are being managed by South Africans, and interest in labor practices is apt to vary more according to personality and to home office pressure than it does by nationality.

The greatest outside pressures on companies in South Africa have come from the United States. The pressures are being brought on home offices by stockholders and other critics and, in turn, passed on to subsidiary managers in South Africa. The pressures in western Europe or Japan, occasionally pushed by unions or by government, have been neither as severe nor as sustained, nor have they succeeded in enlisting the collective corporate response that pressures have in the United States. The Sullivan principles reflect a collective corporate recognition of pressures and, at the same time, provide a framework for further pressures. The result has been, at least in the short term, a set of emerging trends that show some differentiation of company performance by nationality.

A major difference between American companies and their non-American counterparts has been their response to the codes of conduct. Where many European companies have tended to view the EEC code as an unwarranted effort by government to interfere in their activities in South Africa, American companies, by and large, and sometimes reluctantly, have agreed to endorse the Sullivan principles. The South African subsidiaries of American companies, unlike the subsidiaries of European companies, have frequently heard from their home offices on the need to develop guidelines and programs for implementing the principles. There have been exceptions, of course, among both sets of companies. A number of American companies have yet to endorse the principles, some home offices have signed but done little to enforce them, and a few subsidiaries take a position like that of one representative that the principles were the home office's doing, not the subsidiary's.

At the same time, subsidiaries of Rank Xerox, ICL, Unilever,

Barclays and a number of other European companies have been encouraged by their home offices to take steps to develop more progressive practices. More British companies have recognized African unions than have their American counterparts. Anglo American, South African Breweries (an Anglo subsidiary), Barlow Rand, AngloVaal and other South African companies have taken steps to encourage development of better employment practices. Surveys show that South African companies are more likely to make worker evaluations and to define job categories than are foreign companies. Nevertheless, efforts taken under the Sullivan code have had a visible impact on some companies' performance, affecting the practices of many of the signers and to a lesser extent affecting the approaches of managers in other companies. Two areas in which the performance of American companies has differed from that of others are affirmative action and desegregation of facilities. Both are areas in which the somewhat unique American experience has had a particular meaning for many American companies.

A number of European managers and several South Africans commented to IRRC on what they saw as the relative irrelevance of efforts to desegregate facilities. In general, American companies had made greater efforts to desegregate, and their European and South African counterparts said that they saw such efforts as a low priority. They did not understand, they said, why it mattered who used which toilets, and one manager told IRRC that Africans were perfectly happy with facilities that were separate as long as they were equal. A Barlow representative commented that without the American example, the company would not have moved to desegregate its facilities when it did.

Similarly, some managing directors of South African and European companies hesitate to accept the concept of affirmative action. Ken Maud, a director of Altech, described affirmative action as an American phenomenon, and as such, he said, it had a low priority in the company. The managing director of Philips told IRRC that "affirmative action and the inclination to quantify changes is foreign to our European minds," and General Mining, an Afrikaans-speaking mining house, opposes the idea of quotas, designating job slots for blacks, or establishing affirmative action programs that might appear to encourage reverse discrimination.

American experience with desegregation and affirmative action programs, therefore, makes it likely that American subsidiaries in South Africa will be more responsive in these areas than their counterparts. It does not ensure, however, that American companies across the board will suddenly adopt practices that are models for the rest of South Africa's business society. Many companies in the United States have had difficulties with affirmative action. It is unrealistic to think that similar difficulties do not exist in South Africa. The U.S. experience creates a predisposition toward progress along these lines, but it does not guarantee it. What it means is that the more progressive American companies may move more quickly to institute changes in areas that are less immediately visible to non-American managers. The bulk of American companies, however, may well stay just about where the rest of the companies are in South Africa, adopting changes as they seem necessary and feasible.

Chapter V Sources

Books

Desaix Myers III, Labor Practices of U.S. Corporations in South Africa, Praeger Publishers, New York, 1977.

Articles

Financial Mail:

> "Pauleus--how we struck gold," July 25, 1975, p. 309.
> "The awakening giant," July 28, 1978, p. 304.
> "TUCSA: looking blackwards," Sept. 22, 1978, p. 1059.

Other:

William McWhirter, "America's South African Dilemma," Time, Sept. 18, 1978.

Herman Nickle, "The case for doing business in South Africa," Fortune, June 19, 1978.

Roger M. Williams, "American business should stay in South Africa," Saturday Review, Sept. 30, 1978.

Reports

Fine Spamer Associates, "1978, 1979 Report on Asiatic, Black, Colored Advancement in South Africa," op. cit.

Arthur D. Little, "First Report on the Signatory Companies to the Sullivan Principles," Cambridge, Mass., November 1978.

> "Second Report on the Signatory Companies to the Sullivan Principles, April 2, 1979.

> "Third Report on the Signatory Companies to the Sullivan Principles, October 15, 1979.

J.F. Potgeiter, "The Household Subsistence Level in the Major Urban Centres of the Republic of South Africa, April 1979," Fact Paper No. 30, University of Port Elizabeth Institute for Planning Research, May 1979.

Government Reports

United Kingdom:

> "Code of Conduct for Companies with Interests in South Africa," Department of Trade, Press Notice, February 15, 1979.

VI. THE CONTROVERSY OVER SANCTIONS
AGAINST SOUTH AFRICA

Critics of apartheid have talked of some form of international economic sanctions against South Africa since the early 1960s. The UN Security Council in 1963 adopted a resolution calling for a voluntary embargo on military arms sales to South Africa. The Security Council made the embargo mandatory following the death of Steve Biko and the bannings and arrests of Oct. 19, 1977.

Some countries have also taken unilateral steps affecting their commercial ties with South Africa. In November 1973 the Arab members of OPEC—at the request of the Organization for African Unity--placed an embargo on all oil sales to South Africa. The United States has restricted the availability of Export-Import Bank facilities to South Africa. In 1976 it adopted a policy limiting sales of computers to South African government departments and public agencies, and it 1978 it adopted a policy designed to curb sales to the South African police and military. In 1977 Canada withdrew its commercial consuls from South Africa and ended the availability of its Export Development Corp. facilities for sales to the government in South Africa. The Swedish government in 1979 introduced a bill requiring an end to all new investment in South Africa--including reinvestment of earnings as well as new capital flows from Sweden--which is likely to pass.

Demand for further actions against South Africa continue. In early 1979, the UN General Assembly adopted 15 resolutions affecting South Africa, including a call for an oil embargo, a ban on trade and foreign investment, an end to credits from the International Monetary Fund, and full economic sanctions. The resolutions are not binding unless adopted by the UN Security Council, but if negotiations on a settlement in Namibia continue to stall or if South Africa is seen to be impeding a resolution of the conflict in Rhodesia, it is likely that the Security Council will consider action on these or similar proposals.

Economic sanctions against South Africa continue to be an important aspect of public campaigns in the United States to force changes in the government's political policies. Many students are pressing universities to sell their stock in companies doing business in South Africa as the first step toward economic withdrawal; church groups, students, some unions, and several members of Congress are supporting a campaign to end bank loans to South Africa; and in 1978 public pressures led Congress to put new limitations on Export-Import Bank services to South Africa.

The aims of the advocates of economic sanctions vary. Some State Department officials see a limit on trade or investment as a means of restricting U.S. involvement with the South African government and its policies and of demonstrating sympathy for the concerns of the black-ruled states in Africa. One U.S. objective in limiting sales to the military and police, according to State Department spokesmen, is to prevent exports that would increase the operational capacity of South Africa's military or police. Restrictions on sales or investment may be seen as either punitive or persuasive. By temporarily withdrawing its commercial attache from Johannesburg in 1977, the United States was signaling displeasure with the South African government's actions against the black consciousness movement. Moves in Congress to tie investment to implementation of the Sullivan principles or campaigns by members of the public to persuade banks to curtail loans until the South African government ends apartheid are aimed at persuading the government to change its policies. Some restrictions, such as those imposed on computer sales in 1976 by the United States, may be largely an effort to put U.S. policy in a favorable light in the rest of Africa rather than a real attempt to deny technology to the South African government. And some campaigns, such as the efforts to force divestiture of stock in companies active in South Africa, may be undertaken as much in an attempt to make a moral statement as to effect change in South Africa.

White South African Attitudes Toward Economic Sanctions

Political rhetoric: Responding to years of threats by members of the United Nations, the South African government has developed an approach on several levels to the possibility that foreign capital or technology will be curtailed. On the surface, the government has denied the effectiveness of the threat. It has made it a political issue, using it to rally support for National Party policies and to create the image of a nation under siege, beleaguered by external powers that neither understand nor care about South Africa. At the height of talk about economic sanctions, following the death of Steve Biko and the arrests and bannings of October 1977, former Prime Minister Vorster accused the United States of attempting to "strangle South Africa with finesse." In the heat of a parliamentary campaign shortly thereafter, Foreign Affairs Minister Roelof Botha accused the United States of being a worse enemy of South Africa than the Soviet Union. National Party politicians railed against what they saw as the hypocrisy of the West, and Prime Minister Vorster challenged South Africa's critics to "do their damndest." South Africa, he said, would survive.

The political rhetoric of the fall of 1977 was most effective. The National Party won 66 percent of the popular vote and 135 of 165 seats in parliament, its greatest victory since it came to power in 1948. And the polarization of its position--South Africa against the outside world--led many South Africans to believe that sanctions were inevitable. They looked at the Rhodesian experience, assessed their resources, and argued that there was little to fear. One prominent government official told IRRC that white South Africans would "ride bicycles and eat mealie pap" (a staple food among rural Africans) before they would give in to economic pressures that would force them to adopt the one-man, one-vote policy suggested by Vice President Walter Mondale in a meeting with Vorster in Vienna in early 1977. He said it was unlikely that sanctions would require such a drastic change in living style, however, and argued that, in fact, the country not only could make it alone, but it would benefit from sanctions.

A number of business analysts accepted the position that, at least in the short term, sanctions could help rather than harm South Africa. Professor Arndt Spandau of the University of Witwatersrand Business School argued that in the short to medium term sanctions could be a boon, allowing for an "exuberant phase" of import substitution.

A.P.J. Burger, president of the Afrikaanse Handelsinstituut (AHI), the Afrikaans-speaking chamber of commerce, admitted that sanctions would have a detrimental impact in the long term, but argued that they would act as a spur to local manufacturers. A 1977 study by the Federated Chamber of Industries, AHI, and the Steel and Engineering Industries Federation reported that South Africa had an import substitution potential of some $1.65 billion annually--equal to 25 percent of South African's merchandise import bill.

Moves to anticipate sanctions: Despite such reassurance, however, there is evidence that the government has developed some protections against the threat of sanctions. The South African Department of Industries set aside nearly $9 million in 1975, $25 million in 1976 and $11.5 million in 1977 for assistance to companies stockpiling under the National Supplies Procurement Act. To those stockpiling goods enumerated in the act, the government provides low-interest loans for inventories and subsidies on bank loans. The government in 1977 wrote to businesses in what it considers strategic areas, suggesting that they increase their inventories. "If any businessman reckons he handles a strategic product," one government official told the Financial Mail, "it's worth his while to contact us." A number of local analysts estimate that South Africa has about three years of oil stocks stored in abandoned coal mines in the northern Transvaal at current rates of consumption. Besides oil, the Financial Mail reported in December 1977, "the products being stored with financial backing from the government include chemicals, machine parts, aircraft spares and special stock."

In addition, government and business have supported a program to encourage South African consumers to "buy South African." Finance Minister Owen Horwood told the public in September 1978 that "it should be the duty of all of us--manufacturers, dealers and consumers alike--to buy and to use competitive South African products." The government has long had a policy of encouraging the use of local content in motor vehicle manufacture. Since 1969, the government has mandated that an ever increasing portion of the content of each automobile manufactured in South Africa be produced there. The local content stipulation has grown from 12 percent in 1960 to 66 percent in 1976. Local content provisions will be extended to light trucks in 1980, and the government announced in November 1978 that it planned to construct a $300-million diesel engine plant to promote South Africa's self-sufficiency in truck manufacture.

Perhaps the most important move the government has taken to protect itself against sanctions is the construction, through the government-owned South African Coal, Gas and Oil Corp. (Sasol), of a plant to synthesize oil from South Africa's vast coal reserves. The first Sasol plant produces an estimated 4,500-5,000 barrels per day of petroleum distillate, equal to about 1.5 percent of South Africa's total oil requirements. A second $3- to $3.5-billion plant, capable of producing about 45,000 barrels per day, is scheduled to be completed by 1980; some experts estimate it will satisfy up to 25 percent of South Africa's oil demand, although this figure is disputed. Following the revolution in Iran, the South African government announced in February 1979 its intention to expand the Sasol project, constructing a third plant, doubling the project's capacity at a cost of nearly $4 billion. Analysts estimate that by 1982-83, South Africa's coal-to-oil plants will supply 30 to 40 percent of the country's oil demand.

Although significant, the government's moves to anticipate sanctions have been limited. "As the government sees it," one official told IRRC, "sanctions are a business risk, and business will have to weigh the risk and react to it for itself." The government may assist through its stockpiling program, but it has neither issued guidelines to business nor taken any actions to force companies to prepare for sanctions. A risk almost as great as sanctions, one economist argued, was that the threat of sanctions might lead the government to make decisions that would misallocate scarce resources; making non-productive expenditures on defense, public relations, security or building up inventory, he said, could have a serious impact on the pace of real growth in South Africa.

Many businessmen in South Africa recognize the relationship between foreign capital and technology and growth. They argue that any thesis that sanctions will assist South African industry is painfully short-sighted. Some business officials have urged changes in the political system to encourage new capital flows, but many remain on the sidelines, hoping that as the economy picks up, foreign investors will return on their own.

U.S. Government Policy on South African Sales and Investment

State Department officials state that the U.S. government's policy is to encourage South Africans to work for "a society in which there could be full rights, justice and political participation for all of her people." The department says that to obtain this objective, it continues to follow the "even-handed" policy of the Nixon and Ford administrations, putting some pressures on the South African government, but closing few doors. The policy is one of encouraging gradual change, not major confrontation. Investment in South Africa by U.S. corporations is neither encouraged nor discouraged. U.S. opposition to apartheid is made clear, and U.S. investors are urged to become forces for change by taking steps to help their non-white employees.

Restrictions on sales: At the same time, the administration has said that the wide range of relations between South Africa and the United States is under review. Secretary of State Cyrus Vance reported in 1978 that the U.S. government "had made clear to the South African government that a failure to make genuine progress toward an end to racial discrimination and full political participation for all South African citizens can only have an increasingly adverse impact on our relations." Immediately following Jimmy Carter's election in November 1976, the Commerce Department instituted a policy to restrict sales of computers and computer technology to the South African military and police, as well as to government agencies handling African affairs and atomic energy. All companies with general distribution licenses for computer sales to South Africa were informed that future sales to these agencies would require a validated license. A general license allows exports without prior approval on each individual sale; a validated license requires assurances on each export that the item exported will not be diverted to an unauthorized destination. The effect of this change in policy--which was never published as an official regulation--has been to end sales of all computers and computer-related items to these agencies.

The administration has sought since November 1977 to ensure, in the words of one official, "that the United States should act in no way to increase the operational capacity of the South African military and police." Responding to South Africa's arrests and bannings in October 1977, the Commerce Department issued regulations in February 1978 designed to curb sales of products and technology to the South African police and military.

The Feb. 16, 1978, regulations are intended "to strengthen United Nations Security Council Resolutions of 1963 and 1977 regarding exports of arms and munitions to South Africa." The 1977 resolution imposed a mandatory embargo on arms sales to South Africa. The intent of the new restrictions is to tighten up on "grey area" sales to South Africa. "Grey area" items encompass materials of a non-military nature that could be converted on short notice to military or police use such as light airplanes, specialized computer systems, certain electronic components and strategic spare parts.

The regulations require purchasers of U.S. exports to certify that goods purchased will not be sold or used in any way by the military or the police. The regulations also state: "Parts, components, materials and other commodities exported from the United States may not be used abroad to manufacture or produce foreign-made end products where it is known...the end products will be sold or used by military or police entities" in South Africa and Namibia. Finally, the Commerce Department has placed restrictions on the transfer of certain types of technical data that could be used in a strategic manner by the South African government. "Beyond these measures," a State Department representative told IRRC, "it is not the intention of the regulations to hold American firms responsible for actions over which they have no control and of which they are unaware."

The new regulations represented the first time the United States had chosen to apply controls to all goods that might be used by specific institutions in a foreign country, regardless of the nature of the goods and their possible uses. A Commerce Department official explained that this "literally means anything as trivial as paper clips or toilet paper that might be destined for use by the military or police" is prohibited. He admitted that enforcement of the regulations is somewhat subjective and requires a good faith effort on the part of the companies. Officials at the Commerce Department say that they have rejected some 25 applications for sales to the South African military and police since the embargo took effect. The rejections involved more than $9 million.

In September 1978, the Office of Export Administration of the Department of Commerce, the agency responsible for enforcement, issued a bulletin which defined the entities to be considered police and military as including municipal and provincial traffic inspectors, members of the Bureau of State Security, the South African Railways Police Force and Armscor (the Armaments Development and Production Corp.). The Office of Export Administration has received a number of inquiries from companies as to application of the regulations and some requests for exemptions. Pharmaceutical suppliers, for example, who are obligated to sell through a central supplies office administered by the Minister of Defense to private hospitals, requested exemptions. Goodyear and General Tire also asked for exemptions or clarifications.

A major unresolved question is the degree to which companies should be expected to try to prevent sales of U.S. technology from their European or other subsidiaries located outside the United States to their

South African subsidiaries. In a Dec. 26, 1978, letter to James G. Lubetkin of Oberlin College, Lewis Macfarlane, acting director of Southern African affairs in the State Department, wrote, "Existing U.S. statutes do not control the sale of non-U.S.-origin commodities and technical data by overseas subsidiaries of U.S. corporations to the South African police and military. Such sales have the effect of lessening the impact of what U.S. policy seeks to accomplish--keeping essential goods and services from the South African military and police. While not a violation of U.S. law, such sales run counter to the policy objectives of the United States." A second State Department official qualified Macfarlane's letter, however, describing it as "an opinion about the impact of auto company sales," part of the department's factional debate and not an authoritative departmental policy statement. And in a subsequent letter to Oberlin, Macfarlane amended his interpretation of U.S. policy to say that the objective of the regulations was "to prevent exports of U.S. origin goods to the South African military and police." He went on to say that "in view of the fact that the United States has not made it a policy objective to keep essential goods and services from reaching the South African military and police, and that such sales from overseas subsidiaries of U.S. corporations and from non-U.S. corporations are not affected by U.S. law, I believe that my statement that 'such sales run counter to the policy objective of the United States' may have been misleading." A State Department official told IRRC that the second Macfarlane letter is the "standing interpretation" of the regulations.

This interchange demonstrates the limited nature of the steps the administration has taken to date to affect its relations with South Africa. It has consistently opposed more drastic steps--such as those suggested in three bills introduced in Congress in 1978--that would have curtailed loans or investment in South Africa or made them contingent on following equal employment practices. Administration representatives testified before the House Subcommittee on Africa in 1978 that legislation restricting investment in South Africa would be untimely, would limit U.S. ability to negotiate with South Africa on issues of mutual concern--specifically Rhodesia and Namibia--and would be ineffective. C. Fred Bergsten, Assistant Secretary of the Treasury for International Affairs, said passage of the bills would be "contrary to the national interest." Implementation of the legislation, he said, "would be difficult and burdensome on both the government and business firms in the United States." Moreover, "such action could provoke retaliatory actions by the government of South Africa that could be harmful to U.S. economic interests." And, he concluded, political restrictions on investment run counter to U.S. policy on foreign investment worldwide.

Despite administration opposition, legislation was enacted in 1978 prohibiting the Export-Import Bank from extending credit for any export that would contribute to the maintenance of apartheid by the South African government. In addition, the legislation prohibits the bank from extending credit to the government of South Africa for any other export unless the President determines that it has made significant progress toward the elimination of apartheid and transmits this finding to Congress in writing. It also prohibits the bank from extending export credits to private purchasers in South Africa unless the Secretary of State certifies that the purchaser has endorsed the Sullivan principles.

Implementation of this legislation has posed difficulties to the administration, and the State Department has failed, thus far, to provide guidance on the regulations that must be drawn up to enforce it. Its failure to do so has had, on its own, the effect of restricting Eximbank facilities--no Eximbank loans or credits have been approved since the law was passed.

A positive view of investment: Collectively, the positions taken by the administration during the last two years reflect what William Raiford, formerly of the Congressional Research Service, described as "a preference for the maintenance of a normal business relationship with South Africa." Members of the administration have consistently expressed a belief in the relevance of the "Atlanta experience" to the situation in South Africa. Then-UN Ambassador Andrew Young described that experience in a speech to South African businessmen in May 1977: "When in Atlanta, Ga., five banks decided that it was bad for business to have racial turmoil, racial turmoil ceased." Similarly, in Birmingham, he said, "100 businesses negotiated an end of apartheid, in spite of the fact that on the books of law it was still illegal to desegregate anything." His speech emphasized his belief that "change can come through the marketplace."

The belief that companies can play a useful and active role in South Africa is one that has been expressed by President Carter as well. In an interview with the Financial Mail, in November 1976, then President-elect Carter said he thought that economic sanctions could be counterproductive, and that "the weight of our investments there, the value South Africans place on access to American capital and technology can be used as a positive force in settling regional problems." The administration has supported the endorsement of the Sullivan principles by U.S. companies, although it has not gone so far as to make them mandatory. In a statement to institutional investors in March 1979, Richard Moose, Assistant Secretary for African Affairs, said, "No initiative to date has had as much influence as the Sullivan principles....We believe the Sullivan effort merits our support as a potentially major force for change in South Africa."

Factors Working Against Sanctions

The U.S. policy on economic sanctions against South Africa, like that of most of South Africa's major trading partners, is affected by a number of factors perceived as relating to national self-interest. The administration representatives opposing restrictive legislation in 1978 testified that prohibiting investment in South Africa would be ineffective and untimely. They saw sanctions as having, on balance, greater costs than benefits. There are several factors affecting the balance--the cost of sanctions to the United States and its allies; attitudes of Americans toward South Africa; public willingness to accept economic costs for political objectives; the question of whether any action taken by the United States would win support among its allies (especially the United Kingdom because of the size of its interests in South Africa); and, finally, the issue of whether sanctions would produce the intended results in South Africa.

Cost of sanctions abroad: The immediate cost of sanctions depends on their nature, their length and the degree to which the South African government wishes to or is able to retaliate. Economic sanctions could take a variety of forms, focusing on trade, on loans or on direct investment. Countries could restrict landing rights for South African planes or docking rights for ships; could place an embargo on the importation of South African goods; or could prohibit exports to South Africa. The embargo on imports or ban on exports could be limited to specific items. Rep. Charles Rangel (D-N.Y.) has introduced a bill to prohibit imports of South African coal, and members of the United Nations have recommended a ban on the sale of oil to South Africa. Or it could be limited to certain types of equipment, such as arms, or to certain purchasers such as the South African police or military.

Trade bans such as the existing Commerce Department regulations have distinct and often measurable costs to businesses with operations in South Africa. General Tire & Rubber says it has been forced to suspend indefinitely, at a cost of about $1 million a year, its technical agreement with a local South African firm because the firm sells some tires made with General Tire technology to the South African government for military and police vehicles. Burroughs reported that export licenses for two orders totaling more than $2 million were refused the company, and Hewlett-Packard reported a loss of about $1 million a year because of Commerce Department regulations. In a letter to Commerce Department Secretary Juanita Kreps, the American Chamber of Commerce in South Africa wrote in 1979 that the regulations cost U.S. exports and local manufacture of $75 million in 1978 and $100 million in 1979.

The cost of broader sanctions would be far greater, of course. U.S. imports from South Africa in 1978 were valued at $2.3 billion, equal to about 1.3 percent of total U.S. imports. U.S. direct investment in 1978 amounted to $1.8 billion, and indirect investment through securities and bank loans was about $3.9 billion. Exactly what proportion of U.S. trade, investment or loans would be affected would depend on the extent of the sanctions and on the South African government's response. Should the United States decide to ban new investment, for example, the South African government could refuse to allow repatriation of dividends and interest from existing investment. In the short term, at least, the result would be a net gain for South Africa's balance of payments. In 1976 and 1977, American companies in South Africa repatriated $126 million and $103 million, respectively, in interest and dividends; reinvested profits came to $71 million and $94 million in each of those years, respectively, while only $13 and $34 million in new investment was made from sources outside of South Africa.

The minerals question--Similarly, should the United States ban future loans to South Africa, the South African government could order a hold on repayment of interest and principal for existing loans. And a ban on exports to South Africa could lead South Africa to withhold scarce minerals from the world market. (Some analysts, however, discount this possibility in light of South Africa's heavy demand for the foreign exchange earned by mineral exports, but South Africa could withhold a strategic mineral--manganese, chrome or platinum, for example--without drastically affecting its balance of payments. Although important collectively to South Africa's exports total, these minerals individually represent a relatively minor portion of total exports.)

The United States buys only 5 percent of its total mineral imports from South Africa, but a substantial portion of what are termed strategic minerals are of South African origin. South Africa now supplies between 40 and 50 percent of American imports of chrome, ferrochrome, ferromanganese and platinum. It provides 56 percent of U.S. vanadium imports. Of these, chrome appears to be of critical importance to the West. Alternative sources of platinum, manganese and vanadium exist in the United States and in Canada and could be developed with a lead time of two to three years under extreme conditions to replace South African supplies. The United States maintains a stockpile of chrome large enough to cover eight years of South African supply. A settlement of the conflict in Rhodesia that allowed access to Rhodesian chrome could reduce substantially U.S. dependence on South African chrome.

Attitudes in the United States: The willingness of U.S. policy-makers to accept the costs that could result from sanctions against South Africa is greatly affected by their perception of public attitudes toward the situation there. A Louis Harris poll taken in 1978--and largely confirmed by the findings of a subsequent poll in 1979 done by the Carnegie Endowment for International Peace--found that by a nearly two-to-one margin--46 percent to 26 percent--Americans thought that the United States and other countries should put pressure on South Africa to provide blacks greater freedom and participation in government. More than half of those interviewed--51 percent versus 24 percent--supported a halt to arms sales; they favored--46 percent to 28 percent--U.S. companies putting pressure on the South African government; and they supported preventing new investment by 42 to 33 percent. They rejected, however, a halt to operations of U.S. companies in South Africa (51 to 21 percent) and opposed any military action against South Africa (73 to 7 percent).

For most Americans, South Africa is an issue of marginal importance. Analyzing the Harris Poll data, Deborah Durfee Barron and John Immerwahr wrote in the January/February issue of Public Opinion that, "almost any question asked about South Africa will evoke a response of 20 to 25 percent 'don't knows,' and the 'don't know' response is only the visible part of the iceberg," Barron and Immerwahr say. "It is deceptively low since many people are reluctant to say 'I don't know.' They answer questions even when they have no firm opinion about the matter." Barron and Immerwahr argue that much of U.S. opinion is probably not firmly entrenched and is likely to be shaped by a desire for noninvolvement that is a lingering effect of Vietnam, by fear of communism and by a cautious concern for human rights. The conflicting pull of these themes tends to make attitudes toward the American foreign policy in southern Africa unstable but, Barron and Immerwahr argue, it imposes certain limits on any administration in formulating foreign policy. The public is likely to oppose a purely cynical policy of economic self-interest, yet it is unwilling to make real economic sacrifice to force possible change in South Africa. Without substantial change in public attitudes, policy-makers will be hesitant to advocate greater involvement in South Africa. Attitudes could change, however, as events in Rhodesia and Namibia unfold and as pressures mount within South Africa. Whether they will become more or less favorable to a stronger U.S. position on South Africa remains to be seen.

Attitudes of South Africa's other trading partners: The effectiveness of any major economic action that the United States might take against

South Africa would depend in part on the stance of South Africa's major trading partners in Europe and Japan. This is not to say that the United States cannot act unilaterally. It has done so twice--placing stricter licensing controls on computer sales and limiting sales to the military and police. But the goal of these moves was to ensure that American companies were not participating in the sales and to send a message of discontent to South Africa; they were not efforts to cut off the entire supply of these products to the South Africans. Any effort that seeks to do more--by denying South Africa access to certain products or markets or by damaging the South African economy--will require a certain amount of collaboration between South Africa's trading partners.

One factor inhibiting joint action against South Africa is that although its major trading partners--in the EEC, the United States and Japan--may share similar concerns about the situation there, they have different interests, pressures and perspectives. Few countries besides the United States and the United Kingdom have experienced widespread public pressure on corporations doing business in South Africa. The exceptions are countries such as Sweden and Denmark with relatively little financial stake in South Africa that can afford to take strong stands along the lines of Sweden's proposal to end new South African investment. Countries such as West Germany, France and Italy, with little public agitation over corporate ties to South Africa, can accept the EEC code in principle without strong compulsion to introduce rigid enforcement. Relying on South Africa as an important supplier of strategic minerals, and lacking the stockpiles that exist in the United States, few European countries are anxious to take steps against South Africa that might interrupt supply, and most are hesitant to jeopardize what has been a small but nevertheless important export market.

For the United Kingdom the situation is particularly complex. The United Kingdom's relationship with South Africa is unique. Its lengthy historical relationship with that country has produced ties of "kith and kin" that greatly intensify the debate over Britain's role there. The depth of Britain's economic involvement encourages critics of apartheid to press for its use as a lever for change. In response, business representatives and government officials argue that it is exactly the depth of British involvement in South Africa that makes the use of economic sanctions difficult and costly, if not impossible. About 40 percent of South Africa's white population is English speaking. Until 1961 South Africa was a member of the British Commonwealth, and a significant proportion of South Africa's English speakers hold British passports (more than 300,000), have gone to school in England, and continue to maintain close ties with the United Kingdom. These ties are strengthened by the enormous commerce between the two nations. According to the United Kingdom-South Africa Trade Association, British direct investment in South Africa is currently about $6.8 billion--equal to about 10 percent of the United Kingdom's total direct investment abroad. Its indirect investment is an additional $5.1 billion, and the total accounts for about 55 percent of all foreign investment in South Africa.

Britain's earnings from South Africa are substantial. Earnings from exports to South Africa amount to $1.28 billion; income from invisible earnings--investment income, insurance services, dividends, shipping--is about $1.7 billion. Britain earns an additional $501 million from re-export sales--sales of goods like diamonds imported from South Africa and later sold outside Britain. The United Kingdom's imports from South Africa in 1978 were $1.45 billion, much of which was minerals and metals.

For Great Britain, the consequences of a trade boycott against South Africa would be severe. South Africa is the purchaser of miscellaneous inorganic chemicals, electrical power machinery and switching gear, and telecommunications equipment. According to a study done by Lawrence Franco for the Carnegie Endowment for International Peace, South Africa is the second largest buyer of metal-working machinery and motor vehicles from Britain. Trade with and investment in South Africa accounts for more that 2.3 percent of British GNP, Franco estimates, adding that the figure is "almost certainly an underestimate." By comparison, business with South Africa accounts for 0.24 percent of U.S. GNP, according to Franco, and only in woven textiles is South Africa as high as the third largest buyer of American goods. In few product areas does South Africa provide more than 1 percent of the U.S. market. For the United Kingdom, on the other hand, South Africa represents between 6 and 9 percent of the market in nine sectors. (See chart, Appendix G)

At the same time, Britain depends heavily on imports, particularly minerals and metals from South Africa. More than 60 percent of Britain's chrome, 59 percent of its manganese and 50 percent of its platinum comes from South Africa. The United Kingdom-South Africa Trade Association estimates that an end to imports from South Africa could close a number of manufacturing operations in the country--costing British workers as many as 180,000 jobs.

The importance of South Africa to the British economy is great enough to make economic sanctions an unattractive option. Few politicians are interested in accepting the political risks inherent in supporting an embargo on trade with South Africa and the new conservative government has opposed such an action. Despite the strength of the anti-apartheid groups in London and some union opposition to continued trade with South Africa, support for stronger economic action against South Africa is unlikely to grow substantially unless prompted by dramatic developments in southern Africa or by mounting pressures from Arab and African states.

The black African nation factor--In the last several years, there have been stirrings of African pressures on British companies that do business in South Africa. Nigeria has taken the lead among African countries. Its foreign minister said in November 1977 that "an all-embracing package of economic sanctions against South Africa is essential....Any positive action in the right direction must include the cessation of new loans and investments and the progressive dismantling of existing ones." The same year, Nigeria established an Economic Intelligence Unit to review the activities of companies doing business in Nigeria that also operated in South Africa. The periodical Business Europe said in 1978 that companies entering into agreements in Nigeria have been required to sign a statement that they have no business in South Africa. No American company has reported actions against its operations because of South African involvement, but the Nigerian government moved in 1978 to withdraw public sector deposits from Barclay's Bank and to force a repatriation of Barclay's British employees in Nigeria in response to a bank statement that it intended to continue business in South Africa.

Nigeria's posture could influence British policy in the future or even that of the United States, which is a major importer of Nigerian oil. Britain's exports to Nigeria are now nearly double those to South Africa, and in 1978 Britain's Under Secretary of State for Trade, Michael Meacher, told Parliament, "I am sure that most companies will draw their own conclusions from recent events; South Africa is likely to be an increasingly risky proposition."

But for now, South Africa continues to be a critical trading partner. Responding to a confidential survey conducted by the Department of Trade and Industry in 1978, most British companies said that they considered their business ties with South Africa more important than those with the rest of Africa, and they reported that they thought South Africa offered greater potential. Any threat to business in South Africa would bring the corporate lobbyists out of the woodwork, one British government official told IRRC in 1978. "They would lobby as they have never lobbied before."

Impact of Sanctions

The economic consequences of sanctions against South Africa depend on the form the sanctions take. A curtailment of new investment, the withdrawal of old investment, an end to bank loans and an embargo on trade have all been mentioned as types of sanctions that might be applied. The effectiveness of each would differ. Most analysts agree that investment sanctions or withdrawal would be likely to have far less impact on the economy than a trade embargo, but there is considerable debate over how pressures on South Africa's economy will be translated into political change.

Withdrawal: The debate over withdrawal often overlooks the mechanics involved that would severely limit its real impact on the South African economy. It is simply not possible for a company to pick up its plant, put it on a freighter and ship it home. The government instituted strict foreign exchange controls after the mounting flight of capital in the early 1960s that was touched off by Sharpeville. If an American company with a subsidiary operation in South Africa decides to withdraw from that country, it can follow one of three courses of action:

• It can sell its South African operations to another investor in return for non-South African cash or equities.

• It can sell its holding to a South African investor in return for local currency, and then repatriate the sales proceeds in accordance with certain procedures required by the South African government.

• It can follow a strategy of scaling down its South African investment, repatriating abroad all profits earned after Jan. 1, 1975, and repairing old machinery without replacing it, until its assets are so small that they can be abandoned and written off.

The sale of foreign-owned assets in South Africa to another foreign company may be conducted freely without interference from the South African government. This would allow an American company to extricate itself from South Africa but would have no real economic impact on South Africa; South Africa's level of foreign exchange would remain the same.

The other two processes for disinvestment--sale to a local investor and scaling down--are subject to foreign exchange control regulations and, possibly, to the National Supplies Procurement Act as well. Foreign exchange regulations make it virtually impossible for a company to repatriate assets invested before February 1979 without accepting a loss of close to 30 percent; the rand earned from the sale of assets can be exchanged for dollars only at a discounted rate. An alternative is to invest earnings from the sale of assets in government or non-resident bonds for a period of five years, after which time they can be redeemed at full value plus interest in foreign exchange.

The "withdrawal" of foreign companies from South Africa, rather than affecting the country's foreign exchange balance negatively, might actually have a positive impact, at least in the short run. For the last decade, companies have been repatriating in interest and dividends more foreign exchange than they have been investing in South Africa. Investment by subsidiaries in South Africa has been primarily reinvestment of local currency from the subsidiaries' earnings, not a transfer of new funds from the home office. The sale of a South African subsidiary to a South African company--and the high degree of liquidity in the South African economy now makes it likely that any foreign subsidiary would be purchased by a local concern--would reduce the amount of foreign exchange South Africa was required to ship abroad each year as dividends or interest.

Even if a decision to withdraw reduced the flow of foreign capital to South Africa, there is some debate over what impact such a reduction would have on South Africa's economy. Arndt Spandau at the University of Witwatersrand Graduate School of Business argues that a ban on investment in 1976 would have cost South Africa an estimated 40,000 jobs for whites and 80,000 jobs for blacks. Richard Porter, professor of economics at the University of Michigan, on the other hand, says foreign capital flow is not directly related to the growth of the South African economy. In the early 1960s, there was a net flow of foreign capital out of South Africa for seven years, but the real rate of gross domestic product growth was 5 to 6 percent per year.

An end to foreign investment in South Africa would be most serious because of the loss of technology that would accompany it. Should foreign companies decide to close their operations in South Africa, there would be a potential loss of know-how, management skills and technology. Even in this area, however, the loss may be less than it would first appear. In only about half of the American subsidiaries in South Africa is the managing director American, and it is likely that he is the only American working for the company. Most of the rest of the top-level management is South African. What South Africa would lose would be the access to on-going and future technology and the benefits of the research and development going on in home offices abroad.

Porter questions the impact that an end to loans would have on South Africa. He argues that South Africa could respond to an embargo on capital flow to South Africa by banning capital outflows. Even if "short-term financing had also become unavailable," Porter said of a five-year model of the South African economy constructed to test the impact of sanctions, "and South Africa had to alter its imports each year so as to maintain a zero basic balance under investment sanctions, its total imports for the five-year period would have had to contract by less than 4 percent."

Embargo on trade: Import trade is far more important to South Africa than continued foreign investment. Both Spandau and Porter say a meaningful embargo on South Africa's exports is not feasible, but they agree that a ban on imports could be serious. Porter comments, "Nearly half of South Africa's exports are foreign exchange and need no purchaser to convert them into it: gold. And one-half of the remaining exports are readily marketable mineral outputs, raw or slightly processed, which are sufficiently homogeneous to enter world markets with few distinguishable South African markings." Imports are much more vulnerable. A study by the South African Nedbank shows that more than half of South Africa's imports are capital goods. In 1976, it says, "imports of machinery alone accounted for 54 percent of the disclosed merchandise import bill." Porter says that "it is still accurate to say that South Africa imports almost all of its capital equipment--with domestic industry providing essentially only the plant in which it is housed." A curtailment of imports, he says, would be effective in the sense that "South Africa's growth as a modern industrial economy could be dramatically interrupted." Spandau estimates that a 20-percent embargo on sales to South Africa would increase whites' unemployment in South Africa by 90,000 and put 343,000 additional blacks out of work. A 50-percent boycott would raise the unemployment level by 1.1 million and would generate what Spandau describes as "inconceivable hardship."

South Africa's vulnerability to lost imports is increased to some extent by its increased reliance on a relatively limited number of suppliers--the United Kingdom, West Germany, the United States, Japan, France and Italy, which together provide a major portion of South Africa's imports.

To a limited extent, South Africa would be able to respond to an export embargo by these countries through an import substitution program. According to a study by the Federated Chambers of Industry and the Afrikaanse Handelsinstituut, 10 to 17 percent of current imports could be replaced by building new facilities.

But it is unlikely that South Africa could absorb the shock of a total embargo without a substantial and costly restructuring of its economy and the life styles of its citizens. A major change, for example, would have to come in its pattern of energy consumption. In addition to the country's need for imported capital goods, it remains dependent on imported oil to meet 20 to 25 percent of its energy demand. South Africa has made a major commitment to the development of oil from its abundant coal supplies, but energy independence is still a long way off.

An effective oil embargo would have serious implications for South Africa. The government, anticipating the possibility, has stockpiled anywhere from two to 10 years' oil supply in abandoned coal mines in the northern Transvaal. In the most comprehensive study of South Africa's oil situation available, Martin Bailey and Bernard Rivers asserted that an oil embargo would have an "enormously disruptive effect" and estimated that the country would "probably not be able to survive for more than two years." Professor Spandau maintains that South Africa could survive both in the long and the short term with reasonable success, but he does not account for the dramatic, if indirect, impact a reduction in oil availability would have on many sectors of the economy, on the production of automobiles and related goods, or the demand for steel, glass and rubber, and on the development of the petrochemical industry.

An embargo on other items--such as computer spare parts--could also have a serious impact on the economy. As one banker told IRRC, "Without spare parts, our computers would be down within two years. Without computers, we would need 2,000 trained bookkeepers. And where would we get 2,000 bookkeepers?"

Political impact: There is much debate among policy analysts as to the political impact of economic sanctions. Those favoring sanctions and withdrawal argue that the decline in the economy that would follow the termination of trade and investment would significantly demoralize the white-minority regime and accelerate progress toward majority rule. They assert that it would increase unemployment of blacks as well as whites, encourage strikes and work stoppages, and force a re-thinking of the political structure. Supporters of withdrawal argue that the suffering endured by blacks in the short term would be offset by long-term gains following the eventual redistribution of economic and political power.

Those analysts opposed to sanctions say that the blacks are likely to be hurt the most by a further decline in the economy, and they argue that there is no way to foretell what impact the decline in the economy might have on the political process. They say that the government could well become more conservative than liberal and more repressive than progressive. Adopting sanctions, they say, may only promote South African intransigence to domestic political change while placing an unacceptable strain on western economies that would be deprived of South Africa's vast mineral wealth.

There is considerable evidence to show that blacks would be the first to suffer from economic sanctions. Unemployment of blacks begins to rise as the economic growth rate falls below 5.5 percent. Many of the blacks who would be hurt by layoffs would be those who could afford it least. Africans living in urban areas could be forcibly removed to the homelands. And a recession in South Africa would affect a number of other countries in the region that are heavily dependent on South Africa for trade--Botswana, Swaziland, Lesotho, Malawi, Rhodesia, and to a lesser extent Mozambique and Zambia.

At the same time, economic pressures in South Africa over the last several years have greatly increased the number of questions being raised about government's political policies. The black demonstrations in Soweto in 1976 occurred during a period of recession following a period of economic boom. Economic gains made by blacks during the boom years were not matched by social and political gains--if anything, political legislation became more repressive--and a slowdown in economic growth increased black dissatisfaction.

The recession also encouraged dissent by whites. As has been seen, business as a sector only began to become actively concerned with the political situation during the years of sluggishness in the economy. During the boom years of the 1960s and early 1970s, very few businessmen questioned the government's social policies, but the recession of 1975-77 and the accompanying political unrest increased general disenchantment with the situation within South Africa. Whites questioned the causes of the recession, emigration rates shot up (although primarily among English speakers) and, despite overwhelming support for the National Party in the November 1977 elections, the dissatisfaction among whites in South

Africa has become increasingly visible as the Department of Information scandal unravels.

It is not possible to say what level of recession, unemployment, increased emigration, and concern about the future will trigger a rebellion or force those people responsible for making political policy to alter a system deeply entrenched in a combination of ideology, history, religion and self-interest. The inability to determine confidently at what cost, both to those people already suffering within South Africa and to those countries that trade with it, meaningful political change can be achieved by economic sanctions holds most policy-makers back from their advocacy. Policy-makers are likely to turn to economic sanctions only in a rare case where the objective--such as a settlement in Namibia--can be well defined, is not apt to be viewed by South Africa as directly affecting its internal national security, and is possibly achievable in a short period of time, before any counter-sanctions by South Africa are able to have an effect. They are more inclined, in dealing with issues internal to South Africa, to avoid serious economic sanctions but to test first the less costly, and most probably less effective, methods of using business as a tool for gradual change through improved labor practices and lobbying pressures.

Chapter VI Sources

Books

Arndt Spandau, Economic Boycott Against South Africa, Normative and Factual Issues, unpublished manuscript, Johannesburg, May 1978.

Articles

James Baker, J. Daniel O'Flaherty, and John de St. Jorre, "Full report public opinion poll on American attitudes toward South Africa," Carnegie Endowment for International Peace, Washington, D.C., 1979.

Deborah Durfee Barron and John Immerwahr, "The public views South Africa: pathways through gathering storm," Public Opinion, January/February 1979.

Richard Deutsch, "Nigerians prod U.S. on African policy," Christian Science Monitor, April 27, 1979, p. 6.

Laurence Franco, "South Africa: the European connection," unpublished paper for the Carnegie Endowment for International Peace, April 1978.

Richard C. Porter, "The potential impact of international sanctions on the South African economy," unpublished paper, University of Michigan, Oct. 1, 1978.

Financial Mail

"U.S. bending the rules," Aug. 18, 1978, p. 587.
"Sanctions: the West stalls," Sept. 29, 1978, p. 1151.

Reports and Letters

U.S. Government

"United States Private Investment in South Africa," hearings before the Subcommittees on Africa and on International Economic Policy and Trade of the Committee on International Relations, House of Representatives, June 27, July 12, Aug. 10, 15, 17 and Sept. 7, 1978, U.S. Government Printing Office, Washington, D.C., 1978.

U.S. Department of State

Letter from Douglas Bennet, Jr., Assistant Secretary for Congressional Relations, to Mr. Hillis, July 12, 1978, Washington, D.C.

Lewis Macfarlane letters to James G. Lubetkin, Director, Office of College Relations, Oberlin College, Ohio, Dec. 26, 1978, and March 2, 1979.

William N. Raiford, "South Africa: Foreign Investment and Separate Development," Library of Congress, Feb. 16, 1979.

Other

Die Afrikaanse Handelsinstituut, SA Federated Chamber of Industries, Steel and Engineering Industries Federation of South Africa, "Survey into the Gross Import Substitution Potential for South African Manufacturing Industry 1975-1980," Pretoria, June 1977.

American Chamber of Commerce in South Africa, letter to Juanita Kreps, March 13, 1979, Johannesburg.

CONCLUSIONS

An accurate assessment of the role of business in South Africa depends in large part on an accurate assessment of the implications of the changes taking place there. Both evaluations are elusive. There is little doubt that important changes are occurring in the labor practices of corporations and in aspects of government policy and that the pace of change has increased in the last few years. But interpretations of the implications of these changes and perceptions of their significance vary widely among observers both in South Africa and abroad.

To many white South Africans the pace of change in the last few years appears to have been dramatic. In 1973, South Africa's ambassador to the United Nations said that the South African government did not condone racial discrimination and Prime Minister John Vorster argued that the world should "give South Africa six months' chance" to change its policies. Since then, whites in South Africa say there has been considerable change--change that has gone largely unrecognized by the outside world. Between 1976, when the government first introduced its policy of "normalization" in sports, and 1978, 1,900 interracial competitions were held; before 1976 only 128 had occurred. The government has initiated a policy of "internationalizing" hotels and restaurants, permitting blacks to use their facilities. By the end of 1978, 50 of some 1,400 hotels in South Africa had been opened to blacks. A few schools have been permitted to admit limited numbers of blacks to their classes, and now, in total, more than 1,000 African and colored students are attending schools that were exclusively white two years ago. In March 1979 the first African was able to obtain a 99-year leasehold for land in a black urban township. Restrictions on certain jobs have been lifted, controls on black traders trading in black townships have been eased, and training opportunities for blacks in certain industries have been expanded. Most recently, in May 1979, the government announced its acceptance of recommendations affecting the rights of African workers to join recognized trade unions, the Minister of Labor recommended dropping laws and regulations requiring the segregation of facilities in the work place, and the Riekert Commission has called for adjustments in the pass laws.

The government has proposed limited political changes as well. It has suggested scrapping the existing single white parliament for a system of three parliaments, providing for political participation of coloreds and Asians as well as whites. Africans living in urban areas are excluded from the new parliamentary configuration but would be allowed greater political participation through locally elected community councils. The principal area of African political representation remains the homeland, and the South African government has maintained its plans to award independence to individual African homelands. And P.W. Botha has requested a study of the current allocation of land to Africans and has suggested that major revisions are necessary.

A number of whites in South Africa argue that these changes are significant. The government describes them as representing a move away from discrimination based on race, but not from the National Party's vision of separate development. Many critics of the government, including a number of people in business, see them as an admission of apartheid's failure and the beginning of a slow evolution of an alternative policy.

Most blacks in South Africa are unenthusiastic about the changes introduced by the government during the last several years. The homelands policy is almost universally opposed by urban blacks. The community councils have won little support and have been strongly opposed in the more politicized African townships such as Soweto. Changes such as desegregating public facilities, providing greater access to training, and agreeing not to destroy the black community at Crossroads all represent minor advances to most blacks. On balance, however, they fail to deal with the major complaints about restrictions imposed by the system.

Critics of apartheid see real limits in the changes introduced by the government over the last several years. Rights to occupy land obtained under the 99-year lease may not be extended to children of those who obtained the original certificate of title. The construction of homes for squatters in Crossroads is limited to those who are "legally" residents in the Cape. Under South African law, as many as 20 percent of those people living in the Crossroads community may be living there as illegal residents and therefore liable for removal to the homelands. Expanded trading rights for Africans living in townships still do not allow Africans to trade freely on an open market--they are not allowed to own shops or factories in white urban areas. The right to join registered unions is being extended to Africans who qualify as "permanent residents" in the urban areas, but it is being denied to migrant workers. The Riekert Commission recommended a number of relaxations in the pass laws, ending curfews on Africans in urban areas, allowing workers to be joined by their families, and giving Africans permanently resident in white areas expanded opportunities to trade, engage in industry and sell their labor on an open market. At the same time, these expanded opportunities are not extended to those Africans with migrant status. In fact, the Riekert Commission suggests that controls on migrant labor be tightened and that employers be drawn into the system of controls by being held responsible for hiring any Africans who lack the proper papers. Thus the changes being proposed, while creating new opportunities for many Africans, are not available to all Africans and do not threaten the basic structure of apartheid.

To some extent the perception of gains being made in the private sector parallels the perception of progress in public policy. Views on the performance of foreign companies and the importance of changes they are introducing vary just as views vary on the changes being introduced by government. There is no doubt that the employment programs at many companies have improved in the last several years and that the codes of conduct have what business representatives in South Africa describe as a "conscientizing" effect on their operations. There have been real gains, particularly in three areas: desegregation of facilities, access to skills training and housing. Business efforts in these areas have forced the South African government to recognize inadequacies in its policies, and business pressure has contributed directly to change in government policies in all three areas. There have been some gains in a fourth area as well--African labor union representation. Again codes of conduct --particularly the EEC code--and pressure by companies helped create an environment for a change in government policy, and the Wiehahn Commission recommendations demonstrate the impact of the activities of foreign companies. Actions by foreign companies and pressures from abroad, particularly on the union issue and on desegregation of facilities, are directly reflected in the Wiehahn Commission's report.

Just as in the public sector, however, the gains that have been made by companies in the last several years, although important, should not be exaggerated. Despite companies' efforts to desegregate facilities, workers may still be separated by race, with most African workers placed in hourly positions and most whites treated as salaried staff. The number of workers involved in training, housing or education programs, while growing, is still a small percentage of the total work force. And the gains being made by some black workers in some sectors of the economy are by no means universal. Moreover, they are not equal, for the most part, to those opportunities available to the white worker.

In addition, many of the changes made to date are among the easiest to achieve. Removing signs designating separate facilities by race, for example, posed few problems for most companies. Actual desegregation of facilities, and the beginning of integration, has been far less traumatic than originally anticipated. Improved training of Africans has encountered slightly greater resistance, but in most places where it is occurring, the economic justification--the shortages of whites for the jobs--is such that any opposition that exists can be answered quite simply. Housing programs have not required significant new contributions by companies; financial commitments have been limited. And in worker representation, the few companies with experience with an African union, such as Ford, report that the unions have been generally reasonable in relations with management and effective in representing black workers.

The real problems to be encountered by companies trying to follow progressive practices are likely to come as companies try to move beyond the early steps, to close the wage gap, to train and move blacks into white-collar and management positions, to assist black entrepreneurs, and to end the system of migratory labor and separation of families. In these areas, little progress has been made and the systemic constraints and economic realities are likely to be much more severe. Perhaps most importantly, the changes made within the business sector do not alter the reality of apartheid. The ability of business to affect political policies of the South African government either by improving its own practices or by placing direct lobbying pressures on government officials or politicians is limited. Events taking place on the factory floor or in workers' housing, while of real importance to the workers and their families that are involved, have very little impact on the greater structure of separate development. Moreover, the changes made affect only a limited number of workers. U.S. companies probably employ a total of no more than 50,000 to 70,000 black workers in South Africa. Even making the reasonable assumption that each worker supports a family of five, were all American companies to improve working and living conditions for all their employees, the total number of people directly affected would be under 500,000. More important would be the unquantifiable psychological impact on other workers and their employers.

The degree to which business might be able to effect further political change through direct pressure--in effect, through lobbying--is largely untested in South Africa. Traditionally, business has hesitated to involve itself in political issues. Companies have long been willing to make presentations to the government on subjects of business concern, but traditional distrust between a business sector dominated by English speakers and a government run by Afrikaners has discouraged communication on political issues. Few companies have volunteered to speak out on policy issues. In the major examples of business efforts to influence policy, the Urban Foundation lobbied extensively to persuade the government to alter its policies on the rights of Africans to land tenure in urban areas and in Crossroads. The results, after extensive efforts, are the 99-year lease in the first case and housing for many but certainly not all Crossroads residents in the other. The two cases clearly reflect both the potential and the limits of lobbying by business on political issues.

Whether business will have a greater impact now under P.W. Botha is unclear. Certainly there are new opportunities, but there is considerable question as to the degree to which business--which has only begun to prod the edges of the government's political policy--would be interested in trying to push for political change now that the economy has started to ease its way out of the recession. The economy, in the doldrums since 1975, appears to have turned around, bolstered by the phenomenal growth in the price of gold. The economic recession had been a major incentive to business interest in political policy in South Africa. Companies now may well lose interest in political policy should South Africa's GNP grow at the estimated 3.5 to 4 percent, and the potential role that business began to play--with some influence in the reports of both the Wiehahn and Riekert Commissions--would never be fully explored.

Because of the limits on the ability and willingness of business to affect the situation in South Africa, some opponents of apartheid argue that foreign companies should withdraw. There is no sign, however, that public pressures are likely to force companies to withdraw, nor is there likelihood in the immediate future that the policies of foreign governments will mandate withdrawal. In fact, in light of the elections in Britain and a more conservative trend in U.S. congressional politics, the possibility of sanctions against South Africa appears increasingly remote. Even if sanctions should be imposed, their potential impact on the political configuration in South Africa is unclear. Certainly sanctions would be perceived as supportive of blacks' demands, but whether they would prove an effective incentive for political change remains a major question of debate. There is evidence, in developments such as the recommendations of the Wiehahn Commission and in the negotiations over Namibia, that outside pressures like the threat of sanctions have influenced certain South African decision-makers. Like pressures from business itself, outside economic pressures may persuade the South African government to adopt changes in certain areas of its society; whether they can produce major political change remains an untested conjecture. The threat of sanctions may well be more effective in influencing policy than sanctions themselves, just as the call for withdrawal, while unsuccessful, has been a successful goad to get companies to begin to alter business practices in South Africa.

The changes produced in labor practices through business pressures in South Africa or through the pressures for withdrawal have yet to touch the core of South Africa's policy of apartheid--although the results that flow from greater black opportunity and increased interactions between the races may soften the attitudes that support it. They do not directly threaten the structure of the society nor do they represent the major changes being sought by many blacks and by critics of the South African government. But they may serve to strengthen the position of those pushing for major change and act as a precondition to it. In this sense, they can be seen as contributing to a fragile momentum for major change in the society.

II.
Four Case Studies
of Foreign Investment

A. THE OIL INDUSTRY IN SOUTH AFRICA

No sector of the South African economy appears more vulnerable to international economic sanctions than the oil industry, and there is no sector where multinational companies play a larger role. South Africa has no known oil reserves within its boundaries and thus it is obligated to import virtually all of its oil requirements from abroad. Although the country needs oil to supply only 20 to 25 percent of its total energy requirements—far less on a percentage basis than in other developed nations--refined oil products are critical to the successful operation of its industrial and transportation sectors. Five foreign oil firms dominate all aspects of the industry, handling importing, refining, marketing and distribution for some 85 percent of the country's petroleum products.

Oil is at the center of a continuing debate in the United Nations over the possibility of sanctions against South Africa. Many experts believe that an oil embargo would be the first significant step toward comprehensive sanctions against South Africa if the United Nations approved such an action. Advocates hope that sanctions would place pressure on South Africa to play a more cooperative role in granting independence to Namibia (South West Africa), to cease supplying oil and oil products to Rhodesia, and to take meaningful steps toward majority rule within its own borders.

The role of foreign oil companies in South Africa has also been questioned in connection with allegations that they have violated the long-standing UN embargo on sales to Rhodesia. The allegations of sanctions-busting have become a concern of shareholder activists, and resolutions stemming from their concern were proposed in 1978 and 1979 to two U.S. oil firms with operations in South Africa.

This study discusses the structure of the oil industry in South Africa, the industry's strategic importance to the South African economy, the involvement of U.S. companies in that sector and concerns about that involvement. This study contains the following sections:

I.   South Africa's energy economy.

II.   South Africa's oil requirements.

III. The role of foreign companies in South Africa's
      oil industry.

IV.   The role of the South African government in the
      oil industry.

V.   The oil sanctions debate.

VI.   IRRC analysis.

I. South Africa's Energy Economy

South Africa is the largest producer and consumer of energy in Africa. With 6 percent of Africa's population, it generates more than 50 percent of the continent's electricity. In 1976, South Africans consumed roughly eight times as much energy on a per capita basis as those people living in the rest of Africa.

Pushed by a booming economy, the country's rate of energy consumption has skyrocketed over the last two decades. Between 1960 and 1976, according to UN statistics, total energy use jumped 115 percent, in comparison with about 66 percent in the United States. Demand for energy is expected to remain high through the end of the century. South Africa's Department of Planning and the Environment projects that the country's total energy consumption for the period from 1980 to 2000 could grow at an average annual rate of 4.7 to 5.2 percent, depending on economic conditions.

Breakdown of demand: The South African government divides the country's energy demand into four sectors: industrial/commercial, household/agricultural, transportation and mining.

The largest user of energy in South Africa is the industrial/commercial sector, consuming an estimated 62 percent of all energy produced. Among its most energy-intensive sub-sectors are the iron and steel industry, the chemical industry, the glass industry and the cement industry.

The second largest consumer is the household/agricultural sector, which uses some 14 percent of all energy produced. Most of this energy goes to home heating and electrification, street lighting, domestic transportation and the operation of agricultural machinery.

The transport sector is the third largest consumer of energy, using roughly 13 percent of the total produced. The largest consumers in this sector are the South African Railways and the road transport industry.

Finally, the mining sector uses 11 percent of the country's energy, with the gold mining subsector requiring the largest portion.

The South African government expects that energy demand in the years to come will continue to break down into approximately the same proportions. By the year 2000, for example, estimates show the industrial sector using 61.0 percent, the transport sector using 14.0 percent, the household/agriculture sector using 13.3 percent, and the mining sector consuming 11.7 percent.

Principal energy sources: South Africa now obtains most of its energy from coal and coal derivatives, which account either directly or indirectly for 75 to 80 percent of the country's energy requirements. Oil satisfies an estimated 20 to 25 percent of South Africa's domestic energy needs. The contribution of hydroelectric power to the energy sector has been negligible so far, and experts believe that this source of power will never contribute more than 1 percent of the total energy consumed. South Africa's first nuclear power station--now under construction at Koeburg--is scheduled to be commissioned in the early 1980s. The station's two 900-megawatt reactors are expected to satisfy about 4 percent of South Africa's energy requirements when complete.

South Africa's extensive reliance on coal for the bulk of its energy needs is due to the abundant deposits within its boundaries and the low cost of mining the mineral. Estimates of South Africa's extractable coal reserves vary considerably, but there is agreement that they are substantial. According to the 1975 report of a special government commission of inquiry on coal in South Africa, an estimated 25 billion tons of coal can be recovered using existing methods. However, mining industry officials' estimates of recoverable reserves range as high as 61 billion tons.

In 1978, South Africa produced some 90.4 million metric tons of coal. At present rates of production, recoverable coal reserves would stretch a minimum of 300 years, excluding any new discoveries. Despite its sizable coal deposits, South Africa may experience shortages of specific grades of coal. Although coal will continue to meet the bulk of South Africa's energy needs, the majority of the country's coal reserves are inferior in quality, having a very high ash content and a low calorific value. Specialty coals, used as feedstock in the production of coke and char--crucial energy sources for the steel and chemical industries--are particularly scarce and are being depleted at a rapid rate. According to the Financial Mail, Dawie Kotz, director of energy for the Department of Planning, has warned that the annual production of certain high-grade coals may not be sufficient to satisfy the country's needs in 15 years. Aware of potential constraints on supply, the South African government has placed a long-range quota on exports of high-grade coal, limiting the industry to 620 million tons over the next 20 years.

South Africa's dependence on coal is expected to increase in the future as a result of the government's efforts to get industry to convert its plants to coal from other fossil fuels. A number of manufacturing subsectors either have substituted or plan to substitute oil-based products, notably heavy furnace oil, for coal. Interest in converting to coal has been stimulated since 1973 by spiraling oil costs and by the government's desire to reduce South Africa's reliance on foreign oil imports.

In addition, the demand for coal is likely to be greatly exacerbated by the government's commitment to a $6.5 billion crash synthetic fuels program centered on the conversion of coal to oil. Since 1950, the government--through the state-owned subsidiary, South African Coal, Gas and Oil Corp. (Sasol)--has owned and operated the world's only successful oil-from-coal plant, which is called Sasol I. The plant produces an estimated 4,500-5,000 barrels a day of petroleum distillates, satisfying about 1.5 percent of South Africa's total oil requirements. As part of its effort to respond to the threat of an international oil embargo, the government is constructing two more coal liquefaction plants--Sasol II and III--with roughly 20 times the productive capacity of their predecessor. The plants are scheduled to go into operation in 1980 and 1982 respectively, and the government hopes that they will eventually supply up to 50 percent of the country's current oil needs. When operating at full capacity, the two plants are expected to consume between 30 and 60 million tons of coal a year. (For more details on the Sasol plants, see Section IV).

South Africa's growing dependence on coal has already created some logistical problems. Government officials are concerned that South African Railways may have difficulty in transporting extra coal from Transvaal, where it is mined, to coastal areas, especially during winter months when the demand is high. They say that several coastal cities--notably Port Elizabeth and Capetown--already have been subject to acute shortages of coal for limited periods during the winter, and that without increased stockpiling in these areas or dramatically improved railway service the problem is expected to persist.

II. South Africa's Oil Requirements

Although coal is South Africa's principal source of energy, the country imports oil to supply roughly one-quarter of its energy needs. This figure compares favorably to other industrialized countries such as Japan, Italy and France, where foreign oil imports represent more than 65 percent of total energy consumption. Nonetheless, experts consider oil to be a crucial--if not indispensable--contributor to South Africa's energy economy, particularly in the area of transportation.

Because of oil's strategic nature, the government has limited the publication of information on the importation, production, marketing and consumption of oil and oil products for security reasons. In May 1979, restrictions were tightened when the government imposed a complete clampdown on the dissemination of information related to the country's oil needs, reserves and sources of supply. Unauthorized release of such information is punishable by an $8,400 fine and seven years in jail. As a result of these measures, figures used in the discussion of oil production, consumption and demand in this study are inevitably approximations.

The most recent and widely publicized estimates of South Africa's oil requirements are contained in a study released in June 1978 by two British economists--Martin Bailey and Bernard Rivers--entitled Oil Sanctions Against South Africa. The study was prepared at the request of the United Nations Special Committee Against Apartheid. It estimates that South Africa imports some 400,000 barrels of crude and 15,000 barrels of refined oil products each day. When the output of a government-owned oil-from-coal plant is added to the volume of daily imports, the total amount of oil available to South Africa is roughly 420,000 barrels a day, (b/d), according to the study. The study shows the use of this oil in South Africa and Namibia as follows:

Oil products used in consuming sectors	240,000 b/d
Oil products exported	77,000 b/d
Crude oil added to government stockpiles	70,000 b/d
Oil consumed as refinery fuel	26,000 b/d
Oil products consumed in electricity generation	7,000 b/d
TOTAL	420,000 b/d

Another widely quoted estimate of South Africa's crude oil consumption is 320,000 b/d--an estimate contained in a May 1978 report by Prof. Arnt Spandau of the University of Witwatersrand on the impact of comprehensive economic sanctions against South Africa. It is not clear, however, whether this figure includes the government's daily contribution to strategic stockpiles and the country's daily oil exports because the report does not provide a breakdown of the estimate.

Oil consumption by sectors: The oil needs of each of the consuming sectors vary considerably. Consumption patterns are dictated by several factors including general economic conditions, each sector's interest in converting to alternative energy sources and its ability to do so. A summary of oil consumption in the consuming sectors in South Africa and Namibia, taken from the June 1978 study, appears at the end of this study.

Transport sector--The transport sector in South Africa is the consuming sector most dependent on oil; oil is estimated to provide some 79 percent of its overall energy needs.

In 1974, cars, buses and trucks accounted for 87.1 percent of all petroleum products consumed in this sector, followed by aircraft at 6.6 percent, railways at 4.2 percent and local shipping at 2.1 percent, according to the Department of Planning.

Forecasts of demand for petroleum products in the transport sector are correlated primarily to expected increases in the motor vehicle population in South Africa. Government statistics show that the number of vehicles has grown significantly in the last decade. The Department of Planning reports, for example, that between 1970 and 1975 the number of automobiles in South Africa increased approximately 36 percent and the number of commercial vehicles jumped some 82 percent. The government estimates that as many as 12 million vehicles could be on the road in South Africa by the year 2000, roughly four times the number now in operation. By that time, the transport sector could require between 486,000 and 595,000 b/d of petroleum products, depending on the pace of economic growth, according to government forecasts. The average annual growth rate for 1980 to 2000 used in these projections ranges from 4.8 to 5.4 percent.

The estimate of transport needs was made with the assumption that oil would be available to South Africa in sufficient quantities and at a reasonable cost through the end of the century. Officials point out, however, that various factors--such as the widespread development of mass transit and new engine designs--could alter the projected size of the motor vehicle population and anticipated fuel consumption rates and thus ease the overall demand for oil in the transport sector. Demand could also be tempered by average annual growth rates lower than those used in the forecast, they say.

Industrial/commercial sector--Although the industrial/commercial sector is the largest user of energy in South Africa, only 8 percent of its energy requirements are furnished by oil. As shown by the table on p. 183, overall consumption of oil products in this sector has declined in recent years, largely because of oil price escalations and increased interest in substituting coal for oil. The principal petroleum products used in this sector are heavy furnace oils, diesel fuels, kerosenes and liquid petroleum gas.

Some of the industries requiring oil or oil derivatives for more than 25 percent of their total energy needs are the glass industry, motor vehicle manufacturers, rubber tire producers, food processors and metal product fabricators. No industry is more dependent on petroleum products for its operation, however, than the chemicals industry. According to a major study on energy utilization in South Africa released in 1978 by the Department of Planning, petroleum products--used either as an energy source or as a feedstock--account for more than 25 percent of total energy required to produce the following: ammonia (37.6 percent); industrial gases (46.4 percent); fertilizer (61.3 percent); synthetic resins (26.9 percent); medicines and pharmaceuticals (42.2 percent); soap, cosmetics and toiletries (38.7 percent); polishes, waxes and dressings (94.1 percent); and miscellaneous plastic products (38.0 percent). No figures are available for the volume of oil products used exclusively as a feedstock.

Because it is the largest user of petroleum products in the industrial sector, the chemical industry has also been the focal point for fuel conversion projects. In its study on energy utilization, the Department of Planning writes: "An important future development in the South African chemical industry is likely to be a trend toward the greater use of coal both as a fuel and feedstock.... Where technology allows, it is obviously in South Africa's interest to utilize local coal deposits rather than imported oil-based energy sources." Other industries that have undertaken or given serious study to fuel conversion projects include the glass industry; pulp and paper producers; and the cement industry. Assuming widespread fuel conversions are carried out, the Department of Planning estimates that the industrial sector's oil requirements will drop 50 percent by the year 2000, corresponding to an average annual rate of decline of 3 percent.

Household/agricultural sector--Approximately 28 percent of the energy needs of the household/agricultural sector are supplied by oil. Most residential energy requirements are satisfied by electricity, although oil products are used in the form of liquid petroleum gas and paraffin. The agricultural sector, however, is heavily dependent on refined oil products, primarily diesel fuel to power mechanized farm equipment and to ship produce to rail heads for distribution or export.

The prospects for substituting alternative energy sources for oil are limited in both these areas, but the government is stressing energy conservation measures to domestic consumers in an effort to curb overall demand. The Department of Planning has forecast that the petroleum requirements of the household/agricultural sector will grow at an average annual rate of between 3.7 to 4.2 percent through the year 2000.

Mining sector--The mining sector is the least dependent of the consuming sectors on oil products for its operations: In 1974, only 3 percent of the mining industry's energy needs were satisfied by oil. The principal source of energy for the sector is electricity generated in coal-fired plants, which supplies about 87 percent of all the power consumed in mining activities, according to government statistics.

Although the mining sector's need for oil is relatively small compared with that of other consuming sectors, its anticipated growth in demand for oil is the highest of any area of the economy. The Department of Planning predicts that petroleum consumption in the mining sector could grow at an average annual rate of 7.2 to 8.1 percent over the next two decades. At this rate, the sector could require as much as 22,200 b/d by the year 2000, more than four times its present rate of consumption. The upswing in demand is expected to stem from a surge of new mine openings and expansions planned in the near future.

Future growth in oil consumption: According to the Department of Planning, oil will provide about 17 percent of South Africa's energy requirements in its consuming sectors by the year 2000, a measurable decrease from its current contribution of 20 to 25 percent. Despite this drop, however, the demand for oil in South Africa is expected to rise sharply over the next two decades as overall energy consumption increases. Depending upon economic conditions and the accessibility of oil, the Department of Planning estimates that the overall demand for petroleum products will grow between 4.5 and 5.5 percent each year. By the end of the century, domestic oil consumption is expected to reach three to four times its present level, and crude oil imports could reach 750,000 to 940,000 b/d, according to Department of Planning forecasts.

Oil exports: For a number of years, South Africa has exported refined oil products to neighboring countries in southern Africa and elsewhere. Its principal customers are Botswana, Lesotho, Swaziland and Rhodesia, which together receive an estimated 23,000 b/d, the majority of which is channeled to Rhodesia. (The role of foreign oil firms in shipping oil to Rhodesia is discussed extensively in part V.) For the most part, these countries are entirely dependent on South Africa to supply their oil needs.

In addition to direct oil exports, South Africa supplies ships sailing around the tip of Africa--primarily tankers from the Middle East--with bunker oil for fuel. South Africa's bunker exports have declined in recent years, due largely to the opening of the Suez Canal and the growing popularity of supertankers that do not require refueling stops. Nevertheless, the UN study calculates that in 1978 some 50,000 b/d--equivalent to 21 percent of the total daily consumption of oil in the consuming sectors--was exported in ships' bunkers.

Stockpiling: The South African government has been stockpiling crude oil in large quantities since the late 1960s. Originally, crude stocks were stored in tanks above ground, but cost factors and security considerations forced the government to shift its storage operations to abandoned coal mines in the Transvaal province. The size of South

Africa's crude stocks is a closely guarded secret, although most experts believe that the stocks on hand represent a two to four-year supply for that country if they can be rationed properly. (See part IV for a further discussion of stockpiling.)

Sources of supply: Accurate information on South Africa's sources of oil, like much of the data on its oil industry, is difficult to obtain. Before 1973, South Africa received the bulk of its oil from a host of Middle East producers including Iran, Iraq, Qatar, Saudi Arabia and the United Arab Emirates. In November 1973, the Arab members of OPEC—at the request of the Organization of African Unity--placed an embargo on all oil sales to South Africa. The Iranian government, however, refused to accept the cartel's decision and continued to supply crude to South Africa.

UN trade data on international oil exports indicate that Iran supplied an average of 87 percent of South Africa's total crude requirements during 1974 and 1975. Bailey and Rivers assert that in 1977 approximately 91 percent of South Africa's total crude imports originated in Iran. Their estimate is based upon a study of tanker movements in and out of South African ports for part of that year.

Other experts maintain that the commonly quoted figure in the neighborhood of 90 percent is too high. Kenneth Maxwell, a highly respected technical authority on the South African motor industry, claimed in his December 1978 newsletter that Iran's actual contribution to the country's overall oil imports was closer to 40 percent. The balance, he said, was supplied in more or less equal proportions by Saudi Arabia, Iraq and other small Persian Gulf states. When asked about Maxwell's estimate, Secretary of Commerce Tjaart Van de Walt told To the Point magazine, a South African news weekly, that the figure was too low but declined to be more specific.

The debate over Iran's contribution to South Africa's oil needs is moot for the time being, however, because all oil shipments to that country were terminated after the downfall of the Shah in January 1979. For the most part, South Africa's sources of supply since the Iranian cut-off have remained a mystery. Through the first half of 1979, it is known that South Africa purchased large quantities of crude at premium prices on the international spot market to meet its immediate needs. In some cases, South African customers paid a premium of 80 percent or more over listed prices, according to Business Week. In June 1979, it was reported in the House of Commons that the British government had authorized British Petroleum to trade North Sea oil to an anonymous European oil firm in exchange for arrangements by that company to deliver oil to the Shell/BP refinery in South Africa. A January 1979 report in the London Guardian quotes Western diplomatic sources in South Africa as claiming that the white minority regime had secured guarantees for delivery of oil in exchange for gold from Saudi Arabia and certain other Middle East states.

Nigeria has also been named as a potential source of supply. A January 1979 report in the Cape Times claimed that South Africa had negotiated a secret oil deal with Nigeria through Arab middlemen and an unidentified small American oil company. Although the Nigerian government emphatically denied the report, it conceded that there was a possibility that Nigerian oil might be shipped to South Africa through intermediaries without its knowledge.

Other oil imports--In addition to crude, South Africa buys limited quantities of refined oil products from Western countries. These purchases--estimated at 15,000 b/d in 1975--represent close to 4 percent of South Africa's total oil imports by volume, according to Bailey and Rivers. Many of the products--such as specialized lubricants and certain light oils--are not produced in South Africa. Trade statistics from the Organization for Economic Cooperation and Development indicate that the chief suppliers of these products to South Africa are Italy, Britain and the United States.

Cost of oil imports--No hard information is available on South Africa's oil import bill: The South African government has excluded oil purchases from its published trade statistics since 1973. Nonetheless, government officials have occasionally made reference in speeches and interviews to the cost of oil imports. For example, South Africa's Secretary of Commerce, Tjart Van der Walt, said in a 1977 speech that the country's 1976 petroleum imports were valued at approximately $1.5 billion--a figure that represents about 22 percent of South Africa's total import bill for that year.

Bailey and Rivers calculate that South Africa's 1978 oil imports cost more than $2.25 billion. If correct, this amount would represent an eight-fold increase over the 1973 figure of $273 million, the last year that oil import figures were officially made public. Recent figures from South Africa's Federated Chamber of Industries estimate that the 14.7-percent increase in OPEC oil prices will cost South Africa more than $115 million in 1979.

Because of OPEC price hikes and its heavy buying on the international spot market, South Africa's oil bill for 1979 could conceivably double. In June 1979, when South Africa was paying more than $35 per barrel on the spot market, the Johannesburg Sunday Business Times predicted that the country would need as much as $6 billion to pay for the oil imports required to meet the government's 4 percent economic growth target for that year. It is believed, however, that South Africa's balance of payments benefits derived from the rocketing price of gold will more than offset the high cost of oil imports.

Oil exploration--The South African government has been actively engaged in oil exploration for a number of years through the Southern Oil Exploration Corp. (Soekor), a state-owned enterprise. Soekor was formed in 1965 to explore for oil and gas deposits within South Africa's boundaries. According to Willem van Zyl, the company's financial manager, Soekor has spent some $132 million on exploration activities since its inception. So far, no oil has been found on the South African land mass and the company is now concentrating its search efforts offshore. Soekor is using two offshore drilling rigs built and operated by the Dallas-based Zedco Inc. in the hunt. In November 1978, a tentative strike was made 160 kms. south of Mossel Bay, but the quality of the oil was poor and did not justify commercial production.

Foreign oil firms operating in South Africa have periodically sunk test wells in search of exploitable reserves, but they have not made any notable discoveries so far. Several U.S. oil companies--Texaco and Standard Oil of California, joint owners of the Caltex subsidiary in South Africa, together with Phillips Petroleum, Getty Oil and Conoco--were engaged in oil exploration off the coast of Namibia but halted activities in 1975 after failing to find sufficient oil for commercial development.

III. The Role of Foreign Companies in the South African Oil Industry

The oil industry in South Africa is dominated by the subsidiaries of five multinational oil companies: Shell, British Petroleum, Mobil, Caltex and Total. With the exception of Total, all the foreign oil subsidiaries are owned in their entirety by their parent firms. (Local investors have a one-third minority interest in Total-South Africa, and Compagnie Francaise des Petroles holds the balance.) According to the Financial Mail, the five oil majors collectively control close to 85 percent of the petroleum market in South Africa and operate 91 percent of the service stations.

Four smaller companies--Sasol, Esso, Trek Beleggings and Sonarep--control the remaining portion of the market. Sasol is a subsidiary of the Industrial Development Corp., a major government-owned enterprise. Esso is a wholly owned subsidiary of Exxon Corp. Trek is the only oil company in South Africa controlled primarily by local investors; Shell and BP have minority interests, each holding 17.5 percent of the outstanding stock. Sonarep-South Africa is a subsidiary of the Portuguese company Sociedade Nacional de Petroleos, which used to process and distribute petroleum products in Portugal's former African colonies.

In July 1977 the Financial Mail published a list of oil companies operating in South Africa, their respective market shares and the number of service stations under their control. The five main oil companies had 84.8 percent of the market and controlled 4,242 service stations, compared with 15.2 percent of the market and 419 stations for the smaller companies. The list is found in the tables on p. 183.

There is no hard information on the combined annual turnover of oil companies in South Africa. Bailey and Rivers calculate that in 1976 the total sales of the five oil "majors" were close to $2.42 billion. If the estimate of the market share of the smaller companies is accurate, the annual combined turnover of all oil companies in South Africa could be estimated at $2.85 billion for that year.

Bailey and Rivers also estimate that the combined assets of the five main oil companies in South Africa are now worth more than $1.15 billion, accounting for some 11 percent of total direct foreign investment in the country. This amount could increase 50 percent or more over the next decade, based on the announced expansion plans of these companies. (See below for discussion of new investment.)

A breakdown of estimates of sales and assets of the five main oil companies in South Africa by Bailey and Rivers is included in the tables on p. 184.

Employment: Although the oil industry is regarded as capital-intensive, the multinational oil companies operating in South Africa are among the larger foreign employers in that country. A breakdown of employees by color for U.S. firms is presented below:

	Total	White	Colored	Asian	African
Mobil	3,054	1,640	302	195	917
Caltex	2,057	1,195	334	54	474
Exxon	527	337	26	23	141

Like other industry groups in South Africa, the oil industry's unskilled and semi-skilled jobs are held primarily by blacks--and skilled, supervisory and management positions are dominated by whites. All oil firms have training programs to promote job advancement for blacks, and on the average their collective record is considered to be superior to that of most other employers in that country. In addition, wages in the oil industry are higher than the national averages for both blacks and whites. At Mobil, for example, black employees earn more than two-and-a-half times the national average for their population groups; whites take home two-thirds more.

There are no established labor unions--white or black--in the oil industry. Oil companies have organized black liaison committees at installations where there are large numbers of black employees to discuss periodically with management matters related to working conditions.

Refineries: There are four major refineries in South Africa. Their combined output satisfies approximately 95 percent of the demand for refined oil products in that country. They are capable of producing a wide range of fuels and other distillates including gasoline, diesel, kerosene, liquid petroleum gas, aviation fuel, lubricants, greases, waxes and solvents. Reliable private sources have provided IRRC with the following breakdown of refined oil products produced in South Africa in 1975:

Product	Average b/d
Motor gasoline	49,050
Aviation gasoline	6,570
Kerosene	37,260
Aviation turbine fuel	13,150
High speed diesel	79,450
Light diesel	57,800
Fuel oil	77,260
Lubricants/grease	8,220
TOTAL	328,760

Two refineries--one owned by Mobil and the other jointly owned by Shell and BP--are located in Durban, where 85 percent of South Africa's crude imports are delivered. A third refinery--owned by Caltex--is near Capetown, where the balance of that country's crude imports are brought ashore. The fourth refinery--located inland near Johannesburg--is owned by NATREF and operated by Total. NATREF is South African-controlled, with Sasol holding 52.5 percent of the outstanding shares. Total has a 30-percent stake in the firm, and the National Iranian Oil Co. controls the remaining interest. The NATREF refinery is supplied with crude by a special pipeline from Durban.

South Africa also has two lubricant refineries and two lubricant re-refining plants for processing waste oils owned and managed by the oil "majors." These four facilities have a combined capacity of 7,200 b/d. Details on the ownership, location and capacities of South Africa's major refineries and lubricant plants, taken from the UN study, are presented in the table on p. 185.

Marketing and distribution: Although oil companies in South Africa have service stations scattered around the country and in neighboring countries, their principal marketing areas tend to be clustered in their assigned refinery zones. Refinery zones were established to minimize the costs of transporting refined oil products to distribution outlets. Under an industry-wide agreement, an oil company will supply a competitor's service stations and customers within a certain distance of its refinery. Because the agreement is reciprocal, the competitor will perform a similar service for the company's facilities situated in the competitor's refinery zone. For example, all the oil majors operate service stations in the Cape Province. These stations are supplied primarily by the Caltex refinery in Capetown. In return, Caltex's service stations outside its refinery zone are supplied by the refinery nearest them, irrespective of which company owns it. This arrangement effectively eliminates the costly burden of having to transport refined oil products thousands of miles to distant distribution centers.

Because their refineries are located in Durban, Shell, BP and Mobil do most of their business in the eastern half of South Africa and in Lesotho, Botswana and Swaziland. Products allocated for Swaziland are shipped to Maputo in Mozambique and then carried to their final destinations by truck or rail. Otherwise, oil products are shipped directly from the Durban refineries by truck or rail to service stations or storage facilities. Two pipelines carry oil products from Durban to Johannesburg--South Africa's most heavily populated area--to expedite distribution in that region.

Caltex, with its refinery in Capetown, does the bulk of its business in Cape Province, southern Orange Free State and Namibia. Most of the company's products move by truck or rail, with the exception of oil bound for Namibia, which is hauled in coastal tankers.

Products from the NATREF refinery are sold primarily in Orange Free State, Transvaal and Lesotho under Sasol or Total brand names. Sasol has no stations of its own, but, under an agreement with other oil firms in South Africa, stations in Orange Free State and Transvaal are obligated to install one Sasol pump if requested to do so by the state-owned firm.

Investment: The South African subsidiaries of foreign oil companies have made considerable new investments in the last few years. Greater investment has been discussed, although plans for major new investments appear to be in abeyance as oil companies wait for a clear picture of South Africa's economic and political future.

In mid-1978, Caltex finished a controversial three-year project to expand its refinery at Capetown from 58,000 b/d to 108,000 b/d. The expansion effort cost the company approximately $135 million, and it increased South Africa's total refinery capacity by 11 percent. In 1976, church investors submitted shareholder resolutions to Texaco and Standard Oil of California--Caltex's parent firms--asking them not to expand their subsidiary's operations in South Africa. The investors were concerned that Caltex's plans to increase its production capacity would undermine the spirit of the U.S. arms embargo against South Africa by making strategic petroleum products more available to the military there. The resolutions received the support of 2.29 and 2.10 percent, respectively, of the shares voted at the two corporations' 1976 annual meetings.

Smaller investments are being made by Mobil, Shell and BP. The companies are currently spending close to $70 million to install secondary processing equipment at their Durban refineries to increase their yields of light or "white" petroleum products, particularly motor gasoline. In addition, a Mobil subsidiary--Condor Oil--has recently opened South Africa's second largest lubricant re-refining plant, costing an estimated $2.3 million and operating with a capacity of 600 to 700 b/d, according to the Financial Mail in August 1977.

Oil companies in the past have declared an interest in substantial new investment to diversify their operations into other energy-related areas, particularly coal mining. BP and Total have joined forces with General Mining in a coal export venture known as Ermelo Mines. Their financial input into this project could be as high as $230 million over a 10-year period, according to a 1976 statement by BP. Ermelo is now producing approximately 3 million metric tons of coal for export a year. Shell is also involved in coal exports through its joint ownership with Barlow Rand in a mine at Rietspruit.

The involvement of foreign oil companies in coal exports has become a subject of controversy in South Africa's mining industry. Some industry representatives claim that the government has been disproportionately generous to the oil firms in allocating coal export quotas. Shell, BP and Total have been given collectively a 30-percent share of the annual coal export quota of 44 million tons which is valid through 1985. In contrast, the country's largest coal-producing group, the Transvaal Coal Owners Association, was allocated a 23-percent share. In May 1979, then Economic Affairs Minister J.C. Heunis told the Financial Mail that the oil companies' quotas have been tied to the condition that "they continue to fulfill their obligation in supplying liquid petroleum fuels to the country." In the government's view, one official said, the more business the oil majors do in South Africa, the less likely they are to abandon their investment here.

IV. The Role of the South African Government in the Oil Industry

The South African government--acutely aware of the country's dependence on foreign crude imports and on multinational oil firms to process and distribute petroleum products--has taken a number of steps to reduce South Africa's vulnerability to the threat of international oil sanctions, an option that has been widely discussed in the United Nations and other political forums as a means of pressuring the minority regime into relinquishing its apartheid policies.

Broadly speaking, the government has employed a four-pronged strategy to protect South African oil consumers from an abrupt cut-off of foreign supplies. The first part of the strategy is to use a portion of South Africa's extensive coal deposits to synthesize petroleum products, thus compensating for the country's lack of indigenous oil reserves. This is being accomplished through Sasol, the government-owned energy corporation. The second part has been to implement staunch conservation measures to cut overall oil consumption and to urge South Africans to convert from oil to alternative energy sources where feasible. The third part of the strategy has been to build extensive stockpiles of crude and certain refined oil products to cushion the economy from the brunt of an oil embargo until other arrangements could be made. Finally, the government has enacted legislation to ensure that foreign oil companies act in South Africa's interest during times of crisis.

Sasol: Sasol's principal objective is to manufacture petroleum products from coal. The state-owned corporation is regarded by many experts as the world's leader in coal gasification and liquefaction technology. To synthesize oil and petrochemical products from coal, Sasol employs the Fischer-Tropsch method first used by Germany in World War II to supplement its own limited oil supplies.

In the first phase of the process, coal is gasified under high pressure in the presence of steam and oxygen. After the removal of unwanted sulphur compounds in a purification unit, the gas--which is a mixture of hydrogen and carbon monoxide--is reconstituted with the assistance of special catalysts in one of two ways, depending upon the final product desired. Together the two processes yield virtually the entire range of petroleum products derived from regular refinery operations as well as certain basic petrochemical feedstocks, including ammonia, ethylene, butylene, acetone and several alcohols. The raw materials requirements for coal gasification and liquefaction are large: When in full operation, Sasol I--which has an output of 4,500 to 5,000 b/d--consumes more than 22,000 tons of coal and 2,600 tons of oxygen each day.

Sasol II and III: Perhaps the most significant new investment in the oil industry in South Africa is the multi-billion-dollar Sasol II coal liquefaction plant now being built by the government there. The facility--the largest industrial project ever undertaken in South Africa--is scheduled for completion in 1980. According to Sasol's chairman, D.P. de Villiers, "the main object of Sasol II is to diminish South Africa's dependence on imported petroleum and to reduce the heavy outlay in foreign exchange to pay for these imports."

Construction of the plant--now under way 80 miles southeast of Johannesburg near the new township of Secunda--is expected to cost more than $2.8 billion. This cost is more than double the estimate announced by the government in 1974 and does not include township development, interest charges, general sales tax or working capital. Bailey and Rivers estimate that when these costs are added on, the total price tag for Sasol II could exceed $3.45 billion. Financing for the project is coming from three sources: the State Oil Fund ($1.91 billion), appropriations from parliament ($345 million) and foreign export credits ($566 million). The contribution of the State Oil Fund comes primarily from a special surcharge on all fuel sales in South Africa.

The managing contractor for the Sasol II project is Fluor Corp., a California-based process engineering firm. According to Sasol's chairman, all major purchase orders and contracts have been placed with some 60 percent of the project's capital cost being spent in South Africa. Foreign suppliers are primarily French and German: Deutsche Babcock (boilers), Lurgi (gassifiers), Demag Mannesman (heavy transport equipment), Air Liquide (oxygen plant), Dresser-France (compressors) and Heurtey (furnaces). American participation in the project is limited primarily because the U.S. Export-Import Bank--as a matter of policy--will not provide export credits to the South African government or its agencies. Shortly after Fluor was awarded the management contract in 1975, the company tried to persuade the Ex-Im Bank to lift the ban but was unsuccessful. Nevertheless, at least three American firms--Honeywell, Control Data and Raytheon--have business links with Sasol, although informed private sources say that the cumulative value of their contracts is less than $20 million.

Sasol's managing director, Johannes Stegman, has said that when Sasol II is in full operation its output will be about 45,000 b/d with an emphasis on gasoline, diesel and light fuel oil products. Estimates of Sasol II's contribution to South Africa's total oil needs vary widely. Prof. Spandau projects that the new plant will satisfy 25 to 28 percent of oil requirements by 1981. Bailey and Rivers maintain that the plant's actual contribution to the energy sector will be significantly less, representing about 11 percent of South Africa's total production of oil products in 1982.

In March 1979, the government announced that it was planning to expand dramatically the size of the Sasol II complex, effectively doubling its anticipated output, because of the Iranian oil cut-off. The expansion--dubbed Sasol III--is expected to cost close to $4 billion and is scheduled for completion in 1982. According to then-Economic Affairs Minister Heunis, the projected completion date for the project is shortened by two years because the infrastructure and trained work force are already at the site. Heunis said at the time of the announcement that when Sasol II and III are in full operation they will supply some 47 percent of South Africa's current liquid fuel consumption, using 60 million tons of coal a year. To offset part of the cost of financing the expansion, the government has made a $525-million Sasol stock offering to private investors in South Africa. The issue is the largest public offering of stock ever announced in that country.

Conservation measures: Following the 1973 oil embargo against South Africa by Arab members of OPEC, the government announced special conservation measures to reduce consumption of oil products. The steps included lowering speed limits, approving fuel price increases, calling for the recycling of oil and restricting the hours of operation for service stations. As a result of these actions, South Africa's Minister of Economic Affairs reported in April 1977 that gasoline sales had declined some 22 percent since the restrictions were promulgated. Some analysts maintain, however, that the government's conservation measures are having only a selective impact on fuel consumption. They point out that while gasoline sales have declined in recent years, sales of diesel--another critical transport fuel--have continued to rise over the same period, growing at approximately 7 percent a year.

The government also has actively encouraged businesses in South Africa to switch from oil to alternative energy sources--such as coal, coal-gas and electricity--to meet their needs. The steel industry's consumption of fuel oil dropped from 55,000 tons in 1973 to 4,000 tons in 1975, and experts predict that the industry could eliminate its need for oil altogether in the next few years if further conversions are made. The Department of Planning projects that petroleum consumption in the industrial sector will decrease between 5 and 10 percent each year from 1977 to 1980, and thereafter at an average annual rate of 3 percent through the year 2000. Bailey and Rivers consider this forecast overly optimistic, however, and assert that "the most obvious areas where coal can be substituted for oil have probably been exploited."

South Africa has placed new emphasis on fuel conservation following the termination of Iranian oil shipments. In December 1978, the government appointed a four-member committee to consider proposals for further conservation and rationing. In an effort to dampen demand for liquid fuels, the government announced three increases in the price of gasoline and diesel fuel during the first half of 1979. Together these increases raised the price of transport fuels more than 90 percent over this period. In other moves, the government has ordered filling stations closed on weekends and Wednesday afternoons, and the speed limit on highways in metropolitan areas reduced from 54 mph to 42 mph. It is also giving serious consideration to alternative transport fuels such as ethanol--which can be synthesized from maize--and methanol, which can be derived from coal. Several companies in South Africa claim that they could build a chain of alternative fuel production plants within a year that could supply up to 10 percent of the country's fuel needs.

Stockpiling: It has been widely known for a number of years that South Africa has been stockpiling crude oil and refined oil products to reduce the country's vulnerability to an oil embargo. During the 1960s, large storage tanks were used to hold emergency stocks of crude, but toward the end of this period, the government decided to expand its stockpiling program and commissioned an Oklahoma-based company--Fenix and Scission International, an oil engineering firm specializing in underground storage facilities--to prepare inactive coal mines for holding oil. Since then, the government's commitment to enlarging its oil stocks has grown considerably. In 1977, South Africa's Auditor-General reported that the government spent some $641 million on its stockpiling programs, the majority of which was devoted to oil.

Knowledgeable private sources told IRRC that there are three large underground depots now used for storing crude in South Africa, and all of them are believed to be located in the Witbank coalfield area in Transvaal. They estimate that the depots have a combined storage capacity of 261.5 million barrels and a 90-percent recovery rate. This reserve would be close to a two-year supply of oil at estimated 1978 levels of consumption, although it is not clear how far the reserve could be stretched by severe rationing, which certainly would accompany a comprehensive oil embargo. Some experts believe that an immediate 20- to 25-percent reduction in consumption could be achieved under such a program.

The South African press has suggested repeatedly that the country's oil stocks represent a two- to three-year supply that could be extended to four to five years with effective rationing. Prof. Spandau predicts that current oil stocks--which he estimates at 315 million barrels--could last as long as 12.2 years, assuming they are apportioned properly and Sasol I and II are in full operation. These estimates have been challenged by Bailey and Rivers, however, who believe that South Africa's reserves could last a maximum of 18 months without rationing.

In addition to government stocks, oil companies are required under South African law to store minimum quantities of certain oil products. Government regulations specify that companies should have in reserve 13 weeks' supply of inventory cover for fuel sales and 12 months' supply of lubricants, catalysts and other chemicals used in refinery operations. Half of the firms' storage costs for these materials are subsidized by the government.

Government regulations: Under certain provisions of South African law, oil refineries operating in South Africa may be required to set aside a percentage of refined oil for government purchase. The Petroleum Products Act of 1977 gives the Minister of Economic Affairs the authority to regulate the purchase, sale or use of any petroleum product. U.S. oil company officials will not say, however, whether a standing agreement on sales to the government exists. Officials say that information is not available because under South Africa's Official Secrets Act their subsidiaries cannot disclose information on their obligations to distribute their products in South Africa.

In discussions with officials of the U.S. State, Commerce and Treasury Departments, IRRC was not able to obtain an exact description of requirements that might be included in an agreement between private oil companies and the South African government. Commerce officials said an agreement on allocation quotas probably exists in South Africa, as it does in many countries, including the United States. An official of the South African embassy told IRRC there is continuous consultation between oil companies and the government on such matters as projected demand and prices, that the relationship between private oil concerns and the government is very close, and that one could assume that arrangements had been made to meet government needs.

In addition, oil companies are legally prohibited from imposing any conditions on the sale of oil products to creditworthy South African customers. Under this arrangement, oil firms are obligated to sell supplies to South Africa's security forces if asked to do so. Furthermore, since the provisions require oil companies to sell their products unconditionally to any qualified customer, the companies say that they are unable to prevent their products from being re-sold to Rhodesia because South Africa has never agreed to support UN sanctions against that country.

The number of service stations in South Africa is tightly controlled. Under the Service Station Rationalization Plan, the government regulates the number of service station permits available to oil companies and encourages the transfer or closure of stations that prove to be in a poor location or commercially unprofitable. George Birrell, vice president and general counsel of Mobil, reported in testimony to Congress in 1976 that the plan "has held constant the number of stations at the 1960 level while over the same period the average station volume has nearly trebled."

The government also plays an important role in distributing oil in South Africa. Under the terms of the Road Transportation Act, oil companies are required to use state-owned railways and pipelines for transporting petroleum products beyond a 30-mile radius from their refineries or storage depots. The intent of the legislation is primarily to protect the state railroad from competition. Nonetheless, some firms have established subsidiary distribution networks using road transportation by building a chain of storage depots at roughly 60-mile intervals in areas where the demand for oil is high enough to make road delivery economical.

The government taxes retail gasoline quite heavily in South Africa. In inland areas, total direct taxation accounts for approximately 60 percent of the retail pump price; on the coast, taxes claim close to 67 percent. The difference in the rate is due to a special transport charge that is affixed to the price of gasoline sold in the interior of South

Africa. This extra charge boosts the overall price per gallon in these areas, which lowers the percentage represented by total direct taxation.

Tax revenues from fuel sales are channeled primarily into three government administered funds: the National Road Fund for the construction and maintenance of national highways; the State Oil Fund to help finance government stockpiling programs and Sasol construction; and the Acquisition Equalisation Fund to offset the high cost of imported oil purchased on the spot market. The balance is treated as general revenues for the state.

Finally, government regulations cover the processing of petroleum products. By law, all new refinery construction and expansion must be approved by South Africa's Secretary for Industries. Government franchise agreements with the oil companies to enlarge refinery operations are conditioned--in part--on their participation in South Africa's oil stockpile program.

V. The Oil Sanctions Debate

The costs and benefits of instituting oil sanctions against South Africa have been widely debated for a number of years. In 1963, the UN General Assembly passed a resolution condemning South Africa's "illegal occupation of Namibia" and called upon member states to halt all oil exports to South Africa. Compliance with the resolution was voluntary, however, because under the UN charter, only the Security Council can order mandatory sanctions against a nation if a situation is determined to be a threat to international peace.

The sanctions debate has been fueled in recent years by increasing political tensions in southern Africa, particularly in Namibia and Rhodesia, and by broader media coverage of events in that region. In 1974 and in 1977, the United States, Britain and France exercised their vetoes in the Security Council to block moves to impose comprehensive economic sanctions against South Africa. In 1977, however, the Security Council voted in favor of a mandatory arms embargo against the white minority regime.

For the time being, it appears that the implementation of further economic sanctions against South Africa--either by the UN or individual countries--is unlikely. Most Western countries--including the United States--feel that such action would be largely ineffective unless it was taken on a well-coordinated unilateral basis. Nevertheless, if the situations in Namibia and Rhodesia degenerate further and there is no discernible momentum toward satisfactory political settlements in these countries, the discussion of sanctions against South Africa is likely to continue. And many experts believe that a comprehensive oil embargo would be one of the most effective, limited economic pressures that could be used to persuade South Africa to play a more cooperative role in the region.

Costs and benefits: Bailey and Rivers assert that an oil embargo "would be one of the most cost-effective forms of pressure that could be applied on South Africa by the international community: The costs to South Africa would be enormous, but the costs to the international community would be relatively small." They maintain that the costs to the international community would fall into two areas: the costs of actually enforcing the embargo and the costs of providing alternative supplies to those countries in southern Africa that normally import their oil requirements from South Africa.

Critics of an oil embargo, however, argue either that it would be ineffective because South Africa would be able to get sufficient supplies through alternate channels, or that it would rapidly escalate, leading to retaliatory measures by the South African government. It could lead, they argue, to what South Africans would view as an act of war.

Enforcing the embargo--The cost of enforcing an embargo is obviously dependent on the selected method of enforcement. Some experts have suggested that a naval blockade is the only effective way to halt the oil flow to South Africa. The Security Council authorized a naval blockade of Portuguese-controlled Mozambique in 1966 when oil sanctions were imposed against Rhodesia, although oil imports from South Africa thwarted its intent. Others maintain that a blockade would be not only costly but also dangerous because it could lead to confrontations with the South African navy. Bailey and Rivers argue that the principal responsibility for maintaining the integrity of an oil embargo--once imposed by the Security Council--ultimately rests with the international oil companies. To ensure their cooperation if sanctions are imposed, they suggest that the Security Council take steps to require that any tanker that had delivered oil to South Africa be seized the next time it entered a non-South African port. Seized tankers could then become the property of the United Nations or else heavy fines could be levied against their owners, operators or charterers to secure their release, they say. (In April 1979, Nigeria impounded a South African supertanker--the 220,000-ton Kulu--that had docked at Lagos. The ship had been chartered to BP since 1973 and was owned by the Bermuda subsidiary of Safmarine, the South African government's merchant marine corporation. After the $50-million cargo was confiscated, the ship and crewmen were released.)

Bailey and Rivers assert that it would be reasonably easy to identify which tankers had violated the embargo. First, they point out that Lloyd's of London carefully monitors tanker movements in all parts of the world, including South Africa. While actual deliveries are not recorded, they argue, "those tankers which stop in South Africa between two ports in oil-exporting countries can probably be assumed to have delivered oil." Second, they maintain that aerial reconnaissance of South African harbors by either aircraft or satellite also could be effective. Finally, they say a small naval patrol could be organized simply to observe tanker traffic entering South African ports. Once tankers suspected of violating the embargo had been positively identified, the information could then be disseminated to all UN members and appropriate action taken.

The effectiveness of enforcement through identification of ships would depend on the degree to which the embargo was endorsed by other countries. Many observers agree that a system of monitoring such as that described by Bailey and Rivers is indeed possible, but they add that it would be useless unless there was a nearly universal endorsement of the embargo, particularly by countries that might serve as ports of call for ships sailing from South Africa. The universality of endorsement might, in turn, depend on how South Africans view the sanctions, and the degree to which and the means by which they seek to retaliate against those countries participating or vulnerable to the embargo.

Assistance to neighboring countries--One of the most problematic issues encompassed by the sanctions debate is the potential effect of an oil embargo on countries that import their oil requirements from South Africa. The countries in this group include Namibia, Botswana, Lesotho and Swaziland. (The case of Rhodesia is discussed below.) If sanctions were imposed, South Africa's oil exports to these states probably would cease. Former Prime Minister B.J. Vorster stated in 1978 that should oil sanctions be applied, it would be "every man for himself," and that while an embargo would hurt South Africa, "it could kill independent black countries in southern Africa like Botswana and Lesotho."

Although South Africa has frequently highlighted the vulnerability of neighboring states if an embargo should ever be applied, some analysts have challenged the notion that sanctions would entail severe or irreparable damage to these countries' economies. For example, the Financial Mail has stated: "The actual effect of oil sanctions against South Africa" for Botswana, Lesotho and Swaziland, despite Vorster's dramatic warning, are likely to be fairly small. The major suppliers in (South Africa) all have independent companies in the three countries, and are confident that overseas suppliers would export direct" to Botswana, Lesotho and Swaziland in the event of sanctions.

Bailey and Rivers have proposed several assistance schemes for those countries that would be affected indirectly by an oil embargo against South Africa. Generally speaking, these countries would be provided with refined oil products by air, ship or road--depending on their location--from alternative sources. Since the emergency supply schemes would obviously be more expensive than importing from South Africa, Bailey and Rivers suggest that the extra costs be shared by the international community. The schemes, however, are broadly outlined and speculative at best and it seems clear that more detailed feasibility studies are needed before the costs of an oil embargo can be accurately assessed.

The final costs of assistance to neighboring countries are likely to be substantial and could be increased considerably should South Africa elect to take measures against its neighbors in retaliation for the embargo. A shutting-off of trade to Botswana, Swaziland and Lesotho, all of which do considerable business with and through South Africa, could raise substantially the costs to those seeking to impose the sanctions or to those caught in the middle.

Retaliatory measures--Some analysts argue that any assessment of the costs of an oil embargo against South Africa should include possible retaliatory measures by that country's government. They say that South Africa has the potential to inflict considerable economic damage on Western countries by cutting back or halting completely key mineral exports to foreign consumers. South Africa could also refuse to repatriate interest on foreign loans or dividends to parent companies if faced with an oil boycott. Experts say that such action could cost Britain alone close to $2 billion a year, and that worldwide costs would be much higher.

Other analysts maintain that these sorts of retaliatory measures--while painful to the West--would only do further damage to a South African economy already laboring under an oil embargo. They point out that the value of South Africa's exports is the equivalent to roughly 25 percent of its gross domestic product and that the loss of overseas markets through a counter-boycott would drastically curb its economic growth and productivity. Furthermore, they say that a freeze on interest and dividend payments would seriously injure the country's international credit rating and alienate the foreign business community there. In their view, the only situation in which South Africa might take such steps would be if it were confronted with strictly enforced comprehensive economic sanctions imposed by the Security Council.

The impact on South Africa--It is difficult to gauge the impact of an oil embargo on South Africa. Bailey and Rivers assert that this form of pressure would have an "enormously disruptive effect" on that country. They claim in their UN study on sanctions:

> If all oil supplies were cut off, the Republic would probably not be able to survive for more than two years. The economy would grind to a halt: transport would become extremely difficult; industry would be severely hit; production in the modern agricultural sector would rapidly fall; and the armed forces and the police would lose their mobility.

> Clearly, the primary economic impact would be in those sectors most dependent on oil products--transport, agriculture, petrochemicals, local commerce and so on. But the secondary effects could be even greater. The cost of living would escalate rapidly. The motor industry would enter a slump. People would find it difficult to travel to work. An oil embargo would also accelerate the withdrawal of foreign capital.

In contrast, Prof. Spandau maintains that South Africa would be able to adjust to an oil embargo--in both the short term and the long term--with reasonable success. In a recent study on the impact of economic sanctions, he says that if oil imports were abruptly cut off, South Africa would probably take the following steps:

> --Tap its stockpiles of crude oil to keep its refineries in operation.

> --Modify the refineries' production programs in order to increase their output of light and middle distillates such as gasoline and diesel and to restrict their production of heavier products such as bunker oil and industrial furnace oil. (As noted earlier, Shell, BP and Caltex are spending close to $200 million to raise their production of light and middle distillates from roughly 60 to 70 percent of total output.)

> --Introduce a system of rationing designed to cut fuel consumption 25 percent, the maximum decrease allowable without inflicting serious damage to the economy, according to Spandau's calculations; and

> --Restrict the export of bunker oil for international shipping, which would result in savings of approximately 2 million tons of crude each year.

For the long term, Prof. Spandau argues that savings in foreign exchange that would result from an oil embargo--approximately $1.5 billion annually at 1977 prices, according to his calculations--would permit South Africa to finance a new oil-from-coal plant similar to Sasol II every three years. He also envisions the rapid development of non-conventional energy sources, particularly fuel alcohols derived from sugar cane, maize and other agricultural products.

In the event of oil sanctions, the oil industry would be presented at minimum with a stream of government directives regulating output, distribution, sales and prices. The directives would probably be issued under the Petroleum Supply Act or the National Supplies Procurement Act, emergency legislation activated in November 1977 after the United Nations imposed a mandatory arms embargo against South Africa. This legislation, passed in 1970, permits the Minister of Economic Affairs to order any company operating in South Africa to manufacture and deliver goods to the state that the government determines are essential to national security. Compensation for the goods would be equal to the claimed cost plus an extra stipend determined by the government. Should a company fail to comply with the minister's order, he has the power to seize the goods or make use of the facilities to provide the service in question.

It is not clear, however, what role U.S. oil companies would play if their South African subsidiaries received government directives to supply petroleum products directly to the military, although most analysts agree that their subsidiaries would be obligated to comply with such orders because the overwhelming majority of their employees are South African.

Oil sanctions against Rhodesia: Another major facet of the sanctions debate is the involvement of foreign oil companies in circumventing the embargo on oil supplies to Rhodesia. Since 1976, there has been a growing body of evidence that the southern African subsidiaries of the oil majors actively conspired with Rhodesian and South African officials to supply oil surreptitiously to Rhodesia in violation of the UN sanctions imposed against that country in December 1966 following its unilateral declaration of independence from Britain. The sanctions-busting allegations are contained in three major studies: "The Oil Conspiracy," a report prepared by the Center for Social Action of the United Church of Christ based on oil industry documents obtained from anonymous sources in South Africa with the help of Okhela, a secret political organization opposed to the government's apartheid policies; Sanctions Double-Cross: Oil to Rhodesia, a book by Jorge Jardim, former personal envoy of Portuguese Prime Minister Salazar who had intimate knowledge of oil companies' activities in Rhodesia, South Africa and Mozambique; and in the "Bingham report," an official report to the British government by attorney Thomas Bingham released in September 1978 on the role of Shell and BP in evading international sanctions.

Oil and Rhodesia--Rhodesia is dependent on imported oil as a major source of energy, requiring an estimated 15,000 b/d. At the time of the unilateral declaration of independence, it was thought that an embargo on oil supplies would bring down the Smith government; the British prime minister, Harold Wilson, stated that the embargo would bring an end to Rhodesia's independence "in a matter of weeks, not months."

But neither Mozambique nor South Africa chose to participate in sanctions, and oil continued to flow through those two countries to Rhodesia. A pipeline from Mozambique's port of Beira supplied a refinery in Umtali, Rhodesia. After the unilateral declaration of independence, several oil companies refused to supply oil through Beira and the refinery was shut down. Rhodesia was forced to increase its imports of refined petroleum from South Africa, with which it has both rail and road links. It became dependent exclusively on South Africa when an independent Mozambique closed its borders with Rhodesia in 1976.

Following the imposition of sanctions, the Rhodesian government established a government agency, GENTA, which became responsible for purchase of all petroleum products and for sale of these products to the various petroleum marketing companies in the country. The five multinational oil companies operating in Rhodesia--BP, Caltex, Mobil, Shell and Total--were declared "controlled" and ordered to continue in business at the direction of the Rhodesian government. It is assumed that GENTA buys all of its petroleum products from South African suppliers.

The details of Rhodesia's method of supply, however, are not clear. The government has sought to limit the amount of information available in areas that it considers to be of major security importance. Under the Official Secrets Act, the government prohibited "the disclosure for any purpose prejudicial to the safety or interests of Rhodesia of information that might be useful to an enemy." Discussion of anything related to petroleum supply or sales is considered prejudicial to the safety or interests of Rhodesia.

"The Oil Conspiracy"--In June 1976, the Center for Social Action of the United Church of Christ released papers that appeared to demonstrate that the South African subsidiaries of Mobil, Caltex, Shell/BP and Total had played an active role in supplying petroleum to Rhodesia. The papers were contained in "The Oil Conspiracy." They were turned over to the Center by anonymous sources in South Africa. Okhela--which describes itself as a "clandestine organization of white South African patriots who, as militants, are engaged in providing invisible support to the national liberation struggle, headed by the African National Congress--played an intermediary role in transmitting the documents to the Center.

The report asserts that the South African subsidiaries of the five oil companies established a number of paper companies in order to disguise shipment of oil to Rhodesia. According to the report, the subsidiaries sold oil to a South African shipping concern called Freight Services, knowing that the oil, after several intermediate sales, would reach its designated Rhodesian recipient. Freight Services ultimately shipped the oil to GENTA, which in turn sold it to the Rhodesian subsidiaries of the oil majors for public sale. The report says that until 1976, oil was shipped by sea from South Africa to the port of Lourenco Marques in Mozambique, and thence by rail to Rhodesia; since the closure of the Mozambican border, it alleges, oil has gone directly to Rhodesia by rail from South Africa.

The charges contained in "The Oil Conspiracy" precipitated two investigations: Both Mobil Oil and the U.S. Treasury Department's Office of Foreign Assets Control, the agency responsible for administering the Rhodesian sanctions, tried to gather more information on the allegations in an effort to confirm or refute them. In both instances, however, investigators were thwarted from collecting conclusive evidence by South African secrecy laws. Because the Official Secrets Act in that country covers the activities of the oil industry, investigators were unable to examine Mobil South Africa's company files or to question key individuals knowledgeable about the subsidiary's operations there.

In November 1978, the Treasury Department re-opened its

investigation of secret oil sales to Rhodesia. When called by IRRC, Treasury officials said they had "absolutely no comment" on the course or timetable of the investigation. An official confirmed, however, that the government's inquiry had been expanded beyond Mobil's operations in South Africa to include Caltex Petroleum's subsidiary there. Most experts believe that the government's action was triggered by the publication of the Bingham report in Britain in September, although some speculate that the principal reason for the new investigation is to regain the support of Black African states--particularly in the United Nations--that believe the United States has little interest in policing sanctions against Rhodesia.

New allegations--Bingham's and Jardim's documentation appears to reinforce allegations made in "The Oil Conspiracy" that parent oil companies were aware of sanctions-breaking activities by their subsidiaries. The Bingham report identifies several procedures used to evade sanctions from 1965 on. From 1966 to 1968, it appears, both Shell and BP's London home offices were unaware that their South African subsidiary was selling directly to Rhodesia. The shipping agent was Parry Leon and Hayhoe, a South African company later taken over by Freight Services.

A new arrangement that the home offices knew of took effect in early 1968, the "Total swap system." The Bingham report says Total, a French oil company owned by the Compagnie Francaise des Petroles, controlled by the French government, shipped its refined product from South Africa to Lourenco Marques, from whence it traveled to Rhodesia. In return, BP/Shell supplied an equivalent amount of oil to Total inside South Africa. According to the report, the Total exchange ceased about 1972, at which time BP/Shell recommenced direct shipments to GENTA via Freight Services and their Mozambique subsidiary at Lourenco Marques.

The Bingham report suggests that BP/Shell gave assurances to the Rhodesian government before the break from Britain that the unilateral declaration would not keep the oil companies from fulfilling their Rhodesian contracts. To that end, it says, the companies practiced limited stockpiling inside Rhodesia before the declaration of independence.

Jardim makes more specific charges that oil companies facilitated the declaration. He says the prevailing attitude in the Rhodesian government before the break from Britain was one of "unconcern" over the possibility of an oil embargo, because of the Smith government's "absolute faith in the guarantees received from the big international oil companies."

Both Bingham and Jardim allege that top Mobil and Shell management met with South African government officials to discuss contingency plans for shipping oil to Rhodesia in the event of closure of the Mozambican border. On July 4, 1974, they say, Kenneth Geeling, head of Shell South Africa, and William Beck, chairman of the board of directors of Mobil South Africa and a member of the board of Mobil Rhodesia, met with Joep Steyn, secretary of the South African Ministry of Commerce. Geeling's file memorandum of the meeting states: "We also suggested to Steyn that if all supplies were to emanate from South Africa, consideration should be given to Sasol directly handling all these supplies and balancing through intercompany exchanges."

On Sept. 10, 1978, when the Bingham report was drawing headlines in the British press, the London Times charged that BP/Shell was still supplying Rhodesia with oil. The Times alleged that South Africa's Natref refinery was still directing a portion of its output to Rhodesia. The companies denied the charges, stating that they stopped supplying Rhodesia in mid-1977. On Oct. 20, however, BP admitted that its assertion that all links with oil supplies to Rhodesia had been severed previously was incorrect. Company officials said that further investigation revealed that a special market agreement between Shell/BP and Sasol to assist the latter in providing refined oil products to the Smith government had been in effect until Sept. 15, 1978, four days before the Bingham report was released.

Responding to the sanctions scandal, Prime Minister James Callaghan took the unusual step of ordering a high-level parliamentary investigation into certain findings of the Bingham report. The special commission—composed of eight members of the House of Commons and eight members of the House of Lords—is looking into the role of civil servants and government ministers who knew of the sanctions violations by Shell and BP but failed to take appropriate action after learning of the companies' actions.

Lawsuits—Lonrho Ltd., a British multinational, has initiated a suit against several of the oil companies charging that they engaged in an illegal conspiracy to supply Rhodesia with oil by means other than the pipeline that Lonrho operated from Beira in Mozambique. The suit is now in arbitration. Until sanctions forced its closure, the oil companies had agreed to transport all their oil to Rhodesia via Lonrho's pipeline.

Lonrho's financial interest in favorable adjudication of its suit led it to disseminate additional allegations against the oil companies that support some of the claims contained in "The Oil Conspiracy." Bernard Rivers, the principal author of "The Oil Conspiracy," told the House Foreign Affairs Subcommittee on Africa in 1978 that information supplied to him by Lonrho indicated that Rhodesian oil subsidiaries in 1965 had acted to facilitate the unilateral declaration of independence. In addition, Rivers cited Lonrho as a source for his claim that Western oil company officials met regularly with GENTA to discuss the mechanism of supplying oil to Rhodesia.

Information from Lonrho has also provided the basis for a second damage suit, a $2.3-billion claim by the government of Zambia against the five oil companies. The oil companies are accused by the government of depriving Zambia of oil in the mid-sixties in order to build up stocks in Rhodesia, thus damaging Zambia's economy.

Shareholder activism—These complementary sets of allegations and suits formed the basis for shareholder resolutions on sanctions-busting to Mobil, Texaco and Socal. In 1978 a resolution asking Texaco to investigate charges that its South African subsidiary was supplying oil to Rhodesia received the support of 2.97 percent of the shares voted at the company's annual meeting and is not eligible for resubmission. Resolutions submitted to Mobil and SoCal asking the companies to regulate shipment of oil to Rhodesia indirectly by requiring their South African subsidiaries to reduce the volume of oil they import into South Africa received the support of 3.25 percent and 4.15 percent of the shares voted, respectively, in 1978. These resolutions were resubmitted in 1979 and received the support of 1.89 percent and 1.96 percent of the shares voted, respectively. The same resolution at Texaco garnered the support of 2.72 percent of the shares voted in 1979.

VI. IRRC Analysis

A number of factors are likely to ensure that the role of foreign oil companies remains at the heart of the debate over foreign policy toward South Africa. South Africa's demand for imported oil, although limited, still appears to be its point of greatest vulnerability to outside pressures. Members of the United Nations, particularly those from Africa and the rest of the Third World, already have focused on oil sanctions as a possible means of applying pressure to South Africa. Multinational companies dominate the oil industry in South Africa, and concerns about the political nature of their role in the region have grown considerably in the last three years with the publication of "The Oil Conspiracy," the Jardim book and the Bingham report. The Iranian oil cut-off has also illuminated the critical role the oil majors play in South Africa: Industry representatives have met repeatedly with government officials to plan the best way to cope with the growing shortages and higher prices of crude oil available to South Africa.

Future pressures: Excluding for a moment the pressures that have developed as a result of changes in the availability of oil from Iran, the major source of pressure on South Africa's oil supply is from the United Nations. A number of member states have already made it clear that they view oil sanctions as a reasonable step to take should South Africa refuse to assist the United Nations in establishing Namibian independence. Some strategists argue that the situation in Namibia provides a suitable opportunity for the use of sanctions: South Africa is in violation of UN authority in Namibia; sanctions could be tied to limited and specific objectives and imposed for a limited period of time; once South Africa had agreed to the UN plan for Namibian independence, the sanctions could be lifted.

Policy analysts have argued as well that the use of oil sanctions would provide an effective means of forcing South Africa to participate in sanctions against Rhodesia, thus speeding a resolution to the violence there. As with Namibia, they argue, the sanctions could be imposed for a distinct period of time with limited and specific objectives. As the situation in Rhodesia deteriorates, there is likely to be increasing discussion of this possibility.

A third situation for which some critics of the South African government have suggested that oil sanctions might be applied is in South Africa itself. A number of opponents of the government's apartheid policies have argued that oil sanctions can be applied to force South Africa to eliminate its policies of racial discrimination.

Likelihood and effectiveness of sanctions: The possibility of sanctions, as well as their potential effectiveness, is related to the degree to which they can be tied directly to specific and limited objectives and the way the South African government perceives these objectives. It is possible, in the case of Rhodesia or Namibia for example, to imagine sufficient support in the United Nations for sanctions that are limited, both in time imposed and in objective sought. Most Western states are opposed to sanctions, particularly oil sanctions, because they fear the precedent of such sanctions and recognize their own vulnerability. They are also concerned that oil sanctions might quickly lead South Africa to retaliate, either by cutting off supplies to neighboring and dependent states, by refusing to export certain critical commodities, or by freezing capital flows.

South Africa's reaction to sanctions will depend primarily on whether they appear to be a major threat to national security. Sanctions in connection with Namibia or Rhodesia, where the objectives of the sanctions might be considered achievable without major loss of security, are less likely to lead to retaliatory measures than are actions taken against apartheid itself. The government of South Africa has sufficient stockpiles of oil to allow it some time to consider any proposals that might accompany sanctions. It might believe that an agreement could be reached on requests relating to Namibia or Rhodesia before sanctions cause any real damage to the economy. Sanctions applied with the objective of forcing internal changes in South Africa, however, are much more likely to be viewed by the government as requiring it to do what it considers politically unfeasible or unacceptable. In such a case, the government might well seek to use measures that would hurt those participating in the sanctions. Recognizing the greater likelihood that South Africa would respond with retaliatory measures to sanctions imposed to obtain internal changes, the Western states are more likely to oppose such sanctions than they would be in the case of sanctions related to either Namibia or Rhodesia.

Impact of sanctions on South Africa: The dependence of the transport sector, certain industrial processes and commercial agriculture in South Africa on oil gives oil an importance far beyond its quantitative contribution to the country's total energy economy. Oil is required to ship raw materials to industrial centers and to distribute finished goods. It is vital to a variety of manufacturing operations, and it is critical to certain industries such as the chemical industry. It makes a significant contribution to South African agriculture as fuel for sophisticated farm equipment and as feedstock for fertilizer production. A reduction in the availability of oil to any of these sectors, rationing, and an increase in price could have a widespread ripple effect throughout the economy. Without oil, or with a serious cutback in its availability, virtually all sectors of the South African economy would experience severe logistical problems and critical dislocations, and the country's rate of economic growth would decline sharply.

An effective oil embargo would have a serious impact on the quality of life in South Africa. The rate and extent of deterioration are subjects of some debate, but it seems clear that the country's economic growth would be retarded, new investment from abroad would slow to a trickle or cease altogether, and unemployment and the cost of living would rise. Depending on the government's ability to institute effective emergency measures and retain public confidence, its popularity could either be boosted considerably, and probably temporarily, among the conservative white population or be eroded by new political tensions stemming from the crisis. Foreign companies already in the country would probably take a wait-and-see attitude in the short term, closely observing the political situation and the level of business confidence. Large-scale withdrawal of operations triggered by an oil embargo seems unlikely, primarily because the government can be expected to tighten its restrictions on foreign exchange outflows to pre-empt the possibility of panic selling.

The South African government has taken a number of steps over the last 15 years to reduce the country's vulnerability to potential oil sanctions. Through its state-owned subsidiary, Sasol, it has pioneered oil-from-coal technology in an effort to exploit South Africa's vast coal reserves and to lessen the country's reliance on foreign oil. It has also implemented staunch conservation measures for motorists designed to decrease gasoline consumption, and it has encouraged large industrial and commercial oil consumers to convert to alternative fuels where possible to meet their energy needs. In addition, the government has accumulated extensive stockpiles of crude oil in inactive coal mines to cushion the impact of a possible oil embargo, and to buy time until alternative arrangements for oil can be made. Finally, the government has enacted a wide range of legislation to control many of the normal business activities of the oil industry in South Africa. The primary objective of this legislation is to ensure that the subsidiaries of foreign oil companies act in South Africa's interest during times of crisis.

Despite these measures, however, South Africa remains vulnerable to oil sanctions. Some experts say that the estimates of the output of Sasol II and III are exaggerated. They argue that projects on this scale are frequently plagued by unforeseen difficulties and delays when they are first brought into operation. They point out that the Sasol I project was hampered by unexpected delays and design flaws shortly after it was completed. Some of these problems, they say, took several years to correct. They argue, therefore, that estimates of Sasol II's capacity when in full operation may not be valid until the mid- or late-1980s.

In addition, some experts have challenged Prof. Spandau's assertion that South Africa could build new oil-from-coal facilities if it is ever faced with comprehensive economic sanctions. In their view, Sasol's sizable dependence on foreign suppliers for goods and services would prohibit the construction of coal liquefaction plants under such conditions. They point out that the foreign content of Sasol II is close to 40 percent, and they question whether South Africa has the technological expertise to fill this gap if it is cut off from world markets.

There is some debate as well on the degree to which South Africa can conserve oil without seriously affecting the South African economy. Some experts argue that demand for oil in the transport sector and in certain industrial processes where oil products serve as specialized feedstocks must remain at a minimum growth level in order to sustain an acceptable rate of economic growth. They say that large-scale conversion to other energy sources of feedstock substitutes in these areas is not technologically possible at present and that the demand for oil in the industrial sector is highly inelastic beyond a certain point.

Because of the secrecy surrounding information on oil consumption in South Africa and a scarcity of comprehensive, up-to-date statistics on energy utilization there, the minimum level of demand for oil is not accurately known. It seems clear, however, that this minimum level will rise in the long term in tandem with South Africa's overall economic growth. At best, government efforts to assuage demand for oil will slow the rise of this minimum level but will probably be ineffectual in lowering the level in absolute terms.

There appear, then, to be real limits on the extent to which the government can reduce South Africa's demand for imported oil, and its dependence on multinational oil companies to supply it.

The role of oil companies in South Africa: The relationship between oil companies in South Africa and the government there is complicated, but it is not necessarily unusual. Heavy government involvement in an industry as strategic to national interests as oil is a common phenomenon worldwide. What makes the relationship between companies and the government in South Africa controversial is not the high level of government involvement and control over the industry. It becomes controversial because of the dispute surrounding South Africa's role in southern Africa and its policies at home.

The oil industry in South Africa is closely and carefully regulated by the government there. Widespread government control over the day-to-day and long-range operations of the major oil firms is legitimized by a network of statutes and directives affecting pricing, distribution, marketing and storage of oil products as well as companies' expansion plans, borrowing capabilities and foreign exchange situation. This arrangement has precipitated a close relationship between industry representatives and government officials who reportedly meet on a regular basis to discuss matters covered by laws and regulations.

Foreign oil companies operating in South Africa actively participate in the government's stockpiling program. They are required by law to maintain their own minimum reserves of inventory, refinery fuel, lubricants and catalysts to be used in times of tight supply before government stocks are brought into play. In addition, informed observers believe that a portion of the oil sold in South Africa by the oil majors is bought by the government for stockpiling purposes. At minimum, they say, crude oil designated for government stocks is shipped to South Africa primarily on tankers leased or owned by the international oil companies. Oil industry representatives say their hands are tied on this issue because the franchise given to oil companies in South Africa to build or expand refineries is contingent upon their participation in the government's stockpiling program. Moreover, they say that oil firms are bound by law to sell to the government unconditionally if asked to do so.

In addition, the government has the authority under the National Supplies Procurement Act to order oil companies to refine specialized products for strategic purposes regardless of their commercial potential. According to South Africa's Minister for Economic Affairs, the intent of the legislation is to ensure that the subsidiaries of foreign firms act in South Africa's national interest during times of emergency even if their parent companies prescribe another course of action.

The Procurement Act raises some serious questions about the relationship between the oil majors and their subsidiaries in South Africa. It seems likely that directives issued to foreign oil subsidiaries in accordance with this legislation would take precedence over instructions from the home office because the vast majority of the oil industry's work force--up to and including the managing directors--are South African. For South African citizens, failure to comply with such orders could result in arrest and imprisonment as well as seizure of the company's assets. At best, parent firms could terminate shipments of crude and other supplies to South Africa, sever all licensing agreements, and withhold personnel and technology that would be useful to their operations there.

Most experts believe, however, that by the time such action is taken--either voluntarily or in compliance with mandatory oil sanctions--the South African government will already have activated contingency plans to keep the oil industry functioning and will be relying on its emergency stocks.

The relationship between the multinational oil companies and the South African government is complicated. It is likely to become more complex as South Africa develops ways to cope with the Iranian oil shut-off in the short and long term. Companies operating in South Africa, shielded by the Official Secrets Act and compelled by the National Supplies Procurement Act and the Petroleum Supply Act, may be called upon to operate in a manner that runs counter to the spirit, if not the letter, of their home government's foreign policy or law. Some companies have already been accused of performing such a role in relation to oil shipments to Rhodesia.

As events unfold in southern Africa, similar accusations may well be raised about the companies' operations in South Africa itself. There is little doubt--should South Africa fail to make what critics consider to be steady progress toward a settlement of issues in Namibia, Rhodesia and in South Africa itself--that the relationship between oil companies operating in South Africa and the South African government will become increasingly controversial.

Table 1

SOUTH AFRICAN OIL CONSUMPTION BY SECTOR

	1974		1978	
	Consumption (b/d)	Percent of Total South African Oil Requirements	Estimated Consumption (b/d)	Percent of Total South African Oil Requirements
Transport	138,700	66.2	173,000	72.1
Ind/Comm	35,900	17.1	26,000	10.8
House/Ag	31,100	14.8	36,000	15.0
Mining	3,900	1.9	5,000	2.1
TOTAL	209,600	100.0	240,000	100.0

Table 2

MARKET SHARES OF THE OIL COMPANIES IN SOUTH AFRICA

	Market Share	Number of Service Stations
The five main oil companies		
Caltex	19.9%	985
Mobil	18.1	978
BP	17.5	867
Shell	17.5	853
Total	11.8	559
The smaller oil companies		
Sasol	7.4	0
Trek	4.5	228
Esso	2.0	104
Sonarep	1.3	87
GRAND TOTAL:	100.0%	4,661

Table 3

SALES AND ASSETS OF THE MAIN OIL COMPANIES IN SOUTH AFRICA

	Estimated annual sales (and year estimate was made)	Estimated value of investments (and year estimate was made)
Caltex	$575 million (1976)	$334 million (1978)
Mobil	$518 million (1976)	$333 million (1976)
Shell	$506 million (1976)	$288 million (1975)
BP	$506 million (1976)	$161 million (1976)
Total	$338 million (1976)	$178 million (1976)
Exxon	$107.7 million (1977)	$ 16 million* (1978)

* Value of equity capital reported by Exxon officials

Table 4

STATISTICS ON SOUTH AFRICA'S MAJOR REFINERIES AND LUBRICANT PLANTS

	Owners	Location	Year Opened	Capacity (1977)
The four main refineries				
Shell and BP South African Petroleum Refineries (Sapref)	Shell (50%) BP (50%)	Durban	1963	212,400 b/d
Mobil Refining Co. Southern Africa (Moref)	Mobil (100%)	Durban	1953	100,000 b/d
Caltex Oil (South Africa)	Caltex (100%)	Capetown	1966	108,000 b/d *
National Petroleum Refiners of South Africa (Natref)	Sasol (52.5%) Total (30.0%) NIOC (17.5%)	Sasolburg	1971	75,500 b/d
		TOTAL CAPACITY		495,900 b/d
The lubricant refineries				
Shell and BP South African Manufacturing Co. (Samco)	Trek (50%) BP (25%) Shell (25%)	Durban	1968	2,600 b/d
South African Oil Refinery (Safor)	Mobil (32.9%) Caltex (23.8%) Total (19%) Other South African interests (24.3%)	Durban	1973	3,000 b/d
The lubricant re-refining plants				
Chemico	Trek (100%)	Chamdor	1976	900 b/d
Condor Oil	Mobil (100%)	Chamdor	1978	700 b/d

* Includes recent refinery expansion completed in July 1978

Sources

Books

Jorge Jardim, Sanctions Double-Cross: Oil to Rhodesia, Intervencao, Lisbon, July 1978.

Prof. Arndt Spandau, Economic Boycott Against South Africa: Normative and Factual Issues, Labor Research Program, University of Witwatersrand, Johannesburg, May 1978.

Government Reports

South Africa:

Department of Planning and the Environment, The Outlook for Energy in South Africa, prepared for the Prime Minister's Planning Advisory Council, Government Printer, Pretoria, 1977.

Department of Planning and the Environment, Energy Utilization in South Africa (Vols. I, II, III), Government Printer, Pretoria, 1978.

Department of Planning and the Environment, "Energy Trends in the World with Special Reference to South Africa," prepared for the Prime Minister's Planning Advisory Council, Government Printer, Pretoria, 1975.

United Kingdom:

T.H. Bingham and S.M. Gray, "Report on the Supply of Petroluem and Petroleum Products to Rhodesia," prepared for Secretary of State for Foreign and Commonwealth Affairs, Dr. David Owen, M.P., September 1978.

Private Reports

Dr. Martin Bailey and Bernard Rivers, Oil Sanctions Against South Africa, United Nations Special Committee Against Apartheid, June 1978.

Articles

Science, "Synthetic chemicals in South Africa," Aug. 17, 1979.

Rand Daily Mail, "SASOL: Fuel of the future," July 31, 1979.

Johannesburg Sunday Times, "Oil: Heunis was caught off guard," June 3, 1979.

South Africa/Namibia Update:

"Pretoria will bar any publication of information about oil supplies," Feb. 28, 1979.

"Gasoline boosted to $2.42 a gallon, fueling inflation,"
    July 4, 1979.

Financial Mail:

"New generation coal ventures," Sept. 28, 1979.
"ABC of fuel curbs," March 23, 1979.
"Oil supplies: Crunch could come soon," Feb. 9, 1979.
"Oil supplies: Goodbye Iran, hello ?" Jan. 5, 1979.
"Oil sanctions," Sept. 30, 1978.
"Oil stocks: Time's the essence," June 23, 1978.
"Sasol sticks to its guns," March 24, 1978.

To The Point, "Energy: Starting to break the chains," Jan. 26, 1979.

World Business Weekly:

"South Africa's coal oil buildup," March 5, 1979.
"Liquid coal looks good as hunt heats up for other oils,"
    Feb. 26, 1979.

Business Week, "South Africa pays dearly for oil," March 5, 1979.

The Johannesburg Star:

"Petrol will cost 50¢ a litre this year," Feb. 24, 1979.
"Opposition concerned at fuel fund secrecy," Feb. 17, 1979.
"New oil leverage on Rhodesia soon," Jan. 13, 1979.
"Clouds gathering over NATREF," Jan. 13, 1979.
"SA faces higher price for oil from Arabs," Jan. 6, 1979.
"Petrol price has trebled in five years," Dec. 28, 1979.
There's oil for this here land . . . but only at a cost,"
    Jan. 27, 1979.

African Index, "Why Nigeria nationalized BP," July 16-31, 1979.

Financial Times, "Sasol enters U.S. fuel market," Aug. 31, 1979.

The Journal of Commerce, "S. Africa 'outbids' U.S. for Arab oil," March
26, 1979.

The Guardian, "Pretoria ready to censor oil news," Feb. 20, 1979.

The Washington Post, "To cope with embargoes, S. Africa converts coal
into oil," April 27, 1979.

B. THE COMPUTER AND ELECTRONICS INDUSTRY
IN SOUTH AFRICA

As a result of a rapid rate of economic growth and technological development over the last two decades, the demand for effective information management systems and sophisticated electronic equipment has burgeoned in South Africa. The computer and electronics industry is the fastest growing sector of the South African economy, expanding at an estimated rate of 20 to 30 percent each year. Computers and advanced electronic components are not only employed by private industry and commerce, but are also used widely by the government and by public corporations for administrative and technical purposes.

Foreign firms dominate the South African computer and electronics industry; they are responsible for most of the imports, sales, installation and maintenance of high-technology equipment there. Transfer of technology has enhanced South Africa's ability to satisfy a portion of its own requirements for data processing and electronic components. In order to lessen the country's reliance on foreign companies for its high-technology needs, the government has encouraged private firms to design, produce and assemble various electronic components and equipment for commerce and industry, up to and including small data processing systems. This policy has led to the emergence of a small, but dynamic, local computer industry; nevertheless, the country remains overwhelmingly dependent on foreign companies for the development, supply and servicing of computers and electronic equipment.

Because of the increasing demand for information management systems and sophisticated electronic gear in the public and private sectors, and because of the critical role played by multinational firms in making these items available, many experts regard the computer and electronics industry as one of the key strategic areas of the South African economy. As a consequence, the activities of American companies in this sector have become a focal point in the debate over U.S. investment in South Africa. Critics of high technology companies argue that computers and other advanced electronic equipment are a vital part of the apparatus the government has developed to enforce its apartheid policies. They assert that data processing systems--in addition to facilitating day-to-day administrative tasks--are regularly used by the South African military and police for both internal and external security purposes. They also contend that computers and other kinds of electronic equipment play an indirect but crucial role in supporting apartheid by expediting a capital-intensive modernization of the white-dominated economy and thus eliminating jobs.

Company representatives respond that it is not possible to regulate all final uses of their products, but to the best of their knowledge none of their equipment in South Africa is being used for repressive purposes. They maintain that ending sales would not affect the government's political philosophy, and that the most constructive course a company can take is to stay in South Africa and provide increased employment opportunities and technical training for blacks.

Growing concern over the strategic nature of the computer and electronics industry in South Africa has intensified the pressures against multinational firms. Shareholder activists have stepped up their campaign to force several major computer companies to make changes in their

South African operations, and in 1978, the U.S. government tightened restrictions on the sale of computers and other high technology products to the South African military and police as well as other controversial government agencies. In Britain, a number of trade unions representing employees of a major computer firm active in South Africa have openly criticized the firm's involvement there and union officials have met with management on the issue.

This study discusses the importance of the computer and electronics industry to South Africa's economic development, the involvement of foreign firms in that sector, and the array of pressures on multinational companies marketing high-technology equipment. It contains the following sections:

I.   The computer and electronics industry in South Africa.

II.   The role of foreign firms in the computer and electronics industry.

III. Pressures on foreign computer and electronics firms operating in South Africa.

IV.   IRRC analysis.

I. The Computer and Electronics Industry in South Africa

Since the first British-built computer was installed in South Africa in 1959, the market for data processing systems there has boomed. With an average annual growth rate of nearly 30 per cent in its first two decades, the computer industry has emerged as one of the fastest growing sectors of the South African economy. The electronics industry is expanding at a similar pace. South Africa's emergence as a highly sophisticated industrialized nation has intensified demand for electronic instrumentation and components. In turn, the installation of this equipment has aided the modernization process there. The industry's overall sophistication is roughly on a par with its American and European counterparts, and in certain areas--such as uranium enrichment technology--it may even be superior.

Analysts expect the high rate of growth exhibited by these sectors to continue through the mid-1980s. The only possible constraints, they say, would be a shortage of skilled personnel--a scenario that is rapidly becoming a reality in South Africa--or international economic sanctions against that country.

Computers in South Africa: As of the end of 1978, there were more than 2,000 computers in operation in South Africa with an estimated market value of $1 billion. Sales of computer hardware alone for 1978 totaled more than $135 million. Major users of computers include the government and government-controlled corporations, banks, building societies, insurance companies, mining firms, manufacturing conglomerates and universities. Demand for data processing systems is continuing to run at record levels; according to a 1977 survey, only the United States and Britain spend more per capita on general purpose computers than South Africa.

Among the most significant developments in the computer industry in recent years have been the technological advances in integrated circuitry and micro-processors that have paved the way for a new generation of small but powerful mini-computers. The introduction of these compact computing units has intensified demand for information management systems in South Africa by lowering the costs of data processing substantially. The dramatic cost savings brought about by technological advances can be illustrated by the fact that raw computing power priced at $1 million in 1954 is now accessible for as little as $170. As a leading South African business journal wrote in 1977: "Gadgetry not long ago so expensive that only governments could afford it is now available in hobby shops."

The rapidly expanding base of installed computers in South Africa has spawned the development of a computer service sub-sector. The most important businesses in this area are software suppliers (software is the operating system or program that runs a computer) and firms selling items such as discs and tapes that are used by computers and are known as computer peripherals. In addition, the growing demand for effective information management systems has stimulated the growth of bureaux in South Africa. Bureaux are companies with a recognized expertise in data processing that provide computer services for other companies. Customers of bureaux may or may not have their own data processing equipment.

Major users of computers--The government and its agencies are the largest users of computers in South Africa. Data processing systems are used to varying degrees by all departments of the South African government, large municipalities and parastatal corporations. The equipment employed by the public sector ranges from small mini-computers to large "number crunching" mainframe systems that make enormously complicated calculations almost instantaneously. Almost all government computers have been either purchased or leased from foreign suppliers. While most major government departments have their own facilities, computer time-sharing between departments is quite common. Time-sharing is the cooperative use of a central computer by more than one user. Analysts estimate that the government's principal computer facilities are housed in about 15 large installations around the country.

Government computers are used primarily for administrative matters such as accounting, payroll, voter registration, personnel records and budget-planning. In addition, state-owned corporations employ computers for commercial purposes similar to those used by the private sector. These tasks include inventory control, invoicing, making reservations, process control, cost monitoring and market surveys. In some instances, computers are used for research and development activities. The South African Defense Forces, the Atomic Energy Board, the Uranium Enrichment Corp., the South African Arms Development and Production Corp., and the Council for Scientific and Industrial Research are among the more controversial agencies using computers for research purposes as well as administrative tasks. Knowledgeable observers report that there is a great deal of spare computer capacity in existing government installations and that facilities in a number of departments are--for the most part--underutilized.

The largest user of computers in the private sector is the giant South African congolmerate, Anglo American Corp. Reliable sources estimate that Anglo has invested $33 million in computer facilities, although this figure includes equipment based outside of South Africa. In 1978, the company committed more than $4 million to a special in-house computer project designed to reduce production costs in Anglo's gold and uranium divisions by allowing more efficient use of its labor force. The project--known as the Human Resources Information System--may ultimately save the company $5 million each year, according to some analysts.

Other large private sector computer users in South Africa include the auto industry, the oil industry, mining companies and financial institutions. Barclays Bank recently released the details of one of the most ambitious South African computer projects ever undertaken, which is aimed at linking every branch and service in South Africa into its central computer facility. Officials say that once the network is operational, far fewer people will be required to process the movement of money. Barclays has budgeted more than $67 million for the project through 1980, most of which will be spent on installing about 900 terminals in its offices. Standard Bank is also embarking on a similar nationwide link-up of all its branches. Because their technical requirements are similar, the two banks have agreed to share facilities, although the system is designed so that neither bank will have access to the other's records.

Mini-computers—Mini-computers are the fastest growing area in the business technology field, both in South Africa and in other industrialized countries. The demand for them is expected to be so great that International Business Machines Corp. estimates that some 70 percent of its future worldwide growth potential could come from mini-computer sales. While large mainframe systems still dominate the data processing market, small computers now account for more than one-quarter of South Africa's installed computer base on the basis of value. Experts estimate that sales of mini-computers are now in the region of $30 million annually and that the market is growing at 25 to 30 percent each year.

The demand for minis has been fueled largely by the growing popularity of what is called distributed data processing. Under this system, data processing operations are taken out of the head office and into the work places where they are most needed. The decentralization has been made possible by the development of compact, but powerful, mini-computers that are relatively inexpensive to install and to operate. These systems are usually linked by telephone lines to a central computer facility which can then handle those tasks that are beyond the capability of the mini.

Like the mainframe market, the mini-computer market in South Africa is dominated overwhelmingly by foreign firms. Overseas manufacturers descended on the country in large numbers in the mid-1970s after sensing that South Africa represented a lucrative latent market for small data processing systems. In early 1979, more than 36 companies were competing in the field. About half of the mini suppliers do business in South Africa through subsidiaries and affiliates, and the rest are represented on an agency basis. The influx of foreign firms has spurred the growth of the mini-computer market, and intense competition among suppliers has lowered the costs of data processing and made it more attactive to potential users.

Software and peripherals--Reliable sources estimate that the software computer programming market in South Africa--excluding packaged programs such as payroll or pension accounts--generates about $9 million worth of business each year. The dominant software supplier is a locally owned firm, Systems and Programming Ltd., with an annual turnover of about $1.9 million. Most of the market consists of one- to six-man consulting teams operating on a contract basis. Certain computer bureaux are also active in this area. Most experts believe that because of South Africa's relative self-reliance in this field, foreign sanctions on sales of software would not hinder the market there.

The market for data storage media--such as magnetic tapes and discs--is valued at approximately $5 million a year, with Memorex--an American supplier--accounting for an estimated 45 percent of the total sales. Memorex has become market leader within the last three years. Previously, a German media company, BASF, had led in sales until its principal distributor, Dataset--a subsidiary of the British-owned International Computers Ltd.--was closed in 1977.

Computer bureaux--Bureaux services are one of the fastest growing sub-sectors of the South African computer industry, enjoying an annual growth rate of about 30 percent. The bureaux market is valued at close to $50 million annually and is dominated by five companies--ICL Data Services, Computer Sciences Ltd., Leo Computer Bureau, Commercial and Industrial Computer Services and Management Computer Services--which control more than half of all bureaux business.

Companies use bureaux services because, in the words of one South African executive: "We're in our own industry, not computers. Let the bureaux worry about hassles, and finance slip-ups. Bureaux have access to expertise we just couldn't afford ourselves on an in-house installation." Bureaux services are used almost exclusively by the private sector: With the exception of some Department of Treasury and Post Office work, the government provides very little in the way of bureaux business.

The electronics industry: South Africa's demand for electronics is now worth more than $1 billion in business each year, according to industry analysts. Of this total, telecommunications equipment used for telephone, telegraph and telex services accounts for roughly $230 million; entertainment and consumer products such as television sets, stereos and household appliances represent approximately $250 million; and specialized electronic equipment for industry, commerce and the military account for some $575 million. Specialized electronic equipment is a "catch-all" category: Products in this area range from heavy current power transmission equipment to sturdy process control regulators for industrial operations to highly sensitive scientific instrumentation. Military requirements include such devices as missile and ballistics guidance systems, radar equipment, specialized communications systems, aircraft instrumentation and electronic sensors for border control. There are no public figures on what proportion of the specialized electronic equipment category is attributable to military uses.

With the exception of consumer electronics, the industry has been expanding rapidly, with annual growth forecasts ranging from 20 to 30 percent. The fastest growing subsector is the specialized equipment and military requirements, which is expected to grow at 50 percent annually over the next few years. Government business has been particularly important to the health of this subsector. Among those programs increasing demand for specialized equipment are the $3.5-billion Sasol II project--the government-financed oil-from-coal plant scheduled for completion in 1980--and a large power station construction program now underway. The telecommunications industry has gotten a big financial boost recently from the South African Post Office's decision to modernize the country's telephone switching system using domestically produced equipment wherever possible. In contrast, growth in consumer electronics has been fairly stagnant over the last two years. According to some experts, demand has subsided because the white market for these projects is saturated and the black market has yet to develop. The outlook for this subsector remains uncertain.

Specialized equipment--The demand for specialized electronic equipment in South Africa has greatly intensified over the last five years. The upsurge in demand is attributed primarily to the sizable jumps in defense spending that followed Portugal's hasty decolonization of Angola and Mozambique in 1974-75, and to several multi-billion-dollar energy projects initiated by the South African government in the wake of the 1973 OPEC oil price-hikes.

The rise to power of two black anti-South African regimes on South Africa's borders following Portugal's departure from the region in the mid-1970s has caused the white minority government to increase its commitment to defense dramatically. Defense expenditures have risen more than 300 percent over the last five years, jumping from $626 million in 1973-74 to $2.47 billion in 1978-80. In the past, South Africa has generally spent 50 to 60 percent of its defense budget overseas to acquire military hardware. At the same time, the government has given high priority to programs designed to promote self-sufficiency in the production of armaments and advanced weaponry. With the implementation of a mandatory arms embargo against South Africa by the United Nations in November 1977, foreign purchases for defense have dropped off considerably, and new impetus has been given to programs to develop self-sufficiency. The reshuffling of defense resources to favor internal spending has been a boon for local electronics firms. Industry sources say that the two largest suppliers to the military of electronic eqipment and components are Fuchs Electronics, a subsidiary of the South African industrial giant Barlow Rand, and Racal Electronics, a subsidiary of Grinaker Holdings, a large South African construction firm. The value of their contracts with the defense forces and the kinds of equipment covered by them has not been made public.

The construction of Sasol II and the government's large commitment to expand the country's power grid--primarily through the development of nuclear energy--has also required a wide range of specialized electronic equipment. According to Sasol's chairman, D.P. de Villiers, some 60 percent of the project's enormous capital outlays are being spent in South Africa. While it is impossible to estimate the cost of electronic equipment required for Sasol II, informed observers say that Fluor Corp.--the California-based engineering and construction firm serving as managing contractor for the project--has awarded a $13.8-million contract to Honeywell for process-control equipment. It seems safe to say that because of the technological complexity of Sasol II, this sum is only a fraction of the funds budgeted for electronic components and that other firms--both foreign and domestic--probably hold sizable contracts.

South Africa has also embarked on an ambitious power plant construction program in recent years to ensure adequate energy supplies during the next decade. At the heart of the program are two 920-megawatt nuclear generating stations scheduled for completion in the early 1980s. Each station is expected to cost close to $1 billion. While much of the sophisticated electronic equipment required for the plants is being supplied directly by the French contractor, Framatom, the government has made efforts to employ local electronics manufacturers and systems designers where possible.

Telecommunications--While the telecommunications industry has been growing at a rapid pace since the beginning of the decade, it received a further boost in recent years from the South African Post Office's decision to convert the country's telephone system from electro-mechanical switching to fully electronic switching. The ultimate cost of the changeover is not known, but some experts estimate that it could be more than $1 billion. According to government statistics, there were 2.3 million telephones installed in South Africa in September 1977.

The decision to upgrade the country's telephone exchange was prompted by the growing backlog of requests for phone service. In 1971, more than 120,000 orders remained unfilled and it was clear to Post Office officials administering the telephone system that the exchange would have to be modernized to accommodate the growing number of requests for phone installations. In 1974 the Post Office selected Siemens's CP44/CP24 ESK semi-electronic crosspoint switching system for its next generation of public telephone exchange equipment. These systems were considered desirable because local industry had the potential to supply many of the necessary components. The government suspended the Siemens contract in 1977, however, when it became clear that a far more efficient fully electronic switching system had become economically viable because of significant advances in microelectronics in the mid-1970s. Two new systems have since been ordered: the French-designed E-10 from the Compagnie General d'Electricite and the German-designed EWS(D) from Siemens. The principal drawback of the new systems to South Africa is that the prospects for local manufacturing are not as great as they were with the canceled Siemens order. The Financial Mail reports that the Post Office has been discussing the matter with local suppliers.

The Post Office has budgeted more than $115 million over the next four years to expand telephone services for blacks. According to Deputy Post Master General of Telecommunications Christopher Gouw, much of the money will be spent in Natal Indian areas and the Cape Province colored areas because the demand for phone service is significantly greater among Indians and coloreds than it is among Africans. "Our decision to spend the money is not a paternalistic one in the sense of doing something for the blacks, but is based purely on projected demand," Gouw told the Financial Mail in 1978. He said that telephone installation in areas such as Soweto where only a few phones are now in use is extremely costly. "For every telephone we put in there, we need to put up an average of 15 telephone poles," Gouw said. He claimed that progress in extending service to Africans had been severely hindered by the

Soweto riots in June 1976, when the township's small telephone exchange was destroyed. For a year and a half after the riots, the police required Post Office staff to obtain special police permits to enter the township to repair and extend its telephone service.

Entertainment and consumer electronics--The outlook for this area of the electronics industry is uncertain. Demand for entertainment equipment has dwindled considerably over the last five years because of saturation of the white market, and the black market for these products has not yet materialized.

Informed observers say that the television industry has probably sustained the greatest setback of any group of suppliers in this subsector. Television was introduced much later in South Africa than in other industrialized countries: The first programs were transmitted by the South African Broadcasting Co. in 1975. South Africa has an installed television base of between 1.1 and 1.2 million sets. These consist of some 180,000 portable 12-inch sets, 275,000 black and white 24-inch sets, and approximately 800,000 color sets. There are currently six television manufacturers in South Africa. Only one of these firms--Southern Cross Television--is U.S.-controlled, with ITT holding an 85-percent stake; the remainder are held by European or South African interests. Knowledgeable observers estimate that the industry employs some 2,500 people, most of whom are semi-skilled Africans used in manufacture and assembly operations.

Local content in television manufacturing varies from company to company. One analyst told IRRC that South African Television (Pty.) Ltd.--the firm under license to assemble Telefunken sets--probably has the greatest local content of any manufacturer: 44 percent on color models, 50 percent on black and whites and 75 percent on portables. Nonetheless, there are considerable imports of essential components, the most important being the picture tube.

Some experts predict that 1979 will be the worst year for TV sales since the industry began marketing them five years ago. Estimates of the number of anticipated sales of color sets range from 70,000 to 80,000. The outlook for 1980 is slightly better: sales of color sets are expected to be in the neighborhood of 150,000 as whites start to trade in models purchased when TV first appeared in South Africa.

At present, TV sales to blacks are negligible. Experts say that there are three major obstacles to the development of the black TV market. First, the costs of sets--even portable black and whites--are well out of the reach of the average black household. Second, most blacks are not easily able to understand the English and Afrikaans broadcasts used by the SABC. Finally, few black households have electricity, even in urban townships adjoining large metropolitan areas. In 1976 less than 25 percent of the 125,000 homes in Soweto had power. While the government has embarked on a township electrification program, progress has been slow.

Aware of these facts, some observers have questioned the government's decision to spend more than $130 million on a TV service for blacks, scheduled to go into operation in the early 1980s. The government hopes to use TV as a strong propaganda medium to present its policies to the black population. Special TV studios for producing African programs are now under construction in Johannesburg. Officials say broadcasts will probably be transmitted in Zulu and Sotho, the predominant languages among those blacks living in townships around the city. The service would later be extended to Durban and the Eastern Cape.

II. The Role of Foreign Firms in the Computer and Electronics Industry

Multinational computer firms control practically every aspect of the computer industry in South Africa. Foreign companies are also responsible for training the bulk of skilled personnel in the local computer industry. Training programs in South Africa have recently taken on a new urgency because the boom in computer sales and services has led to shortages of specialized workers in the field. These emerging shortages are seen by most experts as the largest obstacle to industry growth.

At the heart of the computer industry are the seven large foreign-owned mainframe suppliers: IBM, Burroughs Corp., NCR Corp., Sperry Rand Corp., Control Data Corp., ICL and Siemens. All firms but the last two companies are U.S.-based firms. ICL is British-controlled and Siemens is German. Another American computer giant--Honeywell Inc.--withdrew its computer sales operation in 1975 for economic reasons.

While foreign participation in the electronics industry has traditionally been large, it is probably not on a scale with the foreign involvement in the computer industry. U.S. firms have a smaller stake in this sector than they do in computers: At best, only 50 percent of all electronics imports are of U.S. origin, according to one estimate. Market leaders in many areas are either European, Japanese or South African firms. Nonetheless, the electronics industry is vital to South Africa's future economic development, and the government has actively encouraged local manufacturing efforts.

Computers and Electronics: The Market Picture

Principal mainframe computer manufacturers: Mainframe computers are extremely expensive and there is no impetus for South Africa to develop a domestic mainframe manufacturing industry.

Until the mid-1970s, IBM held the unquestionable position of market leader in the South African computer industry, accounting in some years for more than 50 percent of all mainframe sales. In 1973, IBM's estimated market share stood at an impressive 56 percent, followed by ICL with 25 percent, Burroughs with 7 percent, NCR with 5 percent, Control Data with 4 percent and Sperry Univac with 3 percent. Since then, IBM's position has been steadily eroded by increasing competition among suppliers and by tighter U.S. restrictions on computer sales to South Africa. (The sanctions and their impact on the South African computer industry are discussed in Section III.) The biggest gainer in the market reshuffling has been ICL, whose sales have increased by close to 50 percent annually over the last five years, according to industry sources. ICL now claims to have overtaken IBM as the new market leader in South Africa on the basis of mainframe units sold in that country, although one analyst told IRRC that IBM still retains a marginal lead in the mainframe market if position is calculated on the basis of value of sales. IBM and ICL each controlled slightly less than one-third of the market in 1977, followed by Burroughs with an estimated 17-percent share, NCR with 14 percent, Control Data with 4 percent, Sperry Univac with 2 percent and

Siemens with 1 percent. (Because of the volatility of the market and of varying methods of calculating market shares, these are rough figures, included only to present a general picture of the mainframe sector.)

Future trends--Forecasting future trends in the mainframe market is difficult, but one expert on the South African computer industry speculated in discussions with IRRC that ICL will probably move into the lead position, taking up to 35 percent or more of all mainframe orders by 1980. She predicted that IBM, Burroughs and NCR are likely to lose ground over this period because customers fear a widening embargo on U.S.-origin computer sales. Siemens has a good chance of capturing 5 to 10 percent of the market in the near future, taking up the slack of American companies, she said. In her view, unless Sperry Univac makes some significant sales soon, the company may be forced to withdraw from South Africa in the next few years. (Sperry's managing director told the Financial Mail in January 1979 that the company was carrying out plans to merge its operations with a local partner and had found a suitable candidate after an extended search. Informed observers believe that Sperry's new affiliate is South Africa's second largest industrial conglomerate, Barlow Rand. Analysts expect that Sperry will assume a minority role in the joint venture, probably holding 49 percent of the equity.)

The mini-computer market: Since the opening of the mini-computer era in South Africa in the early 1970s, the field has been flooded with foreign suppliers. Competition in the mini-market is considerably greater than in the mainframe sector, with more than 35 companies now represented by subsidiaries and agents. Nonetheless, South Africa's mainframe suppliers also dominate the mini-market, accounting for about 60 percent of all sales. Burroughs, IBM, ICL and NCR are considered the leaders in this area. Because of the mini-boom, small computers are coming to represent an increasing portion of these companies' overall sales. For example, NCR derived an estimated 40 percent of its business in South Africa from minis in 1977, and the same year, ICL attributed 35 percent of its sales to small systems, according to reliable private sources.

Some of the smaller foreign companies marketing mini-computers in South Africa have also done well. Among the best selling systems in this category are Datapoint (U.S.), Data General (U.S.), Wang (U.S.), Nixdorf (German) and Philips (Dutch). The largest local supplier of mini-computers is Anglo American's subsidiary, Computer Sciences, with an estimated annual turnover of $16.2 million in 1977.

Most experts feel, however, that the South African mini-market is seriously overcrowded at present and expect the ranks to thin over the next couple of years as firms either withdraw for economic reasons or are bought out by more successful suppliers. These developments have already occurred on a limited scale: In 1977, ICL acquired Singer Business Machines, Singer's subsidiary for handling mini-computer hardware and peripherals in South Africa, and also in 1977 Sperry Univac obtained the Varian agency. In 1978, Wang Computers sold its subsidiary to General Business Systems as a franchise.

Principal foreign suppliers of electronic equipment: Foreign participation in the electronics field is more difficult to pin down than in the computer industry because of the greater tendency of multinational electronics firms to have local partners for business reasons. For example, the British electronics giant GEC had interests in roughly a dozen companies in South Africa in 1977. Nonetheless, foreign suppliers dominate the industry: Experts estimated in 1977 that some 80 percent of all electronic equipment and components was imported.

Only market leaders in the telecommunications field are easily identifiable because of their extensive involvement with the Post Office. The telecommunications subsector is dominated by four major firms, all with varying degrees of foreign participation. Siemens's West German parent--Siemens AG--holds a 52-percent interest in its South African subsidiary, and the balance is controlled by local interests. The other companies are Telephone Manufacturers of South Africa, jointly controlled by the local subsidiaries of two British electronics firms, GEC and Plessey; Fulmen, a subsidiary of France's Compagnie General d'Electricite, now heavily involved in the installation of the new electronic switching system; and Standard Telephone & Cable, a wholly owned subsidiary of Allied Technologies in which U.S.-based International Telephone & Telegraph has a 34.2-percent minority interest. All of these firms do at least 60 percent of their total business with the Post Office.

A number of American companies have subsidiaries or affiliates in the specialized electronics field in South Africa. Those firms identified by the U.S. consulate in Johannesburg in 1979 as marketing specialty instrumentation and electronic equipment and having more than 100 employees include Bell & Howell Co., Cutler Hammer Inc., F&M Inc., General Electric Co., Hewlett-Packard Co., Honeywell Inc., Motorola Inc., and Westinghouse Electric Corp.

Japanese and European firms are generally regarded as the leading suppliers in entertainment and consumer electronics. Market leaders in this area include Sharp Electronics, Sony and Philips.

Employment, Recruitment and Training

Shortages of skilled personnel: While estimates of the number of South Africans employed in the computer industry vary widely--ranging from 18,000 suggested by the Department of Statistics to 30,000 offered by one private consultant--all experts agree that the lack of skilled workers is becoming critical. The electronics industry is also suffering from shortages of skilled workers. The problem has been exacerbated by the extraordinarily high rate of growth in these sectors over the last 10 years, the inability of South Africa's universities to turn out sufficient numbers of adequately trained graduates in these fields and the steady emigration of skilled personnel.

Computer and electronics work is highly technical, and blacks have had difficulty entering the industry because of their lack of basic education. Government statistics indicate that only two out of every 1,000 black students starting school on the primary level graduate from high school. Because high-technology companies feel that a high school education is the minimum acceptable educational background for working in the industry, they say that their efforts to recruit blacks for technical staff positions have been hampered severely by the inadequate number of qualified candidates. For example, blacks do not comprise more than 20 percent of the work force in any U.S.-owned computer firm in South Africa, and in most cases they are assigned administrative or clerical functions rather than technical jobs. Informed observers speculate that there are probably no more than 100 blacks involved in programming and field engineering, although several hundred more may hold less skilled positions in the industry.

According to the Department of Statistics, by June 1977 about 7 percent of all jobs in the computer industry were not filled because of the lack of qualified applicants. In cases where the job is crucial and no candidates can be found, some companies have recruited overseas to fill the position. For example, Control Data told IRRC that its South African subsidiary brought in three people in 1978 from Britain and Israel for specialized slots.

At the heart of the problem is South Africa's educational system. Computer science is an optional subject in white secondary schools and cannot be used to meet university enrollment requirements; in black schools, the subject is not part of the curriculum. While most universities offer courses in computer technology, analysts claim that the subject matter is rarely geared to the needs of the industry. Moreover, the number of white students graduating in computer science is low--only 200 to 300 a year recently.

Rising emigration of skilled computer personnel has also complicated the industry's labor situation. Computerweek, a South African trade journal, reported in 1978 that more than 80 systems analysts have left the country in recent years, some 4 percent of all available systems staff. According to the journal, some of those emigrating are British expatriates returning to the United Kingdom, but departing personnel also include "a strong contingent of South Africans heading for Australia."

Recruitment: Most of the large foreign computer suppliers maintain their own recruitment programs for both blacks and whites. Companies usually recruit two to four times as many whites as blacks. While some recruitment takes place on university campuses, it is not uncommon for firms to make offers to employees at competing companies. Annual employee turnover for whites at some companies may average 35 percent or more, significantly higher than in the computer industries of other developed nations. The volatility of the labor market has caused some industry executives to complain that funds spent on recruitment and training frequently seem wasted because many employees often change firms with little notice.

Some experts have argued that--in addition to the substandard quality of black education in South Africa--another factor inhibiting recruitment of blacks is the cultural bias of the aptitude tests administered to prospective employees. While some firms like IBM--rely on their own standardized tests, many others use the National Institute of Personnel Research examination format. Experts assert that the NIPR test and--to a lesser degree--individual company tests should be revised to reflect the different cultural background of black applicants and their reputed weakness in three-dimensional perception. One expert told IRRC that the Canadians have made great progress teaching computer programming in Zambia after revising the curriculum to take into account cultural disparities, and suggested that similar measures would be useful to black development programs in South Africa.

Training programs: The size and scope of specialized training programs vary in accordance with each company's needs. In general, new white employees are assigned directly to on-the-job training to acquire specific technical skills and to familiarize themselves with various product lines. These programs may last from three months to two years, depending on the complexity of the skills to be mastered. New black employees are usually given special preparatory courses outside the company to help them assume the responsibilities of an entry-level trainee.

Chamdor--One of the best-publicized training centers for blacks coming into the computer industry is based at Chamdor, outside of Johannesburg. Chamdor is an in-service training center staffed and administered by the Business Equipment Association, a trade organization comprised of a number of firms in the business equipment field. Chamdor is one of eight private in-service training centers established under the Bantu In-Service Training Act passed by the government in 1976. Under the terms of the legislation, the government is committed to provide more than $2.3 million in funding for the land and buildings required for each center, and industry, through trade associations, is responsible for staff and administration of the training programs. The Chamdor center is under the auspices of the Business Equipment Association, although companies in other industries use its facilities for their black employees as well.

Chamdor's curriculum has emphasized basic mechanical and electrical skills in the past, but the program has recently been expanded to include non-technical courses on general business operation and employee responsibilities. Most courses range from one to seven weeks, but the center now offers a 29-week program divided into three sections that cover both technical and non-technical subject matter. During the first 12 weeks, the curriculum is devoted to the basic structure of a business enterprise and the roles and expectations of the employees who operate it. One industry representative told IRRC that the intention of this part of the program is to provide blacks with "survival skills" necessary to function successfully in a modern business setting. The next 12 weeks are directed at "pre-product training." During this time, employees are given a basic understanding of the equipment marketed and maintained by their companies. In the final five weeks, employees return to their firms for highly structured on-the-job training.

Chamdor has received the support of a number of American companies selling high-technology products in South Africa, most notably IBM. Joos Lemmer, principal at Chamdor, is an IBM employee on leave for three years to oversee the program. IBM has also donated equipment and funds for housing. Despite this support, however, Chamdor officials say that their facilities are generally underutilized and that the center is barely breaking even financially. Mr. Lemmer maintains that Chamdor could double the number of trainees with very little effort. "It is a shame," he told IRRC, "that we are not being used enough in a time of high unemployment. But we are an in-service institution which means we can provide only for employed people." By mid-1978, six black computer engineers--two for IBM and four for Burroughs--had successfully completed their training at Chamdor.

Other training programs for blacks--Several companies prefer to conduct their own in-house training programs for blacks. For example, in 1978 ICL devoted some $350,000 to a black employee development program. Out of 1,200 applicants, the company gave aptitude tests to 400 blacks and ultimately selected 40 candidates for its program. IRRC was told that 30 participants graduated and were placed as programmers and analysts. ICL's next major training effort will be aimed at increasing the number of computer technicians and operators in the black homelands, according to the company.

Foreign firms have also used at least one private South African company to train black employees in computer operations. The company--Van Zyl and Pritchard--has turned out 11 black programmers since its four-month training program started in 1976. The cost of the training is approximately $1,400 per student, not including living expenses.

Costs of training--Only a few computer firms have revealed their overall annual expenditures for training. Burroughs--the third largest company in the South African computer industry--reported that in 1978 it spent some $450,000 for employee development but was unable to break down this figure by race. Based on the available information, however, it appears that the majority of funds spent by the computer industry for upgrading skills are allocated for whites because whites are more heavily recruited than blacks and occupy all of the senior technical and managerial positions. This is partially borne out by one U.S. computer firm which told IRRC that in 1978 its estimated training costs for white employees totaled some $67,000 while its costs for blacks came to about $3,300. When asked about this discrepancy, a company official said that the costs for whites were higher because several senior management personnel had been brought to the United States for additional training. A number of executives were also enrolled in classes and seminars on information management at local universities last year, he said.

Educational assistance: Many American computer firms have become actively involved in or have developed special programs to improve education for blacks in South Africa. Most companies make regular contributions for black scholarships on the high school and university levels. For example, in 1978, Burroughs spent about $25,000 on education grants to disadvantaged black students. Through their membership in the American Chamber of Commerce, a number of firms have pledged various sums of money to the Chamber's Project PACE (Planned Advancement of Community Education), a multi-million-dollar effort to build and finance a commercial high school and community center in Soweto. One of the largest corporate contributors to PACE so far is IBM, which has pledged close to $300,000 to the project.

Some U.S. firms--among them Control Data and IBM--have become more directly involved in education of blacks through outright contributions of equipment and services. Control Data plans to install a computer-based education system for blacks in stages and has appealed to other American companies for financial assistance to expedite the project. Control Data's chairman, William Norris, has sent letters to the chief executive officers of all companies doing business in South Africa explaining the benefits of the system and asking for their support for the project. The objectives of the system are primarily to help blacks develop basic reading, math and language skills and to expand the vocational training opportunities available to them. IBM has budgeted up to $3 million over the next three years for the production and distribution of a series of video programs to aid and support the teaching of physical science, mathematics and biology in black high schools. Working with the Department of Education and Training and local parent/teacher associations, the company will provide some 40 schools with video cassette players and TV monitors to enable them to use the tapes in classrooms. IBM also plans to develop a small library of other educational and academic cassettes already available commercially.

III. Pressures on Foreign Computer and Electronics Firms Operating
in South Africa

Since 1974, the strategic importance of the computer and electronics industry in South Africa and the role of foreign companies in that sector have come under increasing scrutiny. Critics of the companies maintain that the high-technology products--especially computer equipment-- marketed by their South African subsidiaries and distributors are vital to the enforcement of apartheid policies.

They assert that the white-controlled government--the largest user of computers in the country--is dependent on sophisticated data processing systems for its day-to-day administrative tasks as well as for security purposes. Computers and electronic instrumentation also play an essential role in business and industry: By facilitating modernization and increasing the efficiency of South Africa's economy, computers strengthen the capacity of the minority regime to rule, critics contend. Company officials respond that while it is not possible to regulate all final uses of their products, to the best of their knowledge none of their equipment in South Africa is being used for repressive purposes. They argue that ending sales of sophisticated electronic equipment to South Africa would not affect the government's political philosophy and that the most constructive course of action a company can take is to remain there and provide increased employment opportunities and technical training for blacks.

The widening debate over the activities of high-technology companies in South Africa has expanded pressures against these firms. Perhaps the most significant of these has been a ban by the U.S. government on the sale of U.S.-origin computers and electronic gear to controversial government agencies in South Africa, including the military and police, the Department of Plural Relations, the Atomic Energy Board and the Uranium Enrichment Corp.

In addition, with increasing frequency, institutional shareholders are voicing their concerns to computer firms and other manufacturers of sophisticated electronic equipment about the nature of their operations in South Africa. During the last five years, shareholder activists have submitted a number of resolutions to these companies in an effort to modify their sales and investment policies. In Britain, labor unions representing ICL employees have openly criticized the company's involvement in South Africa, and union officials have had a series of meetings with management to express their views on the issue.

The increasing pressures on U.S. computer suppliers doing business in South Africa have had a sizable impact on the computer industry there. Companies say U.S. restrictions on computer sales to the government have made many South African customers wary of dealing with American firms and have eroded their competitive edge in that country, much to the delight of other foreign suppliers. Sanctions have also spurred interest in import replacement, and several South African companies are now

manufacturing their own computer hardware. Shareholder pressures have
caused at least two companies--Control Data and Burroughs--to adopt a
policy of non-expansion in South Africa and have induced others to
monitor their marketing operations much more closely than they might
otherwise.

Sales to controversial users: To support their contention that
computers are linked directly to the enforcement of apartheid and other
strategic interests in South Africa, critics frequently cite a number of
sales made by U.S. suppliers to controversial government and
government-affiliated bodies there. According to Management (November
1974 and December 1977) and Systems (May 1977), sales to controversial
departments have included:

User	Supplier	Model
Armaments Board	NCR	NCR C100
	Hewlett-Packard	HP 2116
Atlas Aircraft Corp.	Univac	UNI 1106
Atomic Energy Board	IBM	IBM 370/155 (2)
	Control Data	CDC 1700
	Hewlett-Packard	HP 2115
	Computer Sciences	Varian 620/L
Council on Scientific	IBM	IBM 370/158
and Industrial Research	Control Data	CDC Cyber 74
Department of Defense	IBM	IBM 370/40
		IBM 370/145
		IBM 370/158 (2)
East Rand Bantu Admin- istration Board	Burroughs	BUR 3700
Department of Interior	IBM	IBM 370/158 (2)
		IBM 370/155 (3)
Department of Justice	Data General	NOVA (6)
Department of Prisons	IBM	IBM 360/20
Uranium Enrichment	Foxboro	FOX 1 (2)
Corp. (UCOR)	IBM	IBM 370/145

Other controversial users of foreign-supplied computers include
certain public corporations--such as the Iron and Steel Corp., the
Electricity Supply Commission, South African Railways and South African
Coal, Oil and Gas Corp.--and the leading companies in key private sector
industries. Among the latter group are motor vehicle manufacturing,
petroleum refining and distribution, and mining. Computers are also used
for some administrative tasks in black homelands.

Policy on computer sales: In November 1976, the U.S. Commerce Department instituted a policy to restrict sales of computers and computer technology to the South African military and police, as well as to government agencies handling "Bantu" affairs and atomic energy. All companies with general distribution licenses for computer sales to South Africa were informed that future sales to these agencies would require a validated license. A general license allows exports without prior approval on each individual sale; a validated license requires assurances on each export that the item exported will not be diverted to an unauthorized destination. The effect of this change in policy--which was never published as an official regulation--has been to end sales of all computers and computer-related items to these agencies.

The restrictions on computer sales were spelled out and tightened in February 1978 when the Commerce Department issued regulations placing an embargo on all export sales by U.S. companies to the South African military and police. The regulations are intended "to strengthen United Nations Security Council Resolutions of 1963 and 1977 regarding exports of arms and munitions to South Africa." In November 1977, the Security Council imposed a mandatory embargo on arms sales to South Africa. The embargo was enacted in response to the death of black consciousness leader Steve Biko and the South African government's crackdown on political opposition in the fall of that year.

The regulations require purchasers of U.S. exports to certify that goods purchased will not be sold or used in any way by the military or the police. The regulations also state that: "Parts, components, materials and other commodities exported from the United States may not be used abroad to manufacture or produce foreign-made end products where it is known...the end products will be sold or used by military or police entities" in South Africa and Namibia.

Finally, the Commerce Department has placed restrictions on the transfer of certain types of technical data that could be used in a strategic manner by the South African government.

While the February 1978 restrictions on trade have had no effect on computer sales to military and police entities because these sales had already been prohibited under the 1976 Commerce Department policy, they have had a major impact on service agreements between U.S. suppliers and embargoed agencies. Under the regulations, companies holding maintenance contracts with embargoed agencies were given a two-month grace period to notify their customers to make alternate arrangements for servicing their equipment. The regulations specified that the export of spare parts and technical data necessary for the repair of equipment operated by military and police entities would continue during this period, but that export of accessories for future use or for upgrading the capacity of such equipment would not be permitted.

Enforcement problems--The degree to which the Commerce Department can enforce its restrictions on computer sales to South Africa is not clear. Officials charged with putting the regulations into effect are concerned that some U.S. companies will circumvent the controls by simply importing goods into South Africa from their European subsidiaries. Critics contend that this arrangement not only violates the spirit of the regulations, but could well be illegal if parts supplied through this channel are made under patents registered in the United States.

Furthermore, because computers used by the embargoed agencies are similar to commercial models employed by other government departments and by private companies in South Africa, there is no effective way for the Commerce Department to monitor the end use of spare parts shipped to that country.

Other difficulties in enforcing the regulations arise because of the computer time-sharing agreements among various government departments. Because existing government computer installations are--for the most part--underutilized, "there is no way for the U.S. authorities to prevent this capacity from being shared by the defense and police departments," according to one South African computer executive. South African laws may also interfere with the effective implementation of the embargo. The Business Protection Act of 1978 makes it illegal for anyone in South Africa to supply information to any official entity outside the country on any aspect of business without government permission. Under this law, U.S. officials could be prevented from investigating suspected violations of the embargo. The National Supplies Procurement Act of 1970 authorizes the Minister of Economic Affairs to order any company operating in South Africa to deliver goods to the state that are determined to be essential to national security. The government, therefore, has the power to expropriate any computer system or spare part necessary to meet its data processing needs in emergencies.

Possible violations of Commerce Department regulations--On March 10, 1979, the St. Louis Post-Dispatch reported in a copyrighted story that ICL had included Control Data equipment in a computer sale to the South African police (see below). Under Commerce Department regulations, U.S. exporters are required to inform their customers about the embargo on sales to the South African military and police and to receive assurances that they will comply with the ban. Control Data officials were concerned that the company could be in violation of the embargo when the first rumors of the ICL sale to the police surfaced in the summer of 1978, according to an internal company memorandum obtained by the Post-Dispatch.

Control Data maintains that it signed an agreement with ICL in September 1976 asking ICL to comply with the ban on sales of U.S.-origin equipment to military and police agencies in South Africa. The company says it also sent a directive in March 1978 to ICL urging it to use "extreme caution to avoid violations" of the embargo. According to Control Data, the directive said in part: "You are requested to consult with this office before you take action on any order, instruction, request or inquiry which has direct or indirect boycott implications or which could result in a violation of the embargo." Control Data says that because of this directive it is in full compliance with U.S. export regulations.

According to the Post-Dispatch article, ICL claims that it never received the letter referred to by Control Data officials. The article quotes the director of ICL's international division as saying: "It is our understanding of American regulations that any American manufacturer constrained by American law would put a formal request to us to prohibit certain end uses. We have had a number of requests from other U.S. companies. CDC did not make a request, but then they didn't think they had to." The official said, however, that ICL has no further plans to install Control Data equipment in the South African police department and will abide by the regulations, according to the article. When asked to comment on the **Post-Dispatch** article, a Control Data spokesman told IRRC: "Although the ICL official was personally unaware of the CDC request at the time of the interview, Control Data knows for a fact that the directive was sent and received by ICL."

Shareholder pressures: Most computer and electronics companies report that inquiries from concerned investors about their activities in South Africa date back to the early 1970s. According to corporate officials, communications with shareholders about their South African operations have centered on three issues: employment practices, investment plans and business with the government. Originally, most of these inquiries were made by church investors. In the last four years, however, inquiries about South Africa have not only jumped in number, but have come increasingly from other kinds of institutional stockholders, particularly colleges and universities.

In response to growing shareholder interest, many companies have published fact sheets or reports on their South African operations. While these reports describe in varying detail the companies' business activities, most of the texts are usually devoted to discussing companies' labor practices and progress in upgrading black employees, their contributions to community and public service organizations and their views on corporate withdrawal from South Africa. Companies in the computer and electronics field that have prepared these reports include IBM, Burroughs, Sperry, NCR, Control Data, Hewlett-Packard, 3M, Xerox Corp., General Electric Co. and International Telephone and Telegraph Corp.

Since 1976, shareholder activists have filed an increasing number of resolutions with computer and other high technology firms doing business in South Africa, seeking changes in their operations there. During the 1978 proxy season, a shareholder proposal asking Control Data to halt all sales to the South African government received the support of 4.55 percent of the shares voted. Resolutions to Motorola and 3M requesting the firms to withdraw their subsidiaries from South Africa were supported by 1.64 and 1.94 percent of the shares voted, respectively. In 1979, the resolution was resubmitted to Control Data and a similar proposal was filed at Sperry. The resolutions received the support of 3.30 percent and 3.40 percent of the shares voted, respectively. A resolution asking Burroughs to stop sales to the South African government was proposed earlier in 1979 but was withdrawn after the company agreed not to expand its investment in South Africa as long as present social conditions persist and adopted a policy that prohibits the sale of Burroughs equipment that might be used for repressive purposes.

Pressures on ICL: Pressures on ICL have grown considerably following the revelation that the company recently had sold two large computer systems to the South African police. Representatives of nine trade unions--meeting with ICL officials in October 1978--told the company that they were strongly opposed to the sale of computers "for the administration of apartheid." The meeting was held after workers at ICL's Manchester plant declined to work on the two 2960 systems ordered by the police. In addition, 15 employees in the corporate information systems office of ICL's London headquarters informed company officials that they refused to work on any South African projects. A union spokesman said that the workers are opposed to the police order on moral grounds and that they believe ICL's links with South Africa jeopardize the company's business relationships with important Third World customers, such as India and Nigeria.

Company spokesmen deny that the new equipment will be used to enforce apartheid laws. They say that its main function will be to store police personnel records and assist with payroll and accounting procedures. They assert that all of ICL's business in South Africa is conducted in accordance with British law and UN resolutions. Moreover, they say that ICL's South African sales provide work for some 900 employees in Britain and that its subsidiary in South Africa is strongly committed to the career development of its black workers.

While the British government--which has a 24.4-percent stake in ICL--has not taken a formal stand on the controversial sale, industry officials claim that the Commander of the British Empire title recently awarded to ICL's managing director in South Africa, John Starkey, constitutes an official stamp of approval for the company's operations. Mr. Starkey received the honorary title in January 1979 for his "services to British commercial interests in South Africa."

Impact of the pressures: The growing pressures on multinational computer companies active in South Africa have had a substantial impact on the computer industry there. Perhaps the most significant change has been the increasingly cautious position taken by South African customers on doing business with American computer suppliers since U.S. restrictions on trade with South Africa took effect. Industry sources say that the embargo on sales to the military and police has placed American companies at a competitive disadvantage because, in the words of one executive, "customers are concerned about the long-term commitment of U.S. suppliers to South Africa, particularly as it relates to the after-sale servicing of highly technical products." As a consequence, some customers have turned to other foreign suppliers not constrained by such prohibitions to satisfy their information processing and storage needs.

In addition, the possibility of further sanctions and the growing pressures on multinational suppliers of high technology equipment have spurred local manufacturers to give greater consideration to import replacement. In data processing, South Africa has already designed and assembled small mini-computers successfully. In electronics, the government's unofficial policy of favoring South African suppliers in tender offers to promote self-sufficiency is having some effect, although foreign firms have questioned the policy's long-term value.

Competitive disadvantage placed on American firms--Based on available information, U.S. government restrictions on exports to South Africa appear to have had an adverse impact on the commercial reputation of American computer suppliers and other high technology firms involved there. Before the restrictions took effect, American computer companies expressed concern about their potential competitive disadvantage, both individually and through the Computer and Business Equipment Manufacturers Association, the industry's trade group in Washington, D.C. In a letter from CBEMA to Assistant Secretary of Commerce Frank Weil in December 1977, discussing the then-pending restrictions, industry representatives argued that the restrictions would force U.S. computer companies to default on existing maintenance contracts and would be "seriously injurious to their reputation and ability to sell throughout the world." CBEMA wrote that the regulations would "strengthen the contention of foreign competitors who argue that potential customers abroad cannot rely on U.S. multinational companies to meet their existing contractual commitments because of increasing U.S. government intervention."

It is not certain that the worldwide business of American computer conglomerates has suffered because of the Commerce Department's restrictions, but officials at several computer companies have said that the regulations have measurably diminished their sales in South Africa. In a letter to IRRC, Dan P. Lutzeier, director of corporate communications for Burroughs Corp., said:

> The February 1978 Commerce Department regulations regarding the export of goods and technical data to South Africa have affected Burroughs. There have been two instances where we had signed orders for computers and had export licenses denied. One order was for the West Rand Bantu Board and the other for East Cape Bantu Board. The dollar value for these orders was over $2 million.
>
> In addition, because of the ill-defined interpretation being implemented by the Commerce Department, potential customers in South Africa are increasingly reluctant to place orders with American companies. In approximately five instances where bids had been submitted and Burroughs was considered the favored vendor, we were withdrawn from consideration after the regulative changes were announced. These potential orders involved over $22 million.

(Despite the drop in business attributed to the Commerce Department restrictions, Burroughs's managing director in South Africa, Tom Brown, said in an interview with the Financial Mail: "I don't know of any deals which have not gone through because of anti-American feelings. Some customers ask questions, but we point out that the embargo applies to certain government agencies and not to products." Mr. Brown said that Burroughs's South African subsidiary is heading for a record year in sales.)

David Kirby, director of public relations at Hewlett-Packard, told IRRC that his company estimates that the regulations have resulted in a loss of about $1 million annually for its South African subsidiary, approximately 10 percent of its business.

Officials at IBM declined to comment on whether the regulations have placed a financial burden on its South African subsidiary. Some analysts believe that the regulations were probably an important factor in IBM's loss of its traditional position as market leader in computer hardware in South Africa to ICL.

U.S. firms marketing electronic equipment other than computers in South Africa have also been affected by the recent trade restrictions. For example, the chairman of Motorola Corp., Robert W. Galvin, said in a letter to IRRC that the February 1978 regulations "have affected the company's capacity to complete certain substantial contractual obligations entered into prior to the enactment of the stated regulations." While calling the costs "significant," Mr. Galvin said that no accurate estimate could be made until negotiations between the company and its affected customers are resolved. A Motorola spokesman told IRRC that the products assembled in South

Africa include automobile regulators, alternators and electronic ignition systems; two-way mobile radios; portable radios; fixed transmitters; and paging equipment.

Trend toward self-sufficiency--The mounting pressures on overseas computer and electronics suppliers and South Africa's overwhelming dependence on them for high technology has made import replacement programs for strategic items more urgent. Public awareness of the country's vulnerability in these areas is limited, however, and support for import replacement is--for the most part--confined to certain segments of the government and business community. Prof. J.T. Steele, head of the computer center at the University of Witwatersrand, told the Johannesburg Star in December 1978: "We are almost totally dependent on imports for our computer requirements. A faulty chip costing no more than R150 ($172.50) can bring a whole system to its knees if it cannot be replaced. Our utter vulnerability in this vital field is not generally appreciated by the public, but is causing grave concern in official circles and serious attention is being given to the matter."

These concerns are responsible for the fact that several companies have already started to market locally assembled mini- and micro-computers of their own design. One of the most successful models has been the Commander, manufactured by Messina (Electronic) Development Co., formerly a subsidiary of the South African mining and engineering conglomerate Messina (Transvaal) Development Co. that was acquired in mid-1979 by Allied Technologies, a local electronics firm in which ITT has a 36.3 percent interest. The Commander--a micro-computer--has been on the market since April 1977, and in its first year chalked up sales of roughly $675,000. About 90 percent of the company's orders have come from the private sector--particularly industrial users--while the remainder have originated with the government.

The Commander was originally developed to improve the efficiency of Messina's copper mining operations. The company wanted to speed up rock hoisting and to expedite communication between surface and underground work teams, but was unable to find a compact computer that could operate at high temperatures underground. Messina then decided to build its own system and came up with Commander.

Eighty percent of the parts used to manufacture the system are produced in South Africa, with specialty components coming from the United States, Europe and Japan. Company officials are trying to push local content even higher in an effort to reduce costs because imported computer parts carry a 15-percent surcharge under South Africa's tariff regulations. This surcharge has made the Commander system slightly more expensive than competitive imported micro-computers.

While Messina claims that its micro-computer is not only more rugged than other small systems, but more versatile as well, the Financial Mail reports that the Commander has encountered some initial market resistance because of what company officials call "the credibility gap." The credibility gap is an outgrowth of the history of foreign domination of the South African computer industry--the belief among some customers that South Africa lacks the knowledge and resources to put together a computer that measures up to its imported counterparts. The Commander's early track record is changing this view, however, according to company representatives.

Other firms concentrating on the local design and assembly of small systems include Data Corp. of South Africa, Data Management Services, Datakor and Anker Data Systems. While many of their products have only recently come onto the market, they are generally expected to sell well and to gain preferential treatment from government agencies expanding their data processing facilities. One industry expert told IRRC that locally produced equipment will most likely erode American sales "to the small commercial company which is looking to computerize but is uncertain about the reliability of supply from the U.S."

The threat of sanctions has also stimulated considerable interest in self-sufficiency in the electronics field. Siemens, for example, claims to have boosted the local content of its South African manufacturing and assembly operations to 80 percent, up from 65 percent in 1976. To encourage import replacement and local control of technology, government departments have been instructed to favor when possible South African electronics suppliers over foreign ones when disbursing contracts, even if they have to pay a premium on locally produced items. The Post Office and the Armaments Production and Development Corp. have been the greatest proponents of this policy. In the words of an ARMSCOR executive interviewed in the Financial Mail in 1978: "We balance our needs against South Africa's industrial capacity. It's not a question of cost."

Experts say that the government's policy has provided a sizable incentive for multinational suppliers to take on South African partners. While a number of foreign firms have merged all or part of their South African operations with local business interests, some companies--such as Plessey, Siemens and Philips--are reluctant to surrender a majority stake. They argue that if a majority interest were held by local enterprises, the parent company would probably restrict the flow of important technology and take less interest overall in its affiliate's well-being. Moreover, some overseas suppliers argue that the government's push for local control of technology is an affront to firms that have been established in South Africa for a number of years. Philips's managing director, Jan Timmer, told the Financial Mail: "If you've been in a country for 50 years and have invested R70 million ($80.5 million), you like to think that you have proven yor commitment without fashionable window dressing, like increasing local shareholding."

It is not exactly clear, however, how far South Africa has come toward self-sufficiency in electronic components. Post Office officials claim that local industry could probably supply all of the country's telecommunications needs, if necessary. In 1976, the government-financed Council on Scientific and Industrial Research opened a plant to manufacture custom-designed integrated circuits, a highly complex project. Allied Technologies has started to produce certain kinds of semiconductors, diodes and crystals, and plans to invest more than $3.4 million in research and development in 1979. Barlow Rand has joined forces with the Department of Electrical Engineering at the University of Pretoria to establish a special laboratory for applied research in electronics. The primary purpose of the laboratory is to bridge the gap between basic research and economic production of electronic equipment more efficiently.

Despite these developments, some experts are skeptical about the industry's progress toward self-sufficiency. Prof. Louis van Biljon, head of the Department of Electrical Engineering at the University of Pretoria, said in an interview with The Citizen in October 1978: "In spite of talk of high local content and other red herrings that are drawn across the trail from time to time, the horrible truth is that if we are not able to buy components such as diodes, integrated circuits and transistors, we cannot make anything. All that we can do at present is to assemble mini- and micro-computers. Until we develop the necessary manpower, and make everything we need in this country, we will be dependent on other countries. Even if we made everything except one vital component, we would be like the building industry that lacked only cement."

IV. IRRC Analysis

During the last 20 years, the computer and electronics industry has come to play an increasingly strategic role in South Africa's development. It not only has been crucial to the rapid expansion of the country's industrial capacity, but it also has expedited the government's task of handling the growing number of administrative responsibilities that have accompanied modernization. Moreover, the economic importance of the industry is considerable: It now accounts for more than $2 billion in sales and services each year, roughly equivalent to 4.4 percent of South Africa's 1978 gross domestic product.

Foreign firms dominate the computer and electronics fields and are responsible for the transfer of a wide range of technical data, components and equipment to South Africa. U.S. firms control roughly two-thirds of the computer market there. Through the marketing operations of multinational suppliers, South Africans have access to some of the most sophisticated computer systems and electronic instrumentation in the world. These companies also administer most of the training programs for skilled personnel in these areas.

Because foreign suppliers control so much of this strategic industry, it is possible to argue that their activities lend support--both directly and indirectly--to the government's apartheid policies. Historically, the country's rapid rate of economic growth and development--largely facilitated by computers and other kinds of sophisticated electronic equipment--has been a buffer against the threat of international economic pressures for change in South Africa. As a consequence of this growth, the government has accumulated the technology and capital to develop a domestic armaments industry and to acquire advanced weaponry for its military forces. More directly, advanced information management systems have increased the ability of the government to monitor and supervise the affairs of South Africa's various population groups with greater efficiency, an essential component of its apartheid strategy. Agencies charged with these responsibilities--such as the Department of Plural Relations, the Department of Interior and the Department of Justice--rely extensively on computers for record-keeping and other administrative functions.

Increasing public awareness of the involvement of American companies in this controversial industry has made their activities in South Africa one of the focal points of the debate over U.S. investment there. This attention has put a variety of pressures on American computer and electronics suppliers active in that country, the most significant of which has been a U.S. government ban on exports of equipment to the South African military and police.

While the intention of those restrictions is to further U.S. foreign policy objectives on human rights and to strengthen the United Nations arms embargo against South Africa, it appears that the ban has had little or no effect on the availability of high technology products to the embargoed agencies. In cases where American suppliers have had to cancel contracts or forego business opportunities because of the ban, European and Japanese companies have filled the gap. While it is impossible to be certain whether the ban has forced the embargoed agencies to sacrifice some measure of quality or service by buying equipment from non-U.S. suppliers, it seems safe to say that they probably have not suffered any major setbacks. Thus, the principal impact of U.S. trade restrictions against South Africa has been the loss of business by American firms selling to military and police entities there, accompanied by an increasing South African wariness about doing business with these and other American companies. In addition, the ban has stimulated a number of South African suppliers of high-technology products to give serious consideration to programs aimed at making themselves self-sufficient.

In light of these factors, it seems unlikely that the U.S. government will apply further sanctions against South Africa in the short or medium term unless such action has multilateral support. The prospect of further sanctions has also been lessened by the U.S. desire to convince South Africa to assume a more cooperative role in Namibia and Rhodesia.

Nevertheless, shareholder pressures on computer and electronics firms active in South Africa are likely to remain. In the view of some investors, high-technology companies have limited opportunities to act as progressive agents for social change in that country because they employ only small numbers of blacks. Moreover, efforts to recruit and train more blacks have been stymied by the limited pool of qualified candidates available. Because of the burgeoning demand for high-technology products and the accompanying need for greater numbers of skilled personnel, technical training has--out of necessity--focused on whites. Training programs for blacks in this area have been limited and relatively unsophisticated. Some analysts believe that these factors have forced computer companies and other high-technology suppliers to take a more active and visible role in community and educational projects than firms employing larger numbers of blacks. Critics of these firms suggest that in some cases this image may even be illusory; they say high-technology companies tend to publicize their social service record in South Africa more heavily than other companies because of their limited opportunities to upgrade their labor practices.

In the United States, a consensus seems to be emerging among those groups concerned with the situation in South Africa that high-technology companies occupy a special position in the controversy over American corporations doing business there: They dominate a particularly strategic industry in South Africa; they train and employ only a small number of blacks; and the South African government is the largest user of their products. In response to these pressures, high-technology firms are likely to continue or step up their public service activities. Increasing attention may also be paid to problems in black recruitment and training although substantive benefits from these efforts may not be realized for some time to come. In addition, U.S. suppliers with high visibility in the industry will probably view any plans to expand their operations in South Africa very cautiously even though market conditions--in spite of the Commerce Department ban on certain exports--make such a move tempting. In the electronics field, some American firms may follow the lead of other foreign investors and seek local partners for their South African subsidiaries. While this sort of merger may be made largely for business reasons, it could also be motivated by a desire to defuse pressures on the parent firm. It appears, however, that pressures on high-technology firms operating in South Africa will grow as long as that country's political tensions remain unresolved.

Sources

The South African Computer Users Handbook 1977/1978, Systems Publishers, Johannesburg 1977.

Richard Leonard, Computers in South Africa: A Survey of U.S. Companies, The Africa Fund, New York, November 1978.

Department of State Airgrams:

"Research into Best Prospects List--Communications Equipment; Electronic Components," American Consulate, Durban, July 20, 1978.

"South African Import Replacement Program: Local Company Develops and Assembles Micro-computer System," American Consulate, Johannesburg, June 6, 1978.

"South African Telecommunications: Latest Developments Indicate Accent on Self-Sufficiency," American Consulate, Johannesburg, March 21, 1978.

Developments of Interest in South African Data Processing Market," American Consulate, Johannesburg, Jan. 31, 1978.

"Industries and Commodities: State-of-the-Art in Integrated Circuit Production--South Africa," American Consulate, Johannesburg, Aug. 19, 1977.

"Developments in Television Manufacturing Industry in Neighboring Swaziland and Market Penetration in South Africa," American Consulate, Johannesburg, May 13, 1977.

"New South African Television Industry Already in Trouble," American Consulate, Johannesburg, Nov. 30, 1976.

"Further Developments in the South African Telephone System," American Consulate, Johannesburg, Sept. 27, 1976.

Financial Mail:

"Communications: plain talking," Aug. 29, 1979.
"Computers: the ever-booming market," April 27, 1979.

"Computer hardware: an industry is born," March 16, 1979.
"Telephones: hello Soweto," Feb. 23, 1979.
"Import replacement: joys and woes," Feb. 16, 1979.
"Univac's local partner," Jan. 12, 1979.
"Sanctions: U.S. bending the rules," Aug. 18, 1978.
"Some will, some won't," July 14, 1978.
"The sky's the limit", special supplement on telecommunications,
    June 2, 1978.
"Messina: undercover strength?" special supplement, May 26, 1978.
"The ban bites," March 10, 1978.
"Siemens returns," Feb. 10, 1978.

The Johannesburg Star

"Computerless chaos on the cards," Dec. 28, 1978.
"R59 on nationwide computer chain for Barclay's," Dec. 16, 1978.
"UK campaign to outlaw South African computer sales", Nov. 4, 1978.
"Computer for South Africa sparks protest," Oct. 19, 1978.

The Corporate Examiner, "Computing apartheid: the role of U.S. computer companies in South Africa," June 1978.

Johannesburg Sunday Times, special supplement, "Computers in the Eighties," June 24, 1979.

To the Point, "Computers: drawing the sting of sanctions," June 16, 1978.

Gail Purvis, "Computers, Electronics and Telecommunications in South Africa," unpublished manuscript, November 1978.

C. THE MINERALS INDUSTRY IN SOUTH AFRICA

The role of foreign companies in South Africa's mining sector is likely to be the subject of continuing debate during the next several years. The mining industry is critical to the South African economy, accounting for 65 percent of its total exports in 1978. It has contributed significantly to greatly increased state revenues, spurred economic growth and cushioned effects of the oil crisis which followed the fall of the Shah in Iran. In addition, the abundance of South Africa's mineral reserves, some of the world's richest, and the country's proven ability to mine and refine these minerals, have made it one of the world's most important sources of a number of strategic materials.

Most of the development of South Africa's mineral reserves was financed by foreign capital and made possible with foreign technology--primarily from Britain, but increasingly from the United States and Germany. Although many of the current and anticipated development projects can be financed with domestic funds, a substantial need for foreign financing and a lesser need for foreign technology remain.

The debate over American involvement in the South African mining industry has spanned nearly a decade. Since the early 1970s, shareholders have questioned some of the largest U.S. mining companies about their investments and plans for expansion in South Africa. In the last several years, shareholder resolutions have been proposed to Kennecott Copper Corp., Phelps Dodge Corp., Newmont Mining Corp., U.S. Steel Corp. and Union Carbide Corp. requesting them to cease expansion or to withdraw from South Africa.

Until recently, criticism has focused on two major concerns--the conditions under which Africans work in South African mines and the possibility that investment decisions and actions taken by foreign mining companies have supported the South African government's policy of apartheid. Notoriously low wages, physically demanding and dangerous working conditions, and the extensive use of migrant labor have led many observers to criticize foreign capital investment in this sector. Critics are also concerned about the influence of the powerful Mine Workers Union, which represents many white South African mine workers and which has been outspoken in its opposition to most moves that would permit an upgrading of skills and greater opportunities for Africans.

Critics of apartheid also contend that mining, as the major export sector, contributes significantly to South Africa's foreign exchange earnings, strengthening the South African economy and supporting the white minority regime. They accuse the industry of providing wealth for the white minority but few benefits for the majority African population. Moreover, they claim that many mining companies, by locating their smelters in the government's border development areas adjacent to the African homelands, rather than within the homelands near mineral deposits, assist the government in its policy of separate development.

Foreign companies operating in South Africa deny that their investments constitute support for apartheid. They argue that the investments and the labor practices followed by their subsidiaries contribute directly to the well-being of all South Africans, black as well as white. Several companies have endorsed the equal opportunity principles developed by Rev. Leon Sullivan, and most say that they make efforts to improve the working and living conditions of their workers. Mining companies argue that they have a responsibility to shareholders to mine where minerals are available; their presence in South Africa does not reflect their approval of the government's racial program. Those companies that have located near to or in the homelands argue that they have little choice--the mines are on top of the minerals, the smelters are near the sources of power and water as well as existing transportation grids. At present almost all of these facilities are outside of the homelands. They also argue that the lease fees and taxes that they pay to homeland governments and wages paid to African workers provide critical income to economically depressed areas.

In the last three years, a third issue relating to South Africa's minerals has begun to emerge--the question of the strategic value of those minerals to the West. As calls for partial or total economic embargoes against South Africa have come with greater frequency, opponents of such actions have argued that the West cannot afford to participate in an embargo because it is dependent on certain essential South African minerals and dares not risk the possibility of retaliation.

Other policy analysts have been concerned that recent actions taken by the Cubans and the Soviets in Africa raise the possibility that Soviet influence could come to dominate South Africa and result in a cutoff of supplies of strategic minerals to the West.

This study discusses the role of minerals in the South African economy, foreign involvement in the industry, the labor situation in the mines and the issue of the strategic value of South Africa's minerals. The study contains the following sections:

  I. Minerals and the South African economy.

  II. The role of foreign companies in mining.

  III. The strategic importance of South Africa's minerals to the West.

  IV. IRRC analysis.

I. Minerals and the South African Economy

Apart from the Soviet Union and the United States, southern Africa has the largest and most varied known resources of minerals in the world. In a region rich in minerals, South Africa's deposits are the most abundant. South Africa has the world's largest reserves of gold, vanadium, platinum, manganese, chrome and fluorspar and it has the technological and financial ability to mine and refine vast quantities of these and other minerals. It is the world's largest producer of gold, platinum, vanadium and chrome, and it ranks among the world's top 10 producers of a host of other minerals ranging from copper and tin to uranium and asbestos. In part because the world's second largest producer of many of these items is the Soviet Union, South Africa's production is of great significance to policy planners in the West. Moreover, four minerals--platinum, chrome, manganese and vanadium--are considered strategic to the West because they are essential to industrial processes and are in limited supply.

South Africa's minerals are not only important to the world market, they are also of critical importance to South Africa itself. For more than 100 years, mining--first of diamonds and gold and later of a wide variety of non-precious minerals--has been the key to growth for South Africa's industrialization process. South Africa's minerals have been central to attracting manpower, expertise, capital and technology to the country and have provided the wealth required to cover the burgeoning import demands of industrialization. For years minerals have been South Africa's major export, providing more than 50 percent of total export earnings. Gold alone is responsible for more than 30 percent of exports, and a $10 fluctuation in the price of an ounce of gold can amount to a shift of more than $220 million in annual foreign exchange earnings. During the inflationary year of 1977, the $40-per-ounce increase in the price of gold produced about $1 billion in additional foreign exchange. Although the price of gold remained virtually unchanged in terms of the strong Swiss and Japanese currencies, its gains of some 10 percent in terms of the British pound and 25 percent to the dollar were important to South Africa because the United States and the United Kingdom are the major suppliers of its imports. South Africa's Financial Mail commented in January 1979:

Thank heavens, at least, for gold, whose international role shows no signs of diminishing. Back home, this boosts the balance of payments and the state coffers, as well as being a major source of employment and investment capital. Thank heavens, too, for diamonds, platinum, coal, uranium, asbestos, iron and manganese, and chrome, other major contributors to our healthy current account.

In addition to the contributions mining makes to the balance of payments, state revenue, employment and investment, it also plays a vital role in South Africa's quest for energy independence and, some would argue, in the government's efforts to defend what it considers its strategic interests.

In the last eight years, despite fluctuating world metal prices and a world recession, South Africa has benefited both from a steady increase in the quantities of minerals produced and from an even more rapid rise in their value on world markets. Overall production from South Africa's mines, excluding gold, grew 45 percent in volume between 1970 and 1977, and the decline in the amount of gold produced has been more than offset by the dramatic rise in its price. The total value of all mineral production in South Africa grew from $2.2 billion in 1971 to $7.9 billion in 1978 and it is estimated that in 1979 this figure will rise to $10.3 billion; the value of gold production grew from $1.2 billion to $4.4 billion during that period.

Balance of payments: The boom in minerals production has been of particular importance to South Africa's balance of payments. More than 80 percent of all minerals produced in South Africa are exported. At a time when South Africa was mired in a recession along with most of the world's economies, Pretoria increased its earnings from mineral exports by some 64 percent, from $3.9 billion in 1976 to $6.4 billion in 1978. (See table, p. 245) Of the $2.5-billion surge in mineral exports between 1976 and 1978, some $1.7 billion came from increased sales of gold. And it is estimated that South African gold output in 1979 will be in the region of $7.2 billion--some 60 percent of the value of the 1978 gold output.

Without gold, South Africa would run a consistent deficit in its balance of payments. In 1978, with gold exports of $4.4 billion, South Africa's balance on current account was $1.6 billion.

Krugerrands: Gold exports have been boosted by the development in 1970 of the Krugerrand, a coin containing one troy ounce of gold. It is legal tender in South Africa, but the vast majority of the 22.5 million Krugerrands sold from 1970-78 have been exported, principally to Germany and the United States. For those wishing to own gold it is an attractive item--its weight and purity are assured by the South African government, its status as legal tender exempts it from the 11-percent-value-added tax applicable to gold bullion sales in West Germany, and the small premium (3 percent) added to the market value of the gold in the coin is the lowest of any of the gold coins available in the world.

Aided by these factors and the energetic marketing of Intergold, the marketing arm of the South African Chamber of Mines, Krugerrand sales took off in 1975, reaching a total of 3.2 million coins that year. In 1978, 6 million Krugerrands--valued at $1.15 billion--were sold, bringing the South African government more than $30 million in foreign exchange from the premium payments alone. Half of the sales were to Americans, and the $15 million Americans paid in premiums that year was greater than the $11 million U.S. mining companies made in direct investments in South African mining ventures.

World demand for Krugerrands continued to be high during 1979 as serious inflation weakened the dollar.

Payments to the government: The South African government has been a major beneficiary of the growth in mineral production. Lease fees and income taxes paid by South Africa's mining companies have made up between 8 and 22 percent of the central government revenues each year during the 1970s. Within the mining sector, gold mines have been far and away the dominant contributors.

The government receives 42.5 percent of the profits from the mining of all non-precious minerals, coal and platinum. The rate of taxation on gold mine profits is determined by the ratio of the mine's profit to its total revenue, and can range from zero to slightly less than 60 percent. Thus as gold prices and profits increase, the South African government collects a larger proportion of the return. As an example of what this means in practice, the chairman of Anglo American's Orange Free State gold mines has pointed out that:

> ...of the increased benefits of some R155 million accruing to Anglo American Orange Free State mines from the higher gold price (in 1978), the state benefited to the extent of R113 million and the stockholders only R34 million.

Overall, during 1978, some 1,078 million was paid by gold mines in taxes and leases, twice as much as was collected during 1977.

Mining and employment: As a major employer, mining makes an important contribution to South Africa's economy. In 1978, the mines employed nearly 700,000 workers; approximately 11 percent of the African workers and 4 percent of all white workers make their living in the mines.

Because of the increasing degree of mechanization in the

mines--which requires a larger proportion of skilled labor--the ratio of black employment relative to white has been declining since 1972.

Strategic importance of minerals to the economy: South Africa's minerals play a key role in the country's strategic planning. By expanding coal production, constructing larger facilities for converting coal to oil, and developing a nuclear power capability, South Africa can use its minerals to reduce its dependence on imported fuels. Although about three-quarters of South Africa's energy needs can be met by coal, South Africa is dependent on imported oil--90 percent of which used to come from Iran--to meet the remaining 25 percent of its energy demand. The country has abundant coal reserves, however, and has developed one of the most sophisticated methods of converting coal to oil in the world. The South African Coal, Gas and Oil Co. (Sasol) currently operates a coal gasification plant that supplies close to 3 percent of South Africa's petroleum demand. The government estimates that a second Sasol plant, expected to be completed in 1980, should further increase South Africa's coal gasification capability to enable it to meet nearly 25 percent of its oil needs through coal. And in response to the cutoff of Iranian oil early in 1979, the South African government in the summer of 1979 began work on a third Sasol plant equal in size to Sasol II. Some energy experts have expressed doubt that this level of oil production can be attained, and speculate that a more realistic figure is in the neighborhood of 11 percent.

South Africa is also taking steps to develop an independent nuclear power generating capacity supplied with South African uranium enriched in a South African enrichment facility. Expansion of the existing uranium enrichment plant, originally built using West German technology, is scheduled to be completed by late 1984 and will permit South Africa to produce more than the 300 tons of enriched uranium required each year to fuel two atomic power stations now under construction near Capetown.

Outlook: The mining industry will continue to dominate the South African economy for the indefinite future, but may be plagued by increased production costs and low world prices for some minerals. The lack of skilled labor, a union agreement allowing white miners to work fewer shifts, wage increases and hikes in the cost of electricity and transportation all contributed to an average increase in production cost of 23.7 percent for the industry in 1977 and 13.7 percent in 1978. For some base metals--copper, manganese and iron--the increased production costs and low world prices cut deeply into profits, lowering production and closing some mines. Gold mine owners complain that production costs have increased at the same rate as the rise in gold prices.

Nevertheless, the increased price for gold and the growing importance of a number of other minerals--uranium, coal, chrome and platinum--should more than offset any reduction in production of gold or base metals. And most businessmen and government planners are relatively optimistic about the future. The South African government estimates that fixed investments in mining will increase at an annual rate of close to 6 percent in the next two years, and Basil Landau, director of South Africa's Union Corp., predicts that South Africa will spend almost $12 billion on mining, metallurgical and related developments during the 10 years from 1979 to 1988. The outlook for the major minerals is sketched below:

Gold--It is unlikely that there will be a marked increase in gold production in the near future--in fact, production may continue on a slight downward trend--but the introduction of new mines and new methods of recovery of gold from mine wastes and a steady high price for gold will assure that it maintains its critical role in the economy. The February 1978 Financial Mail reported that mining houses, buoyed by high prices for gold and uranium (often mined as a by-product of gold mining in South Africa), were planning to develop five new gold mines in the next five years. Moreover, new methods of retrieving gold, uranium and sulphuric acid from mine wastes should allow one company--the Anglo American Corp.--to produce the equivalent of 2 percent of South Africa's total annual gold production (14,000 kilos) and 400 tons of uranium a year.

Uranium--In the last few years the amount of uranium mined and its value on the world market have both increased dramatically. The world price for uranium jumped from $7.70 a pound in 1974 to $43.00 a pound in 1978, and profits from South African uranium mines grew from $21 million in 1975 to $76.5 million in 1977 and were expected to exceed $115 million in 1978. The U.S. Consulate in Johannesburg estimates that uranium export sales totaled some $245 million in 1978 compared with $104.4 million during 1977.

Most of South Africa's largest mining companies and several international oil companies are engaged in extensive uranium prospecting, and capital investments of $300 million begun in 1977 are expected to double uranium production by 1980 and to raise South Africa's output to that of Canada, currently the second largest producer of uranium in the West (the United States is the largest). South African uranium has a competitive advantage over most of the world's uranium because of its relatively low production costs and because it is mined as a by-product of gold.

Coal--The opening of the new Richards Bay bulk ore handling port in 1977 was the key factor in the dramatic jump in South African coal exports that year--the value of coal exports increased 250 percent over 1976. By year-end 1979, 20 million tons of coal worth approximately $600 million will have passed through Richards Bay and, if a planned double-tracking of the rail line from the coal fields to that facility is completed on schedule, the tonnage will more than double by 1984. With Japan alone planning to import 20 million tons of South African coal from 1983 onwards, export earnings from coal could exceed $1.8 billion annually by the mid-1980s. In order to expand coal production and permit more substantial exports, close to $1.15 billion was invested in coal mining during the three-year period from 1977 through 1979.

Chrome--Since 1975, when the South African government determined that chrome ore and chrome-related products--ferrochrome and stainless steel--had the greatest potential of any commodity for replacing the decline in gold output, there has been a tremendous push to spur chrome exports. The government announced a program of incentives including export subsidies, low-cost loans, tax concessions, and rebates for energy and transportation costs, and companies have moved actively into what is known as beneficiation--the refining of ores into semi-manufactured goods. Both programs promise notable success. Chrome ore production is expected to rise from 3.3 million tons in 1977 to 5.3 million tons in 1980, and by 1980 half of all chrome ore mined will be converted to ferrochrome. Only one-third of production was converted in 1977.

In 1970 ferrochrome exports earned only R13.2 million. By 1978 that figure had shot up to R185.6 million and South Africa was supplying more than 60 percent of the West's ferrochrome imports.

There may be some restrictions on future expansion of South African ferrochrome exports. Both the United States and the EEC have introduced "trigger prices" which lead to the levy of additional duties if the price of imports drops below the trigger. In addition, there appears to be growing concern on the part of Western nations about becoming too dependent on South African sources of supply. If they react by stockpiling and by developing alternative sources of ferrochrome, they would seriously alter the market for South African ferrochrome.

Platinum--The platinum market is small, volatile and heavily dependent on the actions of the three major producers--South Africa, the USSR and Canada. Platinum mines have been plagued by sharply rising production costs, which forced some mines to reduce their output substantially in 1977. The price per ounce rose 75 percent in 1978 to $330 an ounce and hit $380 in August 1979, but most analysts remain cautious about the future. If platinum prices hold at the high level attained recently and the mines are able to control production costs, then platinum might be able to take up the slack occasioned by declining gold production. If either of those two conditions is not met--and the odds are good that at least one of the two will not be--then production will fall and platinum will find itself ranked below gold, uranium, coal and chrome in importance.

II. The Role of Foreign Companies in Mining

South Africa's minerals have consistently been the country's major draw for foreign capital and technology. Between about 1870 and the beginning of World War II, nearly one-half of all the private capital from abroad invested in South Africa had gone to finance development of gold mines near Johannesburg, and the exploitation of South Africa's minerals has continued to attract substantial foreign investment. South African economist Hobart Houghton says South Africa's mineral wealth has also been important to the country's economic development by attracting "men from abroad with drive, energy, vision and courage to take chances." People drawn by the mines stayed to become entrepreneurs and to provide a cadre for industrial leadership. Houghton comments, "whether this enterprise would have arisen without this input from abroad is doubtful."

There is little debate that without foreign capital and technology, development would have taken much longer than it did. Foreign capital not only allowed the import of technology and equipment from abroad for the gold mines--which in fact were relatively non-capital intensive--but also permitted the import of equipment required for manufacturing and permitted local capital to be used in other non-mining ventures. Workers were also imported. Before World War II, although the bulk of the mine labor force consisted of Africans hired in the tribal areas, without the skills of trained miners from Wales, Cornwall and parts of Germany--and 50,000 miners from China--development of the mines would have been hobbled.

The mining houses: The first South African mining involved

extracting diamonds and gold from surface deposits. As the industry grew, mining became increasingly complicated. Most of the gold was deep; miners had to be assured ventilation, water removal, power supply; the process became sufficiently expensive to force individual independent mines to group together under the aegis of finance houses that could provide capital and technology. The houses found their primary backers in England and, to a lesser extent, Germany and the United States. The company that was to become South Africa's largest--the Anglo American Corp.--began in 1917 with one million British pounds in capital investment from England and the United States. Today, British and American stockholders own approximately half of its shares, and the corporation has assets of 1.7 billion rand and produces 40 percent of South Africa's gold, 37 percent of its uranium and 33 percent of its coal. The Anglo American Corp. is part of the broader Anglo American Group which also has other investments ranging from automobile manufacturing to breweries. Mining constitutes 69 percent of the group's activities.

In addition to Anglo American, South Africa has six other major mining houses. Like Anglo American, several of those, including Gold Fields and Johannesburg Consolidated Investments (JCI), were heavily financed with British capital in the beginning. British control was maintained for years--JCI moved its headquarters from London to Johannesburg only in 1963. It is now 50-percent owned by Anglo American. Gold Fields is 49-percent owned by Consolidated Gold Fields (U.K.). The other major mining houses are Union Corp., which had German backing, and AngloVaal, which was started with local capital but later received European financing. Rand Mines is controlled by Barlow Rand, a South African industrial conglomerate run by English-speaking businessmen. The seventh major company, General Mining, was sold by Anglo American to Federale Mynbou in 1964 and became the first Afrikaans-controlled mining house in the gold mining sector.

The mining houses continue to dominate the minerals industry. From an almost exclusive interest in gold, they have expanded into the breadth of South Africa's mineral wealth. AngloVaal has interests in manganese, chrome, iron and copper. General Mining mines coal, uranium, asbestos and uranium, as well as gold; and Gold Fields is actively developing one of the world's largest lead mines.

Foreign interests: The diversification from gold into other minerals has been heavily assisted with foreign capital, and foreign stockholders continue to control a portion of the mining houses indirectly. Foreign stockholders, through purchase of stock in South African gold mines, control indirectly more than 50 percent of a number of South Africa's largest mines; at the end of 1977, Americans held 25 percent of all the shares issued by South Africa's gold mines. But foreign companies are active directly as well, usually in partnership with South African mining houses, in the exploration and development of a wide range of minerals--titanium, chrome, lead and uranium.

Using figures from the U.S. Department of Commerce and the South African Reserve Bank, IRRC estimates that in the mid-1970s at least $3.3 billion of the $17-billion total investment in the South African mining sector came from the United States and the EEC countries. Of that $3.3 billion, close to $300 million is in the form of direct U.S. investment (i.e., a U.S. company owning 25 percent or more of a South African mining concern), and an estimated $1.7 billion is indirectly invested in South African gold mines through the purchase of gold mining stocks by American citizens and financial institutions. At the end of 1973, the EEC countries had some $900 million worth of indirect investments, more than double their $400 million in direct investments. Thus, when the indirect and direct investments of the EEC countries and the United States are combined, they represent approximately 20 percent of the value of the estimated total investment in South Africa's mining and mineral industry.

Foreign capital has also been available to South Africa in the form of loans either to the mining houses, to their foreign partners or to the South African government (to allow construction of harbors, power lines or roads that benefit the mining industry). It has also come through long-term purchase arrangements. This is particularly common for uranium, where foreign purchasers may provide a no-interest loan to be used for the development of a uranium mine and processing facilities, with the loan to be repaid by discounts on the contract price. In 1977, the French Atomic Energy Authority signed a 10-year uranium delivery contract that will begin in 1980. A $103.5-million interest-free loan was included as a part of this contract.

The mining houses and a number of foreign companies--primarily American and British--are connected in what often becomes an intricate network of direct investment, ownership of shares and participation in joint ventures. In general, the major British involvement is indirect, through shareholding, while U.S. involvement is both indirect and direct. U.S. companies have assets valued at a minimum of $475 million in South African and Namibian mining and smelting operations as well as in South African ferroalloy production.

In a number of cases, foreign companies are involved jointly with South African companies in exploration on a contingency basis; in others, foreign companies may be expected to supply technology. AngloVaal, for example, has arrangements with U.S. Steel in which the American company is to provide the capital for financing joint prospecting efforts. If the efforts succeed, U.S. Steel will have the opportunity to become a minority partner in the new mining projects. (The $75 million U.S. Steel has invested in South Africa represents more than two-thirds of the total assets it has outside of North America.) Quebec Iron and Titanium (two-thirds owned by Kennecott Copper and one-third owned by Gulf & Western Industries Inc.) has a 39.3-percent interest in a $290-million titanium sands project; the remaining interest is divided equally between the government-owned Industrial Development Corp. of South Africa and the Union Corp. Quebec Iron and Titanium is responsible for overseeing the smelting operation. Newmont Mining has a 28.6-percent interest in the Palabora Copper Mine managed by Rio Tinto Zinc, a British firm, and a 57.8-percent interest in O'okiep Copper Mine. Union Carbide is active with General Mining in ferrochrome smelting and Phelps Dodge with Gold Fields in lead mining.

To a lesser extent, South Africa is also dependent on foreign technology in mining. As labor costs have risen at the mines in recent years, capital-intensive forms of underground mining have received increasing attention. The most talked about method is "long-wall" mining which utilizes equipment capable of carving one continuous swath through the mineral seam, removing the same amount of ore as the traditional methods but using considerably less manpower. Three U.S. firms--Joy Manufacturing Co., Dresser Industries Inc., and Ingersoll-Rand Co.--supply the bulk of this new technology, and manufacturing plants in South Africa are now being constructed by the first two firms. In 1979, when production at these plants begins, 65 percent of the content of the finished product will be locally produced. This share will rise to 90 percent when final development plans are completed.

South Africa's open pit mines, where enormous quantities of rock must be removed, import almost all of their loading and transporting equipment. Ore crushers large enough to handle the stream of rock pouring out of these mines are also imported. In 1976, capital expenditures by all South African mines for all machinery, transport and other equipment came to $294 million. The United States in that year exported to South Africa mining and construction machinery valued at $74 million. Although these two figures are for categories of goods that do not entirely overlap, they give an idea of the dependence of South African mines on imports from the United States.

The Labor Situation

A major early concern of critics of U.S. business involvement in South Africa's mining industry focused on labor practices. South Africa's mines were built with migrant labor drawn from within South Africa and from neighboring countries. Work in the mines has been tough, dirty and dangerous. The migrant labor system has offered workers little bargaining power to protect their interests, and pay at the mines has been lower than any sector except for migrant farm labor. Opponents of the South African government and critics of business's role there have often cited the plight of African miners as evidence of the cruelty of apartheid.

Wages: Wages for Africans in the mines have historically been among the lowest in South Africa. In 1971, the average monthly wage of an African mine worker was 18.44 rand and the average for a white mine worker was 386 rand. Because of inflation, this meant that African workers had actually achieved no increase in their real wages since the Chamber of Mines began collecting statistics in 1911. In October 1972 African real wages fell in all sectors of the economy as inflation more than negated any wage increases. A wave of strikes began, first in the manufacturing sector in and around Durban, spreading within a few months to the mines. During the two years from February 1973, there were 54 strikes by African workers in 34 mines. The strikes became violent and by the end of the final strike nearly 200 Africans had died and almost 2,000 had been injured.

Mine owners reacted quickly to the strikes. Anglo American Corp. increased its basic monthly wages for African miners by 70 percent between March 1972 and December 1973. At the Tsumeb mine in Namibia, more than half-owned by two U.S. companies--Newmont Mining and Amax Inc.—average wages for African workers rose 57 percent during 1976. As the table on p. 245 shows, Africans obtained impressive wage increases (in percentage terms) in 1973, 1974 and 1975. The rate of increase slowed considerably in the following three years.

While these rapid wage increases have diminished the ratio of African wages to those of whites from 1 to 20.9 in 1971 to 1 to 7.1 in 1978, mining still pays poorly when compared with many other sectors. For example, in 1976 the wage ratios in manufacturing were 1 to 4.4, in central government employment 1 to 3.1, and in construction 1 to 5.2. Moreover, although the income ratios for African and white miners improved during the 1970s, the actual gap between the monthly wage paid to Africans and that paid to whites widened from 367.56 rand in 1971 to 669.25 rand in 1977. In addition, the new minimum wage rates for unskilled mine labor set in July 1979 (R20.04/week for underground labor, R13.50/week for surface work), are below the amount necessary for an African family to meet its minimum subsistence needs.

In interviews or special reports to shareholders, several companies have noted the widening gap between African and white wages. However, the companies argue, the quickest solution for this inequity--massive across-the-board wage increases for Africans--would cause many mines to close, thereby throwing out of work those people whom the increases were intended to help.

In their discussion of wages, the mining companies also point to the free room and board provided the African miners--valued at 50 rand per month in 1979--as a factor that must be considered in any comparison of African and white wages. However, as one critic of South African mining practices has pointed out, the same mining companies consistently fail to report the cash value of compensation in kind provided to white employees.

South African laws and African mine workers: The first report of the Wiehahn Commission, released in early 1979, recommended several changes in existing labor laws that would, if enacted, create greater job opportunity for African workers. However, the commission's specific recommendations concerning African labor in the mines will not be released before early 1980, and regulations enacting legislation could be delayed until the end of that year or 1981.

As of late 1979 the following were the key South African laws affecting black mine workers:

• The Industrial Conciliation Act establishes a system of negotiation between trade unions and industry for resolution of conflicts over wages and working conditions. The act creates industrial councils, composed of an equal number of representatives of trade unions and of industry, which meet periodically to negotiate wages, determine which jobs are to be held by union members and negotiate terms affecting labor conditions such as hours to be worked, overtime permitted, sick leave and other fringe benefits. Before the recommendations of the Wiehahn Commission were incorporated as amendments to this act, the term "employee" was defined to exclude Africans and prevented them from joining registered trade unions. Today all Africans except migrant workers drawn from outside South Africa can form unions which are then eligible for formal recognition--registration--by the government. Multiracial unions are still prohibited and, because registration is not granted automatically, it is possible that some newly formed black unions will fail in their attempts to obtain government recognition.

The act also includes a "job reservation clause" providing for the reservation of certain skilled jobs to people of a certain race. Although reservations affect fewer than 3 percent of all jobs, many of those are in mining. The act is used to ensure that the skilled mining jobs of surveyor, sampler and ventilation official are reserved for whites. The Wiehahn Commission has recommended that statutory job reservation be repealed.

• The Bantu Labor Regulations Amendment Act of 1973 defines the rights of African workers in disputes with employers and sets the limits and conditions for the exercise of those rights. The Amendment act replaces the Bantu Labor (Settlement of Disputes) Act of 1953 and was introduced following the strikes at Durban in 1973.

The Amendment act gives workers the right to demand representation through a works committee composed entirely of representatives elected by African workers unless the company has already established a liaison committee. (The difference between the two kinds of committees is important. At least half the members of a liaison committee must be elected by African employees, but the chairman and remaining members may be appointed by management.) The Bantu Labor Act contained no such provision, and as late as 1972, only 150 to 200 committees representing workers existed in the country. Under the new act, by the end of 1974, companies had established 1,819 liaison committees and 274 works committees. An amendment to the act, introduced in 1977, gives liaison and works committees the right to negotiate contract agreements with their employers. It also recognizes a limited right of Africans to strike, but only after strict prerequisites have been met. Many critics consider these prerequisites to be too limiting.

• The Apprenticeship Act establishes the major means by which a person may become a skilled tradesman, recognized as a qualified artisan. Although the act does not differentiate according to race, interpretative custom has set certain patterns that have severely limited training in the trades for Africans.

• The Mines and Works Act of 1926 also limits the categories of jobs open to blacks by prescribing "regulations on certificates of competency required for employment in certain occupations." Blacks are not granted certificates to do blasting, for example, and they must be supervised by a white miner.

• The Factories Act and the Shops and Offices Act are written in non-discriminatory language but provide for a series of regulations on factory or plant conditions--including health and safety of workers--which permit action by a government inspector to correct a situation detrimental to the physical, moral or social welfare of the employees. Separation of facilities--toilets, eating, working and recreation areas--by race is one item included in the regulations, and a company's performance in respect to separation of facilities is subject to government inspection.

• The Workmen's Compensation Act of 1941 applies to those miners who become injured on the job or suffer from an industry-related disease. When a worker is more than 30 percent disabled, compensation takes the form of a lump-sum payment for African workers and a monthly pension for whites, coloreds and Asians. The South African government explains that this method of payment is used because African workers often have no fixed address.

• The Unemployment Insurance Act of 1966 excludes from its coverage African workers in gold and coal mines who are supplied with food and lodging by the company. Because almost all African miners live in company dormitories and eat at company-financed cafeterias, this clause effectively excludes all African gold and coal mine workers from the protection offered by this act.

Working conditions in South African mines: Mining in any country is a dangerous occupation, but the dangers increase in South Africa where some of the deepest mines in the world are in operation. In 1976, 836 South African miners died in mine accidents. Of these, 783 were African. The number of fatalities increased to 953 in 1977, 890 of which were African. In both years, for every 1,000 African miners there were 1.4 fatalities; for white miners the figure was 0.9. The fatality rate for miners in the United States that year was 0.7.

One of the major reasons for the disparity between the fatality rates of African and white miners in South Africa is that underground work is five times more dangerous than surface work and the bulk of the unskilled jobs are underground. Thus, one of the results of the various legal obstacles that prevent African mine workers from moving up into the ranks of skilled labor has been a fatality rate 50 percent higher for Africans than for whites.

Migrant labor: A striking characteristic of African mine labor is the extent to which it is composed of migrants, from both South Africa and other nations in southern Africa, especially Mozambique. Most of the 600,000 African mine workers live in dormitories without their families. Workers from foreign countries usually stay at the mines for 12 to 18 months; labor contracts for South African migrant workers are shorter, averaging six or seven months.

The South African government and many of the mining companies describe the migrant worker as a laborer who comes to the mines in order to supplement the already adequate income he and his family earn from a small farm either in the African homelands of South Africa or in the surrounding southern African nations. Critics of the migrant labor system contend that in reality the homelands are marked by acute poverty and the migrant worker is forced by economic necessity to leave his home and seek work at the mines.

In line with apartheid, the permanent settlement of Africans in white areas of the country is actively discouraged. Thus, mining companies have been allowed to house their workers only on mine property and must obtain permission before constructing married quarters. By law, no more than 3 percent of the African labor force may be housed in married quarters.

Recently, the government has informally relaxed these rules somewhat so that more married mine workers may now live with their families. The South African Chamber of Mines--an association of mining concerns--hopes to see the regulations amended so that at least 10 percent of the African labor force may live in married quarters, but whether the government will be willing to do so is unclear.

Two factors are currently altering the nature of the migrant labor system in the mines. Following the series of violent strikes at the mines from 1973 to 1975, mine owners attempted to reduce the number of foreign African migrant workers who were seen as both instigators of and ready participants in those strikes. These efforts were successful and, in contrast to 1973 when 80 percent of all African mine workers were foreigners, by 1978 only 47 percent of the African workers were from outside South Africa.

The second factor is the increasing realization that because of a shortage of white skilled workers at the mines, more Africans will have to receive advanced training. For the mining company to recover its training costs, the newly trained African worker must remain an employee of the mine for a period of time measured in years rather than in months. Following the lead of mine owners in Zaire and Zambia 10 years ago, South African owners are now beginning to argue that a migrant labor system does not encourage the level of training that is essential if the mining industry is to have enough skilled workers.

The role of white unions: The white Mine Workers Union, the largest of the eight unions representing white workers in the mines, appears to have been one of the chief impediments to a rapid movement of Africans into skilled mining jobs. White miners have historically played a key role in the South African mine labor picture. Skilled immigrant miners from Britain were the first to introduce craft unions in the mines and used them not only to demand higher wages and better working conditions but also to prevent the replacement of any skilled white union member by a non-white worker.

In 1922, when the Chamber of Mines attempted to replace white miners with Africans in a cost reduction drive--from 1913 to 1921 white wages had increased 60 percent while wages for Africans had gone up only 9 percent--white miners provoked the worst labor dispute in South Africa's history. The Rand Rebellion of 1922 left 153 dead as the army crushed the revolt. The chamber won a temporary victory that was reversed following the assumption of power in 1924 by a political party that granted the white mine workers' demands for job protection.

The miners went out on strike again in March 1979 to protest plans to move colored workers into skilled positions at the O'okiep Copper Mine. Fearing that this would set a precedent for replacement of whites by cheaper colored and African labor throughout the industry, the Mine Workers Union called a wildcat stike. Six days after it began the white miners were back on the job. The South African government had studiously avoided becoming publicly involved in the dispute, but it privately assured the Chamber of Mines that it supported their firm stand against the union. Although the Mine Workers Union appears to have lost much of the political clout it once had following the collapse of its recent strike, it retains the ability to frustrate job advancement for African miners.

While the Mine Workers Union has continued to oppose advancement for African mine workers, its views are not shared by all white unions. In 1977, the Mine Surface Officials Association joined the Trade Union Council of South Africa (TUCSA) which has encouraged its member unions to organize parallel unions for Africans and has gone on record in support of fair employment practices since 1973.

Job training for African miners: Although South African laws and the strong pro-apartheid stance of the white Mine Workers Union have prevented Africans from moving into skilled jobs at the mines, a shortage of skilled white labor is forcing a partial lowering of the color bar. The Minister of Labor predicted in 1975 that an average of 5,000 blacks a year would have to step into skilled mining jobs that had previously been reserved exclusively for whites. The mine owners and even the pro-apartheid white unions have responded to this critical shortage with policies whereby, in the words of Harry Oppenheimer, head of the Anglo

American Corp., Africans will "float up" into skilled jobs.

An example of "floating up" occurred in 1973 when the Chamber of Mines and the white trade unions agreed to set up a training program for African artisan aides. These aides work under the supervision of a white skilled worker and perform various semi-skilled tasks.

Francis Wilson, a South African professor who has written widely on mine and migrant labor, says that "floating up" often does little to change the system of race discrimination in job allocation--skilled white workers merely move up one or two rungs on the job ladder and non-whites take their places. This is especially evident in the case of artisan aides who, even when their training is completed, continue to perform their tasks under the supervision of a white worker. However, Wilson also notes that any increase in the training provided African mine workers will make it more likely that employers will seek ways to stabilize their trained African labor force because it would be increasingly unprofitable not to do so. Measures to promote stabilization could include equal pay for equal work and the provision of family housing for those African employees desiring it.

Some of the more liberal mining houses have indicated willingness to go beyond "floating up" in providing more skilled jobs for African workers. Companies like AngloVaal, Anglo American and Union Carbide have developed affirmative action programs aimed at filling more supervisory, clerical and management positions with blacks. Progress has been most rapid at the supervisory level--as blacks "floated up" many took over first line supervisory positions from departing whites. Few blacks moved into the ranks of management, in large part because of the lack of technically trained blacks, according to company spokesmen. The companies hope to surmount this obstacle by indentifying talented blacks and then encouraging them with scholarships for engineering and other technical studies.

Confronted in March 1979 with a shortage of 250 artisans in the gold mines alone, according to a Chamber of Mines survey, and a predicted shortfall of nearly 1,300 by 1985, some mining companies have recently initiated artisan-level training for selected black employees. According to the companies, when the four- to five-year training period is successfully completed, these black employees will be treated and paid the same as white artisans--even if official recognition is withheld by the licensing boards.

Mining and the Homelands

A major aspect of apartheid is the creation of a commonwealth of ethnically distinct states within South Africa's borders, politically independent yet economically dependent on each other. The government has established "homelands" for all Africans within which they will be accorded the full rights of citizens. One homeland--Transkei--obtained its independence in October 1976, a second--Bophuthatswana--became independent in December 1977, and a third--Venda--became independent in September 1979. None has been recognized by any country other than South Africa.

To reinforce its policy of geographical separation of the races, the South African government has extended incentives to corporations willing to invest in the homelands and in border areas adjacent to those homelands. It is pursuing decentralization in order to provide Africans with job opportunities in or near their homelands and thereby lessen their desire to move to the urban centers in the white areas of South Africa.

Locations of mining operations: Several mining ventures are now located either within homelands or in adjacent border areas. Two of the three South African platinum producers have located all or a portion of their mines within the homeland of Bophuthatswana. Rustenberg Platinum has roughly half of its lease area within that homeland, while all Impala Platinum mines are in Bophuthatswana. Impala Platinum is now paying 70 percent of its lease fees and income taxes to the homeland--some 45 million rand in 1978 or more than 35 percent of the Bophuthatswana government's total revenues for that year--with the remaining 30 percent going to the South African government. Rustenberg Platinum pays a lower percentage--20 to 25 percent--to the homeland. Division of the lease fees is determined by the physical location of the minerals, while the formula for apportioning the income tax is based on the location and value of the mining company's assets.

Quebec Iron and Titanium, U.S. Steel and Union Carbide are all involved in new operations that have recently been developed in the border areas. Quebec Iron and Titanium--owned by Kennecott Copper and Gulf & Western--has participated in the construction of a titanium smelter near Richards Bay adjacent to the KwaZulu homeland. U.S. Steel's chrome and fluorspar operations are in areas bordering Bophuthatswana. Tubatse--a ferrochrome-producing joint venture of Union Carbide and General Mining--began operations close to the homeland of Lebowa at the end of 1976.

The decentralization debate: A component of apartheid is the view that African workers are temporary residents in white South Africa who will return to their homelands when their labor is no longer required. The migrant labor system that grew out of this view took as its models the gold and diamond mines with their single-sex dormitories, compounds, and separation of the male wage earner from his family. Because they permit a greater proportion of African migrant workers to live near or with their families, company officials, South African leaders and some officials of the African homelands approve of the current industrial decentralization plans of the South African government. The chief executive councillor of the homeland of KwaZulu, in a 1976 letter to Kennecott Copper on its proposed mining development located on the border of KwaZulu, said that "our people have been forced to go to the metropolitan areas in order to earn a living. This is at the root of the migratory labor system, which has destroyed the African family life....It would therefore be most regrettable if opportunities for my people to get jobs at their doorsteps would not be forthcoming as is envisaged if you do not go ahead with this venture."

However, the policy of decentralization has also been criticized by some officials of the homelands and anti-apartheid activists. They claim that stimulating industrial development just outside the borders of the homelands makes it more, rather than less, difficult to develop industry within the homelands. New mining developments carried out in border areas by Quebec Iron and Titanium, U.S. Steel and Union Carbide have been criticized. In none of these projects was a smelter or ferroalloy manufacturing plant constructed within a homeland. The South African government has directed its expenditure on infrastructure development to growth points in the border areas, rather than to the homelands themselves. Because the ore bodies require only a single smelter, critics argue, by keeping these major fixed assets inside South Africa, the mining companies and the South African government are perpetuating the pattern of apartheid where capital assets are kept in the white areas while African labor is drawn from the homelands as and when needed. The companies, on the other hand, say that they are forced to locate mines where the minerals are and to place support facilities or smelters close to existing rail lines and power and water supplies.

The Performance of Foreign Companies

In the past several years, a number of developments have affected the performance of U.S. and other non-South African companies. In addition to the growing shortage of skilled workers, incentive for training has come from the public pressure building abroad. A code of conduct drawn up by the European Economic Community and the Sullivan principles that have now been adopted by many U.S. companies, both of which call for equal opportunity for African workers, have encouraged a number of companies to take a closer look at their practices and have pushed South African companies to develop their own codes. Some companies--including Union Carbide, Anglo American, and Palabora Mining Co.--have initiated training programs for Africans that are the equivalent of artisan training. A number have raised wages or instituted for the first time a unified wage curve--opening the possibility of equal pay for equal work.

The quality of housing provided black mine workers has also shown significant improvement during the past two years, especially on the new mines. More family housing is being built, and new hostel accommodations for migrant workers have only two or three men per room rather than the 12 to 16 found in the older hostels.

In general, the practices being followed by American companies are about the same as those followed by South African or European companies. U.S. companies are more attuned to the concept of affirmative action and desegregation of facilities as a result of unique American experience, and some U.S. companies have taken steps in these areas that outpace other companies. But some non-American companies have made moves in areas where U.S. companies have been less aggressive. Surveys find, for instance, that South African companies are more likely to make worker evaluations and to define job categories than are foreign companies. In fact, the major determinant of company performance is most likely to be individual management in home offices or in South Africa.

III. Strategic Importance of South Africa's Minerals to the West

Many analysts view the flow of South Africa's minerals to the West as the most important lever South Africa has to use in resisting Western pressures, not because of the quantities that the West imports, but because of the strategic nature of some of South Africa's minerals.

In terms of the quantities imported, most of the West relies only marginally on South African minerals. Britain and the United States both imported about $700 million worth of South African minerals other than gold in 1976, equal to 9 percent and 5 percent of their total mineral imports, respectively. Japan's imports of $445 million constituted about 4 percent of its total imports, and the $362 million that West Germany imported represented about 3 percent of its total mineral imports expenditures in 1976. (Together with France and Belgium, these four countries bought half of South Africa's mineral exports other than gold in 1976.)

Of the $5 billion worth of minerals exported by South Africa in 1977, strategic minerals accounted for $580 million. Strategic minerals are those that are essential to certain industrial processes, for which there are no acceptable substitutes and of which there is limited supply. South Africa produces four minerals that fall into this category--platinum group metals (platinum, palladium, iridium, ismium, rhodium and ruthenium), chromium, manganese and vanadium. The first, the platinum group metals, are highly efficient catalysts used in petroleum refining and in the catalytic converters used in most new cars for emissions control. The last three are essential alloying agents required for specialty steel. There are no known substitutes for manganese, and those for chromium, vanadium and platinum are economically unattractive and less efficient.

South Africa and the Soviet Union together control nearly all of the world's reserves of these minerals. The United States mines none of these minerals, except for vanadium, in any appreciable amount. (Estimates of reserves must be interpreted carefully. They are provided in most cases by mining companies exploring for new sources to be exploited 10 or more years in the future. Because most exploration for a mineral is carried out in regions already producing it, estimates of reserves are biased in favor of those nations currently mining the mineral in question. Some analysts argue that if South African and/or Soviet sources of supply were disrupted, exploration would shift to new regions with the possible result that new ore reserves would be discovered.)

A better measure than reserves of the importance of South Africa and the Soviet Union for the world's supply of strategic minerals is the portion of actual current world production accounted for by South Africa and the Soviet Union. Roughly two-thirds or more of current world production of these four minerals takes place in either South Africa or the Soviet Union. One can assume that these two countries will retain their dominant position as suppliers of strategic minerals for the next decade, as it would take roughly 10 years to develop alternative ore bodies in equivalent quantities.

Policymakers in the United Kingdom, West Germany and the United States have devoted considerable debate to the impact of a disruption in the supply of strategic minerals from South Africa. Official policy papers on the issue are classified, but elements of the debate have been reported in the press. The disruption, reports say, could come from several developments: A South African counter embargo of mineral exports in response to economic sanctions applied by the United Nations against South Africa; growth of Soviet influence in southern Africa and accession to power of governments in the region that would withhold minerals from the market for political reasons; interference in the normal supply of minerals by political dissidents sabotaging South Africa's interdependent power and transportation networks.

In the short run--fewer than five years--the effect of such a disruption on Western powers would depend on the following factors:

- the size of industry and government stockpiles of strategic minerals;
- the percentage of Western consumption for essential purposes;
- the proportion of total demand that could be met from existing alternative sources;
- the existence of techniques for recycling the minerals;
- the maximum capacity of recycling facilities in the short term; and
- the potential supply of material for recycling facilities.

The long-term--more than five years--ability of Western countries to adjust to an elimination of South African supplies would depend on:

- the ability of other sources to expand existing production facilities;
- the ability of consuming nations to find and develop new deposits of these minerals;
- the development of more efficient recycling techniques and increased recycling capacity; and
- the discovery of new technological processes which reduce or eliminate the demand for strategic minerals.

Using these criteria as a guide, how would Europe, Japan and the United States fare in the event of a serious breakdown of South Africa's willingness or ability to export platinum, chrome, manganese and vanadium?

Platinum Group Metals (see table on p. 246)

Imports from South Africa: Tracing the direct dependence of Western Europe, the United States and Japan on South Africa's platinum is somewhat complicated by the fact that Britain, the Netherlands and Switzerland either refine platinum from South Africa for export to other European countries or act as transshipment points. The European countries that receive platinum from these three often fail to report that the origin of that platinum was South Africa. The United States, Japan and the United Kingdom are the largest buyers of South African platinum. They bought 39, 18 and 6 metric tons, respectively, in 1977 and together accounted for 67 percent of South Africa's total sales. Italy, West Germany, France and the Benelux countries imported only miniscule amounts of platinum directly from South Africa; however, they list the United Kingdom and Switzerland as their major sources of supply outside of the Soviet Union and it can be assumed that an important portion of Swiss or British platinum comes orginally from South Africa.

The United States and the United Kingdom buy about one-half of their imports of platinum from South Africa. Japan depends on the South Africans for about 37 percent of its purchases. One may assume that slightly more than half of the 41 metric tons that make up the net imports of platinum by West Germany, France, Italy and the Benelux countries comes from South Africa after having passed through Britain, the Netherlands or Switzerland. Canada is the one Western power that produces platinum in significant quantities--11 metric tons in 1977, about

7 percent of total world production. (The 1977 U.S. production of 0.16 metric tons was equal to 0.07 percent of world production.)

Essential uses: There is some question as to how much of the platinum imported by countries in the West is for essential uses. In Japan, for example, nearly 70 percent of all platinum imported is used for jewelry. IRRC was unable to obtain figures on the end use of platinum in Europe; however, the U.S. Bureau of Mines estimates that 25 to 33 percent of annual U.S. consumption is essential. The remainder is used for dental supplies, glass, ceramics and electronic equipment and as a catalyst in non-essential industrial processes.

Alternative sources: In the event of a disruption in the supply of platinum, a certain portion of that required would be available from recycling. In 1977, secondary recovery of platinum in the United States accounted for 15 to 18 percent of consumption. Because of the relative ease with which platinum can be separated from other materials, nearly 70 to 80 percent of all the platinum being used today is recoverable. The Bureau of Mines has calculated that "If converter catalysts are reprocessed on a large scale, more than 200,000 troy ounces of platinum group metals could be recovered annually beginning in the early 1980s." Thus, one can say that America's reserves of platinum are traveling on our highways rather than lying buried in the ground. For Japan, not only are its platinum reserves rolling over its roads, they are also contained in the substantial amount of platinum jewelry in the country.

Additional platinum might also be obtained in the open market. The Soviet Union, supplying roughly one-third of the Western market, would be a possible source, as would Canada. Canada exported some 11.4 metric tons in 1977, enough to meet 30 percent of the essential platinum needs of Europe, the United States and Japan, if it is assumed that essential platinum needs are approximately 30 percent of total 1977 consumption. Both Canada and the Soviet Union have sufficient reserves to meet short-term world demand. How quickly and to what extent the two countries would be able to increase their production is difficult to say. Russia's interest in expanding production, moreover, might be tempered by political considerations.

Stockpiles: In the event of a shortfall, Western powers could turn to strategic stockpiles. The United States is the only country that publishes the size of its industry and government stockpiles of these strategic minerals. From these figures one finds that if all South African exports were to be cut off tomorrow, the United States, on the strength of its current secondary domestic production (i.e., recycling of materials containing platinum), imports from other sources, and stockpiles, could continue to use platinum at today's rate of consumption for two years and two months. If all foreign sources of platinum were to disappear, the period would be reduced to a year and three months. However, if the United States were to reduce consumption to only the essential quantity required, the stockpiles could last four years.

Most experts say neither Japan nor any European country has government stockpiles of these strategic minerals, but substantial industry stockpiles are thought to exist, and development of a stockpile program would entail relatively manageable costs. Phillip Crowson of Great Britain's Royal Institute of International Affairs has estimated that if a policy of stockpiling strategic minerals had been adopted in 1977, the cost of a 12-month stockpile of platinum for the European Community (18.7 metric tons) would be $160 million plus 10 to 12 percent for annual finance and storage charges.

Long-term requirements: Over the long term, dependence on foreign platinum could be affected by either the development of new reserves or the diminution of demand. The U.S. Bureau of Mines, for example, has estimated that U.S. resources of platinum are large and inadequately explored. It states that, "U.S. dependence could be greatly reduced if, for example, the platinum-palladium deposits in the Stillwater Complex in Montana were developed....This deposit could supply most of the U.S. requirements for palladium and about one-fourth of its platinum requirements." But current wilderness area legal restrictions and air quality standards could curtail this development.

It is possible that the need for platinum could decline in the future. Forty-seven percent of the platinum imported by the United States in 1977, as well as 20 percent of the industrialized world's consumption of this metal in that year, was used in automobile catalytic converters. This use of platinum may become obsolete within 20 years as the auto industry develops stratified charge and leanburn engines and is able to ensure precise control of ignition and carburetion by electronic devices.

Chrome Ore and Ferrochrome (see tables on pp. 247-248)

Imports: The United States, West Germany and Japan are major purchasers of South Africa's supply of chome ore--used in the metallurgical, chemical and refractory (heat resistant) industries--and ferrochrome, which is used in the production of stainless steel. Together they accounted for nearly 84 percent of the South African chrome ore imported by the industrialized nations in 1977.

The former mining editor of the Rand Daily Mail says chrome ore and ferrochrome "probably represent South Africa's most significant raw materials in terms of strategic considerations." South Africa now supplies roughly half of the West's demand for chrome ore, with the Soviet Union, Turkey, Madagascar, India and the Philippines providing the remainder. West Germany, the United Kingdom and the Benelux countries each depend on South Africa to supply at least 60 percent of their demand for chrome ore. Japan and the United States each imported 41 percent of their total chrome ore imports in 1977 from South Africa, and South African chrome met 30 percent of France's needs.

With the exception of the United Kingdom, which produces its own ferrochrome, the dependence of Western countries on South Africa for ferrochrome is similar to their need for its chrome. For West Germany and the Netherlands, about 60 percent of their total ferrochrome imports come from South Africa; for France the figure is 30 percent. South African ferrochrome made up 76 percent and 40 percent of the total ferrochrome imports of Japan and the United States, respectively.

Essential uses: Chrome ore has metallurgical, chemical and heat resistant uses. Its most strategic use is in the form of ferrochrome which is then combined with nickel to make stainless steel. Pure chrome can also be used to form a superalloy for use in jet engines, missiles or other high-stress applications.

A 1976 study of the world chrome ore market prepared by Charles

River Associates for the U.S. National Bureau of Standards found that only about 12 percent of the chrome imported by the United States is used to produce the stainless steel incorporated into critical goods such as jet engines, petroleum-cracking units, refineries and electric power generators. Approximately 40 percent of all chrome is used in decorative stainless steel. The remainder is used in the refractory and chemical industries.

Alternative sources: Turkey and the Philippines now account for 15 percent of world chrome production. According to a Bureau of Mines source, Turkish production cannot be expanded rapidly, and chrome from the Philippines is used primarily for refractory purposes and would not be suited for the production of stainless steel. The Soviet Union, on the other hand, produces roughly 30 percent of the world's chrome, some of which is of a grade that can be used to produce critical goods.

The discovery of the Argon Oxygen Decarburization process of fabricating stainless steel has considerably altered the chrome supply picture. It permits the utilization of lower grade chrome ore for the production of stainless steel. Although there is debate over the impact of the process on the ability to use chrome contained in scrap metals for producing stainless steel, some experts argue that it could improve the prospect of using recycled chrome to produce stainless steel for essential uses.

Stockpiles: The U.S. government stockpiles for chrome ore amount to 2.4 million metric tons; industrial stocks at the end of 1977 were 1.2 million tons. Together they represent the equivalent of almost eight years of imports from South Africa or a four-year supply if imports from all sources were cut off. The U.S. stockpiles of ferrochrome are equal to those of chrome ore.

As in the case of platinum, there is no evidence that government stockpiles exist in either Europe or Japan, but it is assumed that industry stockpiles exist. Crowson estimated in 1977 that the European Community would have to spend $320 million to stockpile a 12-month supply of chrome and ferrochrome (1.8 million metric tons). At the beginning of 1979, a spokesman for one of the major West German chrome producers called on the government in Bonn to finance a stockpile for West German industry containing a two-year supply of chrome at an estimated cost of $165 to $218 million. Two months earlier, a government study sent to the West German cabinet recommended establishment of a one-year stockpile of chrome, manganese, platinum and vanadium.

Long-term supplies: The long-term supplies of chrome ore and ferrochrome will be greatly affected by events in Zimbabwe-Rhodesia. That country has an estimated 60 percent of the world's reserves of metallurgical-grade chrome ore. A peaceful settlement there and an end to economic sanctions could substantially diminish the need for South Africa's chrome. However, should Zimbabwean reserves remain closed to the world, the market for chome ore could become tight over the long term. Currently the United States adheres to United Nations trade sanctions against Rhodesia and imports no Rhodesian chrome.

Other reserves may be uncovered. A major chrome ore deposit on the California-Oregon border was announced in June 1978. It was estimated to contain 100 to 200 million tons of chrome-bearing ore--equivalent to two or three years of current U.S. consumption. Successful development of this and other deposits, as well as the recovery of chrome from waste metals through improved refining processes, could lessen the impact of any halt in chrome exports from South Africa.

Manganese and Ferromanganese (see tables on pp. 249-250)

Imports: Only in the case of manganese is the United States noticeably less dependent on South African imports than are Europe and Japan. With imports from Brazil, Gabon and Australia amounting to 37, 31, and 14 percent, respectively, of the total manganese imports since 1973, the United States finds itself going to South Africa for only 10 percent of the imported manganese it requires. While manganese from Gabon and Ghana does constitute more than a quarter of the total imports of that commodity by France, Italy, Belgium and the United Kingdom, in none of the industrialized countries other than the United States did the import dependence on South African manganese in 1977 fall below 15 percent, and in most cases it was above 50 percent. For Japan, 41 percent of its manganese comes from South Africa.

Of the 791,000 metric tons of ferromanganese used in the United States in 1977, 32 percent was manufactured in South Africa. Another 35 percent came from France, which in turn depended on South Africa for 25 percent of the manganese ore that went into the ferromanganese exported to the United States. Japan, which supplies 14 percent of the ferromanganese needs of the United States, depended on South Africa for nearly half of its manganese consumption. Thus, both directly and indirectly the United States relied upon South Africa for roughly half of the ferromanganese it consumed.

The dependence of other developed nations on South Africa for ferromanganese is unclear because it is sometimes difficult to determine whether South African manganese is used in the ferromanganese produced in one industrial country and exported to another. The reports on European sources of ferromanganese are extremely confusing. For example, Belgium and Luxembourg get 41 percent of their ferromanganese from France. France gets 37 percent of its ferromanganese from Belgium and Luxembourg. The EEC figures show that none of these countries had sizable imports of ferromanganese from South Africa--all are well below 5 percent. The United Kingdom does not disclose where it gets 74 percent of its ferromanganese, but it is, in turn, a major supplier (46 percent) to the Netherlands.

Essential uses: The principal use of manganese is as an alloy in the production of steel--imparting strength and hardness to the steel. No satisfactory substitute has been found.

Alternative sources: Sources of manganese other than South Africa do exist in the world and in some cases production is being expanded. Australia, Gabon, India and Brazil together produce 50 percent more manganese than does South Africa. Moreover, during the next few years, both Brazil and Australia are planning increases in production capacity--in Australia's case, its 1980 production capacity will be twice the volume of its production in 1975.

Stockpiles: Because of the importance of manganese in steel production, the U.S. government and private industry have stockpiled large quantities of it. In 1977, these stocks represented a five-year supply. If imports only from South Africa were interrupted, these stores of manganese would last for nearly 50 years. American stockpiles of ferromanganese are smaller, yet even here they are equal to almost one-and-a-half years of ferromanganese imports from all sources.

It is assumed by many that both the EEC and Japan have large industrial stockpiles of manganese and ferromanganese that could be used in an emergency. Crowson estimated in 1977 that for some $340 million, the European Community could accumulate a 12-month stockpile of manganese and ferromanganese (2.5 million metric tons of manganese ore and 860,000 metric tons of ferromanganese).

Long-term supplies: Expansion of existing production facilities in Brazil and Australia as well as the existence of manganese reserves in the United States and the deep-sea bed indicate that the West's dependence on South Africa for manganese will diminish in the future.

The Bureau of Mines estimates that the United States, which now produces no manganese, would need at least three years to build plants large enough to utilize domestic low-grade resources and make a significant contribution to meeting its yearly needs. Prices for manganese would have to rise substantially before such development would be economically feasible, but the Bureau of Mines believes that if prices should rise, U.S. reserves are sufficient to supply U.S. demand for the next 20 years.

Vanadium (see table on p. 251)

Imports: Because the United States mines two-thirds of the vanadium it consumes, it depends far less on South African imports than does the EEC or Japan. While the Benelux countries receive more than 75 percent of their vanadium needs from South Africa, South African vanadium makes up only 20 percent of U.S. consumption. Figures for the source of vanadium imports are not available for West Germany, Japan and Canada.

Essential uses: Vanadium is principally used as an alloy in steel to improve its strength. However, steels containing other alloying ingredients such as columbium, molybdenum, titanium and tungsten--all minerals mined in sizable quantities outside of South Africa--can be substituted for steels containing vanadium.

Alternative sources: Vanadium is the only strategic mineral for which European sources of supply exist. Finland and Norway have a combined production capacity equal to roughly 10 percent of total world production and supply a portion of the European demand. The Soviet Union accounts for 32 percent of world production and Chile produces another 3 percent.

Stockpiles: U.S. government and industry stockpiles of vanadium now are equivalent to more than a year of imports. Crowson estimated in 1977 that a year's supply of vanadium (9,000 metric tons) could be stockpiled by the European Community for less than $50 million.

Long-term supplies: Large reserves of vanadium in Canada and the United States as well as new methods of vanadium recovery from scrap metals will both serve to reduce the West's dependence on South African supplies. The Bureau of Mines has calculated that with a lead time of two to three years an ample supply of vanadium could be made available from domestic and Canadian sources.

IV. IRRC Analysis

The debate over foreign investment in the South African mining and minerals industry is likely to continue for the next several years, focusing on the following questions:
- Are wages and working conditions improving in the South African mining industry?
- Do the activities of companies involved in mining support the apartheid policies of the South African government?
- Are South African minerals essential for the United States and other industrialized nations?

Labor conditions in the mines: Wages and working conditions for African miners have been among the worst in South African industry. The industry grew up on the basis of a migrant labor system that offered African workers limited opportunities, restricted living conditions, and relatively low wages. Moreover, the conservative white unions, threatened by the possibility of being replaced by African laborers, have acted as a strong constraint on innovation.

Between 1973 and 1975, strikes by African mine workers and a growing recognition among mine managers of the importance of a more skilled and stable work force combined to bring some improvements to the lives of Africans in the mines. By 1978 a number of companies had begun more advanced training programs, a few had improved housing and health care, and some were petitioning the government to allow more families to join Africans at the mine sites.

These advances, while important to individual workers, were limited. Despite substantial percentage increases, because of the traditionally low level of mine wages the earnings of Africans remained low. The ratio of African to white wages was reduced, but the gap between wages paid the two groups actually grew. Moreover, skills training programs for Africans were available to only a limited number of Africans, far fewer than the industry could have used. Finally, the family housing programs, constrained by both law and company will, met the needs of only a small portion of the workers. Most African workers maintained their migrant status, separated from their families.

Particularly in gold mines, the paucity of Africans who have been able to advance in the mining industry is testimony to the apparent inability or unwillingness of the mine owners--despite skills shortages--to confront the white unions on the issue of job reservation. The Anglo American Corp.--South Africa's most liberal mining house--concluded in a report of the results of an internal investigation of employment practices at its headquarters, "Despite the stated intentions of the corporation, there is no evidence of its moving rapidly towards its goal of equal opportunity employment." The Financial Mail, in a discussion of this report, concluded that, "If the record at Anglo's head office is so poor, one shudders to think what it is like in the mines--or in other companies which don't even profess the ideals (of equal opportunity employment)."

The situation is not likely to improve dramatically in the future, although in general it may be better in the non-gold mines than in gold mines. Recent trends in the mining sector may work against significantly improved working conditions for large numbers of black mine workers. The director of General Mining predicts that mines will become increasingly mechanized; if they do, unskilled African employees will suffer as they are replaced by machines. Without retraining, laid-off workers will find themselves joining the 20 percent of the black South African population currently unemployed.

At the same time, the mining industry has been a critical source of jobs, both directly in the mines and in smelters and indirectly through its contribution to the economy. It has drawn workers from all over southern Africa and has provided them with at least minimal training and an introduction--albeit often harsh--to a cash economy. The importance of jobs in the mines to the thousands of workers who seek them should not be underrated.

Mining and the South African apartheid system: Critics of mining in South Africa make a credible case that the industry contributes to apartheid. The sale and export of South African minerals has a significant, positive impact on South Africa's foreign exchange earnings and government revenues. In recent years minerals provided more than one-half of South Africa's total exports, and taxes paid by mining companies accounted for 10 to 20 percent of the government's total revenues. By contributing to the overall growth and well-being of South Africa's economy, the mining industry strengthens acceptance of the status quo--particularly among South Africa's whites. There is considerable evidence that the greatest questioning of South Africa's apartheid policies by whites as well as blacks has come during a period of recession following a period of growth, not during a period of growth. To the extent that minerals sustain growth, therefore, one can argue that mining contributes to apartheid. Moreover, by providing substantial tax income to the government, mining generates funds that may be used to enforce the government's policies.

Perhaps more significantly, mining is the one industry--with the possible exception of agriculture--that is most directly involved in the use of migrant labor. The industry has long been dependent on migrant labor for its work force. Although in the long run mining companies have begun to suffer the costs of skills shortages and an unstable work force, for years they have benefited from a system that has offered them a constant supply of labor with a minimum of expenditure on social services. Neither companies nor the public has been required to pay for the social services that would have been necessary were African workers allowed to move freely with their families to the mine site. The normal costs of providing schooling, public services, housing and hospitalization to the public supplying labor has been largely avoided by the migrant labor system. The social costs have been borne instead by the workers themselves who have been denied the opportunities that would be available under an alternative system.

Finally, in many cases, the placement of mine smelters and manufacturing plants has been supportive of the government's decentralization policy. In few instances where mines are located in the homelands have companies established smelters or ferroalloy manufacturing plants there. The plants have been constructed in border areas adjacent to the homelands. By keeping these major fixed assets inside the white areas of South Africa, mining companies strengthen the pattern of apartheid in which capital assets are kept in white areas while labor is drawn from the black homelands when needed.

The companies say that these decisions on plant location are governed by the availability of power supplies and transport facilities. While this is no doubt true, the accompanying consequences of such decisions severely affect the economic prospects of the homeland areas. Moreover, location in the homelands could permit companies to provide greater opportunities to their African workers. The homelands that have been granted "independence" do not allow discrimination in employment. If the mining companies located their smelters and production plants in the homelands, a number of skilled jobs would be legally open to African workers. When these plants are located in the white areas of South Africa, the companies' training and hiring programs are governed by South African law, which limits training and promotion opportunities for Africans.

The strategic importance of South Africa's minerals: The South African government and several of the leading American mining companies involved in South Africa have claimed that the United States and other industrialized nations would suffer serious consequences if the supply of South African minerals were cut off. Reportedly, confidential studies done for the West German and U.S. governments during the past year have argued as well that South African minerals are important to the economies of the industrialized nations and that serious economic dislocation would result if the supply were cut off. The U.S. report concluded that the loss of South African minerals would compromise the achievement of U.S. policy goals in the fields of environment, energy and employment; the West German study estimated that a 30-percent cut in annual chrome deliveries could result in a 25-percent drop in West German industrial production.

Of the four essential minerals South Africa exports to the West--platinum, chrome, manganese and vanadium--only the disappearance of South African chrome apears to present serious supply difficulties for the West. Alternative sources of platinum, manganese and vanadium exist in the United States and Canada and could be developed to replace South African supplies.

For platinum, both Canada and the USSR are available as alternative suppliers, and U.S. production could be increased significantly if reserves in Montana were developed. Furthermore, the possibilities are good for meeting much of the future need for this metal by recycling the platinum now contained in catalytic converters.

For both manganese and vanadium abundant alternative sources exist, and substitutes also are available for vanadium. The U.S. Bureau of Mines has estimated that with a two- to three-year lead time, U.S. and Canadian reserves of manganese and vanadium could be developed that would meet total U.S. needs for at least 20 years and could potentially meet the essential needs--equal to approximately 30 percent of total needs under normal circumstances--of the United States, Europe and Japan for about six years.

The U.S. stockpiles of chrome are large enough to cover a total interruption of South African chrome exports for eight years. They would have to be marshaled carefully to ensure that chrome would continue to be available for essential and strategic uses beyond that period. Because their stockpiles are probably smaller than those in the United States, Europe and Japan would be affected by a cutoff of South African exports sooner and to a greater extent, but they would be able to withstand a short-term disruption of supply.

In the long term, a continued cutoff of South African chrome would become critical if new reserves were not uncovered and if processes for the recovery of chrome from scrap metals were not successfully developed. Also, there would be pressures on the United States to sell some of its stockpiled chrome to Europe and Japan. A settlement of the political conflict in Zimbabwe-Rhodesia that allowed the West to have access once again to that supply of chrome, however, could ease the critical importance of chrome from South Africa.

However, although there appear to be solutions to the problems of finding alternative supplies of essential minerals, the difficulties resulting from the jump in the prices of these commodities which would occur once South African exports are no longer available would be serious. As was shown when Iranian oil production was reduced following the fall of the Shah, a small shortfall in the supply of an essential commodity can rapidly lead to a dramatic price increase.

More important than the loss of South Africa's minerals to the West would be the effect on the South African economy if it could no longer sell its minerals to the world. Whoever controls South Africa and its mineral resources--whether it be the present ruling Nationalist Party, a black majority government, or even a regime backed by the USSR—has a strong stake in continuing the mineral trade with the industrialized nations. Only in the case of chrome would a South African government hostile to the West (and presumably supported by the Soviet Union) have a near-monopoly on supply and hence the considerable bargaining power that would derive from its ability to withhold chrome from the market. However, the foreign capital and technology supplied to South Africa by the West as well as the food commodities that the West provides the USSR are likely to serve as an effective check on the use of chrome exports for political ends.

Thus it appears that the West depends less on South Africa's mineral exports than South Africa relies on the foreign exchange, tax revenues and employment that result from its minerals trade.

Table 1

VALUE OF SOUTH AFRICA'S EXPORTS

(millions of U.S. dollars)

Year	Total exports (including gold)	All mining and quarry-ing exports (excluding ferroalloys)	Percent of total exports	Gold exports	Percent of total exports
1978	11,611.1	6,366.2	54.8	4,442.5	38.3
1977	9,444.3	5,004.2	53.0	3,214.5	34.0
1976	7,521.5	3,864.9	51.4	2,698.2	35.9
1975	6,840.7	3,693.8	54.0	2,921.3	42.7

Source: Bulletin of Statistics: South Africa Department of Statistics, June 1979.

Table 2

AVERAGE MONTHLY WAGES FOR SOUTH AFRICAN MINERS

Year	African Rand	African % increase	White Rand	White % increase
1971	18.44		386	
1972	21.32	15.6	411	6.5
1973	29.07	36.4	490	19.2
1974	46.92	61.4	581	18.6
1975	79.01	68.4	661	13.8
1976	91.72	16.1	737	11.5
1977	101.75	10.9	771	4.6
1978 (est.)	119.00	17.0	840	9.0

1971-1975:   Rand = $1.45
1975-present: Rand = $1.15

Table 3

DEPENDENCE OF INDUSTRIALIZED NATIONS
ON SOUTH AFRICAN PLATINUM GROUP METALS - 1977
(metric tons)

Country	Total imports	Imports from South Africa (% of total imports)	Exports	Net imports	Other major suppliers (% of total imports)
United States*	79.6	39.1 (49.0%)	12.4	67.2	USSR (29%) U.K. (23%)
United Kingdom	12	6 (50.0%)	17	-5	USSR (8.3%) Canada (8.3%)
Japan**	49	18 (36.7%)	4	45	USSR (50.4%)
West Germany	17	2 (11.8%)	13	4	USSR (58.8%) U.K. (35.3%) Yugoslavia (17.6%)
France	13	0	4	9	U.K. (7.7%) U.S. (7.7%) Switzerland (7.7%) USSR (7.7%)
Belgium- Luxembourg	1	N.A.	0	1	N.A.
Italy	26	1 (3.8%)	2	24	Switzerland (46.2%)
Canada***	1	0.1 (8.3%)	12.4	-11.4	N.A.
Netherlands	3	N.A.	0	3	N.A.

Source: Analytical Tables of Foreign Trade, Eurostat, EEC.
* Source: Mineral Commodity Summaries 1978, Bureau of Mines, U.S. Department of Interior (IRRC recalculation of figures supplied in tables). U.S. Bureau of Mines source.
** Source: Japan Exports and Imports: Commodity by Country, Japan Tariff Association.
*** Source: Imports, Merchandise Trade 1975-1977, Statistics Canada.

Table 4

DEPENDENCE OF INDUSTRIALIZED NATIONS
ON SOUTH AFRICAN CHROME ORE - 1977
(metric tons)

Country		Total imports	Imports from South Africa (% of total imports)	Exports	Net imports	Other major suppliers (% of total imports)
United States*		1,109,102	458,000 (41.3%)	227,000	882,102	USSR (29%) Philippines (18%) Turkey (14%)
United Kingdom		197,616	123,877 (62.7%)	26	197,590	Philippines (25.8%)
Japan**		899,934	372,922 (41.4%)	2,805	897,129	India (15.3%) Brazil (8.0%)
West Germany		415,594	250,769 (60.3%)	3,931	411,663	USSR (14.9%) U.S. (10.5%) Turkey (5.4%)
France		283,133	85,872 (30.3%)	981	282,152	Madagascar (23.5%) Turkey (22.1%) USSR (19.2%)
Belgium-Luxembourg		3,891	1,625 (41.8%)	1,071	2,820	Netherlands (30.7%)
Italy		178,139	53,240 (30.0%)	2,012	176,127	Turkey (47.5%) Albania (6.0%)
Canada***	(1977) (1976)	175,277	0 (0%) 12,350 (8.3%)	0	175,277	N.A.
Netherlands		26,440	26,078 (98.6%)	19,548	6,892	---

Source: Analytical Tables of Foreign Trade, Eurostat, EEC.
* Source: Mineral Commodity Summaries 1978, Bureau of Mines, U.S. Department of Interior (IRRC recalculation of figures supplied in tables). Mineral Industry Surveys, 8/29/78, "Chromium in June 1978".
** Source: Japan Exports and Imports: Commodity by Country, Japan Tariff Association.
*** Source: U.S. Bureau of Mines estimate of gross weight based on reported chromium content of ores and concentrates imported.

Table 5

DEPENDENCE OF INDUSTRIALIZED NATIONS
ON SOUTH AFRICAN FERROCHROME - 1977
(metric tons)

Country	Total imports	Imports from South Africa (% of total imports)	Exports	Net imports	Other major suppliers (% of total imports)
United States*	227,275	94,000 (41.4%)	10,909	216,366	Japan (16%)
United Kingdom	0	0	1,919	-1,919	N.A.
Japan**	104,098	79,254 (76.1%)	16,307	87,791	N.A.
West Germany	129,125	79,986 (61.9%)	36,426	92,699	Sweden (8.2%) Brazil (7.7%)
France	38,690	11,557 (30.0%)	8,255	30,435	Belgium-Luxembourg (15.7%) Italy (13.5%)
Belgium-Luxembourg	35,927	13,859 (38.6%)	14,666	21,261	Finland (19.8%) USSR (18.5%)
Italy	56,863	8,900 (15.7%)	11,586	45,277	West Germany (42.24%) Sweden (17.0%)
Canada***	33,016	less 9,760 than 1,800 (29.6%)		N.A.	N.A.
Netherlands	12,264	7,187 (58.6%)	9,523	2,741	Brazil (13.7%) Spain (8.2%)

Source: Analytical Tables of Foreign Trade, Eurostat, EEC.
* Source: Mineral Commodity Summaries 1978, Bureau of Mines, U.S. Department of Interior (IRRC recalculation of figures supplied in tables). Mineral Industry Surveys, 8/29/78, "Chromium in June 1978". U.S. Bureau of Mines source.
** Source: Japan Exports and Imports: Commodity by Country, Japan Tariff Association.
*** Source: Imports, Merchandise Trade 1975-1977, Statistics Canada.

Table 6

DEPENDENCE OF INDUSTRIALIZED NATIONS
ON SOUTH AFRICAN MANGANESE - 1977
(metric tons)

Country	Total imports	Imports from South Africa (% of total imports)	Exports	Net imports	Other major suppliers (% of total imports)
United States*	1,000,000	28,000 (2.8%)	109,092	890,908	Brazil (37%) Gabon (31%) Australia (14%)
United Kingdom	328,314	193,494 (58.9%)	6,767	321,547	Ghana (13.8%) Gabon (9.5%) Brazil (8.0%)
Japan**	2,736,818	1,124,487 (41.1%)	5,206	2,731,612	Australia (18.3%) India (19.5%)
West Germany	455,243	285,907 (62.8%)	6,983	448,260	Australia (18.1%) Brazil (8.4%)
France	923,065	232,195 (25.2%)	8,325	914,740	Gabon (40.7%) Brazil (18.5%)
Belgium-Luxembourg	206,727	68,415 (33.1%)	9,988	196,739	Ghana (27.3%) Zaire (7.5%)
Italy	268,535	166,153 (61.9%)	34	268,501	Gabon (29.2%)
Canada***	190,979	29,118 (15.2%)	0	190,979	N.A.
Netherlands	81,242	0 (69,730 listed as "undisclosed")	31,557	49,685	---

Source: Analytical Tables of Foreign Trade, Eurostat, EEC.
* Source: Mineral Commodity Summaries 1978, Bureau of Mines, U.S. Department of Interior (IRRC recalculation of figures supplied in tables). U.S. Bureau of Mines source.
** Source: Japan Exports and Imports: Commodity by Country, Japan Tariff Association.
*** Source: U.S. Bureau of Mines estimate of gross weight based on reported manganese content of ores and concentrates imported.

Table 7

DEPENDENCE OF INDUSTRIALIZED NATIONS
ON SOUTH AFRICAN FERROMANGANESE - 1977
(metric tons)

Country	Total imports	Imports from South Africa (% of total imports)	Exports	Net imports	Other major suppliers (% of total imports)
United States*	636,370	256,000 (40.2%)	6,364	630,006	France (35%) Japan (14%)
United Kingdom	86,120	200 (0.2%)	663	85,457	"Undisclosed" (73.9%)
Japan**	5,777	0	48,634	-42,857	N.A.
West Germany	158,512	15,434 (9.7%)	74,037	84,475	Norway (42.7%) France (25.1%)
France	34,864	1,184 (3.4%)	269,538	-234,674	Belgium-Luxembourg (36.7%)
Belgium- Luxembourg	71,742	533 (0.8%)	49,539	22,203	France (41.2%) Norway (33.1%)
Italy	125,483	22,647 (18.0%)	2,143	123,340	France (46.1%)
Canada***	29,465	8,332 (28.3%)	23,153	6,312	N.A.
Netherlands	25,221	1,980 (7.9%)	2,606	22,615	U.K. (46.3%)

Source: Analytical Tables of Foreign Trade, Eurostat, EEC.
* Source: Mineral Commodity Summaries 1978, Bureau of Mines, U.S. Department of Interior (IRRC recalculation of figures supplied in tables). U.S. Bureau of Mines source.
** Source: Japan Exports and Imports: Commodity by Country, Japan Tariff Association.
*** Source: Imports, Merchandise Trade 1975-1977, Statistics Canada.

Table 8

DEPENDENCE OF INDUSTRIALIZED NATIONS
ON SOUTH AFRICAN VANADIUM - 1977
(metric tons)

Country	Total imports	Imports from South Africa (% of total imports	Exports	Net imports	Other major suppliers (% of total imports
United States*	3,759	N.A.	106	3,653	South Africa (56%) Chile (27%) USSR (9%)
United Kingdom	1,589	125 (7.9%)	48	1,541	
Japan**	N.A.	0	0		
West Germany	23,561	0 (22,738 "undisclosed")	860	22,701	
France	801	143 (17.9%)	0	801	
Belgium- Luxembourg	8,435	6,296 (74.6%)	294	8,141	Ghana (22.7%)
Italy	3,544	0	0	3,544	Austria (78.3%)
Canada	N.A.	N.A.	N.A.		
Netherlands	7,629	6,034 (79.1%)	80	7,549	

Source: Analytical Tables of Foreign Trade, Eurostat, EEC.
* Source: Mineral Commodity Summaries 1978, Bureau of Mines, U.S. Department of Interior (IRRC recalculation of figures supplied in tables).
** Source: Japan Exports and Imports: Commodity by Country, Japan Tariff Association.

Sources

Books

Mineral Resources of the Republic of South Africa, Department of Mines, Republic of South Africa, 1976.

Phillip Crowson, Non-Fuel Minerals and Foreign Policy, Royal Institute of International Affairs, London, 1977.

Robert J. Gordon, Mines, Masters and Migrants, Rowan Press, Johannesburg, 1977.

R.W. Johnson, "South Africa's Salvation: The War Over Gold," chapter 4 in How Long will South Africa Survive?, MacMillan South Africa, Johannesburg, 1977.

W.C.J. van Rensburg and D.A. Pretorius, South Africa's Strategic Minerals, Foreign Affairs Association, Johannesburg, 1977.

Francis Wilson, Labour in the South African Gold Mines 1911-1969, Cambridge University Press.

Policy Implications of Producer Country Supply Restrictions: The World Chromite Market, Charles River Associates, Cambridge, Mass., 1976.

U.S. Government Publications:

"Industrial Outlook Report: Minerals South Africa--1978," Parts I and II, Department of State, American Consulate, Johannesburg.

"Industrial Outlook Report: Minerals South Africa--1977," Parts I and II, Department of State, American Consulate, Johannesburg, Jan. 27 and July 28, 1978.

"Industrial Outlook Report: Iron and Steel (and Ferroalloys)," Department of State, American Consulate, Johannesburg, March 10, 1978.

Mineral Commodity Summaries 1978, Bureau of Mines, Department of the Interior.

Report on the Issues Identified in the Nonfuel Minerals Policy Review, Department of the Interior, August 1979.

"Chromium - 1977," Mineral Commodity Profiles - 1, Bureau of Mines, Department of the Interior, May 1977.

"Gold," Mineral Commodity Profiles - 25, Bureau of Mines, Department of the Interior, October 1978.

"Manganese - 1977," Mineral Commodity Profiles - 7, Bureau of Mines, Department of the Interior, October 1977.

"Platinum," Mineral Commodity Profiles - 22, Bureau of Mines, Department of the Interior, September 1978.

"Vanadium - 1977," Mineral Commodity Profiles - 8, Bureau of Mines, Department of the Interior, December 1977.

"Chromium in June 1978," Mineral Industry Surveys, Bureau of Mines, Department of the Interior, Aug. 29, 1978.

South African Publications:

Bulletin of Statistics, South African Department of Statistics, various issues.

Mining Statistics 1977, South African Bureau of Mines.

Statistical Tables - 1977, Chamber of Mines of South Africa.

United Nations Publications:

1976 World Trade Annual, UN Statistical Office.

Ann W. Seidman and Neva Makgetla, "Activities of Transnational Corporations in South Africa," Centre Against Apartheid, Department of Political and Security Council Affairs, May 1978.

Other Statistical Sources:

Analytical Tables of Foreign Trade, Eurostat, European Economic Community.

Japan Exports and Imports: Commodity by Country, Japan Tariff Association.

Imports, Merchandise Trade 1975-1977, Statistics Canada.

Financial Mail Articles:

"Gold," special supplement, Feb. 24, 1978.
"Down under," a special survey of mining, July 28, 1978.
"SA's minerals: not so strategic," Feb. 23, 1979.
"Mine wages: blacker is cheaper," March 16, 1979.
"The miners' strike: useless victory?", March 30, 1979.
"Job colour bar: two tests," March 30, 1979.
"Mine labour: what's going on?" April 13, 1979.
"Ferroalloys: it's all go," Aug. 3, 1979.
"Mine wages: Paulus charges again," Sept. 14, 1979.
"Mining," special supplement, Sept. 28, 1979.

Other Articles:

"Base metals will rule when gold is dethroned," Management, September 1978.

"Politics may bedevil sales of cheap SA ferrochrome," The Johannesburg Star, Dec. 23, 1978.

"The big U.S. stake in South Africa's minerals," Business Week, Jan. 29, 1979.

"Employment and earnings trends in mining," Standard Bank Review, Johannesburg, February 1979.

"Artisan shortfall expected to grow to 5,000," The Johannesburg Star, March 31, 1979.

"56 percent of all '78 mineral sales came from gold," The Johannesburg Star, April 28, 1979.

"Johannesburg--it's now the world's metal Mecca," Johannesburg Sunday Times, Aug. 26, 1979.

D. THE MOTOR INDUSTRY IN SOUTH AFRICA

The debate over the role of U.S. companies in the motor industry in South Africa is tied to controversy over the February 1978 U.S. Department of Commerce regulations forbidding the sale of U.S. products and technology to the South African military and police. A number of companies--including those manufacturing automobiles, tires and component parts--are affected to some degree. There has been conflict within the State Department and between the Departments of State and Commerce over the application of the regulations. Several of the companies have formally expressed concerns about possible interpretations. And shareholders in two companies--Ford Motor Co. and General Motors Corp.--submitted resolutions at the 1979 annual meetings calling for a halt to all sales to the South African military and police.

The availability of U.S. goods and technology to South Africa's automotive industry is likely to be a question of continuing debate until there is major political change in South Africa. Actions to limit U.S. sales to the motor industry affect an area of critical importance to the strategic well-being of the South African economy. There is a real question, however, as to the impact a limit on sales will have on the situation in South Africa or on companies operating there. This study discusses the structure of the automotive and component parts industry in South Africa, the role of American companies in the industry, the relationship between the companies and the South African government, and the pressures being exerted on the American corporations. It contains the following sections:

I.   The motor industry in South Africa.

II.   The role of foreign companies in the auto industry.

III. The debate over U.S. company involvement.

IV.   IRRC analysis.

I. The Motor Industry in South Africa

South Africa supports one of the most sophisticated consumer markets in the world, and nowhere is this more apparent than in the wealth of choice offered the prospective automobile buyer. South Africa's multi-lane highways are packed with a variety of automobiles equal to any in the world. There are 10 major automobile manufacturers--all but one foreign-controlled--that assemble cars in 39 models with 257 variations. Those who can afford them--and very few blacks buy new cars--can select an Alfa Romeo, BMW, Fiat, Ford, Datsun, Toyota, Chevy or Mercedes. The lone South African-controlled company, Sigma Motors, 25-percent owned by Chrysler Corp., produces under license Chryslers, Peugeots, Citroens and Mazdas.

Role in the economy: The motor industry is critical to South Africa's industrial economy. It dominates the country's manufacturing sector. Retail sales of vehicles, component parts and accessories were estimated at $1.4 billion in 1977. The industry buys $46 million worth of rubber,

$43 million worth of iron and steel and $17 million worth of glass each year. The tire and tube industry, highly dependent on the motor market, reported sales of $240 million in 1977. Component parts for the motor industry were valued at $486 million in 1976, and imported component parts cost more than $500 million. The combined manufacture of motor vehicles and component parts, excluding tires, represents more than 20 percent of the manufacturing sector and is equal to nearly 5 percent of the gross domestic product. Until recently, growth in the motor industry had outpaced growth of the economy as a whole. Over the eight years to 1975, the motor industry's real contribution to the gross domestic product grew at an annual rate of 10.3 percent. By comparison, the manufacturing sector's real contribution grew at a 5.1-percent annual rate during this period, and the real growth in gross domestic product averaged 4.6 percent.

The motor industry is also important as a major employer and trainer of labor. According to a statistical report on tariffs prepared by South Africa's Board of Trade and Industries in 1977, companies involved in producing motor vehicles and component parts have been responsible "for the creation of many skills among large numbers of operatives, artisans, engineers, supervisors, technicians, designers, production planners and managers, marketing experts, financial managers, accountants, computer programmers and operators, and other personnel....The acquisition of this knowledge and familiarity with a multitude of techniques in many various fields is the very heart of industrial growth and progress." More than 41,000 workers are employed in car manufacture and assembly; 18,600 more work in manufacturing motor vehicle components, and 10,000 work for the major tire companies. For the most part, the industry is labor-intensive, and the majority of the work force is blue collar and black.

The market: South Africa has been justifiably described as "the world's toughest car market." According to Tony Koenderman in the October 1977 issue of Management Magazine, there are "too many manufacturers, too many car models, and too much productive capacity." He might have added "too few customers."

With 10 major companies assembling and manufacturing automobiles and commercial vehicles for what is a small market by world standards, the competition is fierce. Companies have fought for market shares with vicious price cutting and a proliferation of models and variations on those models. No single company has been able to control enough of the market to benefit substantially from economies of scale. Koenderman writes that "economies of scale are normally related to sales per model of 100,000 units per year." In 1978, 204,000 cars were sold in South Africa (a 22-percent increase over the previous year), and 100,000 commercial vehicles (trucks and buses) were sold--up nearly 10 percent over the last year. Three-quarters of the models sold, Koenderman writes, have "sales below the break-even point of 5,000 per year." By comparison, manufacturers in the United States produce more than 180,000 vehicles a week.

The industry is overbuilt for its current market, and at least temporarily the market appears close to saturation. Chris Griffiths, managing director of Sigma Motors, estimates that the motor industry has the capacity to produce 2.5 times the number of vehicles required by current demand on a single shift basis. If all companies were to go to double shift, it could supply five times the demand. Car ownership among whites is already at 415 cars per thousand persons. Despite estimates by American automakers that the saturation point for automobiles is about 450 per thousand, South Africa's Board of Trade and Industries blames the slow growth in sales on the economic recession in South Africa and the decline in real income to whites. The board forecasts ratios of 472 cars per thousand for whites in 1980 and 609 per thousand in 2000.

Most analysts, however, argue that the real potential for market growth is in sales to South Africa's blacks and in export to nearby African countries. Africans had a 30-percent increase in real income between 1970 and 1975 and, although the pace has fallen off slightly, the overall trend continues. To be sure, the absolute level of Africans' income is still too low to trigger a massive increase in the purchase of new cars. Nonetheless, from an average of 4.2 cars per thousand Africans in 1970, Africans' ownership of cars has increased 157 percent to 10.8 cars per thousand today. The Board of Trade and Industries predicts a ratio of 11.8 per thousand Africans by 1980 and 20 per thousand a decade later.

Africans are already an important factor in the used-car markets. They now own 17.3 percent of the vehicles in South Africa, most of which they have bought used. The publisher of Drum, a monthly black magazine, estimates the African market for used cars, taxis and parts "as at least 20 percent of these markets."

The role of the South African government: The South African government plays an important role in the South African motor vehicle market both as a consumer and as a regulator. In 1977 the central government, primarily through the central purchasing authority responsible for about 90 percent of government purchases, bought 4,000 cars, 5,000 light trucks and 4,000 heavy trucks. Its purchases of heavy trucks, many of which are used by the public freight corporation operated under the auspices of the South African Railways, amounted to 14 percent of total sales in that sector. What portion of these sales went through the central authority to the police or military is not known, and totals on sales to municipal and provincial authorities are not available. General Motors has reported that its sales to the military before 1978 averaged 1,500 units a year, and Ford states that between 1973 and 1977 it sold 128 cars and 683 trucks directly to the South African Ministry of Defense and 646 cars and 1,473 trucks to the South African police. The Goodyear Tire & Rubber Co. estimated in 1976 that about 1 percent of its $4.3 million in annual sales went to South Africa's military and police. The Firestone Tire & Rubber Co. describes its sales to the government as "a very small percentage" of total sales.

In addition to its role as a consumer, the South African government has been central to the health of automakers since 1960 when it began a program mandating that an ever-increasing amount of the content of each automobile be produced in South Africa. Beginning in 1960 with a stipulation that 12 percent of the mass weight of cars be produced locally, the requirement increased to 24 percent in 1962, 45 percent by 1965, 55 percent by 1967 and 66 percent by 1976. The last phase necessitated large-scale capital investment by manufacturers in the production of local components and resulted in "serious financing and cash-flow difficulties" in the mid-1970s, according to the report of the Board of Trade and Industries. Consequently, in 1976 the government granted the motor industry a two-year "standstill" period to solidify its position. In late 1978, the government announced Phase V, designed to encourage an increase in local content to 76 percent by 1980. Whereas the phases of the local content program used tariffs and excise taxes punitively to guarantee cooperation, Phase V is voluntary, using rebates of excise taxes as rewards to manufacturers who choose to upgrade the local mass of their cars. Phase V is not expected to require additional capital investment by automakers. "Increasing local content will lead to fuller utilization of general industrial capacity which has already been achieved," according to the Board of Trade and Industries.

The government's local content program is part of a broader effort that it calls a "rationalization program" designed to shrink or "rationalize" the number of auto manufacturers by placing unacceptable burdens on smaller manufacturers. The government reasoned that because the local content program increased car prices by an average of 5.2 percent (compared with imports) and forced substantial capital infusions, smaller companies would withdraw and leave the larger manufacturers with greater volume. In addition, the government placed mandatory limits on the number of models on the market, theorizing that an abundance of models decreased the likelihood of economies of scale. In fact, the restrictions on models have backfired and perpetuated fragmentation in the industry. Firms with large assets have been precluded from introducing large numbers of new models and preempting the market, while small manufacturers have been able to tolerate tooling costs for new models knowing that the market would not be flooded with competing cars. "The restrictions placed on numbers of models thus tend to create a comparatively large number of medium-sized companies in the South African marketplace. The total company-related costs are therefore maximized," the Board of Trade and Industries said in its 1977 report.

If the local content program has failed to thin the ranks of the auto industry, it has nonetheless succeeded in most of its other aims. The outflow of currency has been stemmed, saving South Africa an estimated $1.7 million in foreign exchange. Although automakers still import components from overseas, the industry has an overall "positive" impact on the balance of payments, the report of the Board of Trade and Industries determined. The program has stimulated the labor market, increased demand for local raw materials, and benefited a host of related industries.

Most importantly, the local content program has made national self-sufficiency a reality in the auto industry. South Africa now possesses the technological foundation and the technical know-how to protect that industry from foreign pressures.

The local components industry is also largely self-sufficient. Beginning with the production of simpler items such as batteries, windscreens and exhaust systems, component makers now produce complex pistons and engine parts. Most car components are "readily available" from local sources, the Board of Trade and Industries noted. However, because the local content program measures content by mass and not by value, automakers tend to buy heavy, less sophisticated components in South Africa and to import specialized engine parts. For example, carburetion equipment, automatic transmissions, gearboxes and electronic components are still largely imported, but body pressings are made domestically, and a subsidiary of South Africa's General Mining Co. expects to produce a full range of gear boxes with 100 percent local content by 1983. Although only one-third of its weight can consist of foreign components, an estimated 40 to 50 percent of the value of a South African car is now in imported parts.

The South African government has taken two steps to increase the self-sufficiency of the truck industry. Light trucks, heretofore exempt from the local content requirements, will be subject to the 66-percent local mass stipulation in 1980. Trucks now contain only 20 to 40 percent local content. Among the imported components are transmissions, axles and chassis. (Company proposals for government-assisted, local manufacture of heavy axles are now under review by the government.)

In November 1978, the South African government announced plans to construct a $300-million diesel engine manufacturing plant at Atlantis in the Cape. The publicly owned Industrial Development Corp. underwriting the plant has contracted with Daimler-Berry and Perkins Engines for technical assistance. The plant will use local components almost entirely and is scheduled to begin production in 1981. By 1983, the corporation hopes it will be producing 50,000 engines annually for local use.

The prime motive for the plant, apparently, is to further the self-sufficiency of the truck industry. The plant will produce 17 engines in place of the 104 diesel engines now available in South Africa, thus forcing manufacturers to standardize their models to accommodate the engines, and the government has requested all manufacturers of heavy trucks to design their vehicles to allow them to accommodate the locally produced diesel engine by the time diesel production begins.

The South African giant chemical corporation, Sentrachem, announced in August 1979 its intention to develop a synthetic rubber plant capable of replacing "virtually all" the natural and synthetic rubber currently being imported. Nearly half of the 85,000 tons of rubber used annually is natural rubber and about 65 percent of this is imported. By 1982, the company estimates, more than 90 percent of South Africa's natural rubber needs can be met by locally manufactured synthetic rubber.

The government has taken other steps to protect what it considers to be strategic national interests inherent in the motor industry. Critics of the South African government have been most concerned that the government would dictate the use of the automakers' manufacturing facilities in the event of a national crisis. The National Supplies Procurement Act, passed in 1970 and activated in 1977, authorizes the Minister for Economic Affairs to order any company operating in South Africa to manufacture and deliver goods to the state that the government determines are essential to national security. Should a company fail to comply with the minister's order, he has the power to seize the goods or make use of the facilities to provide the goods in question.

When the government activated the legislation in 1977--although the move was not seemingly directed specifically at the auto industry--The Financial Mail commented: "It is the general impression that foreign-controlled firms supplying the Department of Defense could be commandeered if their parents instruct them to stop supplying goods which (the government) needs. These go beyond arms and ammunition: motor vehicles...are among the strategic materials produced by foreign-controlled firms."

II. The Role of Foreign Companies

The South African motor industry historically has been dominated by foreign companies. Virtually all automobiles manufactured in South Africa are produced by the subsidiaries of European or American companies or by their licensees. American companies control the major tire companies, and familiar names--Champion spark plugs, Fram filters, Gabriel shock absorbers and Willard batteries--proliferate in the component parts industries.

Auto manufacturers: American firms were among the oldest and, until recently, the dominant auto companies in South Africa. Ford built the first assembly plant in South Africa in 1923, and General Motors entered the market three years later. Chrysler, a relative latecomer, began its South African operation in 1958. Until Japanese and European companies made significant inroads in the 1960s, Ford and GM owned the bulk of the assets in the industry. Today their combined assets, including reinvested earnings, are estimated at $385 million, and both companies would rank among the top 25 companies on the Johannesburg stock exchange.

	Estimated Annual Sales	Estimated Value of Investments*	
Ford	$288.4	$ 119	(1978)
GM	250	127	(1978)
Chrysler	63	35	(1978)
Firestone	NA	25-30	(1973)
Goodyear	58	43.6	(1977)

* excluding reinvested earnings

Ford was the market leader for 1977, finished second in 1978 and dropped to third in 1979. In 1977, Ford South Africa garnered 16.7 percent of the market, and in 1978--led by the Cortina, South Africa's top-selling car--it tallied 17.5 percent on sales of 35,976. General Motors, on the other hand, which as late as 1973 placed second in auto sales, slipped to fifth in 1977. In 1978, the company sold 17,920 cars for an 8.75-percent market share, and dropped to sixth place in 1979, hurt by its heavy concentration in large car manufacture.

German and Japanese companies have challenged the American automakers in recent years. Volkswagen held an 18-percent market share in 1978, surpassing Ford for leadership in South African sales. Mercedes-Benz and BMW hold commanding positions in the luxury car market. Datsun, with sales of 20,671 and a 10-percent market share, held fourth position in the auto derby in 1978, ahead of General Motors. Toyota held sixth position.

Sales by the one South African-controlled company, Sigma Motors, represented only 14 percent of the industry's total in 1978, but the

SEPTEMBER CAR SALES

	1979 September	% of Market	1979 August	% of Market	1978 September	% of Market
Sigma	3 457	21,78	4 138	21,90	2 880	18,78
VW	3 225	20,32	4 520	23,93	3 020	19,69
Ford	2 141	13,49	2 604	13,78	3 004	19,59
Datsun	1 774	11,18	2 055	10,88	1 231	8,02
Toyota/Renault	1 603	10,10	1 842	9,75	1 167	7,61
GM	1 005	6,33	1 002	5,30	1 400	9,13
BMW	763	4,81	640	3,39	575	3,75
UCDD (Mercedes-Benz)	747	4,71	541	2,86	700	4,56
Fiat	520	3,28	772	4,09	481	3,14
Alfa Romeo	440	2,77	560	2,96	330	2,15
Leyland	191	1,20	215	1,14	541	3,53
Other	4	0,03	4	0,02	7	0,05
September total	15 870 (3,48% up on 15 336 last year)					
Jan-Sep total	156 793 (2,66% up on 152 731 last year)					
August total	18 893 (September 16% down)					

COMMERCIALS

	1979 September	% of Market	1979 August	% of Market	1978 September	% of Market
Toyota	2 206	27,94	2 441	28,13	1 390	18,53
Datsun	1 629	20,63	2 197	25,32	1 386	18,48
GM	1 014	12,84	813	9,37	1 000	13,33
Ford	997	12,63	1 080	12,45	1 214	16,19
Sigma	771	9,77	744	8,58	1 064	14,18
UCDD (Mercedes-Benz)	356	4,51	310	3,57	233	3,11
VW	316	4,00	260	3,00	420	5,60
Leyland	294	3,72	389	4,48	383	5,11
Fiat	106	1,34	239	2,75	215	2,87
MAN	77	0,98	75	0,86	40	0,53
Int Harvester	54	0,68	48	0,55	63	0,84
Oshkosh	32	0,41	19	0,22	11	0,15
ERF	17	0,22	12	0,14	9	0,12
Vetsak	11	0,14	12	0,14	19	0,25
Fodens	8	0,10	9	0,10	9	0,12
Magirus-Deutz	5	0,06	18	0,21	24	0,32
VSA	2	0,03	1	0,01	2	0,03
Malcomess-Scania	—	—	10	0,12	18	0,24
September total	7 895 (5,27% up on 7 500 last year)					
Jan-Sep total	72 788 (3,76% down on 75 635 last year)					
August total	8 677 (September 9,01% down)					

Source: Financial Mail, Oct. 19, 1979

company has perhaps the greatest potential of any manufacturer in South Africa. Sigma Motors was formed in 1976 as a result of the merger of Chrysler and Illings--the maker of Mazda cars and Mack trucks. Illings received 75 percent of the stock in Sigma, Chrysler 25 percent. In 1978, Sigma purchased outright Peugeot-Citroen South Africa and followed that up by merging with British Leyland, a merger that has since fallen through. Sigma now markets Chrysler, Peugeot, Citroen, and Mazda cars--which together represented at one time more than 20 percent of the total market.

Related manufacturing: The same firms dominate the sales of light commercial vehicles--vans and panel trucks (called "bakkies" in South Africa). Toyota and Datsun lead with 22-percent and 19-percent market shares, respectively, followed by Ford, GM, Sigma and Volkswagen.

The medium-to-heavyweight truck field boasts a large number of companies turning out these low-volume, high-profit vehicles. The heavyweight market is only about 2,000 trucks a year, yet a large group of firms sell 100 to 300 vehicles each. As a result, their market shares for the entire commercial vehicle market are well below 1 percent each. MAN, International Harvester Co., Magirus-Deutz, Vetsak, Malcomess-Scania, Oshkosh, Fodens and ERF all specialize in heavyweight trucks.

Buses, a division of the truck industry, reached sales levels of 1,200 in 1977 and an estimated 1,500 in 1978. Leyland is the market leader, followed by Mercedes-Benz and Datsun.

Annual sales by the rubber-processing industry amount to about R350 million. The tire industry, which represents about 70 percent of the total sales, has been described as an "asymmetrical oligopoly" by South Africa's Board of Trade and Industries. The remaining 10 percent of sales is rubber produced for industrial uses such as conveyer belts in the mines. Four companies--Dunlop, General Tire & Rubber Co., Goodyear and Firestone--produce tires in South Africa; the latter three hold about equal shares of the market, averaging 10,000 tires a day to supply 80 percent of the nation's tires. Several other companies, including Michelin and Uniroyal Inc., market imported tires. Company officials state that about 90 percent of the tire content is available locally; the exceptions are polymer fibers and natural rubber. Passenger car tires can be made almost exclusively with synthetic rubber which is available from South Africa's coal-to-oil SASOL plant. Tractor tires and tires for earth-moving equipment and airplanes, however, must include an imported component of natural rubber in order to have sufficient durability.

A variety of foreign companies are active in the $1 billion component parts industry. Some, like GM and Ford, manufacture batteries, spark plugs or radiators for use in their own vehicles. Others, like Motorola Inc., Borg Warner Corp., TRW Inc. or Echelin Charger, are involved in local manufacture or imports of components. Slightly more than half of motor vehicle component parts are imported.

The attractiveness of South Africa: For many years, the motor industry represented a particularly attractive investment to foreign manufacturers. The rate of growth for the industry during the 1960s and early 1970s outpaced that for manufacturing as a whole. Earnings as a percentage of equity were also consistently greater for the industry. Between 1960 and 1969, the five major motor vehicle manufacturers reported a return on equity of 36.2 percent annually, compared with 17.5 percent annually for all manufacturing in South Africa. Some years were extraordinarily high; in 1961, the five companies reported earnings of 72.2 percent of equity. By 1975, however, automobile manufacture had slumped deeply. Earnings dropped to 3.5 percent of equity in 1975 and averaged 5.5 percent between 1971 and 1977 compared with an average 11 percent for all manufacturers in South Africa and 14 percent for American companies worldwide. Automakers lost $36 million in 1976 and $58 million in 1977 as sales dropped to 166,000 cars (GM reported losses approaching $7 million in 1977; Ford placed its losses at $8 million). The industry rebounded slightly in 1978, climbing above sales of 200,000 for the first time since 1975.

The profitability and growth of related industries, component parts manufacture, and the production of tires and tubes has been tied to the performance of motor vehicle sales. Component parts manufacture, buoyed by the local content program, grew at an annual rate of 22.6

percent between 1960 and 1975, linked with the rapid expansion of motor vehicle sales. Tire and tube sales grew at a comparable pace and, because of the need for replacement tires, suffered slightly less during the recession than did auto sales.

The future attractiveness of the motor industry is not likely to approach that of its boom years during the 1960s unless drastic change takes place in the market structure--a quick opening of the black market and a transformation of the current limits on the exports to the rest of Africa. The Financial Mail commented in January 1978 that "with the economy still wallowing, white car ownership approaching saturation, political uncertainty abounding, and the new oil crisis unresolved, the outlook is less than bright." And at the end of 1979, the future continued to look poor. Government price hikes imposed at the pump in 1979--largely as the result of the high cost of oil to South Africa following the fall of the Shah and government decision to force conservation--nearly doubled the cost of petrol to consumers. Car sales dropped precipitously as a result, and a market move toward small cars accelerated. Several auto manufacturers cut back on shifts, and at least one tire manufacturer went to a four-day work week. Figures on car sales in the fall of 1979 showed a slight upturn in overall sales, but sales for the year were still predicted to fall short of those in 1978.

Despite the less than cheery future in South Africa, most companies appear committed to stay. Fiat, after a review of its subsidiary, which sold fewer than 200 cars a month in 1976, decided to invest nearly $12 million--about $6 million to launch a new model and $6 million to retool its plant and to advertise. Henry Ford announced his intention to invest $8 million in retooling and upkeep. In 1978 General Motors stated that it would spend $28 million to develop a new range of small cars.

The commitment to stay in South Africa is based on a number of factors. One is the hope that the market, which was better in 1978 than in 1977, will eventually turn around. Moreover, the major manufacturers hope to increase their market shares. Ford maintained its market share in 1978 and expects to better it in 1979. General Motors believes its new models will allow it to make new inroads into the market. Manufacturers also expect future developments to increase their sales. They believe the government program to thin out the auto industry, which already has reduced automakers' ranks from 13 to 10, may reduce them further by 1980 and should benefit the sales volumes of the survivors and reduce their unit costs. GM and Ford are two of the best-capitalized car manufacturers, possessing the resources to sit out a transition and emerge strong. Both firms also await the development of the black market. Neither wishes to be excluded from its enormous potential, nor from the equally great--and equally undeveloped--potential for export to other black African nations.

Perhaps most important is the fact that it is probably less expensive in the short term to stay in South Africa and absorb minor losses than it would be to get out. Little new investment will be required in the future--Ford, for example, is operating at 60-percent capacity and Henry Ford has stated "it will be some years before we'll be able to make full use of the facilities we already have." Given the controls on foreign exchange and repatriation of assets, companies may well find it cheaper to stay and tolerate short-term reverses than to absorb the losses and penalties that would come from selling and repatriating their assets.

Labor practices in the motor industry: The major companies involved in the motor industry, the auto and tire manufacturers, are considered labor-intensive and the majority of their workers are black. A breakdown of employees by color for U.S. firms is as follows:

	Total	White	Colored	Asian	African
Ford	5,376	2,004	2,083	11	1,278
GM	4,000	1,280	2,120	0	600
Goodyear	2,319	536	633	0	1,190
Firestone	2,459	802	445	7	1,205

Like other industry groups in South Africa, the motor industry's unskilled and semi-skilled jobs are held primarily by blacks, and skilled, supervisory and management positions are dominated by whites. At General Motors in 1979, for example, of 1,090 salaried workers, eight were African.

The major U.S. companies in automobile manufacturing--GM and Ford--and in tire production--Goodyear and Firestone--are signers of the Sullivan principles. In 1978 Ford became the first American company to recognize an African trade union; General Motors has agreed to subtract union dues from weekly wages for Africans wishing to participate in an African union and to recognize the union once it is supported by a majority of GM's African workers. Neither of the tire companies has recognized African unions, although both say that they will if a majority of workers are members.

Both auto companies state that their aim is to pay minimum wages above the minimum effective level--50 percent above the poverty datum or minimum subsistence level. Firestone and Goodyear have adopted policies of paying wages above the poverty datum line or minimum subsistence level, and although their minimum wage has traditionally fallen below that of the auto companies, in 1978 it was nearly equal to it.

In the 18 months to January 1979, all four companies have made commitments to desegregate facilities. GM has set aside $4.5 million for new facilities, and Goodyear is committed to spend $2.5 million.

III. The Debate Over the Role of U.S. Companies in the Motor Industry in South Africa

Until recently, the brunt of criticism directed at American automobile companies in South Africa related to the companies' labor practices and to the economic support the operations provided for the South African government. In 1977, church groups affiliated with the Interfaith Center on Corporate Responsibility asked General Motors and Ford to terminate their South African operations unless apartheid ended. A similar resolution was proposed to Goodyear that year. (The resolution at General Motors was withdrawn after the company agreed to make a statement on its operations in South Africa at its annual meeting; at Ford and Goodyear the resolutions failed to receive the 3 percent required for resubmission in 1978.) The churches argued in support of their resolutions that American corporations ultimately supported the status quo in South

Africa. "U.S. business investments in the Republic of South Africa ...provide significant economic support and moral legitimacy to South Africa's apartheid government," they wrote.

The major companies active in the motor industry and in tire production argue that their commitment to racial equality and political opportunity for blacks in South Africa--exemplified by their signing of the Sullivan principles--can improve conditions there. Ford has urged the South African government to "repeal all forms of racial discrimination" in labor laws, and General Motors has said the company recognizes that "the single most important factor in the creation of a more promising investment climate in South Africa is a positive resolution of the country's pressing social problems which have their origin in the apartheid system." And Goodyear states that "we strongly believe that the presence in South Africa of Goodyear and USA industry in general is a force for constructive change."

Critics' arguments: Critics say the presence of the auto companies provides support for apartheid, and debate has increasingly focused on the strategic role Ford and GM play in South Africa. This topic is carefully examined in a recent publication, "The Motor Industry in South Africa," by Karen Rothmyer of the American Committee on Africa.

The critics are particularly doubtful about the auto companies' potential as a force for social progress and cite as evidence two GM memoranda describing a "contingency plan" for continuing production "in the event of serious civil unrest." The memoranda, sent May 6 and July 20, 1977, from GM's managing director to the company's regional director for Africa, state that, in time of emergency, GM would be designated a "national key point" by the government and would be accorded protection by a local "citizen force commando unit." According to one memo, GM's white employees have been "encouraged by the authorities to volunteer to join a local commando unit....The GM commando would assume guarding responsibility for the GM plants and would fall under the control of the local military authority for the duration of the emergency."

Timothy Smith, director of the Interfaith Center, comments that "the memo raises serious questions about whether GM and Ford can be forces for progressive social change in South Africa when they are a key component of South Africa's military effort." He argues that the memo seems to indicate GM's willingness to cooperate with the government on strategic questions and concludes that "GM has contingency plans to become a full-fledged partner in apartheid" through cooperation with the South African military who already view GM as a strategic and militarily significant industry. Jennifer Davis of the American Committee on Africa argues that the documents show that GM's managers in South Africa "see the interests of the company as identical to those of the South African government...." The government, she says, "has well-laid plans to use the companies to protect its system of white supremacy, and these documents make it clear that GM intends to fully comply."

The connection between the South African government and companies in strategic industries such as motor vehicle and tire manufacture is one that has troubled critics of the government for some time. The concern was heightened by the publication of the contingency plan, but it had arisen earlier among a number of anti-apartheid groups with the activation in 1977 of the National Supplies Procurement Act. The act, they argued, could require companies to participate actively in supplying the South African military and police. And with the publication of the Feb. 16, 1978, regulations by the U.S. Commerce Department, many critics saw increased complications in continued sales in South Africa. They argued that any sales to the military and police, including sales of component parts manufactured by American subsidiaries located outside the United States, constitute a violation of the intent of U.S. law. In shareholder resolutions proposed in 1979 to Ford and GM, church shareholders and Oberlin College asked the companies to adopt a policy not to sell "any vehicles or spare parts or provide any services to the South African police or military." They also asked the companies "to ensure to the extent possible that no customer, including the South African government, shall resell or transship vehicles to the police or military." The resolutions were supported by 2.15 percent of the shares voted at Ford and 2.98 percent of the shares voted at General Motors.

The companies' positions: Ford and GM consider vehicle sales to the South African government important to their financial well-being. Ford has stated, "Ford South Africa will continue to follow its practice of submitting bids where government agencies issue calls for competitive bids to purchase vehicles." General Motors fears that its inability to continue sales to the police and military may adversely affect its competitive position in bargaining for contracts for sales to other parts of the government. In a 1977 internal memo, concern was expressed that refusal to sell to South African defense forces "might be interpreted as reflecting doubt on the motives of the company. Such interpretation or a variation thereof could lead to direct loss of other government business and severely affect GM South Africa's share of the vehicle market and very likely threaten its viability."

General Motors told IRRC that the Commerce Department regulations have forced it to stop supplying automobiles to the South African police and military because transmissions and carburetion equipment (among other components) are imported from the United States. Consequently, it said, unit sales to the government dipped to below 300 for the first half of 1978, compared with an earlier average annual level of 1,500.

Truck sales, however, have not been affected as severely by the U.S. government restrictions. GM told IRRC that it continues to supply "commercial vehicles, primarily small trucks, to the defense and military departments as these vehicles are assembled without components manufactured in the United States." Ford says the Commerce regulations have "resulted in some loss of sales of U.S.-origin trucks to certain agencies of the South African government. The numbers involved were small." The overall effect of the regulations on truck sales, Ford reports, has been "marginal."

Neither of the tire companies reported a serious impact on sales. Firestone told IRRC that all new technology used in its South Africa subsidiary came out of its Rome subsidiary rather than from the United States, and thus the regulations had no effect on its operations.

The automobile companies recognize the strategic importance of their operations. GM noted in a 1977 memo that "should economic conditions decline sufficiently far, there could be a directive issued on model build by various companies--firstly, to preserve the capability of building vehicles and secondly, to ensure sources of supply in the case of greater emergency requirements." Moreover, in a letter to the American Committee on Africa, GM's chairman, Thomas Murphy, wrote: "It is apparent to us that manufacturing plants involved in such basic industries as petroleum production and refining, mining primary metals, transportation, machinery--industries which generate the lifeblood of any economy--also assume equally strategic importance in time of emergency. Any of our plants can be converted to war production as clearly demonstrated in the United States in 1941."

General Motors contemplates continuing operation under military supervision during an emergency situation in South Africa. One of the memos noted, "In the event that an emergency situation is declared, it is likely that there will be imposed requirements, e.g., trucks and commercial vehicles to meet national needs." Only when the country is in a virtual state of war will GM consider the possibility of ending its involvement in vehicle production. Under such circumstances, "it is almost certain that...(GM) would be taken over by an arm of the Ministry of Defense which would regulate output and coordinate the entire industrial effort. At such time, operating control of plants like General Motors and Ford as well as others would most certainly be vested in South African nationals and all materials, manpower and production requirements would be tied into the overall national requirements." Faced with complete government operating control, "the question of continuing American participation in South African business might well be finalized and operating control of plants such as General Motors and Ford would most certainly be vested in South African nationals. The terms of such a takeover could only be assumed at this time to be either nationalization of the assets or a negotiated sale under prevailing conditions."

But both companies doubt that government intervention in the industry is likely in the near future. Ford wrote the Interfaith Center, "As to possible actions by the South African government to bring about compliance with the National Supplies Procurement Act, such a situation has not arisen, and we have no current reason to believe that it will." GM's Chairman Thomas Murphy expressed a similar view to the Interfaith Center: "As a producer of commercial vehicles we would not expect the (National Supplies Procurement) Act to have any direct application to General Motors. However, should the South African government through the act attempt to take over the plant we would, of course, oppose this with every legal means at our disposal."

Both companies emphasize their opposition to apartheid and their intention to obey completely the letter of U.S. law. They continue to resist suggestions that they withdraw from South Africa and state, in the words of Thomas Murphy, "We believe that only through our continued participation in the South African economy can we continue to act as a significant force for necessary social and economic change in that country."

IV. IRRC Analysis

Those companies involved in the motor industry and related areas in South Africa face an uncertain future. They have not prospered in recent years, and although industry spokesmen often speak optimistically, companies realistically can expect only mixed economic news in the next few years. American companies are likely to be confronted with an additional burden--a rising chorus of criticism directed at the strategic role they play in South Africa.

A trend referred to hopefully by those in the auto industry is the long-awaited arrival of blacks as a force in the new car market. Despite large gains in real income in recent years, blacks do not yet earn enough to enter this market in large numbers. Thus, in the short term, blacks will not appreciably influence new car sales, but over the long run they should become important. Of course, the development of an African market in South Africa depends on the problematic continuation of economic growth and political stability in South Africa.

Another trend often cited by auto companies is the continuing "rationalization" of the auto industry. The example of Sigma, which has absorbed several smaller concerns and thereby reduced the number of automakers from 13 to 11, has prompted representatives of the big automakers to predict a further reduction in the near future. The South African government, too, encourages rationalization and predicts that it will substantially reduce the price of cars. These predictions appear to be overly optimistic. The government and auto manufacturers constantly refer to rationalization as something that ought to happen rather than a process that will occur. The growth of Sigma can be explained as much by the decision of a major South African conglomerate, Anglo-American, to enter the auto market in a big way as it can by the logic of rationalization, and substantial rationalization in the future appears unlikely.

But the concerns underlying rationalization are real. Constantly rising car prices, chronic underutilization of production capacity, and increasingly heavy cost premiums induced by local production of components have left manufacturers grasping at any solution that will increase sales volume and hold down costs. The government spoke to these concerns in Phase V of the local content program when it simultaneously encouraged reduction in the number of models and makers and made further increases in local content voluntary. While it wished to further self-sufficiency in the automotive industry, the government recognized that it had to avoid pushing all automakers into extreme financial distress.

Self-sufficiency will continue to be a dominant theme in the automobile and related industries--particularly as foreign pressures on South Africa increase. The construction of a diesel engine plant and the enforcement of a local content requirement for trucks suggest greater emphasis on promoting self-sufficiency in the heavy vehicle industry. A push to produce locally some of the expensive, sophisticated components still imported--transmissions, carburetion equipment, electronic components--is also in the cards as a way of protecting the South African economy further from the ramifications of actions such as the U.S. Commerce Department regulations.

A fundamental ambiguity pervades the relationship between the South African government and the automobile industry. In terms of economic incentives, the government alternately dangles "carrots" of rebates for increased local content and wields "sticks" of punitive taxation and heavy local content burdens to reduce fragmentation of the industry and heighten self-sufficiency. Yet, it is a middle course, short of strong government dictation to the industry but well beyond simple advice and nominal regulation. Both manufacturers and the government have suffered from this lack of clarity about who is manning the helm.

For many observers, concern over the nature of industry-government interaction mounts when discussion shifts to the strategic realm. In a "worst case" analysis--a situation of extreme economic stress and racial warfare in South Africa--the government will take over the automobile industry for wartime production. The National Supplies Procurement Act mandates government operation of strategic industries, and both auto companies and outside analysts have concluded that this includes the auto industry.

It is not easy to determine whether the government might become involved in directing production under circumstances short of a national emergency. Allegations persist that some manufacturers rely so heavily on government contracts that their autonomy is in question. General Motors itself has speculated that the government might intervene to preserve vehicle-building capability if the health of the industry deteriorates seriously. The extent to which the government acts now to maintain the viability of automakers is unclear.

Disclosures by GM and Ford about the volume of their sales to the police and military indicate that even if these sales do not represent a large proportion of the companies' aggregate sales, both the automakers and the government consider them important. Obviously, motor vehicles and tires are central to the maintenance of a prepared defense and police establishment. GM especially has been anxious to preserve its supplier relationship with the government, as have the major tire manufacturers, despite current restrictions on such sales imposed by the U.S. government. The companies appear to believe that the government's perception of whether they are willing to cooperate in car and truck sales outweighs the actual volume of sales.

Increasingly, critics have focused on the cooperative attitude underlying the strategic relationship between the automobile manufacturers and the South African government. The significance of GM's contingency plan is that, while it had been apparent that the auto companies were ultimately at the mercy of the government in a wartime situation, critics had been unaware of the company's willingness to cooperate with the authorities in meeting mandated emergency production goals.

There is a basic difference in perspective between critics who see GM cooperating in strategic planning with the government and the company argument that it must plan realistically for an emergency situation. This difference is not likely to be resolved in the near future; in fact, it is likely to be aggravated by differences in perspective over the meaning of the Commerce Department regulations.

The submission of shareholder resolutions to GM and Ford in 1979 resulted, in part, from concern over the propriety of company cooperation with the government in supplying vehicles to the military and company response to the U.S. Commerce Department regulations. GM and Ford are in technical compliance with the regulations, as are Firestone and Goodyear--they do not sell vehicles containing U.S.-made components to the South African police and military. GM and Ford do sell trucks to the police and military, however, and the tire companies may well still supply tires that reach those departments, undercutting the effect the U.S. government intended the regulations to have.

Whether the use of technology from a European subsidiary--in the case of Firestone--or the use of non-U.S.-manufactured component parts supplied by a European or other subsidiary in the case of the auto or component parts manufacturers--constitutes violation of the intent of U.S. policy is the subject of some debate.

In any event, U.S. companies in the motor industry--particularly the auto companies--are likely to encounter continued controversy at a time when their South African operations are not returning much, if anything, in profits. Both GM and Ford suffered losses during the last three years and still face constant under-capacity. The return on their equity is half of the average for foreign companies in South Africa and even less when compared to their worldwide rate of return. Each has announced in 1979 large infusions of capital into its South African subsidiary. Ford injected $8 million for upkeep and retooling, GM $28 million for retooling and upgrading and desegregating facilities. Thus, each company has been constrained to inject foreign capital into operations that now do not return much on their already large assets. Their prospects for the future, while not grim, must reflect uncertainty over the achievement of rationalization, the development of the black market potential, and the availability and cost of oil.

General Motors and Ford are caught between sharp pressure from critics and the continuing poor health of their South African subsidiaries. Although neither company is likely to withdraw, they will face continuing controversy and increasingly difficult trade-offs between economic demands and their political consequences.

The problems for component parts manufacturers and tire companies are similar. The rubber companies--with the exception of General Tire--have not been seriously hurt by the Commerce Department regulations. (General Tire, which has 16-percent interest in General Tire South Africa and a long-term technical service contract with the South African company, has been forced by the regulations to terminate its relationship.) Firestone and Goodyear have both suffered from a drop in demand for tires, although Goodyear's position is compensated in part by its manufacture of rubber conveyer belts for the mining industry, a market that has continued to grow despite the recession.

Sources

Reports

U.S. Department of State:

"Market Developments in South African Automotive Industry: Rationalization, Local Manufacture of Diesel Engines," unclassified cable, July 11, 1978, American Consul General, Johannesburg.

South African Government:

Inquiry Into the Local Manufacture of Motor Vehicles and Compenents," Board of Trade and Industries, Report No. 1777, Government Printer, Pretoria, 1977.

Other:

Karen Rothmyer, "U.S. Motor Industry in South Africa: Ford, General Motors and Chrysler," American Committee on Africa, New York, 1979.

Articles

Tony Koenderman, "Shot in the arm for motor industry," Sunday Times, May 15, 1977; "Local content," Management Magazine, October 1977, p. 14.

Financial Mail:

"Steering a tortuous course," July 15, 1977.
"Car conundrum," June 9, 1978, p. 786.
"Diesel engines, Ford pulls out," Aug. 11, 1978, p. 503.
"The motor industry: in low gear," June 15, 1979, p. 950.
"Stretching a point," Aug. 31, 1979, p. 855.
"Motor industry: getting into gear," Sept. 7, 1979, p. 952.
"Rubber: up and down," Sept. 14, 1979, p. 1057.
"Motor trade: the black bonanza," Sept. 21, 1979, p. 1164.
"Transport: tell us more," Sept. 28, 1979, p. 1274.

To The Point:

"Motoring," supplement to To The Point, Oct. 21, 1977, p. 16.
"Motoring," supplement to To The Point, Oct. 20, 1978, p. 1-36.

Other:

"Anglo in the lead," Economist, July 8, 1978.
"Changing trade trends in the motor industry," African Business, January 1978.

III.

The Domestic Debate over South Africa

I. PRESSURES FROM INVESTORS

South Africa remains a major concern for institutional investors. In particular, educational institutions and religious groups continue to respond to the question of American corporate involvement in South Africa. They have been adopting policies, voting proxies, selling stock and talking to companies about the issue.

Some investors are examining the problem voluntarily, evaluating their investments in American corporations active in South Africa in the light of public concern over and press coverage of that country's apartheid system. Church investors were among the first to raise social concerns before corporations in which they held stock. The United Church of Christ, for example, believes that "social values and social justice ought to be given consideration together with security and yield in the investment of funds held by religious organizations."

Many colleges and universities are looking at the South Africa issue in response to pressure from students who are angry about their schools' investments in companies that profit from South African operations. During the 1978-79 academic year small but vocal activist groups challenged university administrators and trustees. A coordinated "Week of Action Against Apartheid" in early April saw students on a number of campuses holding rallies, occupying buildings and boycotting classes to dramatize their cause. As in previous years, these protests occurred at some of America's most prestigious and well-endowed colleges and universities, including Amherst, Brandeis, Dartmouth, Columbia, Harvard and Oberlin.

Student activists, labor unions, black organizations and some church groups insist on the withdrawal of U.S. enterprise from South Africa. They say that the presence of American corporations in South Africa gives moral legitimacy to the white minority regime, and that it creates a vested American interest in the status quo and the stability of the existing political system. They argue that the supply of capital by American banks and businesses eases South Africa's foreign exchange problems and makes the country less vulnerable to international pressures that would stimulate reform. Sales of certain products, they say, contribute directly to South Africa's military and security forces, and investments in the homelands that the white government has set aside for blacks or adjoining border areas contribute to the South African government's policy of separate development. In their view, the withdrawal of investment and a moratorium on loans would deal a severe psychological blow to the morale of the white regime in South Africa and would constrict the historically high rate of economic growth that many analysts consider crucial to its stability. They contend that these pressures, coupled with increasing international isolation of South Africa, would force the government to abandon its discriminatory practices and work out a system for sharing power with other racial groups. While critics admit that these types of sanctions would be most injurious to blacks in the short-term, they argue that temporary hardships would be offset by eventual economic and political gains.

The majority of institutional investors--as well as corporations operating in South Africa--disagree with the position that economic disengagement would hasten the dismantling of apartheid. While they share the concern about the oppression of blacks under the current political system, they believe that progress can best be achieved through gradual change. Advocates of investment assert that corporations--by liberalizing employment practices in their South African operations--set a positive example for other employers in that country and contribute to the well-being of all races in South Africa. They believe that by increasing economic opportunities for blacks--thus elevating their standard of living and security in the labor market--companies are contributing to a process that will lead eventually to the full integration of blacks into society on all levels. In their view, economic disengagement would only aggravate unemployment of blacks and strengthen the resolve of whites to resist external pressures, and it probably would lead to increased repression of anti-apartheid activists and organizations because the government would feel in its growing isolation less constrained by world opinion in dealing harshly with dissent.

Although educational and religious institutions have occupied center-stage in the ongoing South African debate, they are not the only actors. Institutions that control, administer or benefit from government monies and pension funds have also been considering the issue. Public employee and private unions are beginning to question the investment of their pension funds in corporations and banks active in South Africa. Cities and states are exploring the feasibility of diverting public funds from supporting multinational companies in South Africa to stimulating the local economy.

Unlike schools and churches, unions and municipalities have motives that reach beyond the morality of involvement in apartheid. Unions seek to stem the flight of capital from the United States and to gain some voice in the investment of their pension funds. Similarly, cities and states see advantage in using their dollars to revitalize their immediate environment.

Given the variety of institutional investors, the range of their interests, and the philosophical differences among them, a host of approaches to the South Africa issue has developed. At universities, where students have translated their beliefs in corporate withdrawal into appeals for divestment, some boards of trustees have opted for selective or blanket sale of South Africa-related stocks. Many schools, though, have joined with churches in espousing shareholder activism. They vote proxies, sponsor resolutions, and negotiate with companies with the goal of limiting certain types of corporate activity and improving corporate labor practices in South Africa. They usually do not advocate withdrawal. Public employee and private unions, often lacking control over the disposition of their pension funds, have concentrated on the issue of bank loans to the South African government. They employ the sanction of withdrawing money from banks that make such loans. City governments have used the same kind of leverage.

The Divestment Issue

Advocates of corporate disengagement from South Africa are divided on the question of divestment. While some argue that shareholder activism is more effective, others favor selling stock. Most student groups and labor unions concerned with apartheid argue that divestment of securities in banks and companies active in South Africa (or, in other instances, withdrawal of accounts from those banks) for non-financial reasons by large institutions would dramatically publicize the human rights questions surrounding the role of U.S. investment in that country. Such publicity, they maintain, would force a number of companies to respond by withdrawing their operations from South Africa in order to avoid further adverse exposure and possible boycotts. Even if divestment does not precipitate corporate withdrawal, some students argue, it is justified on moral grounds alone because it is socially irresponsible for investors to profit from holdings in companies that operate in a country where racial discrimination is an institution.

In the fall of 1978, IRRC reported that eight schools had sold or committed themselves to sell all or a portion of their South Africa-related equity holdings. Antioch College, Hampshire College, the University of Massachusetts, Ohio University, and the University of Wisconsin opted for complete divestment. Amherst College, Smith College, and Tufts University announced selective sales of stock.

In the 1978-79 school year, more universities engaged in selective divestment and fewer sold their entire South Africa-related portfolios. Michigan State University sold all of its South African holdings, worth more than $8 million. Hampshire College sold stock in three companies with South African interests which had been purchased since its 1977 total divestment decision. At least 11 schools--Boston University, Brandeis University, Carleton College, Columbia University, Harvard University, Howard University, the University of Michigan, Ohio State University, Vassar College, the University of Washington and Yale University--disposed of selected holdings.

In December 1978 Michigan State trustees voted to sell all their South Africa-related stocks. The decision came after the university had engaged in lengthy discussions with its investment managers over whether divestment could be done prudently. Earlier, the board had received an opinion from the university's vice president for legal affairs that divestiture was likely to come under "close scrutiny by the courts" because the trustees would be neglecting their overriding obligation "to follow a primary policy of prudent investment, with their sole allegiance being to the preservation and enhancement of those public funds under their control."

Michigan State's investment manager, Scudder, Stevens & Clark, advised the school that divestiture would not harm the quality of its portfolio, although the same rate of return could not be guaranteed. "In effect, we were told that it could be done, but it would be harder to do," a university official told IRRC. The university then began gradual divestment of its holdings in all firms active in South Africa.

Selective divestment by educational institutions: The number of colleges and universities that have adopted investment policies that include selective divestment as a last resort is increasing. The criteria employed by universities vary, but in general selective divestment can be prompted by any one of three kinds of corporate behavior: failing to sign and carry out the Sullivan principles of fair employment in South Africa (or to respond forthrightly to requests for evidence of progressive labor practices), selling strategic products to the South African government, or lending to the public sector in South Africa. Educational institutions' South African investment policies usually provide for extended attempts to use the shareholder process to persuade corporations to cease these actions before the school will actually sell its stock.

Employment practices--Perhaps the most important criterion for selective divestment by colleges and universities is a company's labor practices in South Africa. A number of schools have announced policies to this effect, and several schools have gone ahead with disposal of stock because of a company's employment practices. Many policies are built around corporate acceptance of the labor code drawn up by General Motors board member Leon Sullivan, which has now been signed by 135 corporations. (Sullivan principles, Appendix B)

Three divestments involving labor practices occurred in 1978-79. Ohio State University, the University of Michigan and the University of Washington all sold stock after individual companies failed to respond substantively to requests for information about their labor practices in South Africa.

Ohio State queried all of its portfolio companies about operations in South Africa and efforts to upgrade employment practices for blacks there. Only one company, International Flavors and Fragrances, declined to respond satisfactorily, asserting it did not disclose the sort of information the university requested. The trustees then acted in accord with a 1978 policy statement mandating selective divestment where companies fail to demonstrate adequate progress in fair employment and sold some 10,000 shares (worth about $250,000) of International Flavors and Fragrances stock.

Failure to adopt existing codes of labor conduct was the motivation for two other divestments. Black & Decker objected to the University of Michigan's request that it affirm the Sullivan principles: "Our company does not subscribe to the Sullivan code and does not report to Dr. Sullivan's organization as we do not believe that the company's policies should be dictated by, nor the company report to, any special interest group, regardless of the merit of the group's objectives....It is company policy to be governed by the 'golden rule' and we insist on treating our employees fairly....We have been, are, and will be doing the best we can to improve the lot of our employees in all countries where we have operations without interfering in the internal social and political affairs of the host countries." On the basis of that response, Michigan sold 14,613 shares of Black & Decker stock.

University of Washington regents cited the failure of Dresser Industries to issue a separate statement governing their activities in South Africa as the basis for sale of close to $150,000 worth of Dresser stock in November 1978.

A number of universities that have adopted new South African investment policies, including Boston University, Brandeis University, Carleton College, Cornell University and Tufts University, will sell stock in companies that fail to sign and carry out the Sullivan principles or a comparable labor code.

One university that had endorsed sale of stock in companies that did not sign the Sullivan principles has since moved on to a tougher anti-apartheid stance. Howard University, which in March 1978 endorsed the Sullivan principles and sold all securities it held in companies that had not done the same, decided six months later to sell stock in all companies doing "substantial business" in South Africa. "Using the Sullivan principles as a standard just didn't work over here," university treasurer Caspa Harris told IRRC. "Practically speaking, we couldn't know who abided by the principles and who didn't."

Strategic sales--Only in the last year have colleges and universities begun to provide for divestment of stock in companies that sell strategic products to the South African police and military. In October 1978 the Carleton College trustees decided to prudently sell stocks in corporations active in South Africa that supply goods and services to support that country's security forces or its apartheid apparatus. Carleton, which to date has announced no sales under this policy, will determine each company's involvement on a case-by-case basis. The logic behind the strategic sales policy was explained in the majority report to the trustees of Carleton's South Africa advisory committee. Noting that the proviso is aimed primarily at U.S. computer and electronics firms and oil companies with facilities in South Africa, the study said: "The support given to the South African government by these strategic products and technologies overrides the net good which might result from their employment practices."

Brandeis University has taken a similar stance and has already disposed of one security because of the company's role as a strategic supplier to the South African government. In 1979 Brandeis announced a new policy that provided for sale of stock in American corporations that sell items to the police and military that help enforce apartheid. Such companies cause "severe social injury" in South Africa, according to Brandeis's policy. The policy makes ample provision for efforts to change corporate actions via persuasion and shareholder initiatives. In the case of Ford Motor Co., whose South African subsidiary supplies cars and trucks to the police and military, Brandeis ruled that the company's sales were causing severe social injury. Since Brandeis owned no Ford voting stock, it elected to sell a $350,000 Ford bond.

Bank loans--A growing number of universities and colleges have identified bank lending to the South African government and its agencies as a third criterion for sale of stock. Three educational institutions have dissociated themselves from banks after the banks refused to rule out the possibility of extending credit to the South African public sector in the future.

In selling $4.2 million worth of bonds in five banks--Bank of America, Manufacturers Hanover Trust, First National Chicago, Charter New York Corp. and the Export-Import Bank--in October 1978, Vassar College called lending to the South African government "particularly reprehensible." The board of trustees asserted that its selective divestment strategy "may be effective in encouraging change in South Africa."

In spring 1979 Yale trustees sold $1.7 million worth of J.P. Morgan stock and terminated a short-term lending agreement with the bank after Morgan refused to exclude categorically the possibility of making loans directly to the South African government or its instrumentalities. Yale's decision was made in accordance with its South African investment policy, which calls for divestment of stock in banks that lend to the South African government. Yale's Advisory Committee on Investor Responsibility, which recommended the sale, concluded: "Yale holds that a line ought to be drawn at loans to the South African government, even if a particular loan could be said to be of direct benefit to the blacks...." David K. Storrs, Yale's director of investments, told IRRC that loans support the South African government by providing it with capital. Even if the capital is used for the benefit of blacks, he said, a loan frees an equivalent amount of capital that the government can use for repressive purposes.

Unlike Vassar, Yale doubted its divestiture would have any impact on Morgan's lending policy. "Divestiture is of little practical consequence and hence is almost entirely symbolic," the advisory committee noted; however, "symbols and gestures are important in the realm of moral and humane concerns, and are to be taken seriously."

Columbia University sold $2.7 million worth of stock in Detroit Bank Corp., Manufacturers National Bank of Detroit and Rainier Bancorporation of Seattle, when the two Detroit banks declined to disclose whether they had extended, or planned to extend, credit to South African and when Rainier affirmed it would continue to make loans to the government. Under Columbia's policy on South Africa, the school will sell its investments and withdraw deposits in banks "which provide new or continuing access to capital markets for the government of South Africa and which do not announce their intention to cease such activities."

Brandeis, Boston University, Carleton, Cornell and Tufts are among the universities that adopted investment policies in 1978-79 providing for divestiture of stock in banks lending to the South African public sector. Other schools, including Swarthmore, are considering adoption of selective divestment policies for bank stocks. Tufts is debating sales under its new policy, and Yale is "reviewing all banking relationships the university maintains" in order to determine if further divestiture is warranted.

Several universities have tailored their selective divestiture policies regarding bonds to fit the variety of business relationships they maintain with financial institutions. Boston University, for example, is disposing of all of its South Africa-related non-voting holdings because they "confer no investor powers" on the university. Because the university cannot attempt to influence companies in which it holds non-voting stock, it is "in the position of benefiting financially in these cases from companies doing business in South Africa without the offsetting advantages of voting stock." Bayley Mason, special assistant to the president at Boston University, told IRRC that sale of non-voting stock was "a logical prerequisite to defending our voting holdings."

Harvard has also spoken directly to the problem of ownership of non-voting debt securities it holds in banks. The university does not now own equity shares in banks lending to the South African government. "In the case of debt securities," the president and Fellows of Harvard College have written, "recognizing that such holdings do not give us the status of a voting shareholder," Harvard will attempt to persuade the bank not to lend to South Africa, and, if necessary, sell its non-voting holdings.

Pressures on banks from other institutional investors: The specialized policies on selling voting and non-voting holdings in banks that have been adopted by a small but growing number of universities must also be seen in the context of broader pressures on financial institutions. Universities, because of their status as shareholders in banks, are in a position to employ shareholder activist techniques to attempt to change bank lending policies. Other groups, which either possess no investor powers or do not hold stock, have tried other methods to persuade banks not to lend to the public sector in South Africa. One union, the United Auto Workers, lacking voting control of its pension fund equities, has withdrawn its accounts from a bank involved in South African lending. Several church groups have also closed accounts. A few municipalities have attempted to use direct business pressures to influence banks as well by withdrawing idle city funds from bank accounts.

Committee to Oppose Banks Loans to South Africa--Led by the American Committee on Africa, the ad hoc Committee to Oppose Bank Loans to South Africa, comprised of members of Congress, community organizations and student groups, has launched a campaign to pressure banks into withholding loans from South Africa until the South African government modifies its racial policies. The committee has selected a number of banks--including Bank of America, Citibank, Chase Manhattan, Continental Illinois, First Chicago, Manufacturers Hanover Trust, Morgan Guaranty Trust and Wells Fargo--for a nationwide boycott, urging individual institutions to withdraw their assets in protest of the banks' participating in loan programs to the South African regime. The committee says $127 million has been withdrawn from the targeted banks.

The committee is now headed by Dumisani Kumalo, the exiled founder of the Union of Black Journalists in South Africa. The committee held a conference in 1979 in Minneapolis to coordinate local efforts and to plan strategy for the bank campaign nationwide.

Church actions--Continental Illinois has been the target of withdrawals by constituent Protestant denominations of the National Council of Churches. About $4 million has been withdrawn in response to the NCC's decision to ask its member denominations to "undertake" to withdraw funds from banks that participate in loans to South Africa.

The United Church of Christ announced at the Citibank annual meeting in 1979 that it was closing $7 million worth of accounts at the bank because Citicorp is "the most important U.S. financial interventionist in South African political affairs, bankrolling apartheid."

Union actions--Unions in the Northwest have been concentrating their attention on Seattle First National Bank (Seafirst). Although union interest in Seafirst is principally in support of the efforts of the Retail Clerks Union to become the bargaining agent for bank employees, "South Africa is an important element of the campaign to withdraw funds from Seafirst," according to Joanne Lueke, a campaign coordinator. "The unions are sympathetic to the South African cause."

The Seafirst campaign organizers attracted attention when they announced initial pledges from unions and community groups to pull $2 billion out of Seattle First, which has about $7 billion in assets. However, only $65 million worth of accounts has been withdrawn so far. One problem, Lueke acknowledged, was that while a number of unions had pledged to withdraw large pension accounts from the bank, few had the power to make such a move unilaterally.

Unions and South Africa: Spurred in part by concern about South Africa, a number of unions have begun to study aligning their pension fund portfolios to reflect their social priorities. The assets of public and private pension funds are enormous, according to Jeremy Rifkin and Randy Barber, authors of The North Shall Rise Again: Pensions, Politics, and Power in the 1980s. They estimate that these funds, which are growing at a 10- to 12-percent annual rate, total more than $500 billion. Pension funds own 20 to 25 percent of the stock of companies on the New York and American Stock Exchanges and control more than 40 percent of all U.S. corporate debt capital.

However, Rifkin and Barber point out, many union pension funds are overseen by corporate management. Of collectively bargained funds, more than half are controlled exclusively by management and approximately 40 percent are controlled jointly by management and union representatives. "In every case, however, almost all trusted funds are handed over to a third party, usually a bank, sometimes an insurance company or independent assets manager, to invest on behalf of the beneficiaries."

In 1978 the International Longshoremen's and Warehousemen's Union Local 6 requested that its pension plan, administered jointly by employer and employee trustees, divest itself of holdings in U.S. firms operating in South Africa. In addition to selling existing stock, the local asked that no new contributions be invested in South Africa-related companies. To date, the trustees have not adopted the position advocated by the union.

At a recent convention, the ILWU voted a policy statement that addresses both issues of South African investments and pension fund control. Because of their South African investments, the union said, "union members are without their approval drawn into participation in apartheid, and to the extent that those firms profit from apartheid, then union members too are made to profit from it." The delegates also took note of growing union interest in participating in the control of pension fund investments and suggested: "Not only might it be possible to discontinue particular investments that plan participants find objectionable, but it might also be the case that union officers and pension plan trustees can have a decisive say in directing that such funds be put to use in ways that both satisfy the security of the funds and meet broader criteria as to what actions are in the best interests of working people in general."

The AFL-CIO, which has urged U.S. companies to sell their South African subsidiaries, and which promotes black unions in South Africa through its African-American Labor Center, is one of several national unions looking at the pension fund control question.

Thomas Donahue, executive assistant to the president, explained that the AFL-CIO has tentatively identified several kinds of stocks as questionable pension fund investments. These include holdings in non-union and anti-union companies, as well as holdings in companies doing business in South Africa. The union's inquiry has begun by questioning whether these are "proper places for union investments," Donahue said.

The United Auto Workers in 1978 withdrew $20 million in deposits from banks that lend to South Africa and initiated an investigation of whether its pension money should be invested in corporations "that violate standards of decency," according to a union spokesman. As an example, he cited companies that are not progressive employers in South Africa. As part of a tentative labor contract settlement with financially troubled Chrysler Corp. Oct. 27, 1979, the union won the right to blacklist from its pension fund holdings in five companies that it judges to be in violation of human rights standards in their activities in South Africa.

The International Association of Machinists is also studying the questions of pension fund control and investments in companies active in South Africa.

Alternative investment: Clearly, union interest in the American corporate presence in South Africa goes beyond moral concern about apartheid to an issue of fundamental self-interest: control over pension fund investments. Several municipalities in California have an analogous set of concerns. Motivated initially by a desire to pressure banks that lent to the South African government, these cities have also considered the possibility that their financial resources could be used to benefit their own interests. Several states have also pursued this line.

California municipalities--The city of Davis, Calif., which voted in March 1978 to remove city funds from banks lending money in South Africa, will soon begin phased total withdrawal of its funds from these banks. The city council is now considering the report of a nine-member task force appointed to recommend alternative investments. Davis will redeposit its $7 million in surplus funds in banks that do not lend to South Africa. It will also invest, on a small scale, in government-insured mortgages. A task force member told IRRC that approval of these recommendations by the city council was likely.

In the spring of 1979 a similar referendum was overwhelmingly approved by voters in Berkeley, Calif. Berkeley will withdraw its idle funds from banks making loans to South Africa and reinvest the estimated $4.5 million in projects and institutions that directly benefit the citizens of Berkeley. The city is now forming a nine-member community task force to supervise the withdrawal of funds and their reinvestment in community development projects. A spokesman for the coalition of community groups that sponsored the Berkeley initiative told IRRC that about a dozen California cities and towns had expressed interest in Berkeley's step and might consider similar initiatives.

In 1978 the San Diego City Council and County Board of Supervisors created a reinvestment task force to study the investment of idle city and county funds and public employee pension funds. The panel issued a report recommending divestiture of South Africa-related pension holdings, withdrawal of funds from banks making loans to South Africa, and reinvestment in local businesses and economic development projects. The city has not adopted any of the recommendations. The county board of supervisors agreed to ask the public employees retirement board--which administers the country's $250 million pension fund--to limit its South African investments to companies that have signed the Sullivan principles. It also suggested that the retirement board look into investing in the secondary mortgage market.

State pension fund investments--The linked interests in South Africa-related investments and in alternative investments expressed in cities throughout California have been also voiced at the state level.

California Gov. Edmund G. Brown Jr. has stimulated research that could lead to a wide-reaching examination of the state pension fund's investment strategies. The Governor's Office of Planning and Research published "An Urban Strategy for California" in 1978 which set forth specific steps to improve existing housing and encourage new urban development. One step is the investment of a portion of the public retirement system's assets in California mortgages.

The office is now at work on an elaboration of the urban strategy. One provision reportedly will link state pension funds and bank deposits with their economic impact and potential to meet local needs. An analyst noted that this could provide "the philosophical basis" for reinvestment.

The Office of Planning and Research has also been looking at the potential of state holdings for influencing corporations doing business in South Africa.

Brown is expected to name a public investment task force to investigate alternative investment of state pension fund money and to consider the social implications of the state's stockholdings. The task force would consist of 20 to 30 people representing "the whole investment spectrum," according to a spokesman for the Office of Planning and Research.

The stirrings in California merit attention in part because of the sheer size of the state's investments. The State Teachers Retirement System has almost $5.7 billion in assets. The Public Employees Retirement System, worth $10.7 billion, is "the largest portfolio in the world....(It) virtually sets the bond market," according to John Harrington, former consultant to the state legislature's Select Committee on Investment Priorities and Objectives. Gov. Brown appoints members of the boards that administer these funds; in addition, officials in his administration sit on the boards. Brown also serves as ex officio head of the California Board of Regents, who oversee University of California endowment and retirement funds totaling $2.2 billion.

Ferment at the state level in California about South African and alternative investments appears to be principally due to the governor's personal interest in the topics. The exploratory research, for instance, has been carried on by the governor's office of planning and research.

Brown, moreover, was apparently the motivating force behind the decision of the regents in 1979 to vote $7.5 million worth of GM stock in favor of a shareholder resolution asking the company to cease sales to the South African police and military. The California regents had never before supported a shareholder resolution relating to South Africa. Brown has met twice with a group of university students, who encouraged him on the GM vote. One of these students told IRRC he was impressed by the governor's interest in the South African and alternative investment issues.

Other state actions--Two other states have been following the developments in California closely. The Minnesota state senate's Government Operations Committee has been gathering background information and conducting interim hearings on alternative investment.

"We would like to see the state's investment funds out of countries that violate human rights and reinvested in corporations operating in Minnesota," a committee staffer explained to IRRC. A Minnesota representative spent three days in California meeting with California legislators interested in the subject. Although no legislation is pending in Minnesota, the staff aide thought that a bill might develop out of the interim hearings.

The state of Massachusetts has taken the first steps toward governing the investment of public pension funds. The state appropriated $25 million in its 1980 budget as a contribution to the pension reserve fund, which is designed to meet future costs of the $1.3-billion teachers' and public employees' retirement funds. The legislature stipulated that the reserve fund--but not the much larger pension accounts--would not be eligible to receive the new appropriation if it "maintain(s) any investments in any company doing business in or with the Republic of South Africa or any other nation designated a repressive regime, so-called, by Freedom House or Amnesty International after Sept. 1, 1978."

State Sen. Jack Backman, a strong supporter of the investment restriction, told IRRC that there would be "no change in the present portfolio of any Massachusetts pension fund account. The only victory is that future investments in firms doing business in South Africa and certain other repressive nations will be prohibited."

In a separate move, the legislature approved a 1979 Deficiency Budget with a proviso that the state begin to use its pension fund monies to promote the local economy. The "invest-at-home" provision calls upon the state treasurer to "invest and reinvest such (pension) funds, to the extent not required for current disbursements, as much as reasonably possible to benefit and expand the economic climate within the commonwealth so long as such use is consistent with sound investment policy...." Sen. Backman noted that "No one is yet certain what impact this new restriction will have on state pension investment practices."

Backman termed the decisions to limit future investments in South Africa-related securities and to promote local investment as "the first stage in a multi-year program of redirecting our investment priorities."

Opposition to Divestment

Although church groups, educational institutions, unions and municipalities have become involved in using financial leverage to pressure American corporations and banks about business activities in South Africa, there is no strong consensus among institutional investors in favor of divestment. A number of schools, in endorsing divestment only as a last resort, have expressed doubts as to whether it would have any effect of apartheid.

Other schools oppose divestment not because they feel it is an ineffective strategy but rather because they reject corporate social responsibility as a legitimate investment criterion. These universities are often located in the Midwest and South and have not felt pressures from students urging them to consider the moral implications of their investments. Purdue University is typical. Treasurer Winfield Hentschel ruled out avoiding investments in companies active in South Africa, arguing "that's just not good business."

Both Indiana University and the University of Oregon, which adopted selective divestment policies, have faced internal pressures opposing divestment that have slowed the implementation of their policies. In June 1978 Indiana decided to sell stock in companies that do not endorse and carry out the Sullivan principles. In the fall the trustees were informed by Theodore Sendak, the state's attorney general, that the school's new policy might be illegal if it violated the "prudent man rule" covering the investment of public funds in Indiana. Despite Sendak's letter, which was discussed at a trustee meeting, a university spokesman asserted that the informal opinion had no apparent effect on Indiana's policy.

In Oregon, though, divestment of $6 million worth of stock in companies doing business in South Africa has been stymied by a challenge to the State Board of Higher Education's decision from the Oregon Investment Council, an agency that oversees the state's investments. State Attorney General James A. Redden has disputed both the board's authority to make such a decision and the correctness of including political and moral considerations in investment decisions.

In November 1978 a group of university students filed suit to seek adjudication of the questions of authority over investment decisions and propriety of divestment. Associated Students v. Hunt "will be in the courts quite a while," a spokesman for the Oregon Department of Justice said.

In the meantime, the university's Chancellor of Administration indicated to IRRC that the school had voluntarily limited its investments in some ways. "Our investment managers are aware of the Regents' divestment decision and the discussion surrounding it, and decided it was prudent to avoid stocks in companies doing substantial business in South Africa that did not subscribe to the Sullivan principles."

Shareholder Activism

A growing number of institutional investors have turned to the exercise of shareholder rights as a means of influencing corporate operations in South Africa. Universities that have adopted investment policies incorporating selective divestment as a last resort have recognized that shareholder activism provides them with extensive opportunity to attempt to persuade companies to cease their allegedly injurious activity before divestment is invoked. Other schools that have not favored divestment have also embraced shareholder democracy. Other institutions, such as insurance companies, are increasingly considering South Africa-related shareholder resolutions.

1979 shareholder resolutions: A record number of shareholder resolutions on the corporate role in South Africa were presented to corporations during the 1979 proxy season. Shareholders of 24 corporations voted on 27 resolutions concerning American corporate involvement in South Africa, compared with 22 such resolutions in 1978 and 16 in 1977. In addition, 8 resolutions on South Africa were withdrawn by their sponsors after they reached agreement on appropriate actions with the corporations involved. South Africa accounted for more than one-fourth of all the social responsibility shareholder resolutions in 1979. The average level of support for South Africa-related proposals during the spring 1979 proxy season was 3.59 percent, compared with 4.38 percent in 1978.

As in the past the Interfaith Center on Corporate Responsibility coordinated the sponsorship efforts of its member denominations. As in 1978 the church sponsors were joined by several colleges as proponents of resolutions. A private individual and a student group also sponsored resolutions on South Africa.

The South Africa resolutions that came to votes in 1979 fell into five basic categories:

Bank loans--Resolutions submitted to BankAmerica and Wells Fargo sought to bar new loans or the renewal of any existing loans to the South African government and its agencies until meaningful steps are taken toward majority rule in South Africa.

Resolutions proposed to Citicorp, Continental Illinois, First Chicago, Manufacturers Hanover, and J.P. Morgan asked the banks to issue reports on loans to South Africa and on lending criteria and policies regarding that country.

A resolution to INA asked that the corporation refrain from underwriting any securities sold by the South African government or its instruments until the government takes meaningful steps toward majority rule.

Non-expansion--Resolutions proposed to Exxon, Fluor and U.S. Steel asked these corporations not to expand their operations in South Africa until the South African government committed itself to the elimination of apartheid.

Sales to the South African government--Four resolutions dealt with potentially strategic sales to the South African government. One resolution asked Control Data and Sperry Rand to adopt a policy prohibiting sale or lease of computers or their components to the government of South Africa. A second resolution submitted to Eastman Kodak sought to preclude sales of photographic equipment to the South African government, its agencies and instrumentalities, and any third parties that might resell the equipment to the government. As in 1978, Bryn Mawr College co-sponsored the resolution to Kodak. Oberlin College co-sponsored resolutions to General Motors and Ford Motor asking each company to adopt a policy that it would not sell vehicles or spare parts or provide any services to the South African police and military.

Shareholders proposed a resolution to Caterpillar Tractor asking that a review committee be established to examine the implications of the company's involvement in South Africa, with attention to possible use of Caterpillar equipment by the police and military.

Withdrawal--Resolutions submitted to Union Carbide and Phelps Dodge asked the corporations to terminate operations in South Africa unless the South African government committed itself to ending apartheid and began extending equal rights to the majority population. Phillips

Petroleum was asked to withdraw from South Africa if its affiliate there did not carry out the Sullivan principles. Identical resolutions to American Express, General Motors and Timken requested the liquidation of the company's assets in South Africa.

Oil Sales to Rhodesia--Resolutions proposed to Mobil Oil, Standard Oil of California and Texaco asked these corporations to cut back oil imports to South Africa by one-third to help ensure compliance with economic sanctions against Rhodesia.

In addition, shareholders of Mobil also voted on a resolution proposed by a Cornell University student group asking the corporation to adopt the European Economic Community code for labor union operations as its labor policy in South Africa.

Trends in 1979: Of the 27 resolutions relating to South Africa, 15 got more than 3 percent support. Ten received enough votes to qualify for resubmission next year. Nine of the survivors were voted on for the first time in 1979; only a stop loan resolution to BankAmerica had been voted on previously.

Bank loans--The resolutions to BankAmerica and to Wells Fargo were both the highest vote-getters among South Africa resolutions and among the most favorably viewed by institutional investors. Both shareholders in general and institutional investors in particular were less enthusiastic about resolutions requesting reports on lending activities than they were about the requests for a ban on lending to the South African government. Of the "report" resolutions, only one to Manufacturers Hanover received enough votes to be resubmitted the following year.

Non-expansion--Institutional support was equally strong for the non-expansion proposals. Both the Exxon and the Fluor resolutions received enough votes to be resubmitted, and the U.S. Steel proposal came close to the 6 percent required for a third submission.

Sales to the government--Of the resolutions relating to strategic sales, only one to Sperry survived and overall support dipped, but institutional interest in and support of these proposals was high.

Withdrawal--Two of the three church-sponsored resolutions requesting withdrawal from South Africa received enough support to qualify for resubmission--at Phillips Petroleum and Union Carbide. Institutions supported these resolutions at a rate comparable to that of 1978, although they were clearly less favored than lending, sales or expansion proposals. Institutional and overall support for the withdrawal resolutions submitted by Edward C. Calvert to American Express, General Motors and Timken was extremely low.

Oil Sales to Rhodesia--None of the resolutions submitted to oil companies about their alleged sales to Rhodesia received sufficient support to merit resubmission in 1980. These resolutions received approximately the same amount of support from institutional investors in 1979 as they had in 1978.

Sponsoring resolutions: The two educational institutions sponsoring resolutions in 1979 were Bryn Mawr College and Oberlin College. Bryn Mawr co-sponsored a resolution to Eastman Kodak asking the company to avoid sales to the South African government that could be used for repressive purposes. Bryn Mawr first raised the issue of strategic sales in a resolution to Kodak in 1978, garnering 4.74 percent of the shares voted. This year's resubmission did less well, attracting 3.13 percent.

Oberlin's first plunge into sponsorship also dealt with the strategic sales issue. The college co-sponsored resolutions to Ford and GM asking each company not to sell cars and trucks to the South African police and military. The proposal was supported by 2.98 percent and 2.15 percent of the shares voted at GM and Ford, respectively.

Many observers note that the recent sponsorship of resolutions by educational institutions is an important precedent, particularly for those schools that are committed to divestment if their attempts to persuade corporations to change their activities in South Africa fail. Sponsorship thus represents the final--and perhaps the most significant--step in shareholder activism. Church groups, traditionally the principal sponsors of South Africa-related resolutions, are encouraged by university sponsorship. Timothy Smith, executive director of the Interfaith Center, cited the participation of Bryn Mawr and Oberlin as one of the highlights of the 1979 proxy season.

Both Bryn Mawr and Oberlin reported relatively positive experiences as proponents. The coordinator for the Kodak resolution at Bryn Mawr noted several benefits of sponsorship. The major plusses she cited were the capability to control the wording of the proposal and the opportunity to demonstrate extreme concern with South Africa. Important drawbacks included the financial costs and scattered criticism from alumni. An Oberlin spokesman also reported that the college had received several letters from "irate alumni" and from other colleges expressing disapproval of Oberlin's step. As a result, he said, "if we did it over again we'd do it differently. We would try to publicize and actively enlist support for the resolution."

In 1979, a student group for the first time proposed a shareholder resolution. A group of Cornell University students under the name of the Cornell Corporate Responsibility Project, asked GM, IBM and Mobil to adopt the provisions of the European Economic Code, with respect to the recognition of African labor unions, at its operations in South Africa. The project earlier had purchased one share of stock in each corporation. It withdrew the resolution from consideration at both GM and IBM after GM convinced the project that it was already fulfilling the intent of the resolution and IBM argued to the group's satisfaction that the resolution was inappropriate because of the nature of the computer industry in South Africa and worldwide.

Tom Smith, spokesman for the Cornell student group, told IRRC that it proposed the EEC guidelines, which "have a reputation of being tougher" than the Sullivan principles, in order to "find out where Mobil stands" on the question of African unions. "This resolution tests the sincerity of the corporation's commitment to act as a positive force in South Africa," Smith explained. The resolution at Mobil received the support of 2.57 percent of the shares voted.

The trend toward university sponsorship of resolutions appears likely to continue. By mid-1979 Wesleyan University had already announced that it would sponsor a shareholder resolution to Mobil in 1980 in accordance with its South Africa investment policy. The university said it would ask Mobil not to expand its operations in South Africa. Wesleyan's decision to submit a non-expansion resolution to Mobil came after a lengthy study of the role of American oil companies in South Africa conducted by a student-faculty task force.

Church sponsorship--Traditionally, churches have been the leading sponsors of resolutions on South Africa. The United Church of Christ has been in the forefront of this established movement. "Corporate persuasion is likely to be the most effective option available to improve the social impact of a corporation in which a church organization holds an investment. Therefore, the instrument of corporate persuasion should be used continually," according to the church's most recent "Report on Corporate Social Responsibility Actions." The UCC's policy notes that although divestiture is a "generally ineffective" means of altering corporate practices, "the threat of a sale plus the willingness to go through with the threat" is significant.

Divestiture, though not ruled out by the UCC, nonetheless takes second place to a strategy of negotiation over issues raised in resolutions. In 1979, for example, the church first proposed a resolution to First National Boston asking the bank not to lend to the South African government and then withdrew the resolution after the bank agreed to publish in its 1979 proxy materials a statement that it had made no loans to the government or state-owned businesses during the last year. The statement also reports that as of the end of 1978 the bank held $4.6 million in loans to the South African government and that it had lent $200 million to black African nations. Richard D. Hill, chairman of the board of First Boston, said that the bank's decision to stop loans to the South African government "was brought about by the abhorrence of the world, which we share, towards the policies of apartheid" and that the bank would not resume lending "unless the political policies of the South African government are changed drastically." At the First Boston annual meeting, Howard Schomer, Secretary of the UCC's World Issues Office, complimented Hill for his bank's "model openness" in responding to the issue. Schomer announced the withdrawal of the resolution, cautioning the bank that it would "keep in touch with you about future developments in the matter."

Considering shareholder resolutions: Sponsoring resolutions is a comparatively new development among universities, but universities--as well as insurance companies, pension funds and foundations--have engaged for a number of years in elaborate, detailed examination of shareholder resolutions before voting on them. By now investors have formalized their voting procedures, which differ substantially from institution to institution.

In 1972 Harvard University organized an Advisory Committee on Shareholder Responsibility, whose primary duty is to recommend votes on shareholder resolutions. The committee, composed of four students, four faculty members and four alumni, makes formal written recommendations to the Harvard Corporation (the president, treasurer and five alumni of the university), which ultimately votes Harvard's stock. The committee meets regularly throughout the proxy season to consider resolutions and write individual reports on them.

In considering a non-expansion resolution to Exxon, for example, the Harvard advisory committee felt that despite its judgment that the company had "constructive employment practices," expansion by Exxon might be interpreted as "an expression of confidence" in the South African government. For that and other reasons, the committee supported the resolution and the corporation concurred.

At least 33 schools maintain advisory committees to vote proxies or to recommend additional investment policy decisions. Some of these schools—Macalester, MIT and Rutgers among them--have appointed committees to recommend alterations in current policy.

At Wesleyan, a student-faculty-administration-trustee committee votes proxies directly, bypassing formal board approval. The board's investment committee has delegated the job of voting Wesleyan's stock to the seven-member social implications subcommittee. Wesleyan's student-faculty task force on South Africa--which suggested proposing a resolution to Mobil in 1980--is assigned the task of scrutinizing the school's South African investments to determine if additional action is necessary. The task force makes its recommendations to the social implications subcommittee.

Communicating with management: As part of their deliberations on shareholder resolutions, institutional investors have been communicating with managements of companies involved in South Africa with increasing frequency.

The volume of correspondence companies receive varies according to the size of the company's investment in South Africa, the nature of its activities there, and whether a South Africa-related shareholder resolution is pending that year. Institutions generally inquire whether a company has signed and implemented the Sullivan principles, and what the nature of its business is in South Africa.

A number of universities have sent questionnaires to portfolio companies requesting information. More than 50 schools have turned to IRRC's South Africa Review Service to enhance and coordinate their information-gathering efforts on the activities of U.S. companies and banks involved with South Africa.

Many investors also write to companies receiving shareholder resolutions relating to South Africa to explain their votes. Even in some cases where the institutions favored or abstained on the proposal, they wrote to the company to express concern about the resolution. A number of schools inform every company receiving a resolution of how they voted on the resolution. Bryn Mawr and the University of Minnesota are among the institutions following this practice.

Publicizing shareholder activism: Stanford University is among the institutional investors taking unusual steps to publicize its efforts at shareholder activism. The university purchased space in The Stanford Daily, the student newspaper, in 1979 to reprint letters it sent to companies advising of its votes on pending resolutions and the responses received from the recipients of the resolutions. The coverage included a chart of Stanford's holdings and its position on the shareholder proposals.

Stanford was one of the many investors to favor the resolution asking General Motors not to sell to the police and military in South Africa. Stanford and the University of California's decisions to favor the resolutions--together their stock in GM is worth $13.8 million--were given prominent play in the California press.

The GM strategic sales resolution moved Kalamazoo College to send five representatives to the company's Detroit annual meeting to dramatize its concern.

The University of Iowa also decided that an appearance at annual meetings could enable it to publicize its interest in South Africa. Iowa sent two administrators to six annual meetings. "We tried to be physically present at several meetings as a symbol of the university's concern over management's responsiveness to the South Africa question," one of the representatives told IRRC.

Perhaps the most widely noted testimony to shareholder activism in 1979 was a series of "reflections on the ethical responsibilities of the university in society" expressed in open letters by Harvard University President Derek Bok. Bok's letters have been discussed nationally in newspaper editorials and columns with strong reaction pro and con.

In his first letter, Bok set out to draw limits to an educational institution's ethical responsibilities. He argued that the special mission of a university is "not to reform society in specific ways," but rather to proceed with "the discovering and transmisson of knowledge." He said attempts by a university to affect social and political controversies could threaten its academic function by jeopardizing the intellectual freedom of the institution, intruding on its right to make academic decisions free from the outside pressures of society and threatening financial contributions that "are given in trust for educational purposes and not for political and moral causes, however worthy they may be."

Bok added, however, that there "are clearly cases where an institution should declare itself." As part owners of the companies in which they hold stock, universities "have an obligation to vote on issues placed before them concerning the management of the corporation." Therefore, as a stockholder, Bok said, Harvard has taken positions on a long list of shareholder resolutions that raise questions of social responsibility.

In the conclusion to his first letter, Bok wrote: "Neither as stockholders nor as purchasers nor as contractors of services do universities possess sufficient leverage to move large corporations, let along entire governments. One may still ask that the university take account of injuries elsewhere in the world, even if its acts are only symbolic. Nevertheless, there comes a point where symbolism must give way to real threats to academic freedom, real financial losses, and real administrative burdens. If we do not acknowledge this point, we will merely succeed in damaging important functions of the university without doing anything to alleviate the sufferings of others. In seeking to improve the human condition, we may end by only making it worse."

Bok's second letter clearly stated Harvard's opposition to student demands for divestiture of university stock in companies doing business in South Africa. He cautioned that the costs of divestment "would almost certainly run into millions of dollars." Bok said that Harvard's Advisory Committee on Shareholder Responsibility had estimated that the brokerage fees required to sell the university's stock in the relevant companies would range from $5.7 million to $16.5 million, and that the losses that would result from forbidding endowment managers to buy stock in the 350 U.S. corporations active in South Africa could run from $4.8 million to $9.8 million each year.

In addition to these practical considerations, Bok argued, "Divestment may also be less effective than other methods of changing corporate behavior. Universities may not be able to influence corporations whatever they do, but most experienced observers believe that the best available means of persuasion is to vote as a shareholder and continue to communicate in other ways with management. Although shareholder resolutions rarely attract great support, they have probably helped to persuade American companies to pay closer attention to the employment and social conditions of their nonwhite workers in South Africa. On the other hand, we are likely to accomplish nothing by selling our stock except to lose our status as shareholders and pass whatever influence we have to investors who care little or nothing about apartheid. If other concerned institutions were to follow this course, we would soon be left with no shareholders actively interested in pressing corporations to adopt more enlightened policies."

Bok's series of open letters on the ethical responsibilities of a university concluded with two letters not directly relating to South Africa--reflections on the advisability of participating in national boycotts and of accepting gifts that may be tied to immoral practices. His letters constitute one of the most articulate expressions of the "progressive force" argument widely held by institutional investors.

Continuation of pressures: During the 1978-79 school year, some observers wondered whether student concern over South Africa was beginning to fade. A spokesman for the South Africa Catalyst project, a coordinating body for student groups, admitted that some campus groups have found it difficult to maintain momentum on the issue, given strong university opposition to divestment. However, catalyst leaders also appeared content with the decentralized nature of student protests.

Several university officials told IRRC they perceived a decline in student interest in South Africa. In its place they see rising concern with nuclear power questions. A Stanford spokesman told IRRC that concern over South Africa had undergone "a substantial dropoff. SCRIP (a student activist group) really did not make itself felt at all this year." Student leaders acknowledged that South Africa had been overshadowed by nuclear power on several major campuses, notably at Stanford. However, this shift in concern has not been widespread. University officials on many campuses--principally the ones that have been the scene of student pressures in past years--reported continued efforts by vocal student groups in favor of divestiture.

Investor concerns about monitoring: Certainly institutional investors have not lost interest in South Africa. Many investors, having adopted specific social investment criteria over the last few years, are now faced with important questions about implementing their policies. Since institutions have almost without exception made the Sullivan principles the centerpiece of their positions, the most crucial--and most vexing--issue they face is evaluating the performance of American corporations in South Africa to ensure compliance with the Sullivan employment standards.

This concern has been raised at several gatherings of investors. At a March 1979 conference organized by Oberlin College entitled "The Role of U.S. Corporations in South Africa and How that Relates to Colleges and Universities," Rev. Leon Sullivan addressed the question of corporate compliance with the principles as part of his discussion of what the Sullivan principles can and cannot accomplish.

Monitoring was also the subject of a gathering of prominent university, foundation, union and government leaders in June 1979 at the Carnegie Corporation of New York. Alan Pifer, president of Carnegie, convened the meeting, asking participants to consider the strengths and weaknesses of existing monitoring procedures and to suggest more effective criteria and techniques for monitoring. In a memorandum of the meeting Pifer said of the Sullivan principles, "thus far this effort is the centerpiece of the U.S. government, corporate and university interest--the repository of the broadest range of American concern regarding racism in South Africa."

The participants in the meeting agreed "that the Sullivan principles are a responsible but necessarily limited piece of work that needs to be done, but in order to bolster that effort and to satisfy the more rigorous demands of the students and faculty who have called for divestiture, an independent monitoring mechanism should be considered." They agreed to establish a task force of the most interested institutions to make recommendations to the larger group about the scope, operation and financing of an independent monitoring system. Lawrence F. Stevens, administrative assistant in the office of the general counsel at Harvard and secretary of Harvard's Advisory Committee on Shareholder Responsibility said he had noticed "no startling success in existing monitoring efforts." He reiterated, "we have a problem in getting enough data to state with confidence that a company is behaving in the way it should."

Efforts by institutional investors to grapple with the monitoring dilemma are the most noteworthy manifestation of the continuing concern over South Africa. As policy implementation proceeds, no doubt investors' needs and interest will shift, but their examination of corporate performance in South Africa appears likely to continue.

II. PRESSURES FROM WASHINGTON

The steady pressures from institutional investors on America's largest multinational companies in South Africa have been reinforced by pressures emanating from Washington. Although no new legislation or regulations limiting trade and investment in South Africa were enacted in 1979, earlier restrictions on certain kinds of sales continued to be important constraints on the operation of American business there. In addition, Washington focused attention on the issue. The executive branch publicly encouraged corporations to improve their labor practices and legislators in Congress proposed various measures designed either to urge companies on to progressive employment practices or to punish them for not adopting such practices.

U.S. Policy

Aspects of U.S. policy affecting sales to South Africa--restrictions on loans and export credits, the arms embargo, on sales of computers and "grey area" items, and on sales to the military and police--have already been discussed in Chapter VI of Business and Labor in South Africa, "The Controversy over Sanctions Against South Africa." In addition to its efforts to limit certain types of sales to South Africa, the U.S. government has made several formal statements encouraging American companies to improve their labor practices. Secretary of State Cyrus Vance has met with signers of the Sullivan principles several times--most recently at a conference convened at the State Department in November 1979--and has given a strong endorsement to the principles. In a separate meeting, Assistant Secretary of State for African Affairs Richard Moose told institutional investors:

> I think it fair to say, however, that no single initiative to date has had the impact of that launched by Rev. Leon Sullivan....His initiative in launching the six principles, and subsequently in detailing them and setting up reporting and monitoring procedures, has in fact set the pace in this entire area and in our view continues to do so.
> The great strength of the Sullivan initiative, in my view, is that it springs from the private corporate world and that it brings together American companies voluntarily to pursue a common objective. For those who may wish to believe that our present relationship with South Africa is uniquely tied to the Carter administration, I would suggest that they take a hard look at this fact.
> We have given considerable thought to what role, if any, the U.S. government should be playing in this area. Some have proposed an official U.S. code, which would supplement or supplant other efforts already under way. We are disinclined--at least now--to pursue this course of action. Instead, we believe that our best course of action is to give our strong support to Rev. Sullivan's efforts, and to urge that others do the same.

Legislative Activity

While the Carter administration has strongly supported the Sullivan principles, some congressmen have been proposing that the government mandate corporate compliance with the code. Several legislators who have been active on South African questions in the past have proposed that foreign tax credits be used as a lever to ensure that companies follow the Sullivan principles. A second, more moderate, group has suggested that Congress place its stamp of approval on the code as a way of demonstrating the significance the federal government attaches to it. Neither approach is given much chance of enactment in the near future.

The scope and tenor of the South Africa-related legislation introduced in 1979 was more restrained than legislation proposed in earlier years. Moreover, some legislators believe that the 1979 compromise that could eventually lift the Rhodesian trade embargo does not augur well for either the current legislative proposals relating to South Africa or for sustained congressional anti-apartheid sentiment. Not only did the trade sanctions debate overshadow the South African issue in 1979, but some congressmen are also concerned that the conservatism evidenced throughout the debate, especially in the Senate, may thwart future efforts to promote a more activist South African policy.

Formation of Ad Hoc Monitoring Group on Southern Africa: A significant development of 1979 was the formation of the Ad Hoc Monitoring Group on Southern Africa. Forty-five members of Congress joined together to review U.S. policy and to monitor the role of U.S. business there. Formed in January, the monitoring group draws from both the House and Senate, is bipartisan and is headed by Sens. Mark Hatfield (R-Ore.) and Paul Tsongas (D-Mass.) and Reps. Tom Downey (D-N.Y.) and Paul McCloskey (R-Calif.).

The group met in February with Rev. Leon Sullivan and with representatives of six corporations actively involved in South Africa--Envirotech, Ford, General Motors, Goodyear, Mobil and Union Carbide. In February, McCloskey wrote letters to more than 300 companies informing them of the group's interests in the Sullivan principles, asking whether companies had signed the code, and requesting information on steps companies had taken to put the code into effect.

An aide to McCloskey told IRRC that his office had received answers from 150 companies, mostly Sullivan signers, and was "impressed by the seriousness of the responses." Noting the "polished and positive tone" of most of the letters, the aide commented that the corporate responses to McCloskey's inquiries indicate that the Sullivan principles have induced "important progress" in South Africa.

Resolution endorsing Sullivan principles: Encouraged by the results of McCloskey's corporate survey, Rep. Berkeley Bedell (D-Iowa) introduced a resolution in May 1979 that is characteristic of the moderate approach to the South Africa issue. Described by Bedell as "the mildest of alternatives available to our government in opposing" apartheid, the resolution expresses "the sense of Congress that American businesses in South Africa should refrain from engaging in discriminatory business practices, and that they should pursue the affirmative goals for black employees set forth in the Sullivan principles."

Tax credit proposals: Rep. Charles Rangel (D-N.Y.), a member of the

Congressional Black Caucus, introduced two bills in January 1979 that would restructure foreign tax credit provisions to the disadvantage of American firms in South Africa. One bill, HR 1723, would deny all foreign tax credits to American companies for taxes paid or accrued to the government of the Republic of South Africa. The second bill, HR 1724, would reduce foreign tax credits to companies whose subsidiaries in South Africa are not satisfactorily carrying out the Sullivan principles. The tax credit would be reduced by the percentage of its foreign business the company does in South Africa. Under Rangel's second bill, a presidentially appointed high-level "Commission on American Employment Practices in South Africa" would determine whether a company is in violation of the Sullivan principles.

Both of Rangel's bills were referred to the House Ways and Means Committee which took no action on them. However, Downey--a first-year member of Ways and Means--is currently drawing up some South Africa-related legislation that he expects will revive Rangel's bills and force the committee to consider the issue. According to an aide to Downey, Ways and Means "is not very interested in South Africa but is very interested in tax credits. We see the interest that's there on tax credits as a good opportunity to bring forward the South Africa issue." However, some congressional observers are doubtful that Ways and Means will want to tangle with the South Africa question.

Like Rangel's bills, Downey's proposal would use foreign tax credits as leverage against certain American businesses in South Africa. A member of Downey's staff told IRRC that it is uncertain whether the legislation will be "keyed to fair employment practices or the relation of the company to apartheid." The latter standard, he explained, would refer to whether a particular company might supply items integral to the maintenance of apartheid.

The denial of tax credits as a form of pressure on U.S. corporations in South Africa is a new tactic adopted by legislators. It is also one that could have a substantial impact on the profitability of subsidiary operations in South Africa. A Treasury Department official told IRRC that in 1972 American corporations in South Africa paid $46 million in taxes to the South African government on pre-tax income of $118 million. Two years later the figure had almost doubled. In 1974 corporations doing 95 percent of American business in South Africa paid $89 million to the South African government on pre-tax earnings of $234 million.

Senate activity: The Senate has been the scene of little legislative action regarding South Africa, and it is generally conceded that, in the words of a senatorial aide, "the House is the place for South Africa."

In one notable 1979 Senate action involving apartheid, Sen. Tsongas addressed the nation's universities and colleges from the Senate floor at the end of May. Full of praise for the divestment movement, but disappointed by the dearth of actual sales of South Africa-related holdings and wary of the increasingly "confrontational" mood on many campuses, Tsongas outlined a divestment plan he calls "phased-conditional divestiture." Described by Tsongas as "a tactical alternative, one which combines maximum effectiveness in South Africa with minimum disruption of university investment procedures," the plan calls for all universities and colleges to divest one-fifth of their South Africa-related holdings in corporations and banks each year for five years, unless or until

"South Africa commits itself to ending apartheid and takes meaningful steps toward the full political, social and economic incorporation of all racial groups in a single state." The senator believes university and college divestment over a five-year period, as opposed to "one-shot total divestment," will provide investment flexibility more consistent with the fiduciary responsibilities of trustees, as well as greater leverage against the South African regime.

Tsongas pointedly disputes the notion that implementation of the Sullivan principles can improve conditions in South Africa, arguing that "the issue here is not the reform of American companies. The issue--the target--is South African law." Nor should American companies "be expected to blaze a revolutionary path through the morass of apartheid" by breaking South African law in their business and employment practices, according to Tsongas. Instead, they should lobby for and contribute as they can to the rapid reform of South African law--a form of pressure that would be spurred by the systematic sale of South Africa-related stock in the absence of change.

Finally, Tsongas concedes that any plan to topple apartheid will bring hardship to blacks and whites alike, but claims that because "phased-conditional divestiture" is gradual, it "will give South Africa's rulers time to change before the hardships become severe."

Lobbying on South Africa

Until mid-1978, the Washington Office on Africa, a group affiliated with Protestant church denominations, had been the principal anti-apartheid lobby in Washington. In May 1978, black leaders, including members of the Congressional Black Caucus, formed TransAfrica. TransAfrica is the first organization whose stated purpose is to build a grass-roots constituency among black Americans to influence U.S. policy in Africa and the Caribbean.

TransAfrica and the Washington Office on Africa devoted almost all their attention in 1979 to the Rhodesian sanctions question. Their efforts to derail conservative efforts to lift sanctions against Rhodesia overshadowed earlier efforts to promote oil and trade embargos against South Africa. Chris Root of the Washington Office on Africa pointed out that the lobbies cannot promote South African legislation that has not been proposed. At present, she said, "there is no congressional legislative strategy on South Africa."

Public Attitudes Toward South Africa

As stated earlier, the absence of a specific South Africa legislative strategy is in part due to the lack of a well-defined public attitude toward South Africa. Two recent polls--a 1978 Harris poll and a poll conducted in 1979 by the Carnegie Endowment for International Peace--show that the prevailing public sentiment regarding the situation in South Africa is ambivalence born of concern for human rights and wariness about intervention. The public disapproves of South Africa's apartheid policy and believes that the United States should "do something" about it, but there is no broad-based support for the United States to do more than it already is doing.

The two polls show that public support for the general proposition that the United States should act to bring about change in South Africa went up during 1978, while the level of support for diplomatic statements and trade and investment restrictions, particularly when undertaken unilaterally, went down.

Both polls indicate opposition to apartheid and some willingness for the United States to act to change the situation in South Africa, with support for such intervention dropping off as measures call for increasingly high levels of U.S. involvement. The countervailing pulls of concern over human rights and caution over potential involvement combine to produce an ambivalence that handicaps activist legislators. As the Carnegie Endowment concluded, "knowingly or not, the public gave an overwhelming endorsement for the basic outline of current U.S. policy toward South Africa."

III. IMPACT OF PRESSURES ON CORPORATIONS

In recent years, the nature of the pressures on American companies involved with South Africa has not changed greatly. However, as their knowledge of the issue deepens--and as their experience as shareholder activists grows--institutional investors concerned about South Africa have approached corporations with greater sophistication of technique and greater specificity. As noted earlier, many of their policies have come to revolve around the Sullivan principles.

The corporate response to pressures over business activity in South Africa has evolved similarly. Corporations, facing continuing, insistent queries from shareholders, are making considerable efforts to respond. The most common course is to endorse the Sullivan principles and publicize their efforts to comply with them. Many companies have put together reports to shareholders to detail their operations in South Africa and to answer the questions most frequently asked.

Companies have also employed other methods of responding to shareholders. Many have found it useful to meet directly with shareholders, especially with those institutional investors sponsoring resolutions and with universities considering divestment.

A small but significant group of companies have responded to shareholder pressures by placing limits on their business operations in South Africa. Some corporations have agreed to make no further investment in South Africa; some banks are refraining from making loans there.

Corporate decisions to limit involvement in South Africa are not always made voluntarily. The U.S. Commerce Department restrictions on sales to the South African government--in effect for more than a year and a half--have had a limited but measurable impact on American companies there.

The Sullivan Principles

The most frequent corporate response to heightened shareholder interest in investment in South Africa has been adoption of the Sullivan principles as a code of conduct for subsidiary operations. One hundred thirty-five companies have now committed themselves to comply with the principles. Twelve firms were original signatories to the Sullivan principles in 1977. (Principles, Appendix B; signers, Appendix C)

One corporate spokesman noted that the growing business support for the Sullivan principles was matched by--and perhaps partially motivated by--the fact that the principles are central to the policies of institutional investors. "Universities have latched onto the Sullivan principles just as corporations have," he told IRRC. There is "broader acceptance of the Sullivan principles as the basis for initial evaluation" of a company's performance, he said.

Since their original formulation, Sullivan has twice amplified the principles. Both times--in July 1978 and May 1979--he has directed corporations to take new steps. Perhaps the most significant addition, made in 1978, required signatory companies to support "the elimination of discrimination against the rights of blacks to form or belong to government registered trade unions, and to acknowledge generally the right of black workers to form their own union or to be represented by trade unions where unions already exist." Before the amplification, the principles had been criticized in part as failing to mention trade union rights for non-whites, an issue considered by many analysts to be the cornerstone of meaningful labor reform in South Africa.

The 1979 amplification of the principles required signers to "assist in the development of black and non-white business enterprises, including distributors, suppliers of goods and services and manufacturers." Two further amplifications directed companies to lobby for changes in South Africa's racial laws. Companies were told to support the "abolition of job reservations, job fragmentation and apprenticeship restrictions for blacks and other non-whites." They were further asked to "support changes in influx control laws to provide for the right of black migrant workers to normal family life."

A number of the additions to the principles were suggested by task forces established by Sullivan to oversee the implementation and refinement of each principle. (Sullivan, however, makes the final decisions about new inclusions in the code.) Each of the seven task forces is composed of representatives of signatories. Each task force also has a South African counterpart, which includes local company representatives and black community leaders. They meet periodically and make suggestions for cooperative programs directly to Sullivan.

Six of the task forces are assigned to individual principles. The seventh is charged with studying periodic corporate reporting and also economic and community development. A spokesman for Sullivan explained that once this latter group had drafted the original questionnaire used to survey corporations' efforts to carry out the principles it had fulfilled its mandate, and so Sullivan had given it the additional task of studying the question of economic and community development.

Reporting: The Sullivan principles require signers to issue summary reports every six months to enable the Sullivan group to ascertain what progress signatories have made in carrying out the code. Sullivan hired the Arthur D. Little Co., an economic consulting firm, to distribute questionnaires to signers, analyze results and issue the periodic reports. To date, three reports have been published, in November 1978, April 1979 and October 1979.

The lengthy questionnaire asks companies to detail the location of their South African operations, their employee pay scales, common benefit plans, worker representation, skills development programs and non-work-related employee assistance programs. Individual reports are considered proprietary and are not released to the public. The questionnaire itself is still in an evolutionary state. As Arthur D. Little noted in the introduction to the second report, "the report form is necessarily a dynamic one...." It says that the second questionnaire improved on the first one.

The April 1979 report, which dealt with 81 signers, consisted of two parts. Part I placed individual companies in one of three categories according to their relative success in meeting the Sullivan standards. Part II analyzed the aggregate performance of the American subsidiaries in South Africa.

The three classifications used in the report were: "making acceptable progress," "cooperating" and "non-respondents." Sixty-six companies in the first category had completed both Sullivan surveys; had integrated eating, toilet and work facilities (or had committed to do so); and had shown a "substantial commitment" to carry out the other five principles. Sixteen companies identified as "cooperating" had made less progress toward desegregation but had reported to Sullivan on their efforts, and three signatories were "non-respondents."

The October 1979 report, covering 93 signers, said 22 "are making good progress," 62 are "making acceptable progress" and nine "need to become more active."

Desegregation: Seventy-three percent of the Sullivan signers have integrated work, eating and toilet facilities, a 4-percent increase from the first survey. However, only 59 percent of black employees work at wage levels where no whites are employed, and 29 percent of the African employees of these companies work in desegregated work places--defined as a level in a plant or office in which both white and black work.

Promotion and wage levels of blacks: Twenty-six percent of all supervisors and 3 percent of all managers employed by Sullivan signatories are black (about 600 are African). The 500 blacks in training to become supervisors or managers will almost double the existing number. However, almost one-third of all the companies reporting to Sullivan had no black supervisors or managers.

Most companies pay above minimum wage levels, but Africans are generally in lower-level positions. Where Africans and whites overlap, only 20 percent of African employees are at or above the average income for the level.

The Sullivan signatories provide work for 51,488 people in South Africa, more than half of whom are black, the report said.

Visiting companies: In addition to circulating semi-annual questionnaires, Sullivan's administrative organization--now officially known as the International Council for Equality of Opportunity Principles, chaired by Sullivan--sent a team of observers to South Africa in summer 1979 to evaluate 25 companies. Over a three-week period in July, several representatives visited companies selected because of either their prominence in South Africa or their negligence in reporting to Sullivan in the past. Findings are to be incorporated in a future report on companies' progress in implementing the code.

Other Responses to Presssures

Providing information on operations: As requests by shareholders and the public for information about a corporation's South African operations have grown more frequent, many of the largest American firms have prepared periodic reports or fact sheets to meet the demand.

General Motors, for example, devoted eight pages to its South African operation in its 1979 Public Interest Report. The section describes the history of General Motors South Africa, the nature of its operations, employment figures by job category, and employee compensation and benefits. It also details GM's training programs for blacks, progress in promoting blacks, and its programs to assist its employees outside the workplace.

GM's report differs from most others in that it reveals data on the subsidiary's sales and profitability. Additionally, it discloses the size of General Motors' investment in its South African subsidiary. This specific financial information is not generally available from the information most companies disseminate on their South African operations.

Besides the Public Interest Report, GM has begun to make presentations about its operations to minority communities in the United States. A portion of these presentations deal with South Africa. A GM spokesman described this approach as an attempt to "get out and tell our story."

Most corporations say that those who request information find the reports companies have prepared on their South African operations sufficient to their needs. An Exxon representative told IRRC that "95 percent" of the inquiries he receives about the corporation's South African involvement can be answered by its 10-page fact sheet.

The level of shareholder and public interest in the activities of American corporations in South Africa has prompted the first-hand participation of some companies' top management in studying those operations. For example, Caterpillar's home office compiles reports on its affirmative action program in South Africa on a monthly, quarterly and annual basis. The company has also sent senior personnel, including the chairman, to South Africa for a first-hand look at Caterpillar operations.

Dealing with shareholders: Corporations have responded in a variety of ways to the surge of shareholder activism among institutional investors. Some engage in conciliatory dialogue or negotiations with shareholders over resolutions or threats of divestment, while others respond critically to shareholder pressures.

Criticism of pressures--When Michigan State University informed its portfolio companies of its intent to dispose of stock in those that did not plan to withdraw from South Africa, it received several sharp replies. One of the strongest reactions came from Dow Chemical: "Frankly, we are shocked at the position taken by (the) board of trustees. The issue is not whether we approve of apartheid or other policies of the government of South Africa. The issue is what is the best way to improve the situation." Asserting that a "constructive and progressive presence is more effective than withdrawal," the company said: "You have completely rejected this alternative and have issued the ultimatum 'withdraw or we will sell our Dow stock.' That ultimatum borders on blackmail, and is repugnant to us. If it truly represents the considered view of MSU, then we suggest you dispose of your Dow stock."

This sharp reaction, coupled with a legal challenge from a university lawyer, caused the MSU board of trustees to evaluate its position further. When the board announced on Dec. 8, 1978, that it would proceed with divestiture, Dow sent a second strongly worded letter to the school. This time the corporation informed MSU that because it wished to "avoid embarrassment for the university," it needed to find out whether MSU, "knowing some portion of the funds will be derived from our operations in South Africa," could continue to accept grant money from Dow without "compromising its position and principles."

The MSU board of trustees passed a resolution in January 1979 in answer to Dow's query, affirming the university's "strong commitment to cooperation with the corporate world" and stating that the university would accept any corporate gift, regardless of the company's activities, "unless it is intended for harmful purposes."

The board's resolution apparently ended the school's discussions with Dow over its divestment decision. Stephen Terry, Assistant Vice President at Michigan State, told IRRC that Dow has funded "two or three" projects at the school this year. "There is no evidence that their rate of giving has dropped off," Terry said.

Another company, Hewlett-Packard, wrote Michigan State that while it shares the board's concern for the human rights of the people of South Africa, it cannot support the school's position on disengagement. "If, in fact, the university's investment in our company is conditional upon our withdrawal from South Africa, then we respectfully ask that you remove our name from your investment buy list," the company wrote.

As part of its deliberations over selling its Morgan Guaranty stock because of the bank's policy on lending to South Africa, Yale's Advisory Committee on Investor Responsibility met with Morgan vice president Rodney Wagner. In its statement proposing sale of Morgan stock, the committee complimented the bank for sending a representative to set forth its policy. Calling Morgan's policy one "that honorable and morally concerned persons could reasonably have arrived at," the committee nonetheless recommended divestment. Although "divestiture is of little practical consequence and hence is almost entirely symbolic," the committee wrote, "symbols and gestures are important in the realm of moral and humane concerns, and are to be taken seriously."

Walter H. Page, chairman of the board of Morgan and of Morgan Guaranty Trust, its main subsidiary, took the unusual step of publicly criticizing the university's decision to divest. He took issue with Yale's characterization of its divestment as "symbolic." Page commented: "All this time we have thought we were discussing substance, not symbol. We fear that Yale, both by the decision it has reached and by the cynical view it apparently takes of its own action, has trivialized a matter of high concern."

Conciliatory dialogues--In most cases, though, discussions between companies and investors considering divestiture have not been acrimonious. Wesleyan University, for example, has held a number of meetings with Mobil and Standard Oil of California executives to discuss their operations in South Africa.

Some corporations negotiate the withdrawal of shareholder resolutions with proponents. In 1979, eight resolutions were withdrawn after the companies agreed to at least some steps the proponents had proposed. Twenty-seven resolutions were not withdrawn and came to votes. Resolutions to Merrill Lynch and to First National Boston were withdrawn after the companies agreed not to underwrite South African government securities or to lend to the South African government, respectively. Burroughs Corp. agreed to stop sales to the government and not to expand its South African operations; Borg-Warner reached a similar agreement. American Cyanamid also agreed to a non-expansion statement. And 3M agreed to review its South Africa policy and review its literature and media presentations on South Africa.

Two companies persuaded sponsors to withdraw a resolution because it was inappropriate and unnecessary. The Cornell Corporate Responsibility Project, a student group that sponsored resolutions asking GM and IBM to adopt the European Economic Community code as a basis for its labor practices in South Africa, withdrew both submissions after GM presented evidence it was already fulfilling the intent of the resolution and IBM convinced the project that the resolution was ill-suited to the nature of IBM's operations in South Africa and elsewhere. The resolution did come to a vote at Mobil.

Internal disputes--One shareholder resolution precipitated internal disagreement among corporate leadership. At both Ford and General Motors a director of the corporation took the highly unusual step of breaking with management's position and siding with the proponents. Rev. Leon Sullivan, a board member of GM, and Dr. Clifton R. Wharton Jr., a director of Ford, both black, made statements in favor of the resolution brought by church shareholders to ban vehicle sales to the South African police and military. In its 1979 proxy statement, GM noted that Sullivan "agrees with the position of the board that General Motors should remain in South Africa and continue its efforts to promote equality and improve the condition of blacks and other non-whites there; in this regard, he believes GM should remain in South Africa at least for the time being, until it can be seen how effective these efforts can be. Nevertheless, from personal conviction, and to support protection from continuing military and police repression and for other humanitarian reasons, he favors a vote for Stockholder Proposal No. 7."

Wharton's dissent was based on an interpretation of U.S. Commerce Department regulations--which prohibit such sales by U.S. corporations but not by their South African subsidiaries--at variance with Ford's literal interpretation. Wharton insisted that "any Ford Motor Co. vehicles sold to the South African military or police necessarily include some element of U.S. technology if not material. Thus such sales even by a subsidiary constitute a violation of both the spirit and intent of the policy of the U.S. Department of Commerce."

Insurance company responses to client pressures: A number of insurance companies have been trying to respond to client pressures involving South Africa-related stock holdings. Four firms that handle pension accounts for such non-profit institutions as churches, universities, municipal governments and labor unions have detected an upswing in interest by these clients.

Teachers Insurance and Annuity Association-College Retirement Equities Fund (TIAA-CREF) wrote, "We have received some letters from individual policyholders, either requesting that TIAA-CREF divest itself of South African holdings, or that it display particular sensitivity to such holdings. In addition, we received requests from faculties at two participating institutions that TIAA-CREF divest itself of South African or related investments." A TIAA-CREF official noted that although such requests had risen above previous levels, they were nevertheless small in relation to the fund's overall number of clients. He did not anticipate any new responses to deal with the increased number of requests.

Prudential Insurance indicated that although it had experienced a "relatively quiet" year in regard to South Africa inquiries, it had heard from a few pension clients concerned about the placement of their investments. Another company said it engaged in discussions with a city government whose pension fund it managed on the subject of South African investments.

A fourth insurance company that indicated it had felt pressures from both existing and potential pension fund clients attached greater significance to the phenomenon. Although a company spokesman did not express concern over the increasing level of requests for information or more drastic steps regarding South Africa-related investments, he did draw attention to the fact that these pressures were coming from business clients and not solely shareholders. A business relationship is "a more powerful lever" than stock ownership, he pointed out. There is "growing awareness by institutions of the loudness of their voice when they speak as customers," he said. Insurance companies, the official concluded, face "increasing scrutiny of our business activity by clients."

Increased concern about South Africa-related issues marches with the recent trend toward developing mechanisms for considering shareholder resolutions at insurance companies. Among the companies with elaborate procedures for voting on resolutions and communicating their views to management are Connecticut General Insurance and TIAA-CREF.

Costs of the Pressures

Whether their response is to endorse the Sullivan principles, to provide information to shareholders and others, or to engage in negotiations and discussions with shareholders, corporations are finding that pressures surrounding their involvement in South Africa have certain costs. In general, these costs can be divided into three categories: (1) the costs of responding to shareholder inquiries, of publishing reports and of spending executive time monitoring the performance of subsidiaries in South Africa; (2) the costs of implementing the Sullivan principles; and (3) the costs of complying with U.S. government restrictions on exports to South Africa.

Responding to shareholders: Many company officials describe the amount of time spent by executives in the home office working on matters related to South Africa as "considerable" or "substantial." Beyond the day-to-day communication and decision-making by management necessary to the commercial well-being of subsidiary operations there, executives have devoted time to answering the growing volume of shareholder inquiries about their companies' presence in South Africa, meeting directly with investors to discuss the issues connected with doing business in a repressive environment, formulating special policies and programs for their subsidiaries in South Africa and monitoring their subsidiaries' performance in that country.

Corporate representatives point out that they are forced to devote more time and energy to their South African operations than the scale of those operations would normally warrant. A Morgan Guaranty executive told IRRC that the bank devoted "an inordinate amount of time" to South Africa. Exxon's Public Affairs Office reported that it spends more time on South African issues than on the rest of Africa. A spokesman termed this "hassle factor" a "fact of life." Exxon has expended "a disproportionate amount of management time relative to business there," he acknowledged.

Special programs for non-white employees: The signing of the Sullivan principles served as a catalyst for a number of American companies in South Africa to study and improve labor conditions for their non-white employees. In the last year, the most notable advances have been in the areas of desegregation of facilities and training and housing of non-white employees. All of these programs have entailed financial costs for companies. Other special programs include managerial development and recruitment efforts, scholarship and literacy programs and charitable contributions to outside community and educational groups. (For details of these programs, see Chapter V of Business and Labor in South Africa)

Impact of restrictions: The U.S. Commerce Department limitations on sales to the South African government, promulgated in February 1978, have imposed costs on American companies active in certain sectors of the South African economy. For the most part, though, these costs have proven to be less than first anticipated.

The regulations prohibit the sale of non-military items such as transportation, computer and other technical equipment by U.S. companies to the South African police and military. The Office of Export Administration, the branch of the Commerce Department responsible for implementing the regulations, has received a number of inquiries from companies on application of the regulations and some requests for exemptions.

The overall cost of the regulations for American companies in foregone sales is hard to gauge. Officials at the Commerce Department have given a figure of more than $9 million as the value of some 25 applications for sales to the police and military they have rejected since the embargo took effect. Managing directors at American companies in South Africa say the cost has been far greater. Steven Pryke, executive director of the American Chamber of Commerce in South Africa, estimates the total loss of potential American sales as $75 million in 1978 and $100 million in 1979. The Commerce Department restrictions, he said, virtually ruled out successful bids by American companies like Ford and Cummins to participate in a proposed $300 million project for a diesel engine plant. (For details about the impact of the restrictions on U.S. firms in the motor industry and the computer and electronics industry in South Africa, see case studies D and B, respectively)

Corporate Restrictions on Sales and Services

In 1979, three companies issued public statements agreeing to limit voluntarily the type of equipment or services they would provide to the South African government. Previously, Polaroid had decided it would not sell photographic equipment for use in the government's "pass" system for blacks, and Control Data had announced its decision to avoid sales that abridge human rights.

Kodak announced that, like Polaroid, it "does not now and will not...sell photographic equipment or supplies to any agency of the South African government for its passbook system."

Two other companies announcing limits on sales tied the decision to negotiations for the withdrawal of shareholder resolutions submitted to them by church proponents. A resolution to Burroughs requesting the cessation of computer sales to the South African government was withdrawn when Burroughs made a statement that it "hereby formalizes a policy for South Africa directing its employees against knowingly selling equipment for use for oppressive purposes" and "directing its employees against knowingly entering into new contractual arrangements hereafter for the service or repair of its equipment which is being used for oppressive purposes."

Upon withdrawal of a resolution asking for a ban on sales to the government and expansion of its South African investment, Borg-Warner stated, "We have inquired of our subsidiary in South Africa and have been informed that no sales were made to the South African government, the military or police during the past year and none are in prospect."

Promises of Non-Expansion

Borg-Warner was also one of three companies to state in 1979 that it would not expand its operations in South Africa until real changes are made in that country's apartheid policies. In the same statement it made to announce the limits it was placing on sales, Borg-Warner also said: "Our present policy is not to increase our investment in South Africa, and until the social and economic conditions in South Africa become more favorable, it is our intention to continue such policy." The policy is likely to be tested in the near future. The South African subsidiary has recently stated that a $25 million expansion into heavy axle manufacture may be necessary to ensure the long term viability of Borg-Warner's operations in South Africa.

Burroughs also tied its sales limitations to non-expansion, saying it will not "inject new investment capital into South Africa under present social conditions." Proponents agreed to withdraw a non-expansion resolution to American Cyanamid in January after the company wrote that it had "no plans for any major investment or expansion in South Africa."

Seven companies had previously placed a moratorium on investment in South Africa—Control Data, Ford, General Motors, Gulf & Western, Johnson & Johnson and Kimberly-Clark. The last restated its position in a December 1978 pronouncement that new investment was "not necessary and therefore inappropriate." It tied the propriety of further investment to the particular criterion of "the progress of the South African government towards eliminating laws and practices which deprive employees of their human rights."

In its 1979 Public Interest Report, General Motors linked its standing commitment not to expand to both the political and economic environment in South Africa. Noting that political uncertainty and a depressed economy had contributed to a lower demand for GM vehicles, the company said it "has no present need for, nor intention of, expanding its capacity in South Africa." It cautioned that, "Should conditions in South Africa improve substantially, the corporation may consider an expansion of its facilities in that country. Any investment decisions regarding that nation will, of course, necessarily include an assessment of the economic, social and political environment, not only in South Africa, but in neighboring countries as well." Although GM has pledged not to expand, the company in summer 1979 did give its money-losing South African operation a $24 million capital infusion.

Corporate Restrictions on Loans

Pressure from institutional investors on major international banks has been steadily mounting. Publicity about the role of foreign capital in the South African economy and a spate of shareholder resolutions related to such lending during the 1979 proxy season--seven to banks and one to an underwriter--have focused attention on the lending policies of America's largest financial institutions.

Most of the banks that have elaborated on their South African lending policies because of shareholder scrutiny say that they will not extend further credit to the government or its agencies because South Africa's apartheid policies weigh heavily against its international credit rating. These banks' assessments of creditworthiness incorporate social and political factors--as well as strictly economic criteria--as they affect South Africa's ability to repay loans. According to the banks, the effects of apartheid on the political and economic stability of South Africa play an important role in their decision on whether to lend.

First National Chicago, for example, ties the possibility of greater creditworthiness for the South African government to an "amelioration of South Africa's social policies." In its loan decision process, Wells Fargo assesses "the long-term economic and political viability of the country," including "the quality of life of the people." As part of the bank's country analysis, it weighs "the overall acceptance of the government by the people and the effect of its policies--political as well as economic--on the long-term economic development of the country." Generally similar positions have been articulated by a number of banks that include BankAmerica, Chase Manhattan, Continental Illinois, Citicorp, First Wisconsin, Manufacturers Hanover and Morgan Guaranty.

Some of these banks have provided evidence to confirm their statements that concerns about South African economic and political stability have significantly decreased lending to the South African government and its agencies in recent years. First Chicago claims it has extended no loans to the govenment or its instrumentalities since December 1976 and any such financing is "unlikely" until "further progress toward social equality has been or will be achieved." Manufacturers Hanover wrote in its 1979 proxy statement that "lending to the government of South Africa and its agencies is currently on an inactive front." And BankAmerica, which cited a 40-percent decline in its loan exposure in South Africa from the 1977 level of $200 million, said "the corporation's lending activities in South Africa are restrained and will continue to be so."

Detailing a decline in loans to the South African government and its agencies in recent years--and attributing that decline in part to the negative impact apartheid has had on economic and political stability--does not mean that most major international lenders have adopted policies categorically excluding the extension of such credit. In fact, several banks carefully describe types of loans to the government that they are making and will continue to make. Manufacturers Hanover says it will offer public sector loans that "generate improved circumstances for the whole population of the nation" of South Africa, while Morgan, which believes that loans to the government of South Africa need not be "inconsistent with improvement of conditions for blacks and other non-whites in that country," says that through its lending it "seeks to be an influence in the evolution of a more just social system."

To underline its pronouncement, Morgan Guaranty, along with Chase

Manhattan and BankAmerica, announced at the end of 1978 that they would provide a loan to the Urban Foundation for construction of housing in black townships. The three banks together extended $33.3 million. Morgan Chairman Page has strongly defended--in fact, publicized--this loan. He characterized the loan as one that is "likely to contribute to improvement in the social policies (of South Africa)...and in the condition of blacks and other non-whites living there." The loan for home purchase, "while not made directly to the government, would not have been possible without government involvement in the transaction." Page cited this loan as vindication of his bank's belief that "we can have more influence against apartheid by keeping open the channels of economic contact with South Africa and examining each transaction on a careful, case-by-case basis than we could by shutting ourselves off with a rigid policy excluding all loans to the government." Citibank also indicated in 1979 its willingness to earmark loans for housing projects similar to the one partially financed by Morgan, a position that a bank official described as a "change from last year's policy."

At least three financial institutions went on record in 1979 with statements to the effect that apartheid precludes the possibility of lending to the government. Merrill Lynch responded to a shareholder resolution asking it not to underwrite securities sold by the South African government with a declaration that it has never done so and has "no intention of doing so as long as current conditions exist." The resolution was withdrawn.

In a policy announcement tied to the withdrawal of a shareholder resolution asking it not to lend to the South African government, First National Boston stated it had made no loans in the last year to the South African government because of "the abhorrence of the world, which we share, towards the policies of apartheid." First Boston will not resume lending "unless the political policies of the South African government are changed drastically."

Pittsburgh National Bank notified IRRC that "we will continue our practice of not making any loans to the government of South Africa and will not make loans to enterprises owned or controlled by that government as long as it continues its apartheid policy." A series of other banks, including Chemical Bank, the First National Bank of Atlanta, First Pennsylvania Bank, Irving Trust, Maryland National Bank, Merchants' Bank of Indianapolis and Northwestern National Bank of Minneapolis, have similar policies.

Bank officials told IRRC that in addition to these written policy pronouncements, banks are generally approaching loan opportunities in South Africa with greater care and caution. They attribute this in part to the pressures brought against them by watchful shareholders. A Morgan spokesman believed that, "compared to five years ago, some loans we possibly made then--loans whose use was not easily defined--are not made today." Loans to finance the government purchase of trucks, which might be adapted for military use, are the sort of loans "which would come up quickly today for careful review," he said.

IV. CONCLUSIONS

Public interest in the controversy over U.S. corporate activity in South Africa has never been higher. Student protests, divestment actions, investment policy announcements and proxy voting all received prominent coverage in the national press this year. Derek Bok's open letters on the ethical responsibilities of universities reached far beyond their immediate Harvard audience. National magazines featured stories describing the controversy on campus over American investment in South Africa.

There is general agreement that American companies can--and should--effect social change in South Africa, but beyond that agreement the differences of opinion over the proper role for U.S. business remain sharply drawn.

Advocates of U.S. corporate withdrawal from South Africa argue that such a step would be economically and politically damaging to that country's government and would speed progress toward majority rule. Proponents of withdrawal are by no means agreed on the best course for encouraging radical social change in South Africa, however. Students, and labor unions, to some degree, insist that the divestiture of stock by institutional investors would hasten corporate disengagement. Others, principally church groups and academic institutions, contend that shareholder activism is the best way to curtail the American corporate presence in South Africa.

Corporations and most commercial institutional investors have taken a very different position, arguing that U.S. companies can act as a progressive force in South Africa by contributing to the overall economic advancement of its black population. By improving wages, instituting affirmative action programs and providing training opportunities and educational subsidies to black workers, supporters of investment say, American companies strengthen the prospects for gradual and peaceful change.

Since 1978, the philosophical positions of the initiators and recipients of pressures have been unvarying. There has been a noticeable widening, though, of the cast of those bringing pressures. Labor unions and municipal and state governments have become more outspoken proponents of withdrawal and, in some cases, divestiture. This nascent ferment has been largely located in California. The principal sanctions unions and governments possess--divestiture of South Africa-related stockholdings and the closure of bank accounts--have been infrequently employed. These groups are seriously addressing the issue, however, and their potential as activists, as yet largely unrealized, is not be be underestimated.

Most of the pressures forced upon educational institutions have sprung from student movements. Reports of the death of the South Africa cause on campus are greatly exaggerated. On most campuses where it has flourished in the past, student activism about South Africa remains strong. A number of schools experienced confrontations this spring; many others engaged in less dramatic analyses of investment questions. Students championing the withdrawal of U.S. corporations from South Africa and the sale of stock by their alma maters to encourage that end have certainly faced frustration as universities have almost uniformly rejected their position. Student activists and university administrators alike detect a transferral of activist fervor from South African to nuclear power issues, perhaps as a result of such frustration. Yet interest and agitation remained high in 1978-79 for a third consecutive year and gives little evidence of fading on many campuses.

The level of student pressures is, nevertheless, inherently volatile. Perhaps the most significant development of 1979 for those concerned with the role of American business in South Africa, therefore, is growing evidence of steady sophisticated attention to the issue by institutional investors. Many prominent institutions have adopted investment policies that provide for careful attention to the performance of companies, on an individual basis, in South Africa. The implementation of these policies, which generally center on the enforcement of the Sullivan principles of equal employment, promises to be the source of constant pressures upon corporations in the years to come.

The results of the 1979 proxy season underline both the growing sophistication with which institutional investors approach proxy voting and the specificity of their scrutiny of corporate performance. While most institutional investors still hold to the "progressive force" argument in general, an increasing number object to specific types of labor practices and corporate activity by individual companies. The results of votes on shareholder proposals indicate growing support for resolutions limiting bank loans to the government of South Africa, sales of strategic goods, and the expansion of corporate investment there. Investors favoring these steps include certain public pension funds, insurance companies and foundations as well as a growing number of colleges and universities. Support for more drastic moves, such as withdrawal from South Africa, comes mostly from church investors and a few educational institutions.

According to IRRC's survey of investment policies at 115 colleges and universities (see Appendix E), 51 schools have instituted procedures for voting their proxies on shareholder resolutions on South Africa. Of those, 35 schools have policies providing for votes in favor of resolutions encouraging progressive labor practices in South Africa. Thirteen support resolutions calling for an end to bank loans to the South African government. Ten schools have policies that express support for each of three other issues--halts to strategic sales, non-expansion, or corporate withdrawal; most of the schools endorsing such steps have done so only in the last year and support may grow.

Greater specificity about the sorts of shareholder proposals educational institutions will support is often accompanied by a willingness to consider selective divestment as a last resort. If several attempts to alter objectionable corporate practices via shareholder means have failed, 41 schools say they will selectively divest their stock. Twenty-seven will sell stock in companies that have not endorsed the Sullivan principles or given other indications of progressive labor practices, and five institutions have pledged to dispose of holdings in companies that sell strategic items to the government. It is notable that of the 11 university investors that have opted for selective divestment as a last resort in the last year, most have specific criteria for voting their stock.

In sum, institutional investors are becoming more specific and sophisticated in carrying out their "progressive force" positions. They are looking at corporate conduct more critically, focusing on certain types of conduct they find morally repugnant, and some are threatening selective divestment as a final protest. Yet in general, institutions believe they can do more to encourage change through shareholder activism than by the sharper protest of divestiture.

The impact of widespread attempts by institutional investors to implement policies governing South Africa-related investments is already being felt. The meeting of universities and other institutional investors held in summer 1979 at the Carnegie Corp. addressed one concern shared by all those present: monitoring the performance of American corporations in South Africa to ascertain their compliance with the Sullivan principles. Better monitoring techniques may grow out of this common effort, and if they do, investors' scrutiny of corporations will have advanced a step further. The Carnegie effort shows the continuing, evolving nature of investor attention to South Africa.

The impact of pressures on corporations is harder to gauge, because a direct causal relationship between pressures and corporate responses cannot be drawn. It is clear that many corporations take their shareholders' concerns over South Africa seriously. For several years now, companies have been devoting considerable resources to meeting these inquiries. They have assigned executives to respond to shareholder queries and to voice the company's case. They have published reports on their South African operations, and have sent senior personnel to South Africa to view their operations first-hand. Many companies openly admit that these burdens are disproportionate to the business they do in South Africa. Some regard it as a cost of doing business in a controversial country. Shareholder pressures have placed a considerable if not severe burden on corporate management. The "hassle factor," while apparently not a dominating factor in corporate decision-making regarding South Africa, is not a negligible one either.

An area in which the costs of pressures is more apparent is the application of equal employment guidelines. Some companies have invested large sums of capital in South Africa to desegregate their facilities, and to train and otherwise aid their black employees. Often these expenditures have occurred in the context of declining profitability for their South African operations.

For the last several years, the stream of corporate pronouncements upholding the Sullivan principles as the prime response to shareholder pressures has been punctuated by a small number of announcements of more drastic steps. The decisions this year by three companies to limit sales to the government and by three more not to expand operations are due in large part to direct shareholder pressures. These moves may also be attributed in part to greater awareness on the part of the corporations as to the legitimacy of concerns about labor practices in South Africa.

The calculus is equally complicated in the case of banks, where the pressures and their impact have been the strongest. Many American banks say they have curtailed their lending to South Africa because apartheid has created political and economic instability detrimental to the national credit rating. Other banks simply state that the continued existence of apartheid precludes further lending. Banks speak of scattered customer campaigns to withdraw funds because of their loans to South Africa or of shareholder protests bringing unwanted publicity, and these and the "hassle factor" they represent have played an important role in the sharp decline in American lending to South Africa in recent years.

The singling out of bank loans in the investment policies of institutions has been indirectly acknowledged by some banks. Many banks now publicly describe the additional, careful scrutiny potential loans to South Africa undergo. Some also have mounted efforts to publicize loans to South Africa that will tangibly benefit blacks by providing housing or training facilities. Both these steps suggest the impact investor pressures have had on the lending process.

The regulations clamped on sales to the police and military early in 1978 have also had a limited but measurable impact on the operations of American business in South Africa. The Commerce Department has documented the loss of sales by some companies, while several companies have themselves disclosed the extent of the competitive disadvantage they now face. Companies have been forced to adopt elaborate procedures to ensure that no items of American origin reach the South African police and military. In general, though, the Commerce Department regulations have not had the catastrophic effect feared by some companies 18 months ago when they were first put into effect. Although the volume of foregone sales is hard to quantify, the loss of sales does not appear to have been severely damaging. Companies have been inconvenienced, not crippled.

It is unlikely that business will have to cope with further federal restrictions on trade with South Africa. The latest State Department statements have encouraged companies to support voluntary initiatives such as the Sullivan principles. The government is emphasizing the positive social changes that companies can spur through progressive labor practices.

In Congress the trend also is away from consideration of punitive, restrictive legislation and toward incentives to spur progressive corporate steps in South Africa. Some members are sponsoring legislation that takes the new tack of denying tax credits to companies with a poor labor record in South Africa. This initiative, however, is not likely to win approval. Many previously active legislators on South African issues are pessimistic about the climate in Congress. They point to widespread support for lifting Rhodesian sanctions as evidence of the surge of conservative sentiment in the Congress. The findings of polls show that the public--though sympathetic to the plight of blacks in South Africa--is suspicious of any steps that suggest U.S. intervention or a weakened commitment to anti-Communism. Such beliefs clearly undergird the temperament of Congress on South Africa. The strongest voices in the Congress now are moderate ones. They are simply calling for Congress to endorse and put its weight behind the efforts that corporations are making on behalf of the Sullivan principles.

The national administration and legislature is joining the chorus of institutions and companies trumpeting the Sullivan principles. Support for Sullivan is, by its nature, a relatively moderate stance in the spectrum of opinion on the role of U.S. business in South Africa. It does not, however, mark the final resting point of concern. In three years, the movement that began with church and student activists has prompted increasing investor concern about--and corporate attention to--South Africa. The Sullivan principles now stand as the most widely accepted set of steps for corporations to take. The concerns of investors and the responses of companies will, no doubt, continue to evolve.

Sources

Reports

James E. Baker, et al, "Public Opinion Poll on American Attitudes Toward South Africa," Carnegie Endowment for International Peace, Washington, D.C., 1979.

Deborah Durfee Burton and John Immerwahr, "The Public Views South Africa: Pathways Through a Gathering Storm," Public Opinion, January/February 1979.

Beatte Klein, "The Banks Say--On South Africa," Interfaith Center on Corporate Responsibility, New York, N.Y., 1978.

David M. Liff, "U.S. Business in South Africa: Pressures from the Home Front," Investor Responsibility Research Center, Washington, D.C., October 1978.

Tanya V. Light and John C. Harrington, "Socially Responsible Investing: Criteria and Proxy Voting Guidelines," California Senate Select Committee on Investment Priorities and Objectives, Sacramento, Calif., June 1978.

Mary O'Connor, "The 1979 Proxy Season: How Institutions Voted on Shareholder Resolutions and Management Proposals," Investor Responsibility Research Center, October 1979.

Richard Parker and Tamsin Taylor, "Strategic Investment: An Alternative for Public Funds," Foundation for National Progress, San Francisco, Calif., 1978.

"Anti-Apartheid Organizing on Campus---and Beyond," South Africa Catalyst Project, Palo Alto, Calif., 1978.

"First Report on the Signatory Companies to the Sullivan Principles," report prepared by Arthur D. Little Inc., Cambridge, Mass., for Dr. Leon Sullivan, Zion Baptist Church, Philadelphia, Pa., November 1978.

"Second Report on the Signatory Companies to the Sullivan Principles," report prepared by Arthur D. Little Inc., April 1979.

"Model for a Community Investment Fund," Institute for Community Economics, Inc., Cambridge, Mass., January 1979.

"NAACP Task Force on Africa: Report and Recommendations," National Association for the Advancement of Colored People, New York, N.Y., 1978.

"Restrictions on Exports to Namibia and the Republic of South Africa," Export Administration Bulletin No. 175, U.S. Department of Commerce, Feb. 16, 1978.

Articles

Barry   Mitzman,   "U.S.   students   vs.   apartheid: the   divestiture
demonstrations," The Nation, May 13, 1978.

Shelly   Pitterman   and   David   Markum,   "Campaigning   for   divestment,"
Africa Report, September/October 1978.

Stephanie   Urdang,   "Break   all   ties...   student   movement   escalates,"
Southern Africa, June/July 1978.

Roger   M.   Williams,   "American   business   should   stay   in   South   Africa,"
Saturday Review, Sept. 30, 1978.

"Human   rights   policy   affects   export   controls,"   Commerce America,
June 5, 1978.

Appendices

APPENDIX A

LAWS AFFECTING LABOR IN SOUTH AFRICA

Laws Governing Location of Africans

During the last three-quarters of a century in South Africa, a body of legislation has grown up designed to control the location of African workers and their families. Among the most critical laws are:

The Native Land Act of 1913--The act set aside 22.5 million acres as reserves for Africans. Whites were prohibited from owning land in these areas, and Africans were not permitted to buy land outside the reserves. (Recently the prime minister announced his intention to review the act to consider the possibility of expanding the acreage allocated to Africans.)

The Native (Urban Areas) Act of 1923--The act required local authorities to establish separate living areas or "locations" for Africans. The local authorities were to be held responsible for controlling the "influx" of Africans from rural areas and were charged with seeing that any "surplus" Africans were removed to the reserves.

The "Pass" Laws--To meet its obligations under the Native Land Act, parliament has over the years enacted a number of varying laws designed to control the movement of Africans. Collectively known as the "pass laws," they attempted to control the settlement of blacks by such methods as housing permits, work permits and curfews.

The Native (Urban Areas) Consolidation Act of 1945--This act replaced the myriad local pass laws with authorization for the central government to develop a system to control the influx of blacks into white areas. The act, as amended, sets the conditions under which Africans are now permitted to stay in areas that have been "proclaimed" for whites. The conditions state that an African cannot visit an urban area for longer than 72 hours without first obtaining a special permit; he may not reside there unless he has lived there continuously since birth, has worked there continuously since birth, has worked there continuously for 10 years for a single employer, has lived there lawfully for 15 years, is the wife, unmarried daughter, or son under 18 of someone with the right to live there, or has obtained a special exemption. Any African in a white area is to be considered "migratory labor," a "temporary sojourner." He is not permitted to vote or own land, and he can be "endorsed out" if the government determines that he is idle or "redundant." To facilitate monitoring of Africans in white areas, all Africans over the age of 16 are required to carry passbooks at all times. The books include a wealth of information on the individual bearer ranging from his age and birth place to the name of his employer and his last year's taxes.

The Group Areas Act of 1950--The act made exchanges of property and changes of occupation between races subject to government permit. It also authorized the central government to define certain zones by race. Should the government decide that people are living in areas that have been zoned for another race, the government can force them to move.

The Environment Planning Act of 1977 (formerly the Physical Planning and Utilization of Resources Act)--The act seeks to limit the migration of Africans from rural to urban areas by restricting the expansion of business or industrial operations that will require increased numbers of African workers. Industries in certain urban areas must maintain specific racial ratios in their work force and may not increase their black labor force without government permission. For example, in the Johannesburg area, factories that had a ratio of one white worker to 2.5 or fewer Africans before June 1, 1973, will be allowed to expand as long as the ratio remains 2.5 Africans to every white. Factories established after June 1, 1973, can expand as long as the ratio is no more than 2 Africans to every white. No new firms will be allowed to open factories that would require a ratio above 2:1.

Laws Governing Political Dissent

South Africa's body of security legislation severely restricts the opportunity for political dissent. The three most important of the securities laws are the Terrorism Act of 1967, the Suppression of Communism Act of 1950, and the Riotous Assemblies Act.

The Terrorism Act of 1967--Under this act, an individual is deemed guilty unless he can prove beyond a reasonable doubt that he did not commit acts designated as "terroristic" with an intent to endanger the maintenance of law and order. The South African Institute of Race Relations reports an intent to endanger the maintenance of law and order is presumed, unless the accused is able to prove otherwise, "if the act committed was likely to have the effect of encouraging an insurrection or forcible resistance to the government, causing general dislocation or disturbance, furthering the achievement of any political aim (including the bringing about of any social or economic change) by forcible means or with the assistance of any foreign or international government or body, embarrassing the administration of the affairs of the state, causing feelings of hostility between whites and blacks, hampering or deterring anyone from assisting in the maintenance of law and order, seriously injuring anyone or causing substantial financial loss to any person or to the state, promoting the achievement of any object by intimidation, or prejudicing any undertaking or industry or the production or distribution of commodities or the supply or distribution of essential services or the free movement of traffic."

The act under section 6 permits any police officer at or above the rank of lieutenant-colonel to detain without charge people he suspects of being terrorists or of having knowledge of terrorist activities. Suspected terrorists or those suspected of knowing about activities that might be defined as terrorist may be held indefinitely for interrogation. The Minister of Justice is not obligated to provide any information to parliament on people held under section 6, nor does the ministry have to notify family or friends of the detained.

Suppression of Communism Act of 1950--The Suppression of Communism Act defines communism broadly as any doctrine that aims at establishing a system of government based (1) on the dictatorship of the proletariat, (2) on bringing about political, industrial, social or economic change by the promotion of disturbance or disorder, by unlawful acts or omissions, (3) on bringing about change in accordance with directions from a foreign government or international institution, or (4) on encouraging hostility between race groups, with the impact of bringing about a change in government. Amendments to the act provided the Minister of Justice with the power to "ban" persons he considers to be engaged in communist activities, to be promoting communism, or to be engaged in activities that might promote communism. Those individuals served with "banning orders" may be restricted to their magisterial district (county), and be prohibited from publishing and making speeches to more than one person at a time.

The act under section 10 also permits the Minister of Justice to detain for up to 12 months, persons he suspects of engaging in activities that endanger the security of the state. The Attorney General is granted the authority to detain material witnesses for a period of up to six months. Although the act provides for a three person committee to review detentions, decisions on detentions are beyond the courts. The Attorney General can forbid access to any detained person--except a state official or a magistrate who are entitled to one visit per week--and no court has the power to order that a detained person be released or allowed to receive visitors.

The Riotous Assemblies Act--The Riotous Assemblies Act, first passed in 1914 and reenacted with amendments in 1956, authorizes the minister or a magistrate with the minister's approval to prohibit public gatherings, or to prohibit someone from addressing public meetings if such gatherings might endanger public peace or cause racial hostility. The act was amended in 1974 to allow magistrates themselves to prohibit gatherings if they think the public peace will be threatened, and the amendment defined gatherings as "a gathering, concourse or procession of any number of people having a common purpose, whether such purpose be lawful or unlawful." It also provides for the detention of those people who are suspected of violating the act.

Laws Affecting the Rights of African Workers

Current law in South Africa prevents Africans from joining

recognized trade unions; it reserves certain jobs for whites; and it effectively shuts off access to training and advancement by restricting opportunity for apprenticeship training. The key laws establishing these restrictions are the Industrial Conciliation Act, which excludes Africans from government-authorized unions; the Apprenticeship Acts, which left training in the hands of white unions; the Bantu Labor Act, which limits the African's right to representation and to strike; and the Separate Facilities Laws that require separate dining, toilet and, in some cases, working areas for each race.

The Industrial Conciliation Act of 1924--The Industrial Conciliation Act of 1924, enacted shortly after the 1922 mine workers strike and amended in 1937, was designed to establish a system for the negotiation of conflicts between trade unions and employers over wages and working conditions. Its concern was primarily with white trade unions, and its implications for black workers became apparent only with the increased role of Africans in the industrial economy. The act provides for the creation of industrial councils, composed of an equal number of representatives from trade unions and industry, which are to meet periodically to negotiate wages, determine which jobs are to be held by union members, and negotiate items affecting labor conditions, such as hours to be worked, overtime permitted, sick leave and other fringe benefits. Once an agreement has been reached, it is printed in a government gazette and becomes legally binding on employers and employees in an industry.

The act includes three provisions that directly affect black opportunity. First, it defines the term "employee" to exclude Africans and prevents the admission of Africans to registered trade unions. It does not prohibit Africans from joining non-registered, officially unrecognized trade unions, but such unions would not be permitted representation on the industrial council. Thus, Africans are effectively excluded from engaging in collective bargaining on the industrial council. In some cases, white or colored unions have stated their intention to represent the interests of black workers in negotiations with management, and Africans may have observers at the industrial council meetings. But they do not have the right to vote, despite the fact that they are bound by the terms decided upon and promulgated in any industrial council agreement.

The second obstacle posed by the act is the provision in section 77 for the establishment of an industrial tribunal which may recommend to the Minister that certain jobs be reserved for members of a certain race. The Minister, in the past, has reserved specific jobs for whites, but in the last few years, the number of jobs specifically reserved for whites has decreased. In 1976, an estimated 2.3 percent of the labor force was directly affected by job reservations; that year, reservations on six positions were removed, and in 1977, 13 more reservations were cancelled. Current reservations apply to six types of jobs such as motor assemblers; mine surveyors and those charged with mine ventilation; construction workers; traffic police; and fire and ambulance staffs in Capetown. In total, the current reservations affect some 90,000 workers, less than 1 percent of South Africa's work force.

More important than the job reservation clause in preventing black advancement is the act's provision that the Industrial Council Agreement may require a company to reserve positions for union members. This creates a closed shop, with Africans, because they are denied the right to participate in registered unions, excluded from certain positions. The building industry's industrial council agreement, for example, states that only trade union members may be employed on artisan's work. Africans may be permitted to serve as assistants, provided that the employer maintains a strict ratio of African workers to whites. If Africans are promoted, whites are to receive corresponding promotions. Thus if an African is promoted to the operator level, whites in that section expect to be upgraded to "master craftsman" with a corresponding increase in salary.

Apprenticeship Act of 1922--The exclusion under the Industrial Conciliation Act of Africans from the designation "employee" and the denial of the right to join registered unions directly affects the opportunity of Africans to get training under the Apprenticeship Act.

The Apprenticeship Act, while non-discriminatory in language, effectively has been used by white trade unions to exclude Africans and other blacks from apprenticeship training. The act authorizes the formation of a national apprenticeship board and a number of apprenticeship committees composed equally of industry and registered trade union representatives. The committees are charged with setting standards for--and supervising--programs for apprentices. Africans, who are prevented from joining registered trade unions under the Industrial Conciliation Act, are thereby excluded from participation on apprenticeship committees. The committees have not approved apprenticeship training for Africans. Few, if any, white unions have accepted Africans as apprentices, and only a limited number have been willing to take colored or Asian apprentices.

Mines and Works Act of 1911--Like the Industrial Conciliation Act, the Mine and Works Act provides for the restriction of certain jobs according to race. The act prescribes regulations in the certificates of competency required for employees in certain occupations. Blacks are not granted certificates to do blasting, for example, and must be supervised by a white miner.

The Bantu Labor Regulations Amendment Act of 1973--South Africa's Labor Minister said in 1977 that the African was excluded from participation in the Industrial Conciliation Act because "if he was allowed to be absorbed into the trade union system of that time--a system which was too sophisticated for him...he could be exploited and abused." Instead, the government argues that a more "suitable" system is provided under the Bantu Labor Act.

The Amendment Act defines the rights of African workers in disputes with employers and sets the limits and conditions for the exercise of those rights. The Amendment Act replaces the Bantu Labor (Settlement of Disputes) Act of 1953 and was introduced following the 1973 strikes in Durban, when 50,000 African workers spontaneously walked off the job.

The Amendment Act gives workers the right to demand representation through a works committee composed entirely of representatives elected by African workers unless the company has already established a liaison committee. (The difference between the two kinds of committees is important. At least half the members of a liaison committee must be elected by African employees, but the chairman and remaining members may be appointed by management.) The Bantu Labor Act contained no such provision and as late as 1972, only 150 to 200 committees representing workers existed in the country. Under the new act, by the end of 1976 companies had established 1,819 liaison committees and 274 works committees.

The Bantu Labor Act did not permit Africans to strike under any conditions. The new act recognizes a limited right of Africans to strike, but only after three prerequisites have been met: (1) a works or liaison committee has had the opportunity to consider the dispute and a 30-day period has elapsed following the failure of the committee to resolve the dispute; (2) no minimum-wage level for the industry has been set within the last year; (3) the workers on strike are not engaged in industries handling products or providing services that the government deems essential.

The act was amended further in 1977 to permit workers and liaison committees the power to negotiate wage agreements and make other conditions. Agreements reached between management and the committees are binding under civil law and must be displayed on the company premises.

Separate Facilities Laws--The principles of separation of the races have been extended to the work place in order, according to the government, "to reduce the possibility of racial friction. Racial separation is incorporated in the Factories, Machinery and Building Work Act of 1941 and the Shops and Offices Act of 1964. As written, the acts are nondiscriminatory in language but provide for a series of regulations on factory or plant conditions--including health and safety of workers--that permit action by a government inspector to correct a situation detrimental to the physical, moral, or social welfare of the employees. Separation of facilities--toilets, eating, working and recreation areas--by race is one item included in the regulations, and a company's performance in respect to separation of facilities is subject to government inspection.

For example, the Factories Act authorizes an inspector to inform a company that, "If employees of different races or sexes work in the same room such steps as are practicable in order to ensure that the employees of one race or sex work apart from the employees of any other race or sex shall be taken." If the inspector judges the steps taken inadequate, "he may require such further steps to be taken as in his opinion are practicable and desirable." And separation--in the case of "sanitary conveniences"--is to be noted. "The employer or occupier shall cause all closets, privies or urinals to be marked in a conspicuous place in painted or stencilled letters of at least 50 millimeters high to indicate the sex and race for the use of which they are intended."

APPENDIX B

CODES OF CONDUCT

1. SULLIVAN PRINCIPLES

Rev. Leon H. Sullivan in July 1978 published an amplified version of his six principles of equal employment practices for U.S. firms operating in South Africa. The principles have now been signed by 135 U.S. companies. Following is the text of the amplified principles:

PRINCIPLE I - Non-segregation of the races in all eating, comfort and work facilities.

Each signator of the Statement of Principles will proceed immediately to:
● Eliminate all vestiges of racial discrimination.
● Remove all race designation signs.
● Desegregate all eating, comfort and work facilities.

PRINCIPLE II - Equal and fair employment practices for all employees.

Each signator of the Statement of Principles will proceed immediately to:
● Implement equal and fair terms and conditions of employment.
● Provide non-discriminatory eligibility for benefit plans.
● Establish an appropriate comprehensive procedure for handling and resolving individual employee complaints.
● Support the elimination of all industrial racial discriminatory laws which impede the implementation of equal and fair terms and conditions of employment, such as abolition of job reservations, job fragmentation, and apprenticeship restrictions for blacks and other non-whites.
● Support the elimination of discrimination against the rights of blacks to form or belong to government registered unions, and acknowledge generally the right of black workers to form their own union or be represented by trade unions where unions already exist.

PRINCIPLE III - Equal pay for all employees doing equal or comparable work for the same period of time.

Each signator of the Statement of Principles will proceed immediately to:
● Design and implement a wage and salary administration plan which is applied equally to all employees regardless of race who are performing equal or comparable work.
● Ensure an equitable system of job classifications, including a review of the distinction between hourly and salaried classifications.
● Determine whether upgrading of personnel and/or jobs in the lower echelons is needed, and if so, implement programs to accomplish this objective expeditiously.
● Assign equitable wage and salary ranges, the minimum of these to be well above the appropriate local minimum economic living level.

PRINCIPLE IV - Initiation of and development of training programs that will prepare, in substantial numbers, blacks and other non-whites for supervisory, administrative, clerical and technical jobs.

Each signator of the Statement of Principles will proceed immediately to:
- Determine employee training needs and capabilities, and identify employees with potential for further advancement.
- Take advantage of existing outside training resources and activities, such as exchange programs, technical colleges, vocational schools, continuation classes, supervisory courses and similar institutions or programs.
- Support the development of outside training facilities individually or collectively, including technical centers, professional training exposure, correspondence and extension courses, as appropriate, for extensive training outreach.
- Initiate and expand inside training programs and facilities.

PRINCIPLE V - Increasing the number of blacks and other non-whites in management and supervisory positions.

Each signator of the Statement of Principles will proceed immediately to:
- Identify, actively recruit, train and develop a sufficient and significant number of blacks and other non-whites to assure that as quickly as possible there will be appropriate representation of blacks and other non-whites in the management group of each company.
- Establish management development programs for blacks and other non-whites, as appropriate, and improve existing programs and facilities for developing management skills of blacks and other non-whites.
- Identify and channel high management potential blacks and other non-white employees into management development programs.

PRINCIPLE VI - Improving the quality of employees' lives outside the work environment in such areas as housing, transportation, schooling, recreation and health facilities.

Each signator of the Statement of Principles will proceed immediately to:
- Evaluate existing and/or develop programs, as appropriate, to address the specific needs of black and other non-white employees in the areas of housing, health care, transportation and recreation.
- Evaluate methods for utilizing existing, expanded or newly established in-house medical facilities or other medical programs to improve medical care for all non-whites and their dependents.
- Participate in the development of programs that address the educational needs of employees, their dependents and the local community. Both individual and collective programs should be considered, including such activities as literacy education, business training, direct assistance to local schools, contributions and scholarships.
- With all the foregoing in mind, it is the objective of the companies

to involve and assist in the education and training of large and telling numbers of blacks and other non-whites as quickly as possible. The ultimate impact of this effort is intended to be of massive proportion, reaching millions.

PERIODIC REPORTING

The signator companies of the Statement of Principles will proceed immediately to:

- Utilize a standard format to report their progress to Dr. Sullivan through the independent administrative unit he is establishing on a 6-month basis which will include a clear definition of each item to be reported.
- Ensure periodic reports on the progress that has been accomplished on the implementation of these principles.

2. EUROPEAN COMMUNITY CODE OF CONDUCT FOR COMPANIES
    WITH SUBSIDIARIES, BRANCHES OR REPRESENTATION IN SOUTH
    AFRICA

(1) Relations Within the Undertaking

(a) Companies should ensure that all their employees irrespective of racial or other distinction are allowed to choose freely and without any hindrance the type of organization to represent them.

(b) Employers should regularly and unequivocally inform their employees that consultations and collective bargaining with organizations which are freely elected and representative of employees are part of company policy.

(c) Should black African employees decide that their representative body should be in the form of a trade union, the company should accept this decision. Trade unions for black Africans are not illegal, and companies are free to recognize them, and to negotiate and conclude agreements with them.

(d) Consequently, the companies should allow collective bargaining with organizations freely chosen by the workers to develop in accordance with internationally accepted principles.

(e) Employers should do everything possible to ensure that black African employees are free to form or to join a trade union. Steps should be taken in particular to permit trade union officials to explain to employees the aims of trade unions and the advantages of membership, to distribute trade union documentation and display trade union notices on the company's premises, to have reasonable time off to carry out their union duties without loss of pay and to organize meetings.

(f) Where works or liaison committees already operate, trade union officials should have representative status on these bodies if employees so wish. However, the existence of these types of committees should not prejudice the development or status of trade unions or their representatives.

(2) Migrant Labor

(a) The system of migrant labor is, in South Africa, an instrument of the policy of apartheid which has the effect of preventing the individual from seeking and obtaining a job of his choice: it also causes grave social and family problems.

(b) In the meantime employers should make it their concern to alleviate as much as possible the effects of the existing system.

(3) Pay

Companies should assume a special responsibility as regards the pay and conditions of employment of their black African employees. They should formulate specific policies aimed at improving their terms of employment. Pay based on the absolute minimum necessary for a family to survive cannot be considered as being sufficient. The minimum wage should initially exceed by at least 50 percent the minimum level required to satisfy the basic needs of an employee and his family.

(4)   Wage Structure and Black African Advancement

(a) The principle of "equal pay for equal work" means that all jobs should be open to any worker who possesses suitable qualifications, irrespective of racial or other distinction, and that wages should be based on a qualitative job evaluation.

(b) The same pay scales should be applied to the same work. The adoption of the principle of equal pay would, however, be meaningless if black African employees were kept in inferior jobs. Employers should therefore draw up an appropriate range of training schemes of a suitable standard to provide training for their black African employees, and should reduce their dependence on immigrant white labor.

(5)   Fringe Benefits

(a) In view of the social responsibilities, undertakings should concern themselves with the living conditions of their employees and families.

(b) For this purpose company funds could be set aside for use:

-- in housing of black African personnel and their families; in transport from place of residence to place of work and back;
-- in providing leisure and health service facilities;
-- in providing their employees with assistance in problems they encounter with authorities over their movement from one place to another, their choice of residence and their employment;
-- in pension matters;
-- in educational matters;
-- in improving medical services, in adopting programs of ensurance against industrial accidents and unemployment, and in other measures of social welfare.

(6) Desegregation at Places of Work

In so far as it lies within their own competence, employers should do everything possible to abolish any practice of segregation, notably at the work place and in canteens, sports activities, education and training. They should also ensure equal working conditions for all their staff.

(7) Reports on the Implementation of the Code of Conduct

(a) Parent companies to which this code is addressed should publish each year a detailed and fully documented report on the progress made in applying this code.

(b) The number of black Africans employed in the undertaking should be specified in the report, and progress in each of the six areas indicated above should be fully covered.

(c) The Governments of the Nine will review annually the progress made in implementing this code. To this end a copy of each company's report should be submitted to their national government.

3. CODE OF CONDUCT OF THE URBAN FOUNDATION, ENDORSED BY THE SOUTH AFRICAN EMPLOYERS CONSULTATIVE COMMITTEE ON LABOR

Believing that free enterprise has a major contribution to make towards improving the quality of life of all people in South Africa, and believing that the opportunity for men and women to develop themselves to their fullest potential plays a basic role in the quality of their lives, the Urban Foundation, recognizing progress already achieved in matters dealt with below, recommends the adoption by all members of the private sector of a code of employment practice whereby the subscriber is committed, within the provisions of the law:

1. To strive constantly for the elimination of discrimination based on race or color from all aspects of employment practice, and to apply this principle in good faith, in particular in the following aspects:

1.1. The selection, employment, advancement and promotion of all employees;

1.2. The reward of employees;

1.3. The provision of pension, medical aid, leave, sick pay, employee insurance, assistance with housing, and like facilities; physical working conditions and facilities related thereto; training programs or facilities to improve the productivity and skills of employees to enable them to achieve advancement in technical, administrative and managerial positions, in all these instances with due regard to different job categories, fairly determined on basis other than race or color;

1.4. The recognition of the basic rights of workers of freedom of association, collective negotiation of agreements of conditions of service, the lawful withholding of labor as a result of disputes, and protection against victimization resulting from the exercise of these rights.

2. To promote and maintain, through contact and consultation, sound and harmonious relations between itself and its employees, and between all categories of its employees.

3. To cooperate with other organizations and members of the private sector in promoting:

3.1. The accelerated creation of employment opportunities for the South African population at wage rates aimed at the maintenance of viable living standards;

3.2. The progressive transition to a system wherein the rates of remuneration paid and any assistance given by the employer in respect to housing and other practical needs of employees will be such as to render unnecessary any general differential subsidy based on race or color.

APPENDIX C

COMPANIES THAT HAVE SIGNED THE SULLIVAN PRINCIPLES

Abbott Laboratories
AFIA Worldwide Insurance
American Cyanamid Co.
American Express Co.
American Home Products Corp.
American Hospital Supply Corp.
American International Group Inc.
Armco Steel Corp.
Automated Building Components Inc.
Badger Co.
Borden Inc.
Borg-Warner Corp.
Bristol-Myers Co.
Bulova Watch Co. Inc.
Bundy Corp.
Burroughs Corp.
Butterick Fashion Marketing Co.
Caltex Petroleum Corp.
Carnation Co.
Caterpillar Tractor Co.
Celanese Corp.
Champion Spark Plug Co.
The Chase Manhattan Bank
Citicorp
Colgate-Palmolive Co.
Control Data Corp.
CPC International
Crown Cork and Seal Co. Inc.
Cummins Engine Co. Inc.
Cutler-Hammer Inc.
Dart Industries Inc.
Deere & Co.
Del Monte Corp.
Deloitte Haskins & Sells
Donaldson Co. Inc.
Dow Chemical Co.
Eastman Kodak Co.
E.I. du Pont de Nemours & Co.
Engelhard Minerals & Chemicals Corp.
Envirotech
ESB Ray-O-Vac
Exxon Corp.
Farrell Lines Inc.
Federal-Mogul Corp.
Ferro Corp.

Grolier Inc.
Walter E. Heller Overseas Corp.
Heublein Inc.
Hewlett-Packard Co.
Honeywell Inc.
The Hoover Co.
Hyster Co.
IBM Corp.
INA Corp.
International Harvester Co.
International Minerals & Chemicals Corp.
International Standard Brand Inc.
International Telephone & Telegraph Corp
The Interpublic Group of Cos. Inc.
Johnson & Johnson Co.
Johnson Control International Inc.
Joy Manufacturing Co.
Kellogg Co.
Kelly Springfield Tire Co.
Kennecott Copper Corp.
Eli Lilly & Co.
Masonite Corp.
McGraw-Hill Inc.
Measurex Corp.
Merck & Co. Inc.
Mine Safety Appliances Co.
Minnesota Mining & Manufacturing Co.
Mobil Oil Corp.
Monsanto Co.
Motorola Inc.
Nabisco Inc.
Nalco Chemical Co.
Nashua Corp.
NCR Corp.
A.C. Nielsen International Inc.
North Carolina National Bank
Norton Co.
Norton Simon Inc.
Olin Corp.
Oshkosh Truck Corp.
Otis Elevator
Pan American World Airways Inc.
The Parker Pen Co.
Pennwalt Corp.
Pfizer Inc.

Firestone Tire & Rubber Co.
John Fluke Manufacturing Co. Inc.
Fluor Inc.
FMC Corp.
Ford Motor Co.
Franklin Electric
GAF Corp.
Gates Rubber Co.
Gardner-Denver Co.
General Electric Co.
General Motors Corp.
J. Gerber & Co.
The Gillette Co.
Goodyear International Corp.
W.R. Grace & Co.
Sterling Drug Inc.
Tampax Inc.
J. Walter Thompson
Tokheim Corp.
The Trane Co.
TRW Inc.
Twin Disc Inc.
Union Carbide Corp.

Phelps Dodge Corp.
Phillips Petroleum Corp.
Readers Digest
Revlon Inc.
Rexnord Inc.
Richardson-Merrell Inc.
Rockwell International Corp.
Rohm and Haas Co.
Schering-Plough Corp.
Sentry Inc.
Simplicity Pattern Co. Inc.
The Singer Co.
SmithKline Corp.
Sperry Rand Corp.
Squibb Corp.
Uniroyal Inc.
The Upjohn Co.
Warner-Lambert Co.
Westinghouse Electric Corp.
White Motor Corp.
Wilbur-Ellis Co.
Xerox Corp.

APPENDIX D

BLACKS ENROLLED IN TRAINING COURSES

Chart A

Number of Pupils Enrolled in Trade Courses: 1977

Trade	Number of Pupils			
	1st year	2nd year	3rd year	Total
Carpentry, joinery and cabinetmaking	305	218	22	545
Concreting, bricklaying and plastering	379	277	26	682
Painting and glazing	93	-	-	93
Electricians	71	31	-	102
Motor mechanics	204	169	120	493
Welding and metalwork	220	154	-	374
Leatherwork	18	26	-	44
Plumbing, drainlaying and sheetmetalwork	188	113	24	325
Tailoring	47	39	38	124
Upholstery and motor trimming	76	58	-	134
Motorbody repairmen	104	98	-	202
Watchmakers	10	9	13	32
TOTAL	1,175	1,192	243	3,150

Credit: South African Department of Education and Training: Information on Trade Training, Technical Training, Advanced Technical Training, Industrial Training. Pretoria, February 1978

Chart B

Pupils Enrolled for Secondary Technical Courses: 1977

Subject	Standard					Total
	6	7	8	9	10	
Building construction	40	23	30	-	-	93
Electricians	21	20	11	1	-	53
Technical drawing	192	117	190	103	43	645
Motor mechanics	6	-	-	-	-	6
Woodwork	20	30	51	-	-	101
Welding and metalwork	126	44	78	-	-	248
TOTAL	405	234	320	144	43	1,146

Credit: South African Department of Education and Training:
Information on Trade Training, Technical Training, Advanced
Technical Training, Industrial Training. Pretoria, February 1978

Chart C

Number of Students Enrolled at Colleges for
Advanced Technical Education: 1977

Course	Number of Students										
	1st yr		2nd yr		3rd yr		4th yr		Total		
	M	W	M	W	M	W	M	W	M	W	Total
Engineering technicians	22	--	13	--	15	--	8	--	58	--	58
Survey technicians	13	--	9	--	9	--	6	--	37	--	37
Geology technicians	10	--	2	--	6	--	--	--	18	--	18
Telecommunication technicians	23	--	8	--	11	--	--	--	42	--	42
Trade inspectors	5	--	4	--	--	--	--	--	9	--	9
Dental therapy	5	4	12	2	10	2	--	--	27	8	35
Physiotherapy	--	8	--	9	--	6	--	--	--	23	23
Radiography	5	3	3	1	--	--	--	--	8	4	12
Medical laboratory technology	14	6	--	--	--	--	--	--	14	6	20
Community health nursing	--	68	--	--	--	--	--	--	--	68	68
Health assistants	36	--	--	--	--	--	--	--	36	--	36
National diploma in public health	38	--	16	--	21	--	--	--	75	--	75
Water purification operators	26	--	--	--	--	--	--	--	26	--	26
Maintenance workers	30	--	--	--	--	--	--	--	30	--	30
Analytical chemistry	25	--	6	--	--	--	--	--	31	--	31
Dietetics	--	5	--	2	--	--	--	--	--	7	7
Occupational therapy	2	6	2	4	--	--	--	--	4	10	14
TOTAL	254	100	75	18	72	8	14	--	415	126	541

Credit: South   African   Department   of   Education   and   Training:
Information on Trade Training, Technical Training, Advanced
Technical Training, Industrial Training. Pretoria, February 1978

APPENDIX E

INVESTMENT POLICIES OF COLLEGES AND UNIVERSITIES

IRRC has surveyed the 100 American colleges and universities with the largest endowments, as well as selected other educational institutions, regarding their positions on South Africa-related investments. Brief summaries of the stands taken by the educational institutions that have made public their positions on the issue follow. The listing also includes those schools that told IRRC they do not have South Africa-related policies. Detailed information on schools that have sold stock in companies with operations in South Africa is provided in Appendix F.

AMHERST COLLEGE: The board of trustees of Amherst College adopted a South Africa-related investment policy in October 1977. Under the terms of its policy, Amherst is committed to:

- support the adoption and implementation of the Sullivan principles by portfolio companies doing business in South Africa;
- support shareholder proposals to prohibit further bank loans to the South African government; and
- consider selective divestment of stock in companies that fail to carry out the goals of the Sullivan principles or rectify policies that the trustees consider "objectionable."

To implement its policy, the college maintains an on-going correspondence with its South Africa-related portfolio companies and reviews its holdings in companies that, after several shareholder resolutions, do not implement the policies asked of them. Amherst sold its stock in Blue Bell in March 1978. (For details, see Appendix F)

ANTIOCH UNIVERSITY: In May 1978, the board of trustees of Antioch University instructed its money manager to sell all the school's investments in companies with South African ties. The decision affected stocks held in four companies and was made in compliance with a 1963 investment policy that requires the board to consider social and moral issues in its financial affairs. (For details, see Appendix F)

UNIVERSITY OF ARKANSAS: The University of Arkansas' formal investment policy mentions only financial criteria. The university endorses the Sullivan principles, and it supports shareholder resolutions that call for implementation of the Sullivan principles and for a halt to bank loans to the South African government.

BEREA COLLEGE: Berea College has no policy regarding investments in American companies with operations in South Africa.

BOSTON UNIVERSITY: In late April 1979 Boston University trustees, acting upon recommendations made by an investment advisory committee composed of students, faculty, administration officials and alumni, announced that the school will:

- selectively sell stock in any company active in South Africa that "is not constructively seeking to maximize black opportunities and pay and to support an end to apartheid," and in companies where "persistent efforts to change corporate policy have demonstrably failed";
- refrain from depositing funds in, or holding stock in, banks that lend to the South African government;

• sell all its South Africa-related non-voting holdings because they "confer no investor powers on the university."

In accordance with this policy, Boston University began the sale of bonds and non-voting stock and the withdrawal of bank accounts totaling $6.6 million. (For details, see Appendix F)

BOWDOIN COLLEGE: The President of Bowdoin College appointed an ad hoc South Africa investment advisory committee in the fall of 1978 which is developing recommendations.

BRANDEIS UNIVERSITY: In April 1979, the Brandeis board of trustees announced that it would selectively sell and refrain from purchasing stock in companies whose South African business and employment practices cause "severe social injury."

According to the Brandeis trustees, the following activities cause "severe social injury":

• the extension of loans to the South African government or its agencies;
• the sale of items to the South African police or military that are used to enforce apartheid; and
• a refusal to endorse the Sullivan principles or a similar code by companies that employ 50 or more employees in South Africa.

If a portfolio company engages in one of these practices, the school will:

• communicate with corporate management to urge termination of the socially injurious activity or withdrawal from South Africa;
• support shareholder resolutions calling for an end to the socially injurious activity and for withdrawal from South Africa;
• prudently divest its holdings if its inquiry is not satisfactorily answered, if the corporation refuses to cease its socially injurious practices, or if the university's holdings are in companies in which it has no voting rights.

In addition, Brandeis will no longer purchase the securities of corporations whose behavior is socially injurious.

Brandeis University has sold investments in two South Africa-related companies. (For details, see Appendix F)

BROWN UNIVERSITY: After six months of study, in November 1978 the Advisory and Executive Committee of the Brown Corp. issued an investment policy statement on responsible shareholding. The corporation "agrees with the Sullivan principles" and is "opposed in general to loans made to the South African government and will express that view as widely as (it) can."

In January 1979 the Advisory and Executive Committee authorized establishment of a Committee on Corporate Responsibility in Investment. The committee is to evaluate shareholder resolutions, correspond with companies and present recommendations to the trustees.

BRYN MAWR COLLEGE: A committee on investment responsibility has made proxy voting recommendations to the Bryn Mawr board of trustees since 1972. The committee--composed of students, alumnae, faculty, staff and one trustee--makes its recommendations on a case-by-case basis.

In 1978 and 1979, Bryn Mawr cosponsored shareholder resolutions to Eastman Kodak on the subject of strategic sales of photographic equipment to the South African government and its agencies. The resolutions received the support of 4.79 percent of the shares voted in 1978 and 3.13 percent of those voted in 1979. The school also organized a conference on university sponsorship of South Africa-related shareholder resolutions, which was held in October 1978 and was attended by officials from 18 colleges and universities.

BUCKNELL UNIVERSITY: In December 1978, the board of trustees of Bucknell University formed a subcommittee for investment to review and establish guidelines for the school's South Africa-related investments. According to the policy drawn up by the trustee-composed subcommittee, the school will refrain from investing in any company active in South Africa that has not subscribed to the Sullivan principles. The subcommittee also votes the school's proxies. A university administrator told IRRC that the trustees "usually vote with management."

UNIVERSITY OF CALIFORNIA: In 1977 the board of regents of the University of California sent letters to 37 portfolio companies asking about the nature of their South African operations and appointed an advisory committee to recommend appropriate social responsibility investment guidelines. In May 1978, the board rejected the committee's proposal to establish an Advisory Council on Social Responsibility in Investments. At that time, it indicated that it planned no further action on the South Africa issue.

In May 1979, however, the regents voted 129,493 shares of General Motors stock worth about $7.5 million in favor of a resolution asking the company to cease sales of vehicles to the South African police and military. The 15-3 vote by the regents marked the first time the University of California board had cast a vote against management on a shareholder resolution.

Gov. Edmund G. Brown Jr., an ex officio member of the regents, reportedly had discussed the issue witn activist students and strongly urged a vote in favor of the shareholder resolution. Brown characterized the regents' vote as a way "we can put General Motors to the test," according to the San Francisco Chronicle. "If they don't respond to this request, then I think it may well be in order to take the matter up again as to our participation."

CARLETON COLLEGE: In October 1978, the board of trustees of Carleton College adopted a policy sanctioning selective divestment of the school's investments in companies that fail to comply with specific guidelines for corporate behavior in South Africa. The policy, suggested by a student/faculty study group, states that the school will:

- noc invest in firms whose primary business interests are in South Africa;
- prudently sell stocks and bonds in banks that make new loans or increase existing loans to the South African government or its agencies;
- prudently sell stocks in corporations active in South Africa that supply goods and services to support that country's security forces or its apartheid apparatus (determinations of the nature of a company's involvement will be made on a case-by-case basis);

- prudently sell holdings in firms that have not adopted the Sullivan principles or a comparable code of conduct;
- urge companies to disengage from South Africa if they fail to disclose important information about their activities there. If they decline to withdraw, then the school will strongly consider selling its holdings in these firms;
- vote its proxies actively in support of its guidelines on corporate performance in South Africa; and
- establish a student/faculty/administrator/trustee committee that will oversee implementation of the policy.

Carleton sold its holdings in Wells Fargo because of that bank's policy on making loans to the South African government. (For details, see Appendix F)

CARNEGIE-MELLON UNIVERSITY: Carnegie-Mellon University has no specific guidelines for its investments in companies that do business in South Africa.

CASE WESTERN RESERVE UNIVERSITY: Case Western has no investment policy for American companies that do business in South Africa.

UNIVERSITY OF CHICAGO: The board of trustees of the University of Chicago voted in February 1978 not to sell the school's holdings in South Africa-related companies because it was "unconvinced that divestiture would in any way affect the apartheid policies of the South African government."

At that time, the trustees also established a proxy voting policy which states that the university treasurer will examine all shareholder proposals. If management's position is "instructive and responsible," the treasurer will vote the university's proxy in favor of management. Otherwise, the resolutions are submitted to the trustees' Investment Committee for approval or disapproval.

CLARK UNIVERSITY: In May 1979, the Clark board of trustees adopted a five-step policy for its investments in companies that do business in South Africa. Recommended by a committee composed of students, faculty, alumni and trustees, the policy states that the university will:

- consider shareholder resolutions on South Africa issues on a case-by-case basis;
- investigate the possibility of sponsoring such proposals;
- communicate its views to portfolio companies with South African ties;
- sell its stock in firms that are unresponsive to its concerns after all appropriate avenues of communication have been exhausted and publicize its divestment decisions.

COLBY COLLEGE: On April 14, 1978, the Colby College board of trustees adopted guidelines for its investments in companies that do business in South Africa: The policy states that the school will:

- endorse the Sullivan principles;
- seek information from portfolio corporations regarding their South African employment practices and urge them to adopt policies aimed at ending racial discrimination;
- "support and, where appropriate, initiate" shareholder petitions to implement the Sullivan principles; and

- dispose of its holdings in companies that "do not demonstrate adequate initiative" in implementing progressive policies and practices.

The board also formed a committee composed of students, faculty, administrators and alumni to advise the trustees' Investment Committee on all issues of shareholder responsibility.

COLGATE UNIVERSITY: Colgate University devised a general policy of investment responsibility in the early 1970s. In response to growing student concern over university investments in South Africa, the Colgate board of trustees in January 1979 accepted guidelines recommended by a student faculty advisory committee that specifically deal with South Africa. According to the new policy, the school will:

- neither invest in companies whose primary activities are in South Africa nor purchase debt instruments, short-term notes, or certificates of deposit in banks that make direct loans to the South African government;
- support shareholder resolutions that aim to end corporate "aid and support" of apartheid;
- sell its holdings in corporations that are "intractable and insensitive to moral considerations."

UNIVERSITY OF COLORADO: The board of regents of the University of Colorado adopted a slightly reworded version of the Sullivan principles as its shareholder responsibility policy in the spring of 1978. The policy pertains to corporate activities worldwide. The university has notified all its portfolio corporations of its policy, and a university administrator told IRRC that none has declined to subscribe to it.

The university's proxy votes are left to the discretion of its money managers.

COLUMBIA UNIVERSITY: In October 1977, the Columbia academic senate convened a committee composed of three faculty members, one student, one administrator and one alumnus to study the divestment issue. In June 1978, the investment guidelines for South Africa-related companies recommended by that committee were accepted by the board of trustees. Under the terms of its policy, the university will:

- divest itself of holdings in and withdraw deposits from banks that continue to make loans to the South African government;
- divest itself of securities in companies that "respond in a manner manifesting indifference, through act or omission, to the prevailing repressive policies in South Africa"; and
- express to portfolio companies active in South Africa Columbia's concern over the political situation in that country and its intent to consider carefully shareholder proposals that would affect corporate activities there.

In March 1979, the university announced the sale of approximately $2.7 million worth of stock in three banks because of their South African lending policies. (For details, see Appendix F)

CONNECTICUT COLLEGE: Connecticut College does not have a formal South Africa policy. The school's proxy votes are cast by the board of trustees, who receive recommendations made by a multi-constituency committee on shareholder responsibility. Each resolution is judged on a case-by-case basis.

CORNELL UNIVERSITY: In July 1978, the Cornell University board of trustees named an ad hoc committee of trustees to review the university's investment policy in companies with subsidiary operations in South Africa. The committee estimated in its report that total divestiture of Cornell's South Africa-related stock would cost the school $1 million initially and $1 million each year thereafter. The committee also pointed out that total divestiture "would leave the university without a voice to speak to corporations as a concerned shareholder." Instead of total divestiture, the committee recommended--and in December 1978 the board accepted--guidelines for selective divestment. Under the terms of the new policy, the university is to:

- establish a new committee with "broader representation of the Cornell community" to review shareholder resolutions, monitor the activities of portfolio companies in South Africa, and make recommendations to the board of trustees' Investment Committee;
- bar any trustee from voting on "an issue which directly involves his or her corporate association";
- make no investments in companies whose primary operations are in South Africa;
- solicit information from portfolio companies regarding their South African employment and business practices;
- hold no equities in banks that make or extend loans to the South African government or its agencies;
- consider selling its holdings in corporations that refuse to subscribe to a code of fair employment practices, do not act in South Africa "in a socially responsible way," and are unresponsive to university efforts to persuade them to change.

Cornell has informed each of its portfolio companies of its policy.

DARTMOUTH COLLEGE: In response to vocal student protests against Dartmouth's investments in companies active in South Africa, the board of trustees of Dartmouth College in April 1979 adjusted the duties of its six-year-old, multi-constituency Advisory Committee on Investment Responsibility. The revisions were made according to recommendations from the committee itself and empower it to:

- consider proxy votes and make recommendations to the Trustee Committee on Investment Responsibility (in "extraordinary cases," the committee may recommend that a letter explaining the college's vote be sent to the company involved); and
- recommend divestiture of stock held in companies whose "goals, purposes or methods persist in being inimical to the basic goals of the institution."

The advisory committee plans to examine the college's corporate bond holdings and its procedures for purchase of securities. The committee will also study how monitoring of corporate performance on social issues can be improved.

UNIVERSITY OF DELAWARE: In response to rising student concern over the school's South Africa-related investments, the Finance Committee of the University of Delaware board of trustees issued a position paper on the divestment issue in May 1979. The policy of the committee is to monitor the South African activities of companies and banks in which the university holds stock by using adoption of the Sullivan principles as the standard of appropriate corporate behavior in that country. The university treasurer has written to all the school's South Africa-related portfolio companies and reports that 18 have signed the Sullivan principles, and the remaining seven have equivalent policies.

DENISON UNIVERSITY: Denison University follows no formal investment guidelines for companies active in South Africa, and the university has no plans to do so. The school does engage in shareholder activism on the South Africa issue. A Denison advisory committee questioned all portfolio companies with South African ties and reported to the board of trustees that each subscribes to the Sullivan principles or a similar code.

DREW UNIVERSITY: Drew University has no South Africa-related investment policy. The Investment Committee of the board of trustees meets with a committee of students concerned about the South Africa issue before it decides how to cast the university's proxy votes.

DUKE UNIVERSITY: In February 1978, Duke's president, Terry Sanford, announced that the school would vote its proxies in favor of shareholder resolutions calling for non-expansion of investment in, and withdrawal from, South Africa. Sanford's policy statement came in response to recommendations in a report prepared by the President's Committee on the Social Implications of University Investment Policy on South Africa-related stocks. The president refused to endorse a recommendation of the committee that the school sponsor withdrawal resolutions to portfolio companies, saying that taking an activist role would be too costly for the school.

In September 1977, the Duke board of trustees wrote to portfolio corporations involved in South Africa to express its support for the Sullivan principles and to urge firms to recognize unregistered African labor unions.

EARLHAM COLLEGE: Earlham's board of trustees announced in February 1978 a special investment policy for companies doing business in South Africa. The policy calls on companies to adopt the Sullivan principles as guidelines for their South African operations and to recognize the "basic rights of freedom of association, collective bargaining and the 'lawful' withholding of labor in industrial disputes." It says that where adhering to the guidelines requires changes in existing laws and practices governing working conditions, companies should seek such modifications. The board says that it will oppose expansion of investment in South Africa if companies are unable to achieve these goals. Earlham's policy--which the board has communicated to affected portfolio companies--also requests that firms report to shareholders annually on their progress in carrying out the principles.

A committee composed of trustees, students and other members of the college community makes recommendations to the board on issues of shareholder responsibility. The committee operates by consensus, and the board usually accepts its recommendations.

EMORY UNIVERSITY: Emory University has no specific policy for its investments in firms that do business in South Africa. A university administrator told IRRC that the school "generally votes management on shareholder resolutions."

GRINNELL COLLEGE: Grinnell College votes its proxies on South Africa issues, but it has not developed a formal policy on South

Africa-related investments. In casting the college's proxy votes, the trustees consider the recommendations of a campus-wide advisory group, which uses IRRC reports and its own communications with management as the basis for its recommendations.

HAMPSHIRE COLLEGE: In the spring of 1977, the Hampshire College board of trustees established a South Africa-related investment policy which states that the school will hold no investments in companies active in South Africa. (For details, see Appendix F)

HARVARD UNIVERSITY: In late April 1978, the board of trustees of the Harvard Corp.--responding to recommendations made by an advisory committee on South Africa-related investments--announced that the university would:

- refrain from holding debt securities in banks lending to the South African government or its agencies and support shareholder resolutions calling on banks to stop lending to the public sector in South Africa;
- ask portfolio companies with subsidiaries in South Africa to follow progressive labor practices there "even where such action impinges on profitability" (the companies would be asked to implement the Sullivan principles and, in addition, to increase wages and to recognize and negotiate with African trade unions);
- support shareholder resolutions that request withdrawal from South Africa where it is clear that company activities support apartheid policies or when a company refuses to disclose information critical to an evaluation of its operations in that country; and
- support resolutions that request a halt of sales or services that have a strategic significance to the South African government.

The Harvard Advisory Committee on Shareholder Responsibility, which recommends proxy positions to the trustees, has extensively reviewed the school's portfolio holdings in South Africa-related firms. Using IRRC South Africa Review Service questionnaire responses, the committee intends to expand its monitoring efforts and will be sending "forcefully worded" requests for data to companies that have not responded to IRRC's or Harvard's inquiries.

Harvard also sold a debt instrument it held in J.P. Morgan when the bank failed to disclose information requested by the university regarding its lending activities in South Africa. A Harvard spokesman told IRRC that the university and the bank "agreed to disagree" about how much information the bank owed to its shareholders.

HAVERFORD COLLEGE: In 1972, Haverford College formed a committee on investment and social responsibility composed of alumni, students, faculty and administrators to evaluate corporate social responsibility issues. The committee operates by consensus and, unlike most such committees, actually votes the college's proxies.

During the 1978 proxy season the committee supported shareholder resolutions calling for an end to loans to the South African government, a ban on new investment in South African productive capacity, and an end to sales of strategic items to the South African government. The committee wrote frequent letters to managements, both to gain information for its votes and to explain them, and also co-sponsored a shareholder resolution asking Motorola either to stop its sales to the South African government or to withdraw from South Africa. The resolution received the support of 1.64 percent of the shares voted.

HOWARD UNIVERSITY: In March 1978, Howard University endosed the Sullivan principles and sold all its stock in companies that had not signed the principles. In November 1978, the university revised its South Africa-related investment policy to exclude all companies doing "substantial business" in South Africa from its portfolio. In compliance with the policy, the university has sold $1.8 million worth of stock in South Africa-related companies. (For details, see Appendix F)

UNIVERSITY OF IOWA: In 1977, students at the University of Iowa urged the university's board of governors to divest its holdings in seven South Africa-related corporations, to boycott the products and services of those firms, and to state its position on apartheid. After considering these proposals, the governors announced they would not divest or boycott the stocks or firms in question, but they would support "selected shareholder resolutions" pertaining to South Africa.

During the 1979 proxy season, two university administrators attended six annual meetings and delivered statements expressing the university's concern over South African labor conditions.

UNIVERSITY OF ILLINOIS: In March 1979, the board of trustees of the University of Illinois revised the South African investment policy it had established in September 1977. The new policy states that the school will:

- support shareholder petitions for the withdrawal from South Africa of a corporation that refuses to adopt or to implement effectively the Sullivan principles or that is adjudged to contribute more to the maintenance of apartheid than the welfare of non-whites; and
- divest corporate holdings in companies and banks when "persistent efforts to persuade the company to abandon unethical practices have proved ineffective."

The same policy will apply to banks doing business in South Africa. To draw attention to its policy, the school attached a copy to the proxy votes sent to corporate managements in 1979. The university will also monitor corporations' implementation of the Sullivan principles.

INDIANA UNIVERSITY: In a June 1978 statement, the board of trustees of Indiana University resolved to:

- ask all portfolio companies doing business in South Africa to affirm the Sullivan principles, the European Economic Community code of conduct, or a similar code;
- write letters and support shareholder resolutions that urge portfolio companies to take steps to improve the political, economic and social conditions of their non-white employees; and
- dispose of investments in companies that neither follow progressive employment practices nor seek to improve the status of their non-white employees, and refrain from purchasing stock in such companies until appropriate changes in their conduct take place.

One month after the university announced its policy, Indiana Attorney

General Theodore Sendak challenged the action on legal grounds. At the request of a state legislator disturbed by the policy, Sendak sent an informal written opinion to the board which stated, "trustees may not manipulate trust holdings to serve their own political ideologies or to serve any other special interest." A spokesman for the university recently told IRRC that the legal challenge has had no apparent effect on the implementation of the school's policy.

JOHNS HOPKINS UNIVERSITY: In April 1978, the board of governors of Johns Hopkins University published a policy of investment responsibility which states that while "the primary fiduciary responsibility of the university in investing and managing the university's endowment securities is to maximize the financial return on these resources...if the trustees adjudge that corporate policies or practices cause substantial social impact, they, as responsible and ethical investors, shall give independent weight to this factor in their investment policies, and in voting proxies on corporate securities." The university's treasurer, George Stewart, told IRRC that the trustees developed the policy in anticipation of student concern over the South Africa issue.

Under Hopkins's proxy voting policy, a Public Interest Investment Advisory Committee, composed of students, faculty and administrators, considers all resolutions dealing with social responsibility issues and makes voting recommendations to the board of trustees. According to Stewart, the committee has concentrated on corporate activity in South Africa for several years.

KALAMAZOO COLLEGE: After considering the recommendations of a student-faculty-administration Committee on Investment in South Africa, the board of trustees of Kalamazoo College passed a resolution in October 1978 stating that it opposed apartheid and intended to communicate that view to portfolio companies operating in South Africa and to the public at large. In February 1979 the board established an Investment Advisory Committee with student, faculty and administration representatives to advise it on all issues of corporate responsibility brought up in shareholder resolutions.

KANSAS UNIVERSITY ENDOWMENT ASSOCIATION: The policy of the Kansas University Endowment Association regarding South Africa-related investments is to allow any past, present or future donor to earmark contributions for investment in companies with no South African ties. All other investments will be made to ensure maximum stability and return.

A university official told IRRC that a campus coalition of students and faculty members has requested that the university take more comprehensive steps regarding its investments in companies active in South Africa.

KNOX COLLEGE: The trustees of Knox College established investment guidelines for firms with operations in South Africa in May 1979. The new policy supplements an existing investment responsibility policy and states that the college will:

- not purchase stock in companies that have not signed the Sullivan principles or a similar code, nor place deposits in or invest in banks that make loans to the South African public sector;
- ask corporations and banks already in the college's portfolio if

they have signed the Sullivan principles or adopted a policy of not lending to the South African government; and
- divest holdings in firms that refuse to adopt such policies or to disclose such information, or that cannot provide "convincing evidence for warranting an exception."

Banks and corporations in the college's portfolio will be expected to make regular reports on their South African operations. Evidence of inadequate progress or failure to report regularly may be considered grounds for divestment.

LAWRENCE UNIVERSITY: According to a policy statement approved by the board of trustees of Lawrence University in January 1978, the board's Investment Committee will:
- not hold securities in corporations whose activities are "unconscionable"; and
- vote the school's proxies "against any corporate activity which violates the law...or is unconscionable."

In May 1979 the Investment Committee announced to the board that it would support and encourage implementation of the Sullivan principles by its South Africa-related portfolio companies.

MACALESTER COLLEGE: In response to student concern over the South Africa issue, the Macalester College board of trustees in 1979 designated a committee composed of trustees, faculty members and students to study the school's investments in firms with South African ties.

UNIVERSITY OF MARYLAND: According to Comptroller D.A. Milway, the university's general policy on companies with South African ties is to "encourage signing and implementing the Sullivan principles, with no restrictions on investments." The board of regents of the university wrote to its 28 South Africa-related portfolio corporations to ask them about their efforts "to work toward the termination of apartheid." The regents reviewed the replies in June 1977 and have taken no further action.

UNIVERSITY OF MASSACHUSETTS: The board of regents of the University of Massachusetts voted in October 1977 to sell all the university's South Africa-related stock. The school disposed of investments worth about $631,000. The university now invests only in firms with no subsidiary operations in South Africa. (For details, see Appendix F)

MASSACHUSETTS INSTITUTE OF TECHNOLOGY: The executive committee of the MIT board of trustees considered divestiture of the school's South Africa-related holdings in the spring of 1978. The committee concluded that "divestiture would have only the most transient effect on either the South African operations of those corporations or on the state of human rights in South Africa," and instead authorized the use of MIT's shareholder rights to:
- encourage implementation of the Sullivan principles;
- call for corporate policies of non-expansion in South Africa; and
- urge that banks discontinue making loans to the South African government.

An Advisory Committee on Shareholder Responsibility composed of students, faculty and administrators is currently writing a report that will include recommendations to the board for changes in the present policy.

MIAMI UNIVERSITY (OHIO): In April 1978, the governing board of Miami University voted to sell all its stock in South Africa-related corporations and to boycott the goods and services of those firms. At that time, the university held stock in only two companies--Union Carbide and Warner-Lambert--that were active in South Africa.

Three months later, the board rescinded its divestment decision, and it has not adopted an alternative investment policy for companies doing business in South Africa since then. The decision not to divest came after the board heard an opinion prepared by a university lawyer stating that South Africa-related divestiture was probably illegal. The board had also received strong criticisms of its policy from several corporations. (For details, see Appendix F)

UNIVERSITY OF MIAMI (FLORIDA): The University of Miami has no investment policy on companies with operations in South Africa.

UNIVERSITY OF MICHIGAN: In March 1978, after considering the report and recommendations of the Senate Assembly Advisory Committee on Financial Affairs, the board of regents of the University of Michigan resolved to:

- support shareholder resolutions calling for the adoption of equal employment guidelines;
- withdraw deposits from--and discontinue purchasing short-term money market instruments in--any bank that makes loans to the South African public sector, unless the bank proves the loans are not supportive of apartheid;
- write to portfolio companies with South African ties asking them to affirm the Sullivan principles and to make regular reports to the university regarding their progress in implementing them; and
- sell its stock in any firm refusing to abide by its requests.

In compliance with its policy, the board of regents wrote to the school's 47 portfolio corporations that have South African ties and to 41 banks with which it has a depository or investment relation. At its March 1979 meeting, the board reviewed the replies it had received and voted to sell the school's holdings in Black & Decker Manufacturing. According to university investment officer Norman Herbert, the shares were sold because the company "was unwilling to comply with university requests for information regarding labor practices and the Sullivan principles." (For details, see Appendix F)

MICHIGAN STATE UNIVERSITY: The board of trustees of Michigan State University announced in March 1978 that it would begin a program of prudent divestment on Dec. 1, 1978, of stock in firms active in South Africa unless there was clear evidence that designated companies "have adopted and are implementing positive measures to withdraw" from that country.

The board also pledged in its statement to support shareholder resolutions calling for corporate withdrawal from South Africa, and to remove its deposits and refrain from investing in banks that extend credit to entities in that country.

Controversy delayed implementation of the school's policy, but in December 1978 the trustees directed the school's money managers to commence divestiture of all South Africa-related stocks. The decision affected $8.5 million worth of stock--some 45 percent of the school's

$18-million equity portfolio. The sales began in March 1979. (For details, see Appendix F)

UNDERLINED text UNIVERSITY OF MINNESOTA: Although the University of Minnesota has no formal guidelines for South Africa-related investments, it has actively encouraged corporations to adopt and implement the Sullivan principles. In 1978, the university sponsored shareholder resolutions to this effect at 11 companies. At the one company where its resolution came to a vote, management supported the resolution and it gained the support of 99.3 percent of the shares voted. Minnesota withdrew the resolution at 10 other companies after they agreed to it.

The university subsequently considered selling its South Africa-related securities. Despite student pressures, in January 1979 the board of regents defeated the divestment proposal, 4-7. The board resolved instead to "reinforce the university's position as a responsible, informed and active shareholder" and to monitor corporations' implementation of the Sullivan principles.

The school's proxy votes are cast by the board of regents, which bases its decisions upon the recommendations of an advisory committee that has faculty, student, civil service, administration and alumni representatives.

UNIVERSITY OF MISSOURI: In response to rising concern over the school's South Africa-related investments, in spring 1979 the board of governors of the University of Missouri announced that it would take "more selective positions on issues raised by shareholder resolutions." "Rather than vote affirmatively or abstain from voting on resolutions that are ambiguous or not adequately justified, efforts will be extended to gain additional information," the board stated. "If this is not possible, or the information received proves to be unsatisfactory, the particular issue in question will receive a negative vote."

MOUNT HOLYOKE COLLEGE: Mount Holyoke's investment responsibility policy dates back to May 1973 and authorizes divestiture of securities held in a company that commits "grave social injury" and is unresponsive to shareholder efforts to persuade it to change. To focus its policy on the school's portfolio companies doing business in South Africa, the Mount Holyoke board of trustees in 1978 named an advisory committee on social responsibility and asked the college treasurer to prepare a "Cost of Divestiture" study. The treasurer estimated that divestiture of all the college's South Africa-related investments would involve a one-time transaction cost of $81,625 and an investment opportunity cost of $759,720 per year. The board of trustees accepted the advisory committee's recommendations in November 1978, and resolved to:

- consider non-acceptance of the amplified Sullivan principles a form of "grave social injury";
- sponsor shareholder resolutions calling for adoption of the Sullivan principles where other sponsors are not forthcoming;
- refrain from holding investments (not including demand deposits and interbank deposits) in banks that increase their net loan commitment to the South African public sector; and
- ask the college's money manager (Scudder, Stevens & Clark) to construct a hypothetical "clean" portfolio.

In constructing a hypothetical "clean" portfolio, Scudder told Holyoke that excluding all investments in corporations doing business in South Africa from the college's portfolio would "measurably and significantly" reduce the rate of return earned by the college's endowment. However, the firm reported, if only non-signers of the Sullivan principles were excluded from the portfolio, the fund's rate of return would suffer no measurable reductions.

STATE UNIVERSITY OF NEW YORK: In December 1978, the State University of New York appointed a trustee committee to review the university's investment policy. The committee's final report, approved by the board in June 1979, states that with respect to South Africa, the school will:

- consider corporations' adherence to the Sullivan principles as a factor in its investment decisions;
- seek information on the employment policies of companies that do not adhere to the Sullivan principles;
- sell securities in companies that do not provide "satisfactory responses" to its inquiries;
- support shareholder resolutions consistent with its policy.

NORTHWESTERN UNIVERSITY: In November 1978, the board of trustees of Northwestern University adopted South Africa-related investment guidelines recommended by a special trustee committee. According to this policy, the university will:

- seek information from portfolio banks and corporations regarding their business activities in South Africa;
- dispose of its investments in companies that "support apartheid";
- arrange meetings with representatives of the executive and legislative branches of the federal government to discuss South Africa;
- sponsor a conference on corporate activity in South Africa; and
- establish a fellowship program for non-white South Africans.

UNIVERSITY OF NOTRE DAME DU LAC: In October 1978, the Notre Dame trustees enacted a policy of selective divestment under which the university would:

- dispose of holdings in banks that make or renew loans to the South African government and its agencies, or that refuse to disclose information about such practices;
- support shareholder resolutions calling for withdrawal from South Africa to companies refusing to adopt the Sullivan principles or doing "more to strengthen the apartheid regime than to contribute to the welfare of non-whites"; and
- divest South Africa-related stock when "persistent efforts to persuade the company to abandon unethical practices have proved ineffective."

To carry out this policy, the university has informed portfolio companies of its policy, supported appropriate shareholder resolutions, and requested regular reports from portfolio companies on their progress in implementing the Sullivan principles. University investment officer Rev. Richard Zang told IRRC that the responses of one-fifth of the university's South Africa-related portfolio companies to its inquiries were "unsatisfactory." The trustees are reviewing these corporations and, according to Zang, will decide whether to sell the holdings or maintain them and pressure the companies.

OBERLIN COLLEGE: In April 1978, the board of trustees of Oberlin announced that the college would use its influence as a stockholder to persuade banks and corporations--through supporting or sponsoring shareholder resolutions and communicating directly with management to request information on South African operations--to work conscientiously toward implementation of the Sullivan principles, to cease making loans to the South African government, and to withhold investment in and around the Bantustans and in Namibia. The trustees said they would consider divestment of stock in companies whose policies and practices are in conflict with Oberlin's goals regarding South Africa.

During the 1979 proxy season, Oberlin co-sponsored a shareholder resolution to General Motors and to Ford asking each to halt sales to the South African police and military. The resolutions were supported by 2.98 percent and 2.15 percent, respectively, of the shares voted.

In spring 1979, a South Africa advisory committee recommended that the college stop buying stock in companies that have not signed the Sullivan principles. Critics claimed the policy would be too restrictive and the trustees defeated the proposal, 10-11, at their meeting in June.

OHIO UNIVERSITY: In February 1978, the board of governors of Ohio University authorized the divestiture of all the university's common stock held in firms doing business in South Africa. (For details, see Appendix F)

OHIO STATE UNIVERSITY: Under the terms of a policy recommended by the Fiscal Affairs Committee and adopted by the trustees in April 1978, Ohio State University has pledged to:
- support shareholder resolutions calling for adherence to the Sullivan principles;
- "support, where possible, the reduction in the level of business activities in South Africa":
- tell its portfolio companies that Ohio State endorses the Sullivan principles and ask them to do the same; and
- divest its holdings in companies not making adequate progress in implementing the Sullivan principles.

After establishing this policy, the school sent questionnaires to 260 corporations asking them if they were involved in South Africa and requesting information on the nature of their activities in that country. All the companies, with one exception, responded satisfactorily to the school's inquiries; International Flavors & Fragrances told the university it was not company policy to disclose the sort of information requested. On the basis of that response, the university sold its shares of IFF stock. (For details, see Appendix F)

UNIVERSITY OF OREGON: In November 1977, the Oregon State Board of Higher Education voted to sell its stock in companies that do business in South Africa, Namibia and Rhodesia and have more than 50 employees or direct investment or sales in excess of $500,000 in those countries. The board's policy, however, was never implemented because James Redden, the state attorney general, ruled that the decision went beyond the legal limits of the board's authority. Students in favor of the divestiture decision have filed a suit contesting Redden's ruling. The case is slowly proceeding through the courts.

In the interim, the university follows an informal policy of not investing in companies that do substantial business in South Africa and have not signed the Sullivan principles. (For details, see Appendix F)

UNIVERSITY OF PENNSYLVANIA: In 1972, the University of Pennsylvania composed a set of guidelines for investment in publicly held companies which charged the university with the duty to act against any corporate activity that is illegal or "in the judgment of the trustees' Committee on University Responsibility, unconscionable."

The January 1979 report of the committee sets forth its current position on social responsibility issues. The committee:

- endorses the amplified Sullivan principles;
- intends to work jointly with other colleges and universities to monitor American business activities in South Africa;
- votes its proxies in favor of withdrawal and non-expansion resolutions to companies that do not adhere to the Sullivan principles; and
- sanctions divestment of holdings in companies not adhering to the Sullivan principles, as a last resort.

POMONA COLLEGE: Pomona College is the only one of the five Claremont colleges with a policy on the South Africa issue. As part of a general investment responsibility policy recommended by the Investment Committee to the board of trustees and approved by the board in November 1978, the college announced that, with respect to South Africa-related investments, it would:

- support shareholder resolutions calling for withdrawal from South Africa to companies that refuse to disclose information on their activities there and those whose policies "do more to strengthen apartheid than improve the welfare of black workers"; and
- sell its stock in a company when exercising its shareholder rights ("letters, personal contact and voting on shareholder resolutions") has proved ineffective in changing objectionable corporate behavior.

PRINCETON UNIVERSITY: In May 1978, the board of trustees of Princeton University adopted a policy statement on its role as a shareholder in companies with South African ties. In formulating the policy, the trustees studied recommendations made by the Resources Committee of the Council of the Princeton University community, an eight-member student-faculty-administration group that advises the trustees on proxy votes. The Princeton board opposes "disassociation" from any company involved in South Africa but commits the university, in its capacity as a shareholder, to:

- support the adoption and "aggressive implementation" of the Sullivan principles or similar policies in South Africa;
- urge portfolio companies to develop "independent and credible means of monitoring" corporate progress in implementing the code of fair employment;
- oppose direct bank loans to the South African government; and
- follow the lead of the State Department in developing its South Africa policy.

The trustees said they would consider selective divestment "in the context of the full range of the companies' activities" and would undertake divestiture only if they had "a strong sense of the issue at stake" and were "convinced that the university's position was clearly correct."

Student activism on the South Africa issue at Princeton has been considerable, and proponents of total divestment held frequent rallies during most of the 1978-79 school year.

PURDUE UNIVERSITY: Purdue University has no South Africa-related investment policy.

RENSSELAER POLYTECHNIC INSTITUTE: In a policy statement adopted on June 22, 1970, the board of trustees of Rensselaer Polytechnic Institute announced that while as individuals they "recognize the current national and world problems of pollution, poverty, racism and urban blight," their duty as fiduciaries requires them "to invest Rensselaer funds solely for the purpose of ensuring Rensselaer's financial well-being."

A-C Trust, Rensselaer's money manager, has written to portfolio companies doing business in South Africa to request that they endorse and implement the Sullivan principles. Arnold Cogswell of A-C Trust told IRRC that responses to its inquiries have been "mixed."

RICE UNIVERSITY: Rice University has no special policy on its South Africa-related investments.

RUTGERS UNIVERSITY: In May 1978, the board of governors of Rutgers University announced an investment policy that sanctions selective divestment of holdings in South Africa-related corporations. The Budgets and Investments Committees of the university senate drew up the guidelines adopted by the board, which stated that the university would:

- gather information on the South African activities of portfolio corporations;
- urge portfolio companies to adopt non-discriminatory employment policies equal to those in force at their U.S. facilities; and
- sell holdings in companies that do not improve inferior working conditions or that do not respond satisfactorily to the school's inquiries.

In its proxy statement, the board also asked the senate advisory committee to formulate guidelines regarding the school's deposits and investments in banks extending credit to the South African government. The committee recently completed its report, which recommends expanding the existing selective divestment provision to include banks lending to the South African public sector in which the university holds certificates of deposit, short-term loans or demand deposits.

SMITH COLLEGE: Smith College has no formal South Africa-related investment policy, and it votes its proxies on a case-by-case basis. A college administrator told IRRC that there have been several student newspaper articles and one student meeting with trustees about the issue, but that there is "no concerted action."

In October 1977, the college sold its shares in Firestone Tire and Rubber because of that company's refusal to provide the school with information it had solicited regarding Firestone's South African operations. (For details, see Appendix F)

UNIVERSITY OF SOUTHERN CALIFORNIA: The University of Southern California endorses the Sullivan principles and, according to Deputy Treasurer Peter Cheung, "is considering informing companies which operate in South Africa about its endorsement of the code."

SOUTHERN METHODIST UNIVERSITY: Southern Methodist has no

policy regarding investments in South Africa-related companies. The school's proxies are voted by its investment managers.

STANFORD UNIVERSITY: Prompted by widespread student concern over the school's investments in companies doing business in South Africa, in December 1977 the board of trustees of Stanford University adopted a special policy on investment responsibility for the university's endowment. Under the terms of the policy, the university will:

- support shareholder resolutions that seek to eliminate "substantial social injury" caused by corporate actions; and
- prudently divest its holdings in companies that are unresponsive to its shareholder efforts and have been allowed "the maximum reasonable opportunity" to change their practices.

At the same time, Stanford formed a Commission on Investment Responsibility composed of students, faculty, staff and alumni to recommend positions on shareholder resolutions to the trustees. In April 1978, the commission decided to follow a set of proxy voting guidelines formulated a month earlier by the Teachers Insurance and Annuity Association/College Retirement Equities Fund (TIAA/CREF), which call for support of resolutions asking companies active in South Africa to:

- take steps to reduce and eliminate discrimination in the workplace as well as economic and social inequalities that stem from such discrimination;
- develop "mechanisms that promote communications between employees and corporate management" for all workers regardless of race;
- provide adequate information to interested parties that will permit evaluation of corporate accomplishments and "future ability to meet the responsibilities associated with the conduct of business in South Africa";
- refrain from expanding their operations or making additional investment in that country; and
- place a moratorium on the scope of loans to the South African private sector and extend no further loans--or renew extant ones--to that country's private sector.

Only the advisory commission is constrained by the TIAA/CREF guidelines; the board of trustees votes the school's proxies on a case-by-case basis.

SWARTHMORE COLLEGE: In December 1978, the trustees of Swarthmore College adopted the recommendations of an advisory committee on the college's South Africa-related portfolio corporations. The policy states that the college will:

- refrain from investing in South African corporations;
- continue to hold investments in U.S. companies with South African operations, while monitoring their progress in fulfilling the Sullivan principles; and
- selectively divest holdings in corporations whose implementation of the Sullivan principles appears to be inadequate.

UNIVERSITY OF TEXAS: The University of Texas, which has the third largest endowment of the nation's educational institutions, uses only fiduciary criteria to make its investment decisions. Students have openly questioned the university's investment policy "for a couple of years," according to a university investment officer. He added that "the board of regents has discussed the South Africa issue and has tentative plans to study it further."

TRINITY COLLEGE (Hartford, Conn.): Trinity College has a general policy of ethical investment. If a corporation's activities are at odds with the ethical and social policies of the college, the school "may attempt to change the firm's practices by exercising its prerogatives as an investor, including communications with management, voting or withholding proxies, enlisting the support of other investors, or disposing of the investment.

In regard to corporations with South African ties, the college's Finance Committee voted in June 1978 that the Sullivan principles were a reasonable measure of responsible corporate conduct in South Africa and that it was appropriate for the school to encourage their adoption. Since then, the college has written to all its portfolio companies with operations in South Africa asking whether they have subscribed to the Sullivan principles or a similar code.

TUFTS UNIVERSITY: In May 1979, Tufts University trustees adopted a policy of selective divestment of stock in companies that were not carrying out the Sullivan principles or that made loans to the South African government. In formulating the new policy, the school's trustees rejected the call for total divestment made by the student and faculty Advisory Committee on University Investment in January 1979.

Under the terms of the new policy, the university will:

● sell stock in companies that do not make sufficient progress in carrying out the Sullivan principles;

● sell stock in banks that continue to lend to the South African government or its agencies; and

● refrain from purchasing stock in companies that do not endorse and implement the Sullivan principles and in those that sell products to the government of South Africa "for the direct support and maintenance of apartheid."

To carry out its policy, the school has requested information from its portfolio companies with South African operations about their activities in that country. Robin Dushman of the treasurer's office told IRRC that the poor response of one unidentified company that had not signed the Sullivan principles prompted the school to sell its stock in that company. (For details on this and an earlier South Africa-related divestiture, see Appendix F)

TUSKEGEE INSTITUTE: Tuskegee Institute has no formal South Africa-related investment policy. It has, however, endorsed the Sullivan principles. An institute administrator told IRRC that its investment managers have been instructed "to the greatest extent possible to avoid companies that have not signed the Sullivan principles."

UNIVERSITY OF UTAH: The Institutional Council of the University of Utah reaffirmed the university's support for basic human rights and progressive employment practices in an October 1978 trustee resolution. In the statement, the trustees instructed the university's money managers to:

● tell all portfolio companies that the university endorses affirmative employment practices; and

- review shareholder resolutions and refer to the university's president and board of governors "any such resolution bearing upon corporate policies or practices affecting basic human rights in South Africa or elsewhere."

VANDERBILT UNIVERSITY: Vanderbilt University does not follow a special policy for its South Africa-related investments. Outside money managers invest half of the school's portfolio and vote the proxies relating to those holdings; the investment committee of the board of trustees administers the remainder of the portfolio. The investment committee considers shareholder resolutions arising from the portion of the portfolio it directs on a case-by-case basis and, according to a university administrator, "more often than not, sends letters to management that explain its vote."

VASSAR COLLEGE: The trustees of Vassar College in October 1978 adopted a policy of "highly selective divestment after careful study and interaction with companies active in South Africa." Their decision was based largely on the report and recommendations of a student-faculty South African study group. The policy commits the college to:

- establish a student-faculty-administrator-alumni committee on investment responsibility to make recommendations for administration of the policy;
- urge all corporations that do business in South Africa in which the college holds stocks or bonds to adopt and implement the amplified Sullivan principles;
- monitor corporations' implementation of the fair employment code on a periodic basis;
- engage in shareholder activism, without ruling out selective divestiture;
- sell holdings in banks that lend to the South African government.

The trustees also instructed the Investment and Finance Committee to sell debt securities the college held in five banks that made direct loans to the South African government and its parastatal corporations. (For details, see Appendix F)

UNIVERSITY OF VERMONT: In November 1978, the student association of the University of Vermont presented a resolution to the university's board of trustees urging the sale of the university's holdings in eight companies doing business in South Africa. Instead, the board set up an an hoc committee of students, faculty, administrators and trustees "to study the moral and ethical issues raised by university investment and policies." The trustees affirmed the final recommendations of the committee in February 1979.

As a general policy of ethical investing, the university will "seek first to exercise the rights of shareholders and only as a final step to undertake the divesting of securities." With regard to South Africa, the university will:

- support shareholder resolutions "deemed able to influence racial policies in South Africa"; and
- divest its holdings in any company if that company is not responsive to the university's "shareholder and other actions."

The policy also calls on the board to consider alternative investments, particularly those within the state of Vermont that are "socially beneficial." A University Investment Advisory Council consisting of students, faculty, staff and trustees will advise the trustees on social responsibility issues.

WABASH COLLEGE: Wabash College lists "favorable records of recognizing and meeting community and social responsibilities" as one of seven guidelines it follows in purchasing securities. The school has communicated with portfolio companies, and according to college treasurer Daniel F. Evans, "most have endorsed the Sullivan principles, although the investment policy does not specifically require this." Evans also told IRRC that a "small on-campus study group favors divestment" of the school's South Africa-related holdings.

WASHINGTON UNIVERSITY: Washington University's investment policy was drawn up according to a Missouri law entitled the Uniform Management of Institutional Funds Act, which lists only fiduciary criteria for investment.

In January 1979, the board of trustees supplemented its investment policy with a so-called "blind trust" proxy voting procedure. The policy delegates the responsibility of analyzing and voting the school's proxies to its investment advisers and requires them to make annual reports describing each vote and its rationale. Students, faculty and others can express their opinions on proxy issues to investment officers via the university treasurer or vice chancellor of financial affairs.

UNIVERSITY OF WASHINGTON: In an April 1978 resolution, the board of regents of the University of Washington declared "that all U.S. companies which do business in South Africa should adopt the Sullivan statement or a similar statement of principles" as a "standard of responsibility in their operations in South Africa commensurate with the principles of human rights and values followed in university practices." After the announcement of the policy, the regents' Finance and Facilities Committee sent letters to portfolio companies with South African operations which stated the university's commitment to the Sullivan principles and asked for a similar endorsement by the companies. The board found the response of one corporation, Dresser Industries, unsatisfactory and in November 1978 voted to sell the university's stock in that company. (For details, see Appendix F)

WELLESLEY COLLEGE: In March 1978, the governing board of Wellesley College accepted the investment guidelines for South Africa-related stocks proposed by a trustee Investment Subcommittee on Social Responsibility. Under the terms of its policy, Wellesley will:

- continue to consider shareholder proposals that seek to modify corporate behavior in South Africa on a case-by-case basis;
- intensify its efforts to communicate its views on South Africa--both orally and through correspondence--to the managements of portfolio companies;
- reaffirm its present policy of not investing in companies whose principal activities are based in or derived from South Africa; and
- consider the sale of stock in any company that fails to adopt and carry out the Sullivan principles or a comparable program, or that has been unresponsive to the school's request for information on its South African operations.

Wellesley also held two forums where college and university officials discussed college investment policies and American corporate involvement in South Africa. In September 1978, College President Barbara Newell wrote to President Carter to urge his support for a more activist U.S. policy toward South Africa.

WESLEYAN UNIVERSITY: In October 1978, the board of governors of Wesleyan University mandated an extensive, case-by-case review of the university's South Africa-related portfolio companies. Basing their action on the recommendations of a Committee to Investigate Investment Policy composed of students, faculty, administrators and trustees, the board called upon companies with South African operations to prove that their activities in that country did not support apartheid. The board cited these possible justifications for a company's continued presence in South Africa:

- implementation of the expanded Sullivan principles;
- contributions to black employment;
- lack of strategic value of its products or services to the South African government;
- active opposition to discriminatory laws; and
- the likelihood that a foreign buyer would take over the company's operations if it withdrew.

According to the policy, corporations failing to prove the utility of remaining in South Africa will be urged to withdraw from that country, and other companies may be encouraged to adopt policies of non-expansion or to curtail sales to the South African government. To accomplish this, the university may sponsor and support shareholder resolutions, communicate with management, participate in annual meetings, issue public statements, and, if these measures fail, selectively divest its South Africa-related holdings.

Bank activities in South Africa will be evaluated on the same basis, and the university will not make deposits in banks that lend to the South African government or its parastatal corporations.

The task force established to oversee the implementation of the school's policy made a recommendation to the trustees that the school divest its holdings in Standard Oil of California and sponsor a shareholder resolution to Mobil in 1980 requesting that Mobil withdraw from South Africa. The board agreed to propose a shareholder resolution to Mobil but in the form of a request for non-expansion rather than withdrawal, and it instructed the board's social implications committee to continue communications with SoCal.

WILLIAMS COLLEGE: In August 1978, the board of trustees of Williams College issued a statement on the school's holdings in firms active in South Africa. The trustees said they would:

- use their power as shareholders to urge portfolio companies with operations in South Africa to adhere to the Sullivan principles and support efforts to promote trade unions and collective bargaining for workers of all races in that country;
- encourage companies to supply fuller reports on their activities in South Africa;
- ask that banks extend no further credit to the South African government or its agencies "unless such loans would provide significant improvement in conditions for the non-white majority"; and

- consider selling stock in firms that display "intransigent refusal" to contribute to the social and economic well-being of their employees.

An Advisory Committee on Shareholder Responsibility oversees the school's implementation of its policy and advises the trustees on proxy issues.

THE UNIVERSITY OF WISCONSIN: The board of regents of the University of Wisconsin voted in February 1978 to sell all the university's South Africa-related stock purchased after the enactment of a 1973 state law that prohibits the university from holding investments in companies "which practice or condone through their actions discrimination on the basis of race, religion, color, creed or sex." The regents' decision affected stocks and bonds held in more than 24 companies worth approximately $10.2 million. (For details, see Appendix F)

YALE UNIVERSITY: In June 1978, the governing board of Yale University announced a policy of selective divestment which commits the university to:

- support shareholder efforts to liberalize the South African labor practices of portfolio companies involved in that country, using the Sullivan principles as the basis for its policy;
- vote its proxies in favor of "properly drawn" shareholder proposals calling upon firms to comply with the principles;
- collect information from outside sources on the actual performance of portfolio companies in South Africa; and
- strongly consider selling its stock in firms that refuse to commit themselves to the Sullivan guidelines or have failed to implement them in a satisfactory manner.

Yale uses the same procedure to discourage both bank loans to the South African government and corporate activities whose strategic value to the South African government outweighs the relative benefits the company may provide for its non-white employees.

Since the adoption of the policy, the university has asked its portfolio companies about their business and employment practices in South Africa. After extensive discussions with Morgan Guaranty Trust, the Advisory Committee on Investment Responsibility recommended that Yale sell its Morgan stock because the bank refused to categorically deny all requests for loans by the South African government. The Yale Corp. accepted the committee's recommendation. The university has begun divestiture of the $1.7 million of Morgan stock it owns and will make no further investments in Morgan. (For details, see Appendix F)

APPENDIX F

SALES OF STOCK BY COLLEGES AND UNIVERSITIES

Following is a rundown of actions by colleges or universities that have decided to sell stock in corporations active in South Africa.

ANTIOCH UNIVERSITY: The board of trustees of Antioch University voted in May 1978 to dispose of all its South Africa-related investments. At that time, the school held stock in four companies active in South Africa. The market value of the shares was not made public, but Edward Richards, chairman of the trustees' Finance Committee, told IRRC that it was somewhere in "the significant six-figure range." The decision to divest was made in accordance with 1963 guidelines that require the board to consider social and moral issues in its financial affairs.

AMHERST COLLEGE: In November 1977, one month after the Amherst board of trustees announced its selective divestment policy, Treasurer Kurt Hertzfeld wrote to all the companies in Amherst's portfolio with operations in South Africa and requested information about their activities in that country. In March 1978, the college sold some 50,000 shares of Blue Bell, a clothing manufacturer, after the company failed to provide a "positive response" to Amherst's inquiry about the work conditions of its black employees, according to Hertzfeld. With the exception of Blue Bell's reply, the board was satisfied with the responses and has not sold any other South Africa-related stock. Hertzfeld told IRRC that the funds released by the sale of the Blue Bell stock--approximately $1 million--were reinvested in short-term cash equivalents.

BOSTON UNIVERSITY: Boston University is disposing of all its South Africa-related bonds and non-voting stock and withdrawing deposits from banks that lend to the South African government. The gradual $6.6-million divestiture was announced in April 1979.

According to Boston University's policy, holding non-voting stock in companies active in South Africa places the school "in the position of benefiting financially in these cases from companies doing business in South Africa without the offsetting advantages of voting stock." Bayley Mason, special assistant to the president of Boston University, told IRRC that sale of non-voting stock was "a logical prerequisite to defending our voting holdings." He added, "we don't anticipate any loss" from the sale of the securities.

BRANDEIS UNIVERSITY: In June 1978, the governing board of Brandeis University authorized the sale of a $50,000 fixed income instrument held in Crocker National Bank after the bank displayed "a lack of responsiveness" to the school's inquiries about its lending policies to South Africa, according to a university official. The sale was made in compliance with an investment policy established in December 1977 that called for selective divestment of holdings in firms that refuse to disclose adequate information about their South African operations.

More recently, Brandeis sold a $350,000 Ford Motor Co. bond. The school sold the bond as the first step in carrying out the investment policy announced in April 1979 which states that the university must sell its holdings in a company that causes "severe social injury" in South Africa if the school owns no voting shares in the company. University Treasurer

Lester Loomis told IRRC that Ford's truck sales to the South African police and military fell within the board's definition of "severe social injury." The sale did not entail any financial loss for the university, according to Loomis.

CARLETON COLLEGE: Carleton College sold 9,000 shares of Wells Fargo stock worth approximately $285,000 and a $10,000 Wells Fargo bond in June 1979 because of that bank's policy on making loans to the South African government. The decision came after several rounds of correspondence with Wells Fargo and is in compliance with an October 1978 policy that authorizes the prudent divestiture of holdings in banks that engage in such lending.

The Carleton policy also calls for prudent divestiture of stock in corporations active in South Africa that do not adopt the Sullivan principles or a similar code. The school is now reviewing its holdings in companies that operate in South Africa but have not signed the Sullivan principles.

COLUMBIA UNIVERSITY: Columbia University announced in March 1979 that it sold some $2.7 million worth of stock in three banks because of their positions on making loans to the South African government. The banking corporations were Detroit Bank Corp., Manufacturers National Bank of Detroit and Rainier Bancorporation of Seattle. According to the school, the sale was made without financial loss and the funds have been reinvested in other banking institutions.

The divestment was carried out in compliance with Columbia's policy on holding stocks in banks and companies doing business in South Africa. Under that policy, the school will sell its investments and withdraw deposits in banks "which provide new or continuing access to capital markets for the government of South Africa and which do not announce their intention to cease such activities." According to William J. McGill, Columbia's president, the decision to sell stock in the two Detroit banks was made after each had declined for policy reasons to disclose whether it had extended credit to South Africa and if it had plans for future loans. McGill said that the sale of Rainier stock was prompted by the bank's decision to continue to make loans to the South African government.

HAMPSHIRE COLLEGE: In the spring of 1977, Hampshire's board of trustees voted to sell all of the school's common stock--valued at approximately $200,000--until the school could devise an investment policy that incorporated appropriate guidelines on social responsibility. This action followed student protests against Hampshire's holding of $39,000 worth of stock in four companies with subsidiary operations in South Africa. The money raised from the liquidation of the school's portfolio was invested in firms with no South African commercial ties.

However, in August 1978 the college's money managers bought three issues of stock in companies with South African ties. Once college officials realized the new purchases were South Africa-related, they requested and received information on the three companies' operations there. In March 1979 the Finance Committee of the board voted to instruct the college's money managers to dispose of all holdings in South Africa-related corporations and to avoid all such securities in the future.

HOWARD UNIVERSITY: Howard University's first South Africa-related investment policy was established in March 1978 and excluded from the school's portfolio all companies that had not signed the

Sullivan principles. However, "using the Sullivan principles as a standard just didn't work over here," said Caspa Harris, university treasurer. "Practically speaking, we couldn't know who abided by the principles and who didn't." In November 1978 the university changed its policy so that it no longer holds stock in any companies doing "substantial business" in South Africa. Since that time, the university has sold about $1.8 million of South Africa-related securities (about 13 percent of its $19-million endowment) and has not incurred a financial loss from the sales.

UNIVERSITY OF MASSACHUSETTS: The board of regents of the University of Massachusetts--in response to increasing student and faculty concern--decided in October 1977 to sell all of the school's South Africa-related holdings. The divestment decision affected some $631,000 worth of stock in 21 companies, representing approximately half of the school's equity portfolio. Robert Brand, the university's treasurer, told IRRC that all of the affected stock was sold within 90 days of the board's decision, as specified in its divestment resolution. He estimated that the school suffered a total net loss of $90,000 after all transactions were completed. Funds from the sale of South Africa-related securities were reinvested in firms with high growth potential that are not doing business in South Africa, according to Brand.

MIAMI UNIVERSITY: In April 1978, the governing board of Miami University in Ohio adopted a resolution calling for the sale of all stock owned by the school in companies active in South Africa and asking the school to cease doing business with these firms. At the time, Miami's portfolio contained investments in two companies--Union Carbide and Warner-Lambert--identified as having South African operations. These investments had a combined value of approximately $160,000, representing about 3 percent of the university's $5.5-million endowment fund.

The board rescinded its divestment decision in June 1978 after hearing a report from a special committee established to examine the financial and legal ramifications of such action. In a legal opinion prepared by James Irwin, a lawyer assigned by the Ohio attorney general's office to be the school's special counsel on the matter, the trustees were advised that their decision to sell South Africa-related stocks on ideological grounds would probably violate state statutes on prudent investment of public funds. Irwin also said it was probably illegal under Ohio law for the school to discriminate against certain firms in its business dealings.

A Miami official told IRRC that, following the board's original decision to divest, the school had heard from several companies that were strongly critical of the trustees' action. The firms, he said, had hinted that Miami might be excluded from their recruitment programs and that grants and gifts might be withheld to express disapproval of the school's investment policy. The official said that the companies' responses--as well as general community reaction to the trustees' original resolution--were important considerations in the board's decision to drop its divestment plans. The board has not adopted an alternative policy for Miami's South Africa-related holdings.

UNIVERSITY OF MICHIGAN: In March 1979, the board of regents of the University of Michigan voted to sell its stock in Black & Decker after the company refused to supply certain information regarding its operations in South Africa. The decision follows guidelines established in March 1978 that call for divestment of "stock in any firm that fails to...abide by the school's bank policy (no new loans to the South African government except where detrimental to apartheid) or adhere satisfactorily to the Sullivan principles."

The regents' vote was cast after review of the university's correspondence with the 47 corporations doing business in South Africa in which it holds stock. As in all its letters to portfolio companies, the university asked Black & Decker to "(1) affirm the Sullivan principles, (2) endorse political, economic and social rights for all its employees in South Africa, and (3) make regular reports to publicly disclose corporate progress in these matters."

Black & Decker officials responded that "Our company does not subscribe to the Sullivan code and does not report to Dr. Sullivan's organization as we do not believe that the company's policies should be dictated by, nor the company report to, any special interest group, regardless of the merit of the group's objectives....It is company policy to be governed by the 'Golden Rule' and we insist on treating our employees fairly....We have been, are, and will be doing the best we can to improve the lot of our employees in all countries where we have operations without interfering in the internal social and political affairs of the host countries."

On the basis of that response, the regents decided to sell the university's 14,613 shares of Black & Decker stock. University investment officer Norman Herbert reports that the university will not incur any financial loss from the sale.

MICHIGAN STATE UNIVERSITY: The board of trustees of Michigan State University voted in March 1978 to sell all South Africa-related holdings unless designated companies "have adopted and are implementing positive measures to withdraw" from that country.

Divestiture was scheduled to begin on Dec. 1, 1978, but was delayed by controversy over the board's decision. In August 1978, university general counsel Leland W. Carr Jr. submitted a written opinion to the trustees which warned that they might encounter significant legal difficulties if they enforced the special policy on South Africa-related investments. He recommended they seek further advice on the financial feasibility of their policy from outside investment counselors.

In October, the trustees asked the university's money manager, Scudder, Stevens & Clark, whether it would be possible to manage the university's portfolio prudently under the terms of the new policy. The firm told the school in early December that it could probably reinvest the portfolio in stocks of comparable quality, but the same return on investment could not be guaranteed. The board then reaffirmed the policy it had announced in March.

Meanwhile, MSU had informed its portfolio companies with South African ties of its policy, and no company said it would withdraw from that country. Therefore, on Dec. 8, 1978, the university trustees resolved to commence prudent, total divestiture of the approximately $8.5 million worth of stock the university held in firms doing business in South Africa.

According to a divestment procedure agreed upon in March 1979, Scudder, Stevens & Clark is to sell the equities in three blocks. The firm is to dispose of the poorest performers among the affected stocks first, the average performers second, and the best performers last.

A university official told IRRC in fall 1979 that Scudder had already sold the first two blocks of stock and that only the "big winners"--three companies out of the original 13 in the Michigan State portfolio that were South Africa-related--remained to be sold. He said the university experienced a net loss on the sale of the first block, and a "modest" net gain on the sale of the second, so that "the school is almost breaking even so far." The official commented that the net loss was attributable more to holding the poor performers to begin with than to the divestment decision. "Whether our South Africa investment policy is costing us money will only become apparent when we see how the alternative investments perform," he concluded.

OHIO UNIVERSITY: In February 1978, the board of trustees of Ohio University in Athens, Ohio, voted to sell all of the university's common stock in firms doing business in South Africa. The sales took place gradually in order to minimize the financial impact of the transactions on the school. William Kennard, the university's treasurer, told IRRC that the board's decision affected holdings in four firms--Mobil, International Telephone and Telegraph, TRW, and Monsanto--with an estimated combined market value of about $38,000. The stocks accounted for approximately 1.3 percent of the university's $3-million endowment fund.

The funds freed by the sales have been invested in companies that have no direct commercial connections with South Africa, according to Kennard.

OHIO STATE UNIVERSITY: In November 1978, Ohio State University sold some 10,000 shares of stock in International Flavors & Fragrances after the company failed to respond to an inquiry by the school about its activities in South Africa. The shares had an estimated market value of $250,000.

The sale was made in accordance with a policy on South Africa-related investments adopted in April 1979 by the school's board of trustees, committing it to sell its holdings in firms that fail to demonstrate adequate progress in carrying out the Sullivan principles. At that time, Ohio State sent questionnaires to all of its portfolio companies to determine if they had business operations in South Africa and--if they were involved in that country--to determine the extent of their activities and their progress in upgrading employment practices for blacks there. A university spokesman told IRRC that follow-up letters and phone calls were made to companies that failed to respond to the school's questionnaire. In the case of International Flavors & Fragrances, he said that Ohio State had attempted to communicate with the company several times on its South African activities but had not received a substantive answer. He said the firm finally told the school that it is not its policy to disclose this sort of information and that that response prompted Ohio State's decision to divest.

Follow-up communication with other companies that had not responded to the school's original inquiry has resulted in satisfactory assurances from the firms that they are in active compliance with the Sullivan principles, the official told IRRC.

UNIVERSITY OF OREGON: Under strong student pressure, the Oregon State Board of Higher Education voted at its November 1977 meeting to sell its stock in 27 companies doing business in southern Africa. The securities had a total estimated market value of $6 million.

The decision applied to any firm operating in South Africa, Namibia and Rhodesia that has more than 50 employees or that has direct investment or sales in excess of $500,000 in those countries.

Following the board's action, however, the state's attorney general, James A. Redden, ruled that only the Oregon Investment Council, an agency charged with overseeing most of the state's investment accounts--including that of the Board of Higher Education--could authorize divestment. At most, Redden said, the board could recommend action to the Investment Council but it had no power to issue investment commands. In his written opinion on the divestment issue, he said political and moral considerations could play only a limited role in state investment decisions. "It is inappropriate and irrelevant for the investment managers to consider any factors other than the probable safety of, and the probable income from, the investments as required by the statutes (on prudent investing). Only if the investment managers determined that political factors affected either the safety of or return on investments could those factors be considered in making investment decisions," Redden wrote.

In November 1978, the Associated Students of Oregon filed suit contesting Redden's ruling. The case, Associated Students et al. v. Hunt et al., will be concerned with (1) whether the "prudent man" rule prohibits trustees from using other than fiduciary criteria when they make investment decisions; (2) whether the State Board of Education can issue policy directives to the university system's money managers; and (3) whether it is permissible for state agencies to make investment decisions with foreign policy implications.

Redden's legal opinion and the pending court challenge to it have not completely derailed the regents' March 1977 decision. University Chancellor of Administration Freeman Holmer told IRRC that the suit had had "little influence" on the school's investment practices. "Our investment managers are aware of the regents' divestment decision and the discussion surrounding it," said Holmer. "They decided it was prudent to avoid stocks in companies doing substantial business in South Africa that do not subscribe to the Sullivan principles."

SMITH COLLEGE: In October 1977, Smith sold 42,014 shares of stock it held in Firestone Tire & Rubber after the college decided that Firestone had not been sufficiently responsive to questions by the Smith board of trustees about the company's activities in South Africa. The shares had a market value of $687,728.

The previous May, about 600 Smith students, as well as a number of staff and faculty members, had petitioned the board to sponsor and support shareholder resolutions at companies in which it owns stock that have South African subsidiaries, asking the firms to withdraw their operations from that country. If the resolutions failed, the petition said, the college should sell its holdings in those companies, which were identified as Caterpillar Tractor, General Motors, International Business Machines and Firestone.

The trustees did not agree to initiate shareholder resolutions, but they did write to the chairmen of the four companies asking questions about South Africa activities and communicating their strong support for the Sullivan principles. According to Roger Murray, then chairman of Smith's Investment Committee, the trustees received satisfactory responses from IBM, Caterpillar and General Motors, but "in the case of Firestone, the location of a new plant next to reserved living spaces, which had been a particular concern of Smith students, was not covered in the response." Subsequently, "although we directed additional questions to Firestone about the plant location, we did not receive from them the information we needed to evaluate the matter," he said. As a result, the shares were sold.

TUFTS UNIVERSITY: In October 1977, Tufts sold 11,000 shares of Citicorp because its bank subsidiary, Citibank, had made direct loans to the South African government after the Soweto riots in 1976. The sale--made public in February 1978--was "in accordance with university policy that forbids investment in a corporation if their normal practices are discriminatory," according to Tufts' president Jean Mayer. The university's treasurer, C. Russell de Burlo, said that the school's investment policy was not the only factor in the decision to sell, and cited the declining value of Citicorp's stock as another major consideration.

In line with its revised investment policy calling for divestiture of stock in companies not adhering to the Sullivan principles, Tufts has disposed of its stock in a non-signatory company that did not adequately respond to the school's requests for information on the firm's South African operations. The Treasurer's office representative, Robin Dushman, would not identify the company involved, saying "we're not making a big thing of this."

VASSAR COLLEGE: At the same time the governing board of Vassar College enacted a policy of selective divestiture of South Africa-related holdings, it announced the sale of approximately $4.2 million worth of bonds it held in five banks that made direct loans to the South African government and its agencies. The bonds were held in Bank of America, Manufacturers Hanover Trust, First National Bank of Chicago, Irving Trust, and the Export-Import Bank. The sale was made in accordance with Vassar's policy requiring the sale of holdings in banks that lend to the South African public sector.

UNIVERSITY OF WASHINGTON: In November 1978, the board of regents of the University of Washington voted to sell the university's holdings in Dresser Industries, an energy technology corporation that does business in South Africa. The decision was made in accordance with a resolution passed in April 1978 that calls for corporate adherence to the Sullivan principles.

After passing the resolution, the university sent letters to its South Africa-related portfolio companies requesting that they adopt the Sullivan principles. Almost all the companies responded affirmatively. Dresser Industries, however, responded that: "Since we operate in over 100 countries, we do not adopt statements of principle for each country. Our worldwide policy, which applies in each country in which we operate, is to be a good corporate citizen and to operate under the laws and customs of each host country. This, in our view, is the only way we can continue to do business throughout the world." (According to University of Washington's assistant vice president for finance, W.C. Adkisson, the letter went on to indicate that Dresser "is pursuing job training programs to improve South African blacks' capabilities to improve their conditions, though the number of blacks affected by these programs was not supplied.")

"The board of regents felt the situation in South Africa was special enough to warrant a separate statement to govern corporate activities in South Africa," Adkisson told IRRC. "Dresser's lack of a special statement of policy or interest in developing one doesn't conform to our resolution. We felt we were keeping faith with our constituencies by divesting."

Adkisson reported that the university's Dresser holdings, valued at $148,686 when purchased, were sold at a slight profit; the university received $153,615 after transaction costs for their sale.

UNIVERSITY OF WISCONSIN: In accordance with a 1973 Wisconsin law that prohibits the state university from holding investments in companies "which practice or condone through their actions discrimination on the basis of race, religion, color, creed or sex," the board of regents of the University of Wisconsin voted in February 1978 to sell all of the school's South Africa-related holdings purchased after the law's enactment. The school has since divested its $30-million endowment fund of $10.2 million worth of stocks and bonds in more than 24 companies that do business in South Africa.

The board's decision to divest climaxed a prolonged legal controversy that had started in May 1977 when the state attorney general, Bronson LaFollette, informally advised the regents in a letter to sell the university's securities in firms doing business in South Africa. The attorney general's recommendation to divest was based on the state law prohibiting the university from knowingly investing grant money and gifts in companies that practice discrimination. The letter to the board was prompted by growing student concern over the University of Wisconsin's stock holdings in companies operating in South Africa.

In the summer of 1977, the board solicited another interpretation of the statute from a law professor at the university. The new opinion questioned the constitutionality of the law, stating that the discriminatory clause was "invalid if read literally so as to improperly interfere with commerce and international trade" and that matters involving overseas investments were beyond the jurisdiction of the state attorney general.

With both legal opinions in mind, the board voted in October 1977 to sell all stock in those companies doing significant business in South Africa that had not yet adopted the Sullivan principles. The regents defined "significant business" as having more than 250 employees in a company's South African operations. Under this policy, the university sold its stock in one company--Dresser Industries--according to Charles Stathas, the university's legal counsel.

In January 1978, however, the state attorney general reaffirmed his position, calling for comprehensive divestment of all South Africa-related securities in a lengthy legal brief to the president of the University of Wisconsin system. In the brief, LaFollette stated that the "no discrimination" standard is the "emphatic embodiment of the public policy of the State of Wisconsin against unlawful discrimination" and urged the board of regents to "leave the ultimate determination of the constitutionality of the 'no discrimination' clause to the courts." Not wanting to become involved in a protracted court battle, the regents elected to comply with the law and sell their holdings in companies that violated it.

YALE UNIVERSITY: Yale University decided to sell $1.7 million worth of J.P. Morgan & Co. stock in May 1979. At the same time Yale terminated a short-term lending agreement with the bank and announced it would not make any further investments in Morgan.

Yale's decision was made in accordance with its South African investment policy, which calls for divestment of stock in banks that lend to the South African government. Yale's Advisory Committee on Investor Responsibility, which recommended the sale, concluded: "Yale holds that a line ought to be drawn at loans to the South African government, even if a particular loan could be said to be of direct benefit to the blacks...." David K. Storrs, Yale's director of investments, told IRRC that loans support the South African government by providing it with capital. Even if the capital is used for the benefit of blacks, he said, a loan frees an equivalent amount of capital that the government can use for repressive purposes.

The Yale Advisory Committee described Morgan's lending policy as one that "considers all factors it regards as relevant to a loan's prudence but does not categorically exclude the possibility of making loans directly to the South African government or its instrumentalities." Calling this a policy "that honorable and morally concerned persons could reasonably have arrived at," the committee nonetheless recommended divestment. Although "divestiture is of little practical consequence and hence is almost entirely symbolic," the committee wrote, "symbols and gestures are important in the realm of moral and humane concerns, and are to be taken seriously."

APPENDIX G

U.S. AND BRITISH EXPORTS TO SOUTH AFRICA OF SELECTED MANUFACTURED GOODS AS A PERCENTAGE OF TOTAL U.S. AND BRITISH EXPORTS OF THOSE GOODS - 1974

Item	U.S. Exports Percentage	Rank*	British Exports Percentage	Rank*
Chemicals				
Organic chemicals	2	14	2	12
Other inorganic chemicals	3	10	8	1
Plastic, etc., materials	2	9	8	3
Chemicals, n.e.s.**	3	9	3	7
Basic manufactures				
Paper and paperboard	4	8	7	3
Woven textiles non-cotton	6	3	3	13
Iron, steel, univ. plate, sheet	4	4	1	17
Tools	3	8	6	4
Machines, transport equipment				
Power machinery, non-electrical	2	13	2	8
Agricultural machinery	2	4	7	1
Office machinery	1	15	2	13
Metalworking machinery	3	7	9	2
Electrical power machinery, switchgear	2	9	8	1
Electrical distributing machinery	1	13	5	3
Telecommunications equipment	1	13	6	1
Electrical machinery n.e.s.	1	15	4	6
Road motor vehicles	1	9	6	2
Aircraft	1	7	1	12
Miscellaneous manufactured goods				
Clothing not of fur	1	11	1	17
Instruments, apparatus	1	13	3	8

* South Africa's ranking among all other major country markets for each commodity group.

** Not elsewhere specified.

Credit: Lawrence G. Franko, Javier Ergueta, Carnegie Endowment for International Peace, "South Africa, The European Connection," April 1978.

APPENDIX H

SUPPORT LEVELS FOR SELECTED SOUTH AFRICA RESOLUTIONS

1977-1978-1979

The following chart shows the average level of support for South Africa resolutions during the last three years. The first part refers to all shareholders, the second part to the 78 institutional investors responding to IRRC's annual How Institutions Voted survey.

All Shareholders

	1977	1978	1979
Bank Loans			
a. all resolutions	2.3	5.7	5.7
b. stop loans	2.3	6.2	7.9
c. loan reports		5.4	3.4
Nonexpansion	3.5	5.4	5.0
Sales policies		4.6	2.9
Withdrawal	2.4	2.8	2.8
Rhodesian oil	1.8	3.3	2.2

Institutional Shareholders

	1977	1978	1979
Bank loans			
a. all resolutions	15	32	30
b. stop loans	15	33	37
c. loan reports		31	24
Nonexpansion	18	37	38
Sales policies		31	39
Withdrawal	10	12	12
Rhodesian oil	15	26	18

39